BRING ME THE HEAD OF WILLY THE MAILBOY!

A DILBERT® BOOK BY SCOTT ADAMS

BXTREE

First published in the UK 1995 by Boxtree Limited
Broadwall house, 21 Broadwall, London, SE1 9PL

First published in the USA in 1995 by Andrews and McMeel,
4900 Main Street, Kansas City, Missouri 64112, USA

Dogbert and Dilbert appear in the comic strip Dilbert®, distributed by United Feature Syndicate, Inc.

10 9 8 7 6 5 4 3 2 1

ISBN: 0 7522 0136 0

Printed and bound in Great Britain by Mackays of Chatham PLC, Kent

A CIP catalogue record for this book is available from the British Library

For Pam, Sarah,
and Freddie
(in that order)

Introduction

In the introduction to my previous book *(Shave the Whales),* I recommended that people sign my name inside the cover and pass it off as an autographed copy. Unfortunately—due to a typo—it appears I went on to promise I would "verify your clam."

Well, needless to say, I have spent the past year explaining to nervous people that clams do not really need verification. So I agreed to put this book out to correct the misperception. I figure you've got enough problems without worrying if your clam is lying to you.

Clams have annoyed me for years. When I became a vegetarian, I used to say that I "wouldn't eat anything with a face," then I would smile with the self-assured look of a man who is both low in cholesterol and incredibly clever. Then my wise-ass friend pointed out that clams don't have faces, so I should eat them. I argued that they have ugly little faces; it's just hard to tell.

But what sometimes gets lost in all this bickering is that if you put an irritant in a clam, and wait long enough, eventually a beautiful pearl will form. Some people say pearls come from oysters, not clams, but these people don't have the credentials in clam verification that I do.

Speaking of pearls, there's still time to join Dogbert's New Ruling Class (DNRC) before he conquers the planet and makes all non-members his slaves. All you have to do is subscribe to the free Dilbert Newsletter.

The frequency of the newsletter is approximately whenever I feel like it. But the e-mail version will be more timely than the paper version.

To subscribe, write:

E-mail: scottadams@aol.com

Snail Mail: Dilbert Newsletter
United Media
Dept. W
200 Park Ave.
New York NY 10166

Scott Adams

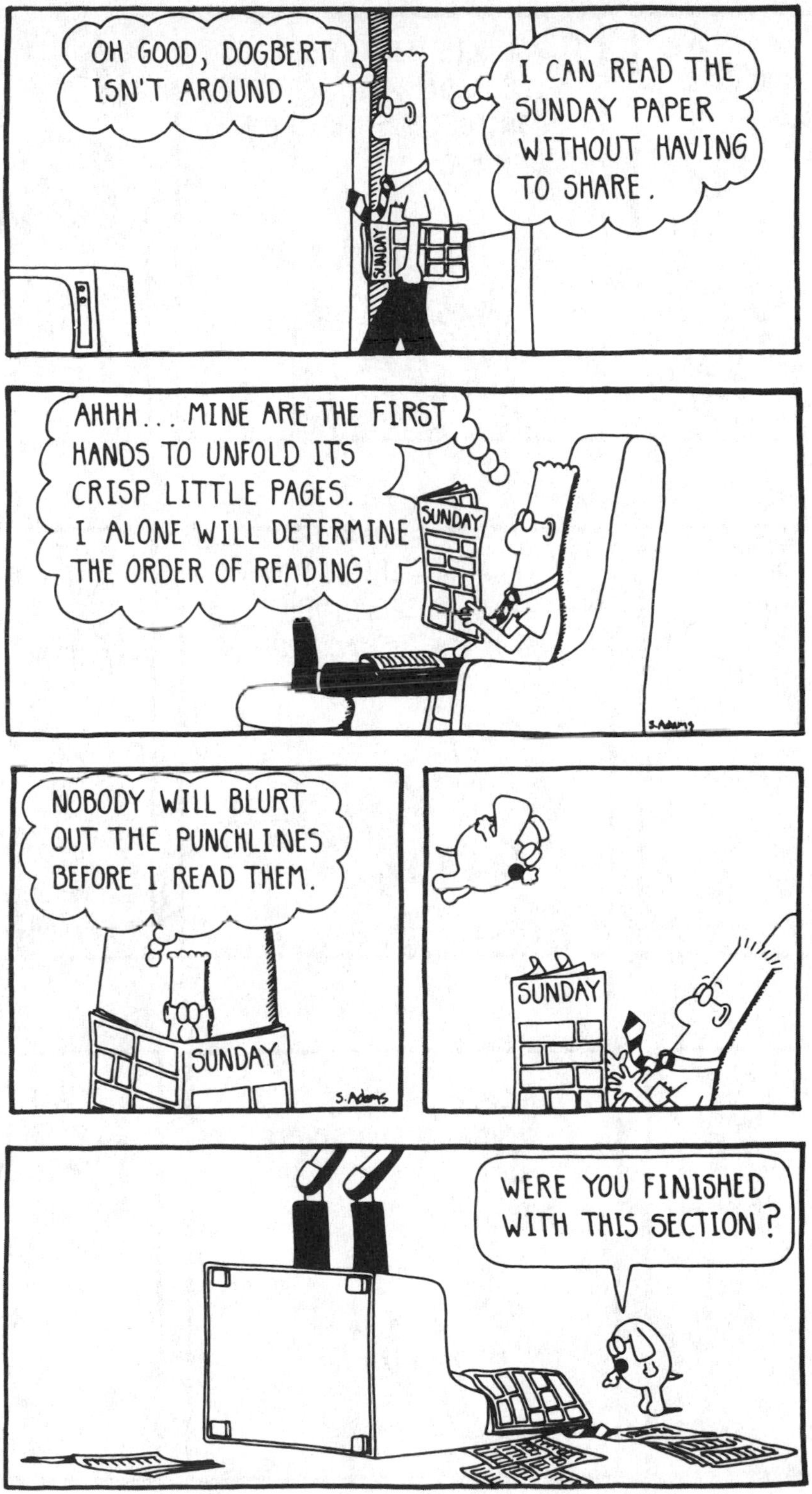
OH GOOD, DOGBERT ISN'T AROUND.
I CAN READ THE SUNDAY PAPER WITHOUT HAVING TO SHARE.
SUNDAY
AHHH... MINE ARE THE FIRST HANDS TO UNFOLD ITS CRISP LITTLE PAGES. I ALONE WILL DETERMINE THE ORDER OF READING.
SUNDAY
NOBODY WILL BLURT OUT THE PUNCHLINES BEFORE I READ THEM.
SUNDAY
S. Adams
SUNDAY
WERE YOU FINISHED WITH THIS SECTION?

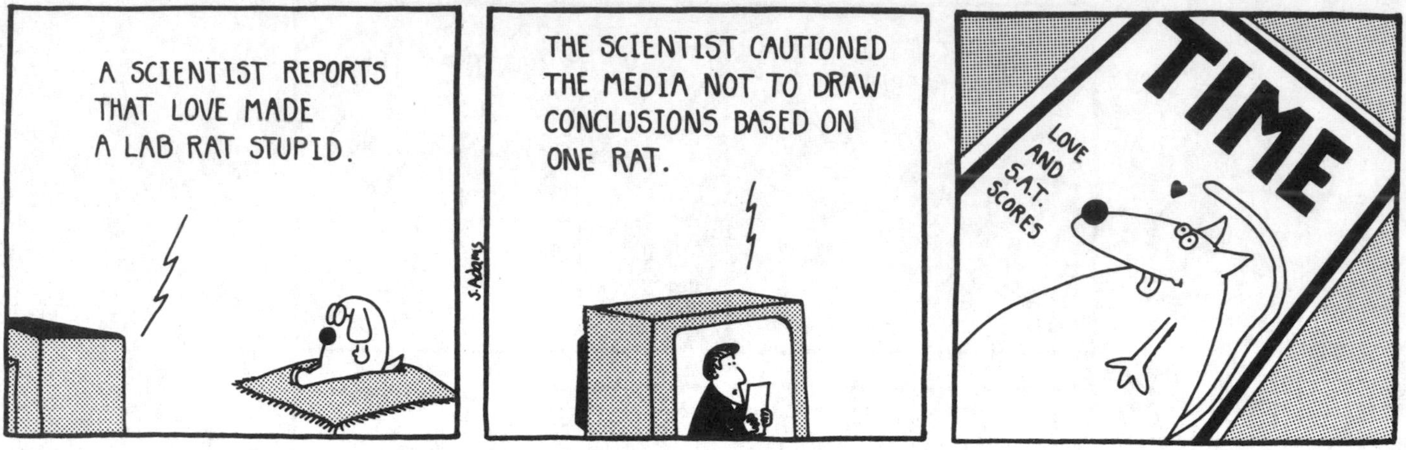
A SCIENTIST REPORTS THAT LOVE MADE A LAB RAT STUPID.
THE SCIENTIST CAUTIONED THE MEDIA NOT TO DRAW CONCLUSIONS BASED ON ONE RAT.
TIME
LOVE AND S.A.T. SCORES
S. Adams

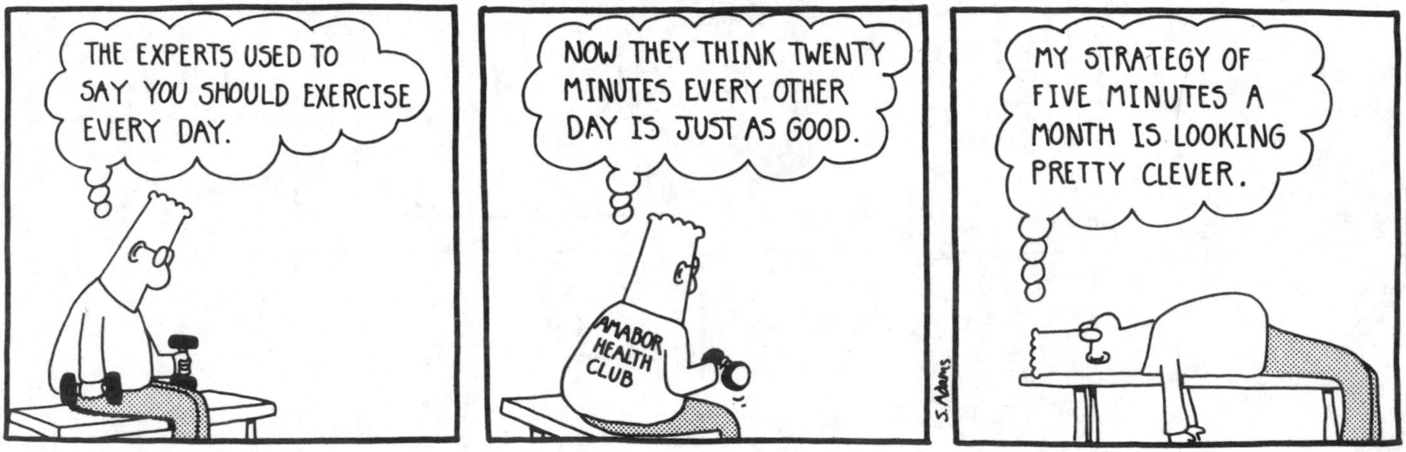
THE EXPERTS USED TO SAY YOU SHOULD EXERCISE EVERY DAY.
NOW THEY THINK TWENTY MINUTES EVERY OTHER DAY IS JUST AS GOOD.
AMABOR HEALTH CLUB
MY STRATEGY OF FIVE MINUTES A MONTH IS LOOKING PRETTY CLEVER.
S. Adams

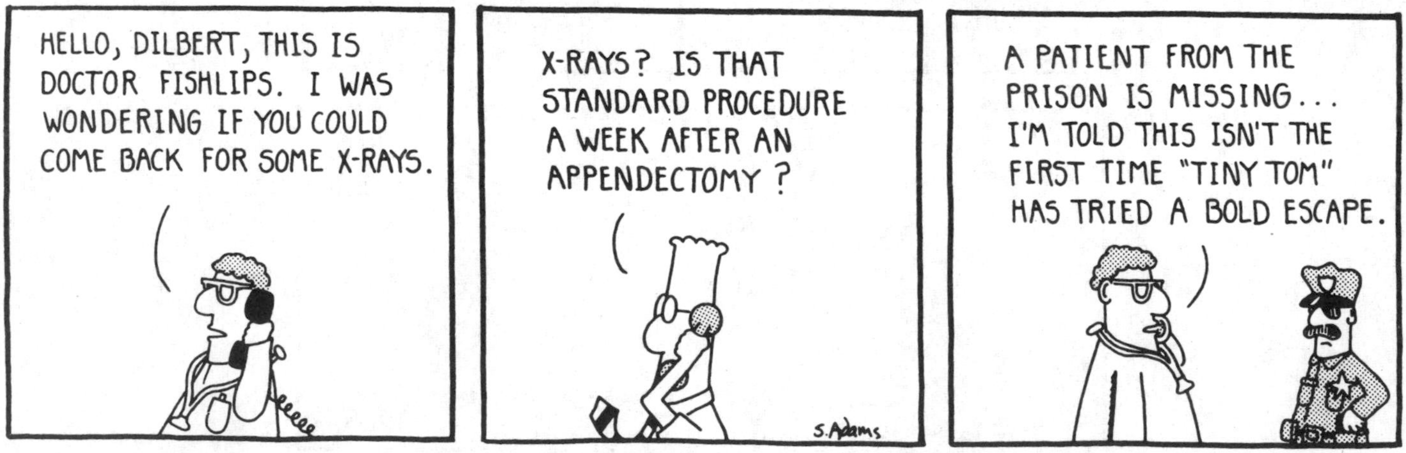
HELLO, DILBERT, THIS IS DOCTOR FISHLIPS. I WAS WONDERING IF YOU COULD COME BACK FOR SOME X-RAYS.
X-RAYS? IS THAT STANDARD PROCEDURE A WEEK AFTER AN APPENDECTOMY?
S. Adams
A PATIENT FROM THE PRISON IS MISSING... I'M TOLD THIS ISN'T THE FIRST TIME "TINY TOM" HAS TRIED A BOLD ESCAPE.

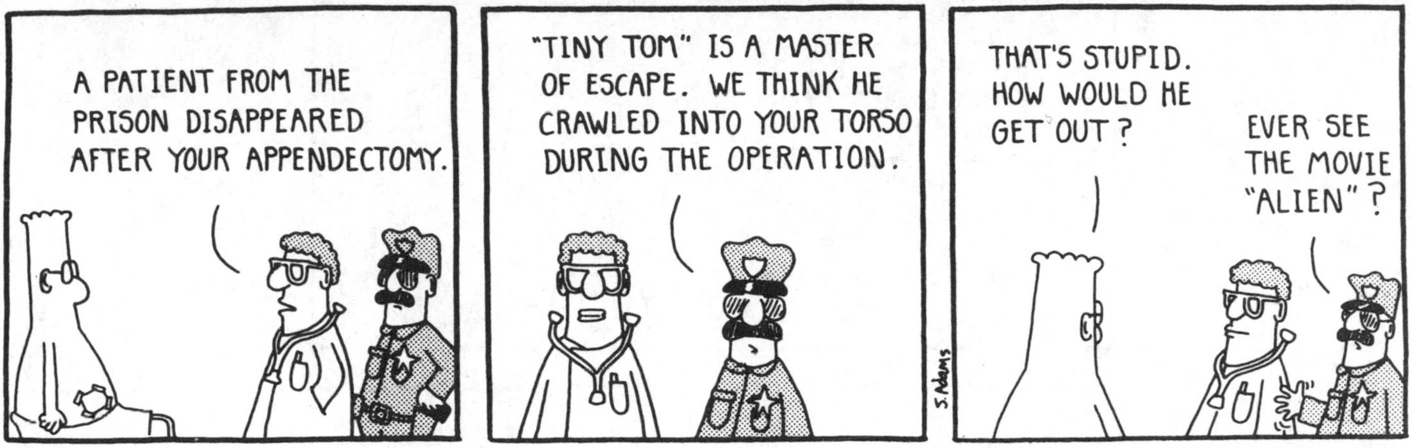
A PATIENT FROM THE PRISON DISAPPEARED AFTER YOUR APPENDECTOMY.
"TINY TOM" IS A MASTER OF ESCAPE. WE THINK HE CRAWLED INTO YOUR TORSO DURING THE OPERATION.
THAT'S STUPID. HOW WOULD HE GET OUT?
EVER SEE THE MOVIE "ALIEN"?
S. Adams

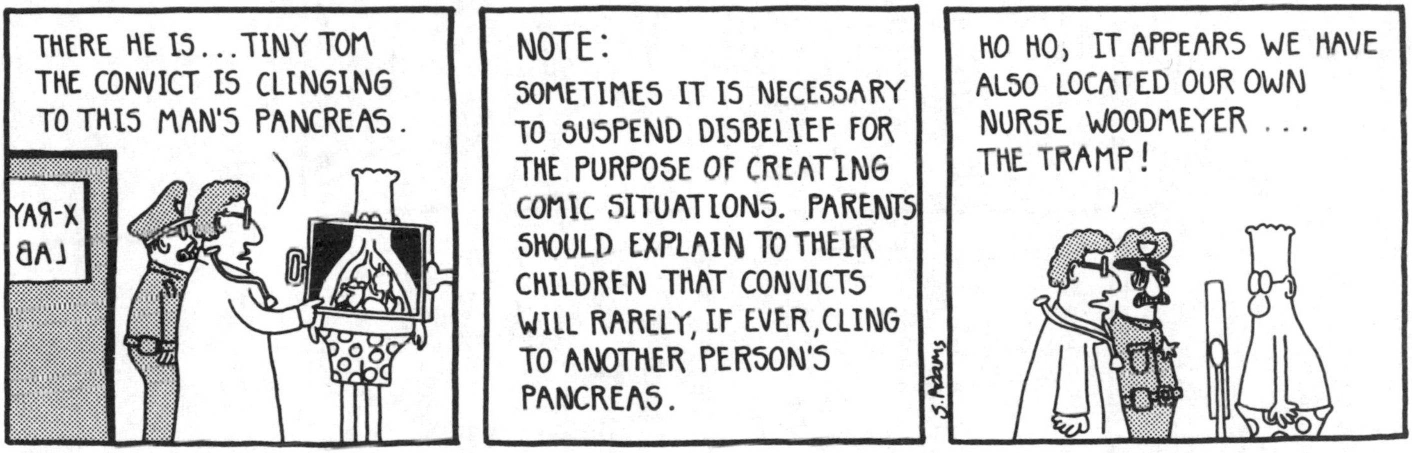
THERE HE IS... TINY TOM THE CONVICT IS CLINGING TO THIS MAN'S PANCREAS.
NOTE:
SOMETIMES IT IS NECESSARY TO SUSPEND DISBELIEF FOR THE PURPOSE OF CREATING COMIC SITUATIONS. PARENTS SHOULD EXPLAIN TO THEIR CHILDREN THAT CONVICTS WILL RARELY, IF EVER, CLING TO ANOTHER PERSON'S PANCREAS.
HO HO, IT APPEARS WE HAVE ALSO LOCATED OUR OWN NURSE WOODMEYER ... THE TRAMP!
S. Adams

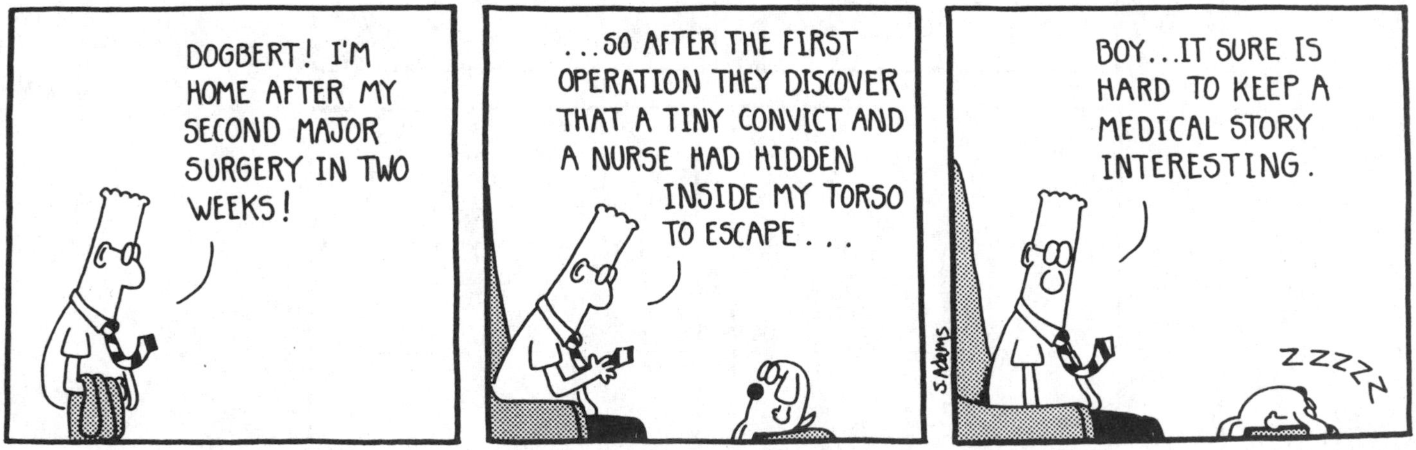
DOGBERT! I'M HOME AFTER MY SECOND MAJOR SURGERY IN TWO WEEKS!
...SO AFTER THE FIRST OPERATION THEY DISCOVER THAT A TINY CONVICT AND A NURSE HAD HIDDEN INSIDE MY TORSO TO ESCAPE...
BOY... IT SURE IS HARD TO KEEP A MEDICAL STORY INTERESTING.
ZZZZZ
S. Adams

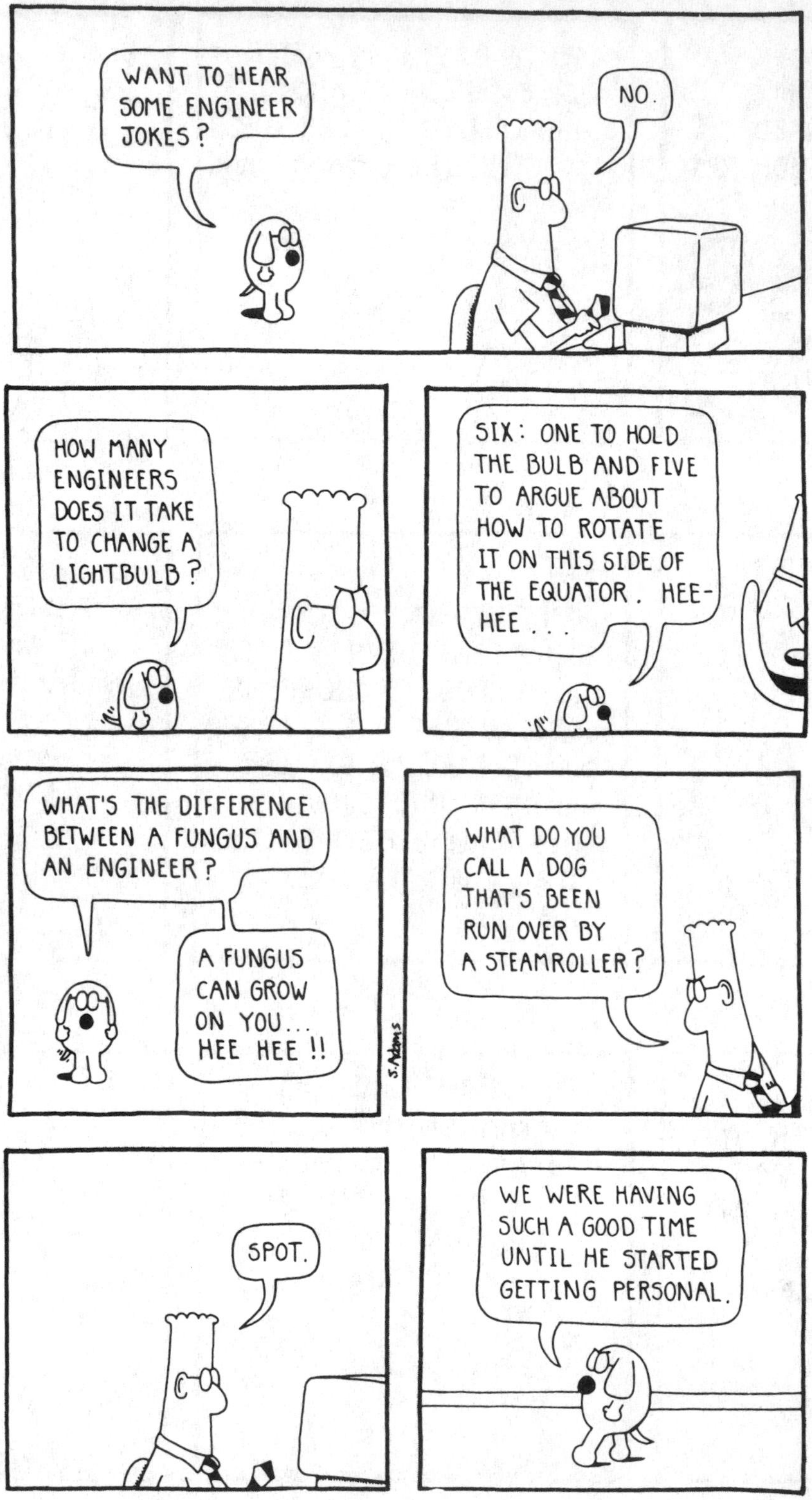
WANT TO HEAR SOME ENGINEER JOKES?
NO.
HOW MANY ENGINEERS DOES IT TAKE TO CHANGE A LIGHTBULB?
SIX: ONE TO HOLD THE BULB AND FIVE TO ARGUE ABOUT HOW TO ROTATE IT ON THIS SIDE OF THE EQUATOR. HEE-HEE...
WHAT'S THE DIFFERENCE BETWEEN A FUNGUS AND AN ENGINEER?
A FUNGUS CAN GROW ON YOU... HEE HEE!!
S. Adams
WHAT DO YOU CALL A DOG THAT'S BEEN RUN OVER BY A STEAMROLLER?
SPOT.
WE WERE HAVING SUCH A GOOD TIME UNTIL HE STARTED GETTING PERSONAL.

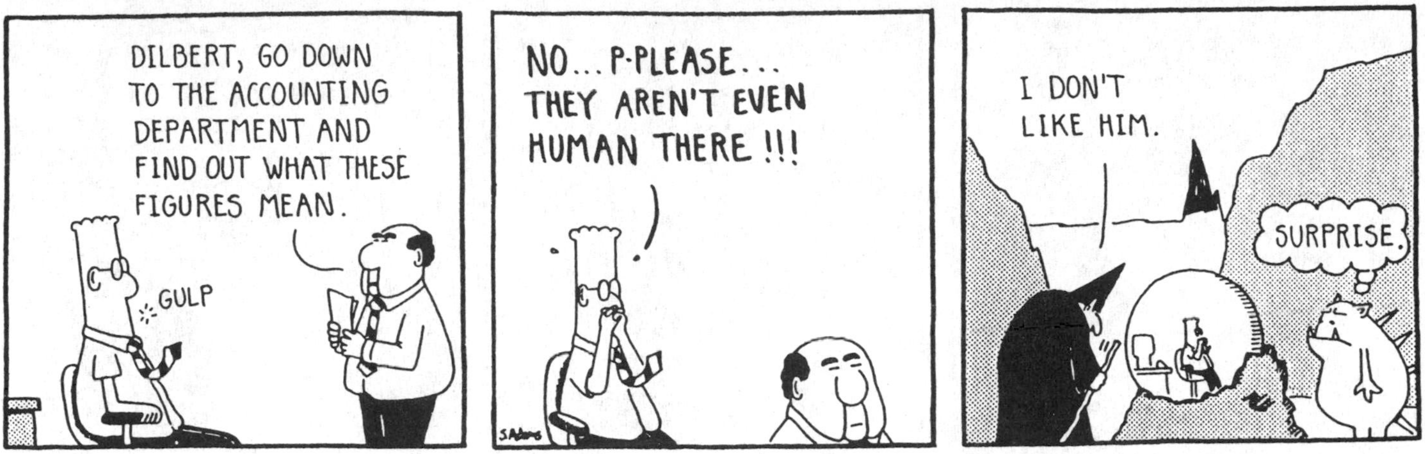
DILBERT, GO DOWN TO THE ACCOUNTING DEPARTMENT AND FIND OUT WHAT THESE FIGURES MEAN.
GULP
NO... P-PLEASE... THEY AREN'T EVEN HUMAN THERE !!!
I DON'T LIKE HIM.
SURPRISE.

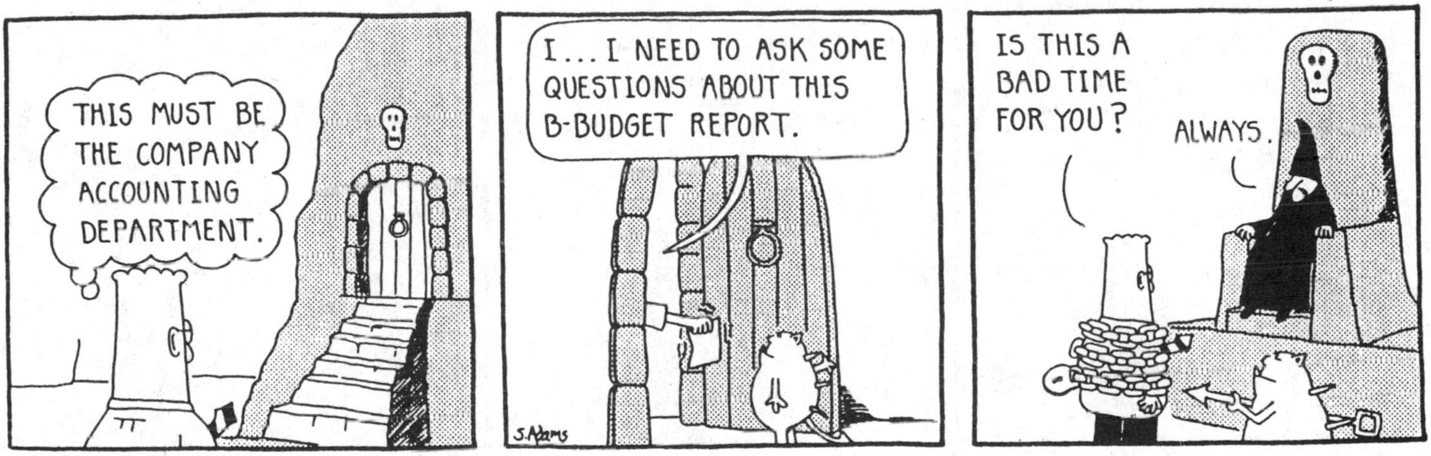
THIS MUST BE THE COMPANY ACCOUNTING DEPARTMENT.
I... I NEED TO ASK SOME QUESTIONS ABOUT THIS B-BUDGET REPORT.
IS THIS A BAD TIME FOR YOU?
ALWAYS.

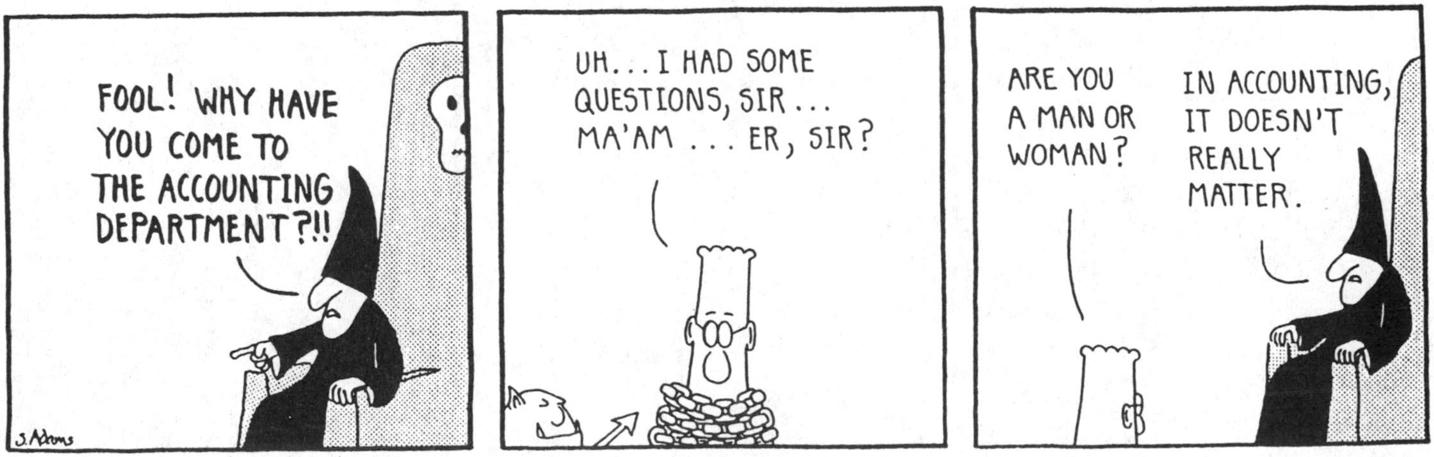
FOOL! WHY HAVE YOU COME TO THE ACCOUNTING DEPARTMENT?!!
UH... I HAD SOME QUESTIONS, SIR... MA'AM ... ER, SIR?
ARE YOU A MAN OR WOMAN?
IN ACCOUNTING, IT DOESN'T REALLY MATTER.

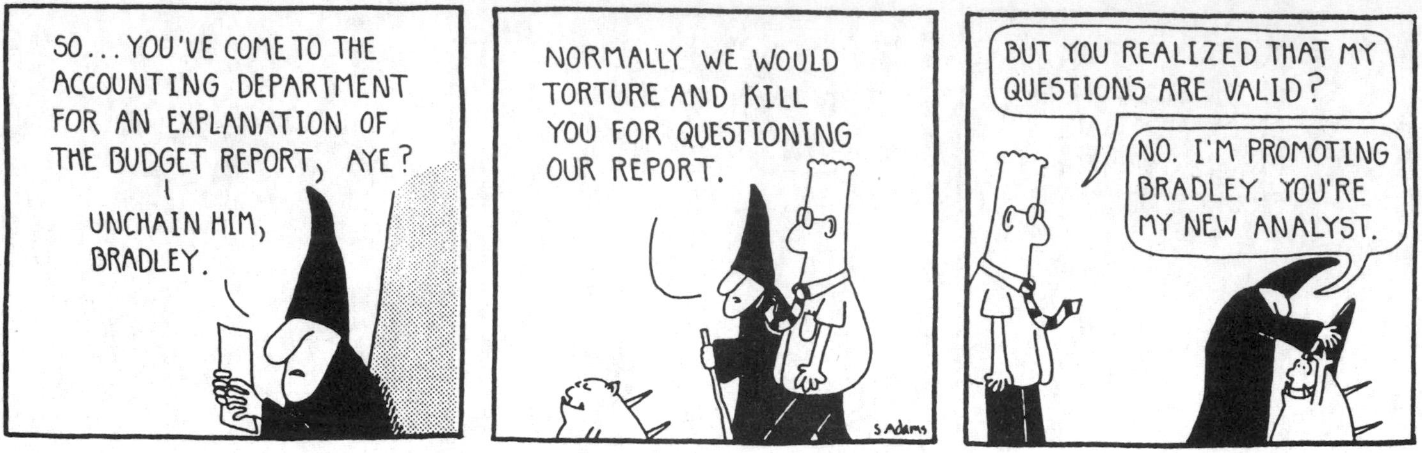
SO... YOU'VE COME TO THE ACCOUNTING DEPARTMENT FOR AN EXPLANATION OF THE BUDGET REPORT, AYE?
UNCHAIN HIM, BRADLEY.
NORMALLY WE WOULD TORTURE AND KILL YOU FOR QUESTIONING OUR REPORT.
S. Adams
BUT YOU REALIZED THAT MY QUESTIONS ARE VALID?
NO. I'M PROMOTING BRADLEY. YOU'RE MY NEW ANALYST.

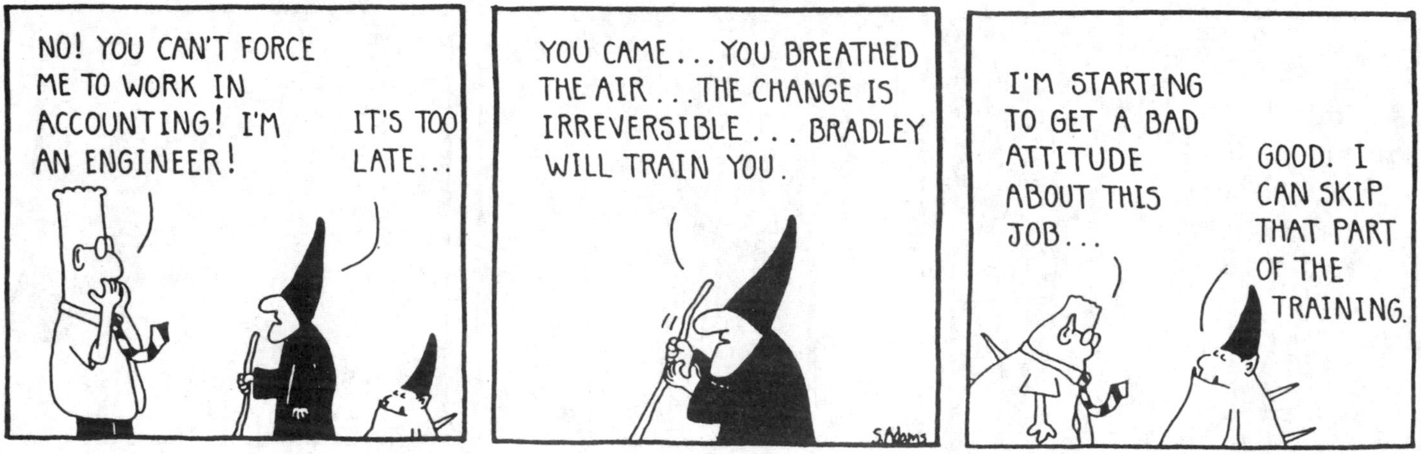
NO! YOU CAN'T FORCE ME TO WORK IN ACCOUNTING! I'M AN ENGINEER!
IT'S TOO LATE...
YOU CAME... YOU BREATHED THE AIR... THE CHANGE IS IRREVERSIBLE... BRADLEY WILL TRAIN YOU.
S. Adams
I'M STARTING TO GET A BAD ATTITUDE ABOUT THIS JOB...
GOOD. I CAN SKIP THAT PART OF THE TRAINING.

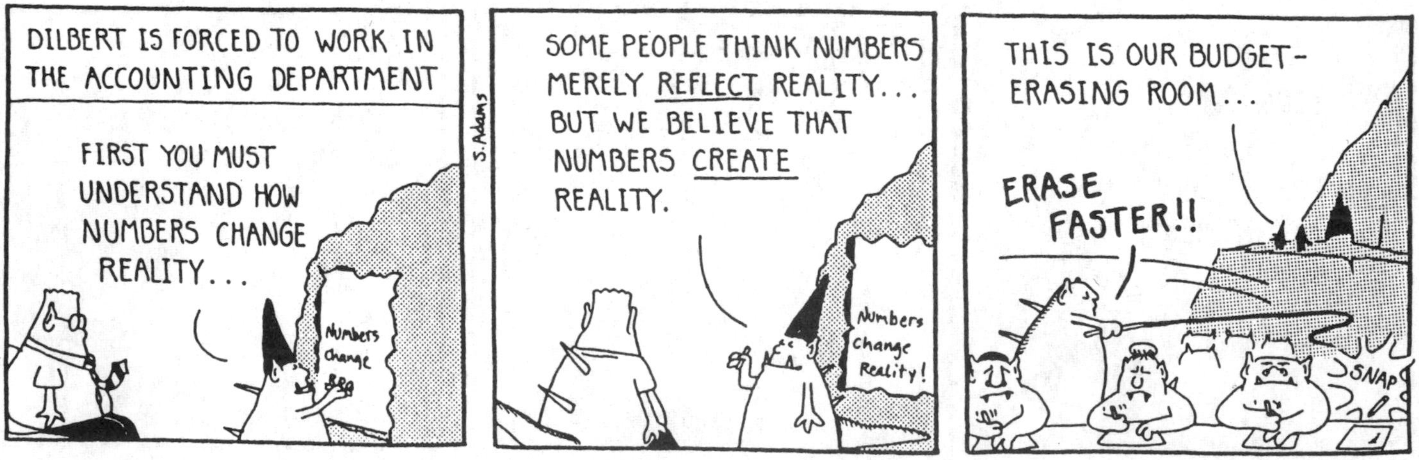
DILBERT IS FORCED TO WORK IN THE ACCOUNTING DEPARTMENT
FIRST YOU MUST UNDERSTAND HOW NUMBERS CHANGE REALITY...
S. Adams
SOME PEOPLE THINK NUMBERS MERELY REFLECT REALITY... BUT WE BELIEVE THAT NUMBERS CREATE REALITY.
Numbers Change Reality!
THIS IS OUR BUDGET-ERASING ROOM...
ERASE FASTER!!
SNAP

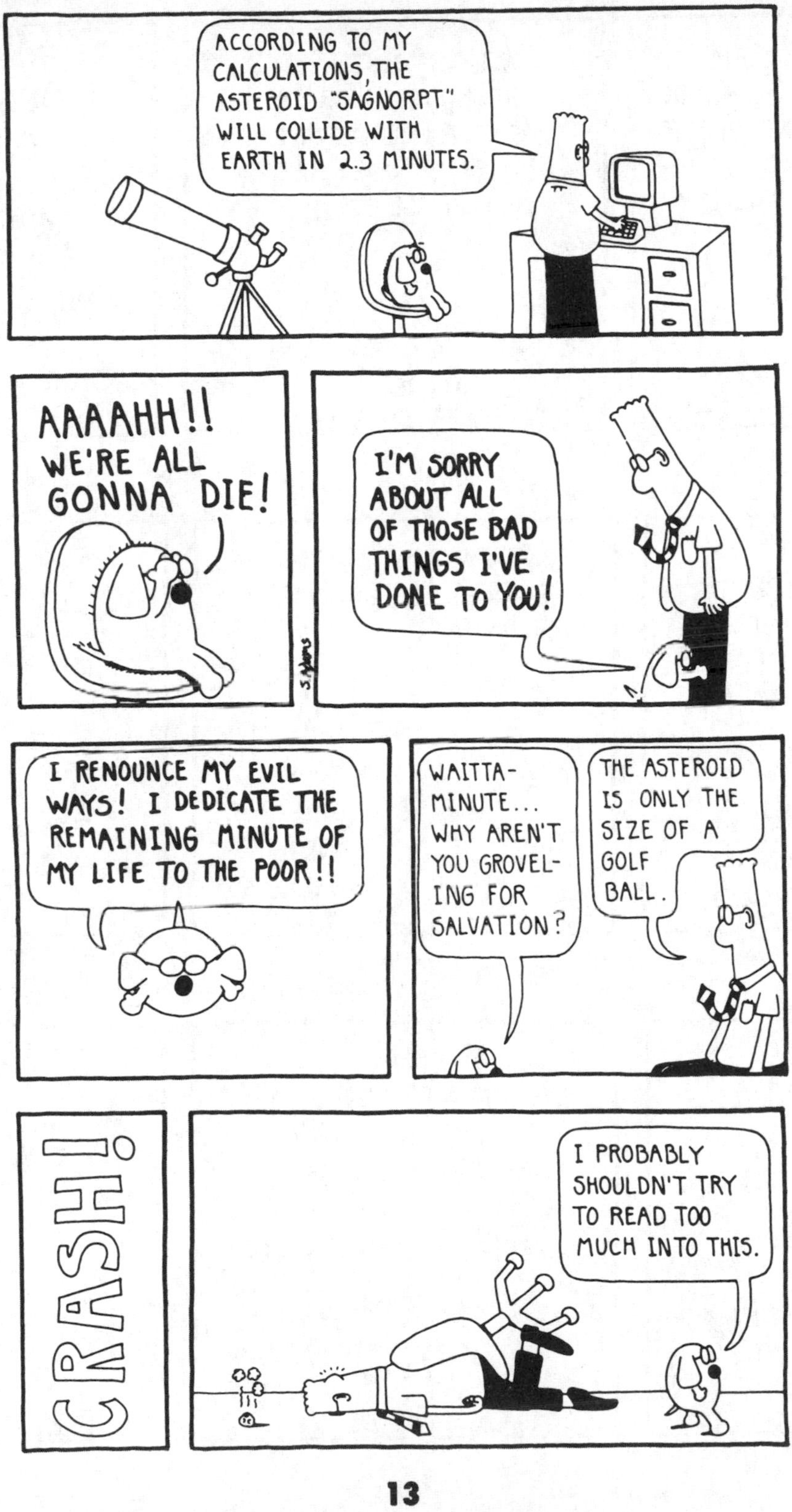
ACCORDING TO MY CALCULATIONS, THE ASTEROID "SAGNORPT" WILL COLLIDE WITH EARTH IN 2.3 MINUTES.
AAAAHH!! WE'RE ALL GONNA DIE!
I'M SORRY ABOUT ALL OF THOSE BAD THINGS I'VE DONE TO YOU!
I RENOUNCE MY EVIL WAYS! I DEDICATE THE REMAINING MINUTE OF MY LIFE TO THE POOR!!
WAITTA-MINUTE... WHY AREN'T YOU GROVEL-ING FOR SALVATION?
THE ASTEROID IS ONLY THE SIZE OF A GOLF BALL.
CRASH!
I PROBABLY SHOULDN'T TRY TO READ TOO MUCH INTO THIS.

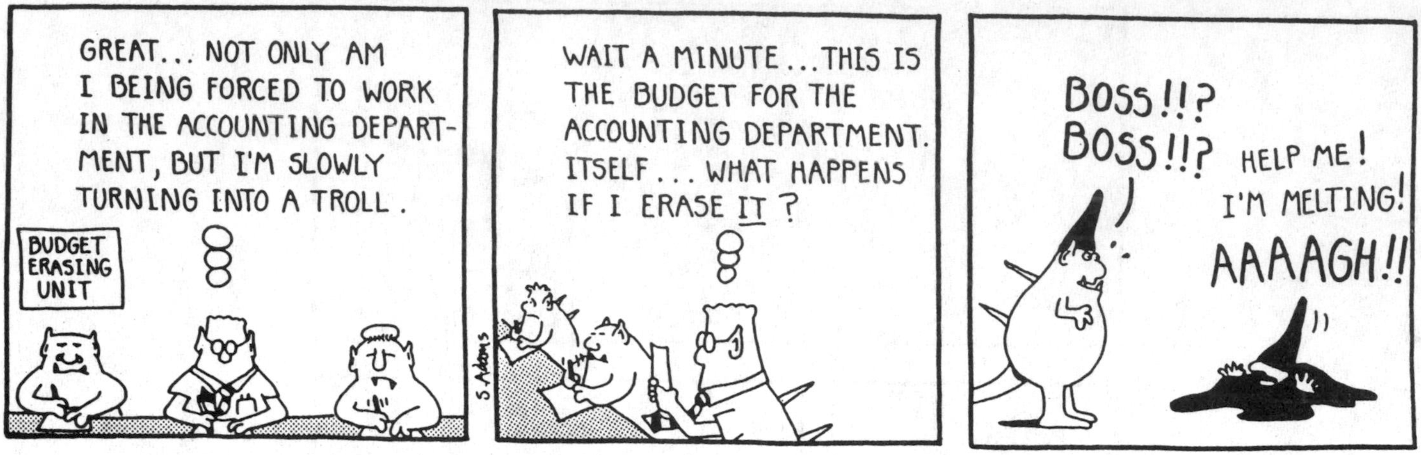
GREAT... NOT ONLY AM I BEING FORCED TO WORK IN THE ACCOUNTING DEPARTMENT, BUT I'M SLOWLY TURNING INTO A TROLL.
BUDGET ERASING UNIT
WAIT A MINUTE... THIS IS THE BUDGET FOR THE ACCOUNTING DEPARTMENT ITSELF... WHAT HAPPENS IF I ERASE IT?
BOSS!!? BOSS!!?
HELP ME! I'M MELTING!
AAAAGH!!

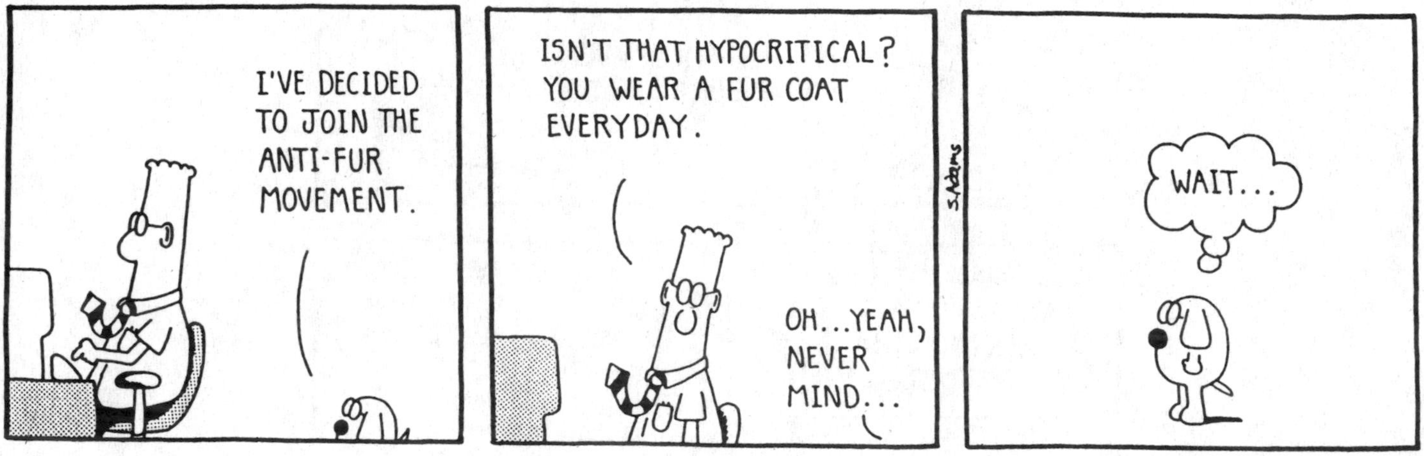
I'VE DECIDED TO JOIN THE ANTI-FUR MOVEMENT.
ISN'T THAT HYPOCRITICAL? YOU WEAR A FUR COAT EVERYDAY.
OH... YEAH, NEVER MIND...
WAIT...

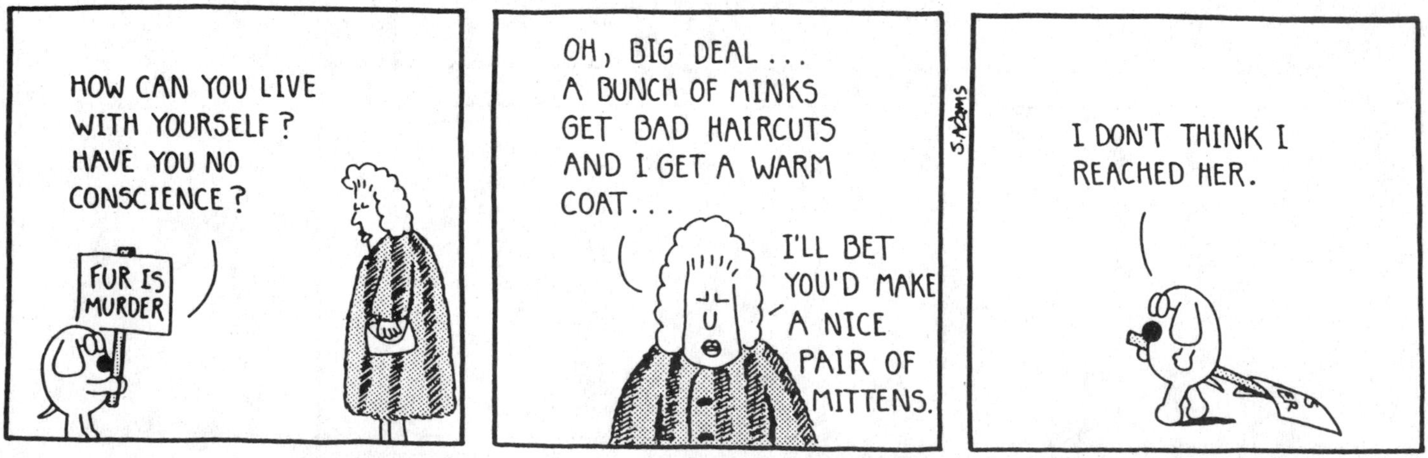
HOW CAN YOU LIVE WITH YOURSELF? HAVE YOU NO CONSCIENCE?
FUR IS MURDER
OH, BIG DEAL... A BUNCH OF MINKS GET BAD HAIRCUTS AND I GET A WARM COAT...
I'LL BET YOU'D MAKE A NICE PAIR OF MITTENS.
I DON'T THINK I REACHED HER.

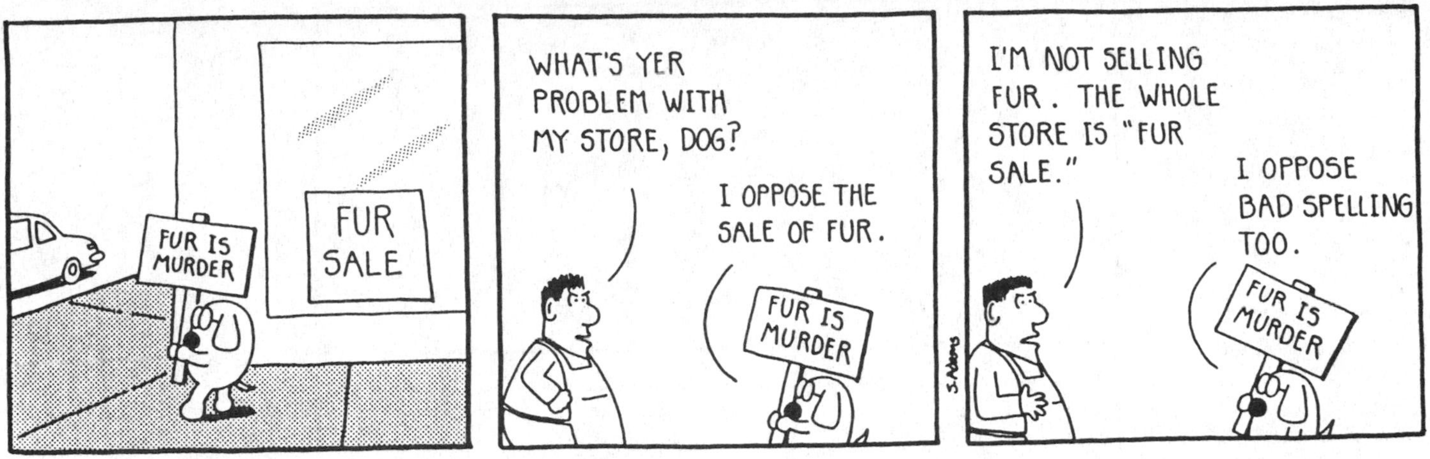
FUR IS MURDER
FUR SALE
WHAT'S YER PROBLEM WITH MY STORE, DOG?
I OPPOSE THE SALE OF FUR.
FUR IS MURDER
I'M NOT SELLING FUR. THE WHOLE STORE IS "FUR SALE."
I OPPOSE BAD SPELLING TOO.
FUR IS MURDER
S. Adams

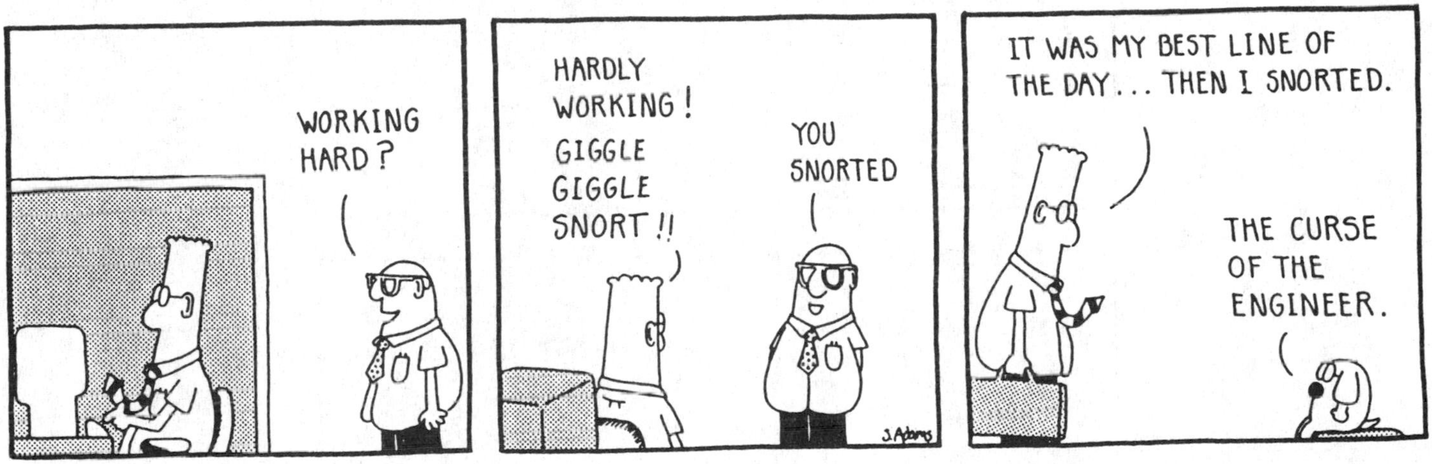
WORKING HARD?
HARDLY WORKING! GIGGLE GIGGLE SNORT!!
YOU SNORTED
S. Adams
IT WAS MY BEST LINE OF THE DAY... THEN I SNORTED.
THE CURSE OF THE ENGINEER.

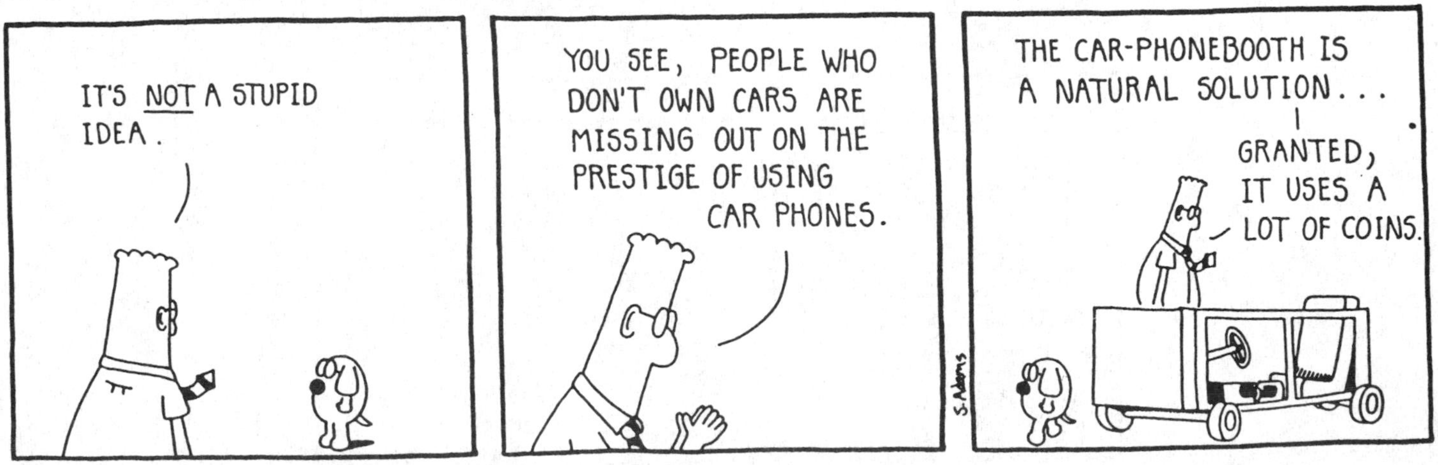
IT'S NOT A STUPID IDEA.
YOU SEE, PEOPLE WHO DON'T OWN CARS ARE MISSING OUT ON THE PRESTIGE OF USING CAR PHONES.
S. Adams
THE CAR-PHONEBOOTH IS A NATURAL SOLUTION...
GRANTED, IT USES A LOT OF COINS.

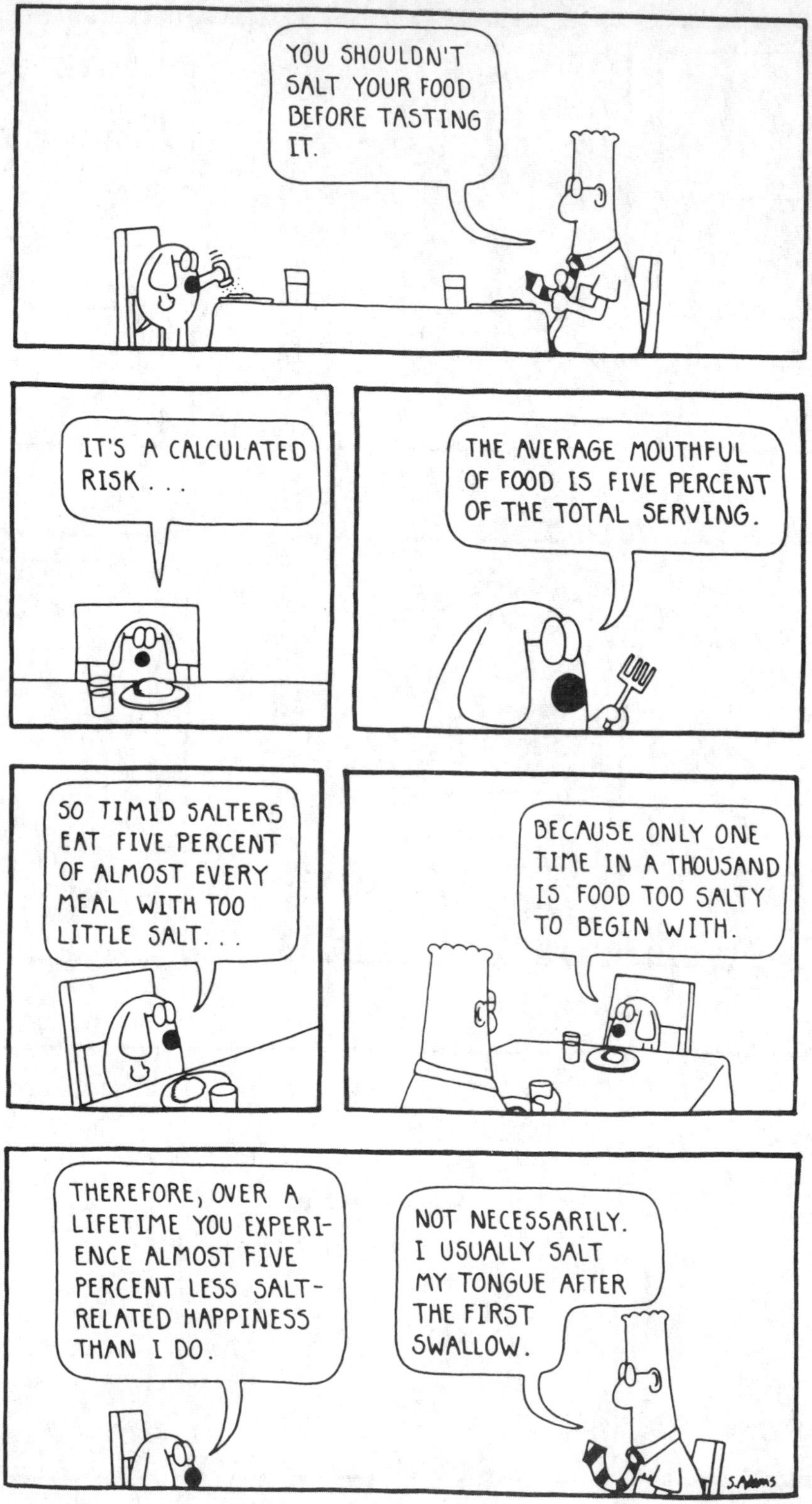
YOU SHOULDN'T SALT YOUR FOOD BEFORE TASTING IT.
IT'S A CALCULATED RISK . . .
THE AVERAGE MOUTHFUL OF FOOD IS FIVE PERCENT OF THE TOTAL SERVING.
SO TIMID SALTERS EAT FIVE PERCENT OF ALMOST EVERY MEAL WITH TOO LITTLE SALT . . .
BECAUSE ONLY ONE TIME IN A THOUSAND IS FOOD TOO SALTY TO BEGIN WITH.
THEREFORE, OVER A LIFETIME YOU EXPERI-ENCE ALMOST FIVE PERCENT LESS SALT-RELATED HAPPINESS THAN I DO.
NOT NECESSARILY. I USUALLY SALT MY TONGUE AFTER THE FIRST SWALLOW.
S.Adams

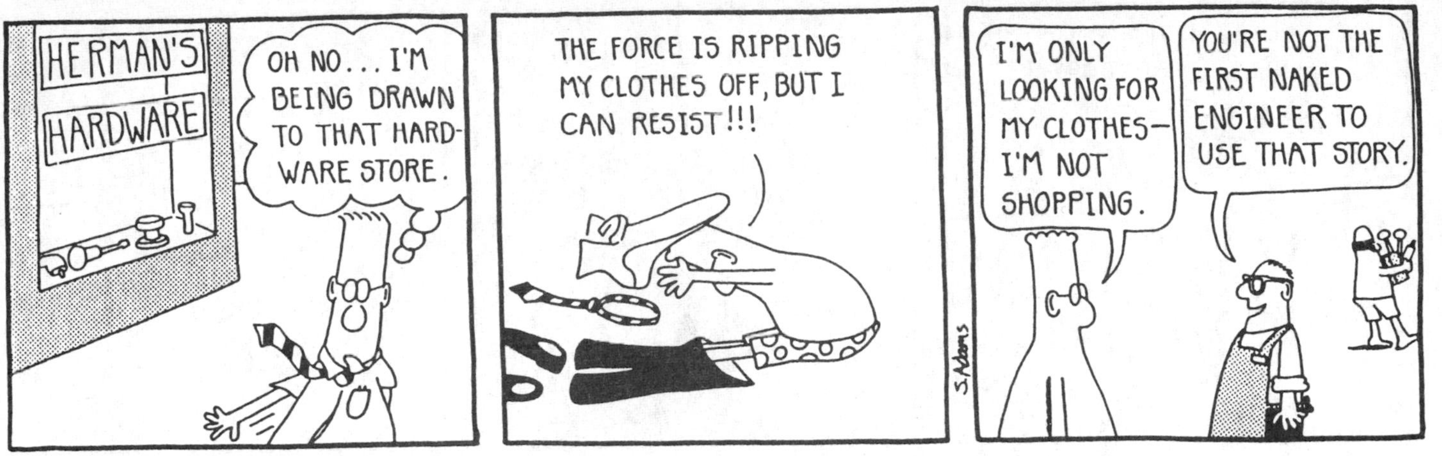
HERMAN'S
HARDWARE
OH NO... I'M BEING DRAWN TO THAT HARD-WARE STORE.
THE FORCE IS RIPPING MY CLOTHES OFF, BUT I CAN RESIST!!!
I'M ONLY LOOKING FOR MY CLOTHES— I'M NOT SHOPPING.
YOU'RE NOT THE FIRST NAKED ENGINEER TO USE THAT STORY.

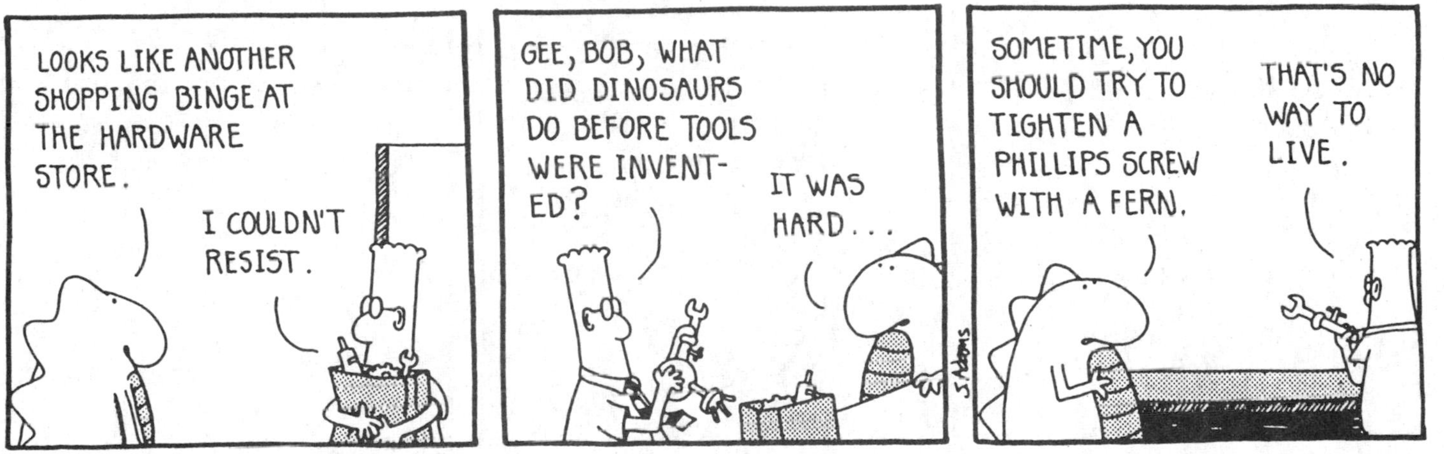
LOOKS LIKE ANOTHER SHOPPING BINGE AT THE HARDWARE STORE.
I COULDN'T RESIST.
GEE, BOB, WHAT DID DINOSAURS DO BEFORE TOOLS WERE INVENT-ED?
IT WAS HARD...
SOMETIME, YOU SHOULD TRY TO TIGHTEN A PHILLIPS SCREW WITH A FERN.
THAT'S NO WAY TO LIVE.

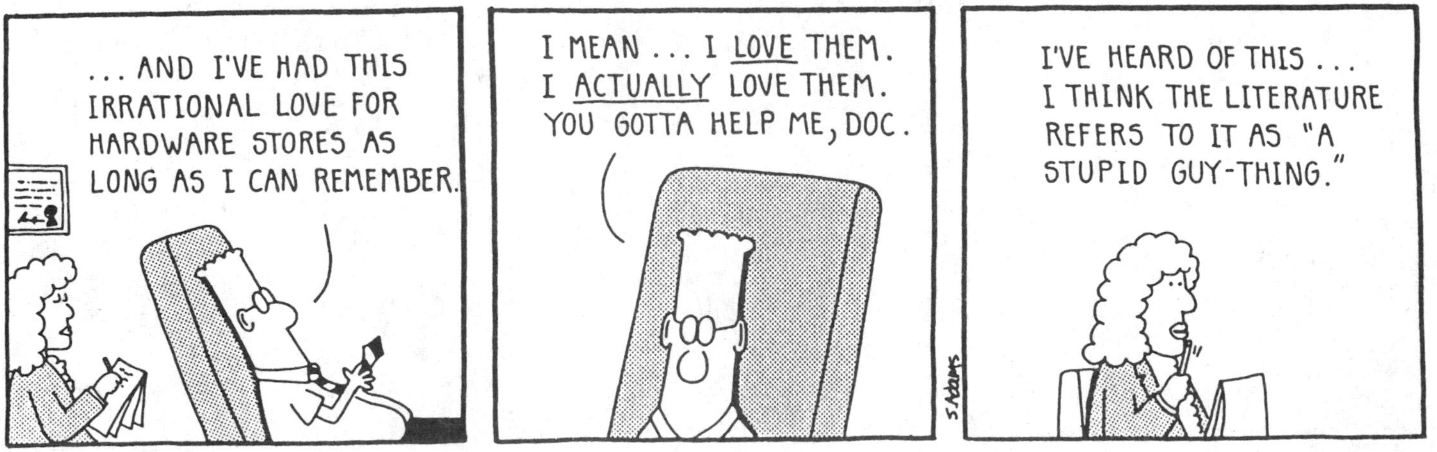
... AND I'VE HAD THIS IRRATIONAL LOVE FOR HARDWARE STORES AS LONG AS I CAN REMEMBER.
I MEAN ... I LOVE THEM. I ACTUALLY LOVE THEM. YOU GOTTA HELP ME, DOC.
I'VE HEARD OF THIS ... I THINK THE LITERATURE REFERS TO IT AS "A STUPID GUY-THING."

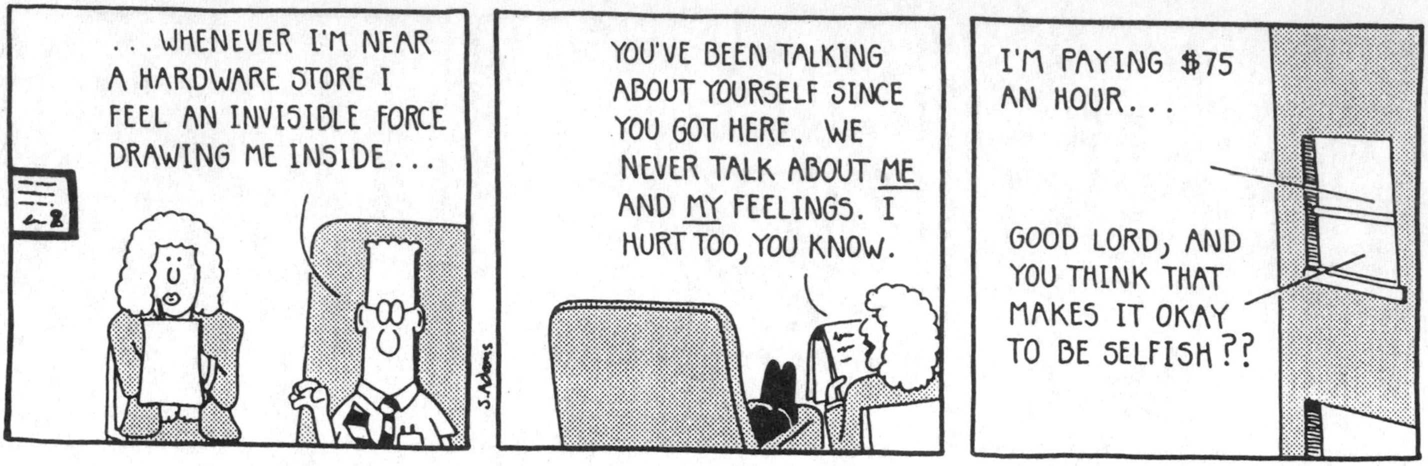
. . . WHENEVER I'M NEAR A HARDWARE STORE I FEEL AN INVISIBLE FORCE DRAWING ME INSIDE . . .
S. Adams
YOU'VE BEEN TALKING ABOUT YOURSELF SINCE YOU GOT HERE. WE NEVER TALK ABOUT ME AND MY FEELINGS. I HURT TOO, YOU KNOW.
I'M PAYING $75 AN HOUR . . .
GOOD LORD, AND YOU THINK THAT MAKES IT OKAY TO BE SELFISH??

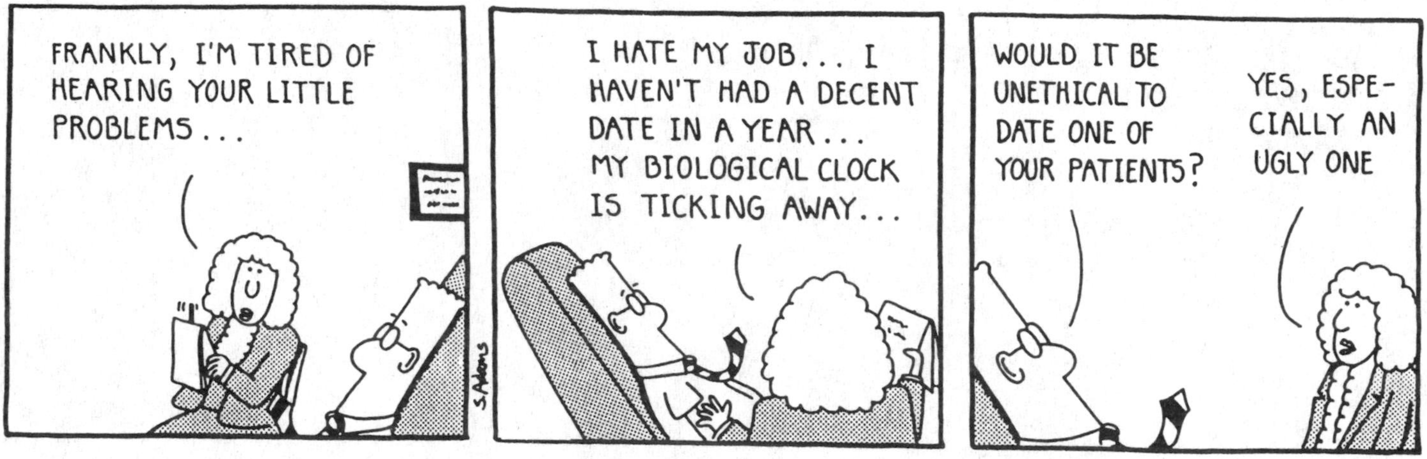
FRANKLY, I'M TIRED OF HEARING YOUR LITTLE PROBLEMS . . .
S. Adams
I HATE MY JOB . . . I HAVEN'T HAD A DECENT DATE IN A YEAR . . . MY BIOLOGICAL CLOCK IS TICKING AWAY . . .
WOULD IT BE UNETHICAL TO DATE ONE OF YOUR PATIENTS?
YES, ESPECIALLY AN UGLY ONE

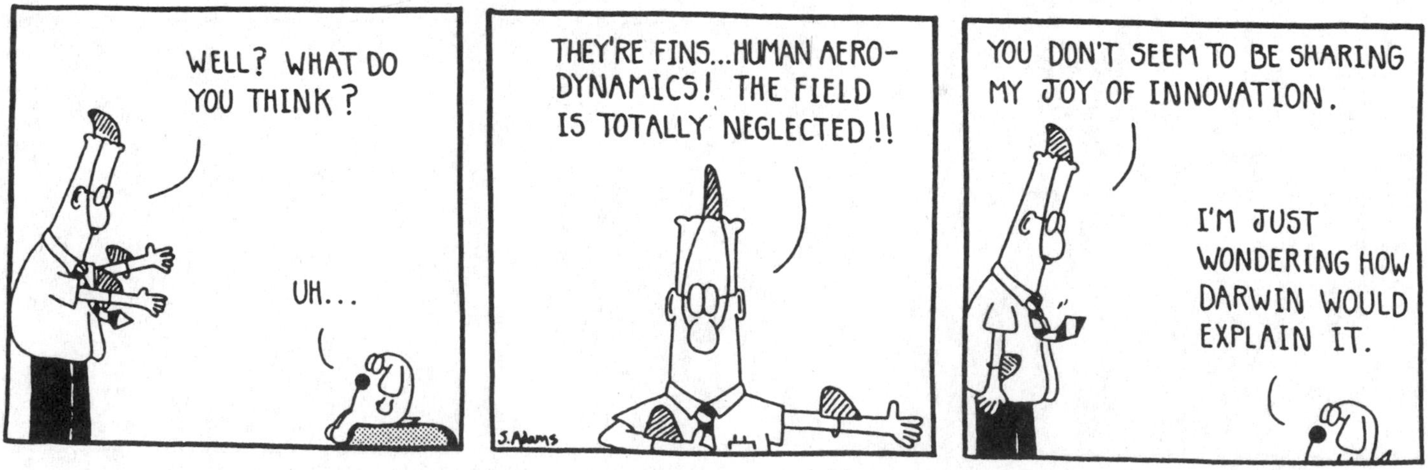
WELL? WHAT DO YOU THINK?
UH . . .
THEY'RE FINS...HUMAN AERODYNAMICS! THE FIELD IS TOTALLY NEGLECTED!!
S. Adams
YOU DON'T SEEM TO BE SHARING MY JOY OF INNOVATION.
I'M JUST WONDERING HOW DARWIN WOULD EXPLAIN IT.

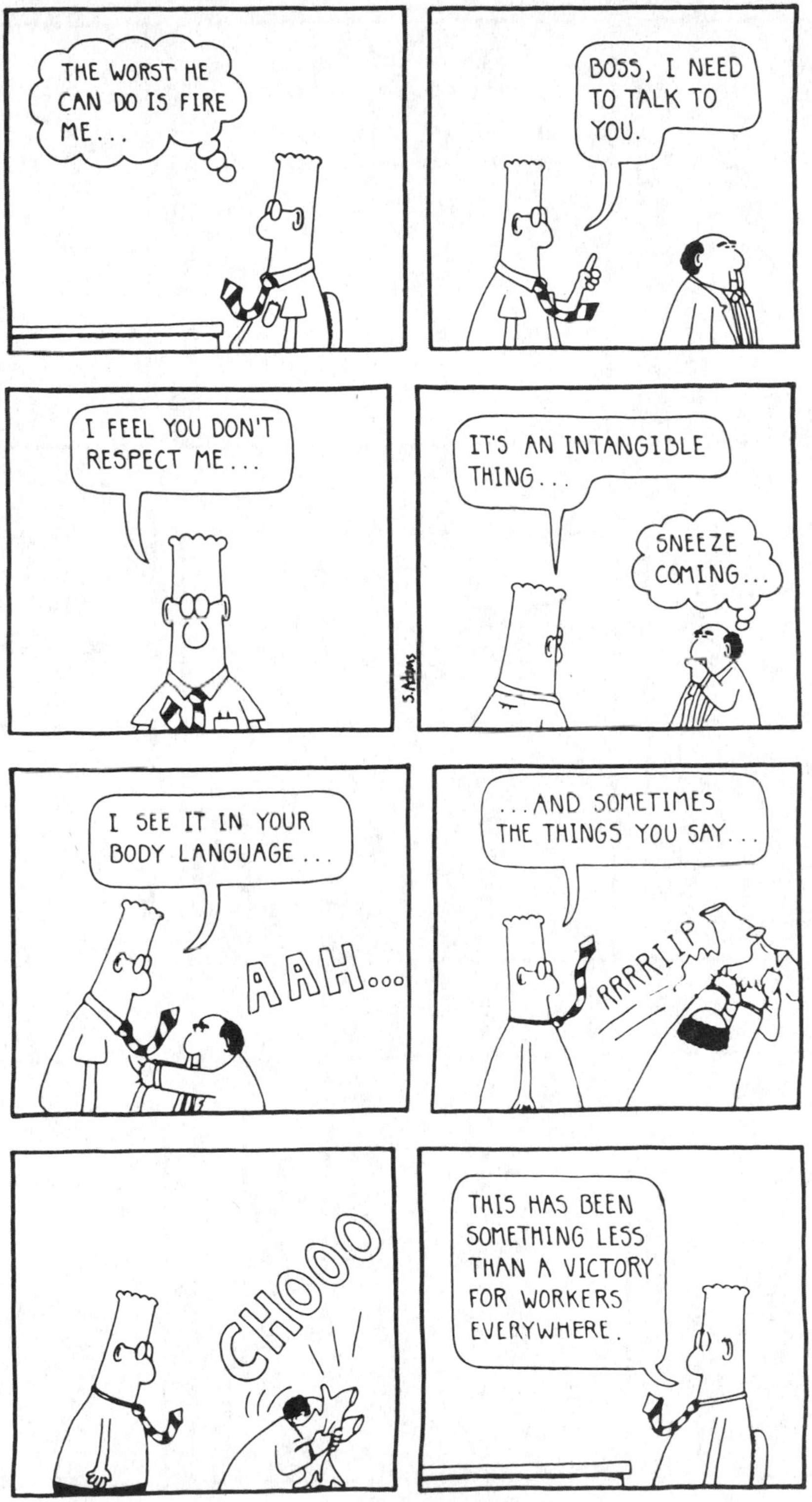
THE WORST HE CAN DO IS FIRE ME...
BOSS, I NEED TO TALK TO YOU.
I FEEL YOU DON'T RESPECT ME...
IT'S AN INTANGIBLE THING...
SNEEZE COMING...
S. Adams
I SEE IT IN YOUR BODY LANGUAGE...
AAH...
...AND SOMETIMES THE THINGS YOU SAY...
RRRRIIP
CHOOO
THIS HAS BEEN SOMETHING LESS THAN A VICTORY FOR WORKERS EVERYWHERE.

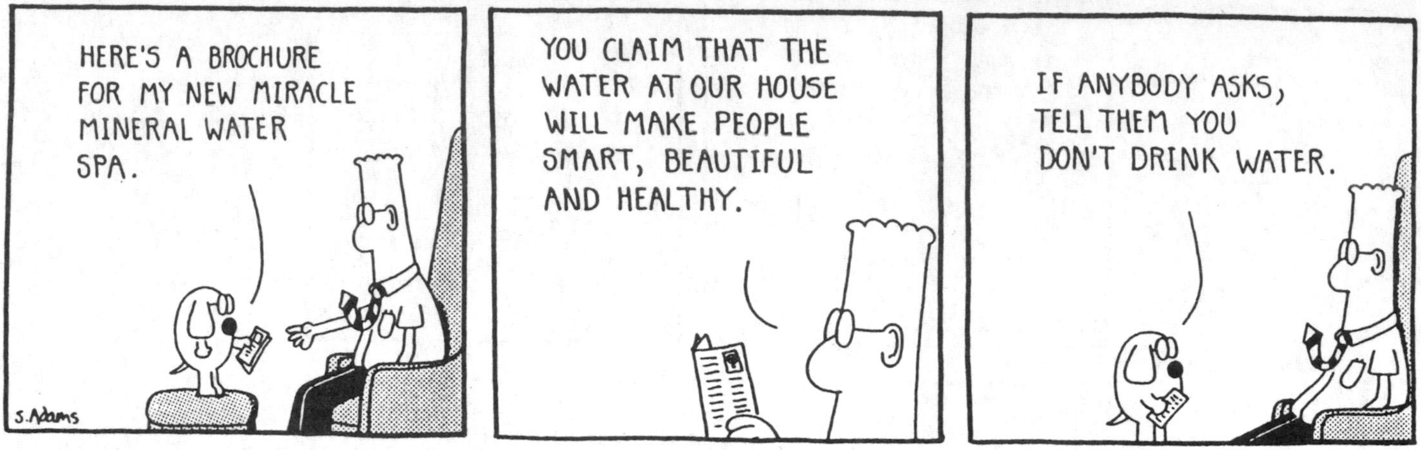
HERE'S A BROCHURE FOR MY NEW MIRACLE MINERAL WATER SPA.
S. Adams
YOU CLAIM THAT THE WATER AT OUR HOUSE WILL MAKE PEOPLE SMART, BEAUTIFUL AND HEALTHY.
IF ANYBODY ASKS, TELL THEM YOU DON'T DRINK WATER.

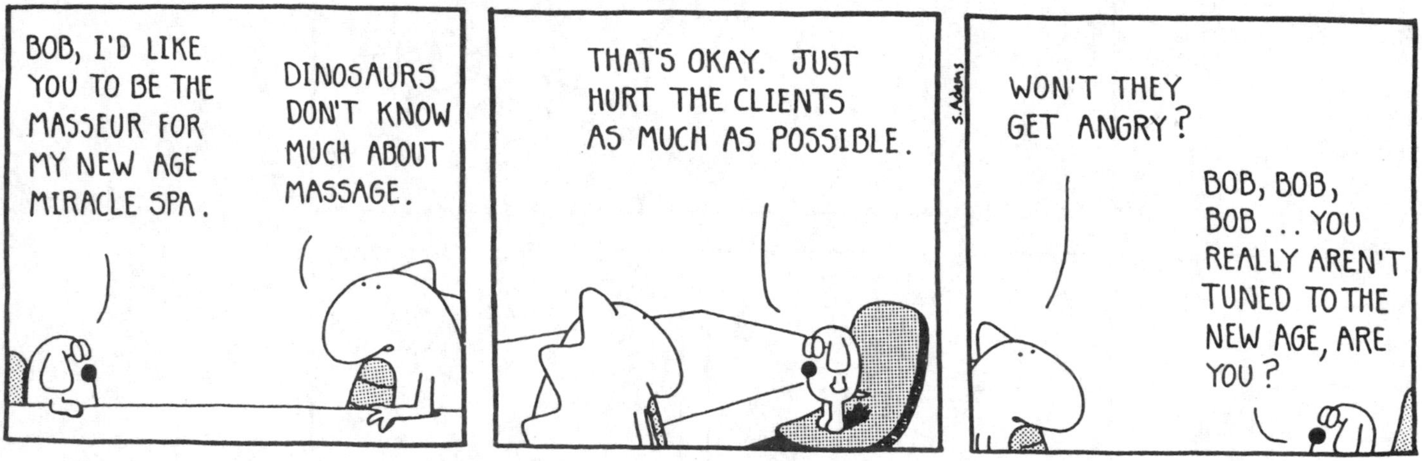
BOB, I'D LIKE YOU TO BE THE MASSEUR FOR MY NEW AGE MIRACLE SPA.
DINOSAURS DON'T KNOW MUCH ABOUT MASSAGE.
THAT'S OKAY. JUST HURT THE CLIENTS AS MUCH AS POSSIBLE.
S. Adams
WON'T THEY GET ANGRY?
BOB, BOB, BOB . . . YOU REALLY AREN'T TUNED TO THE NEW AGE, ARE YOU?

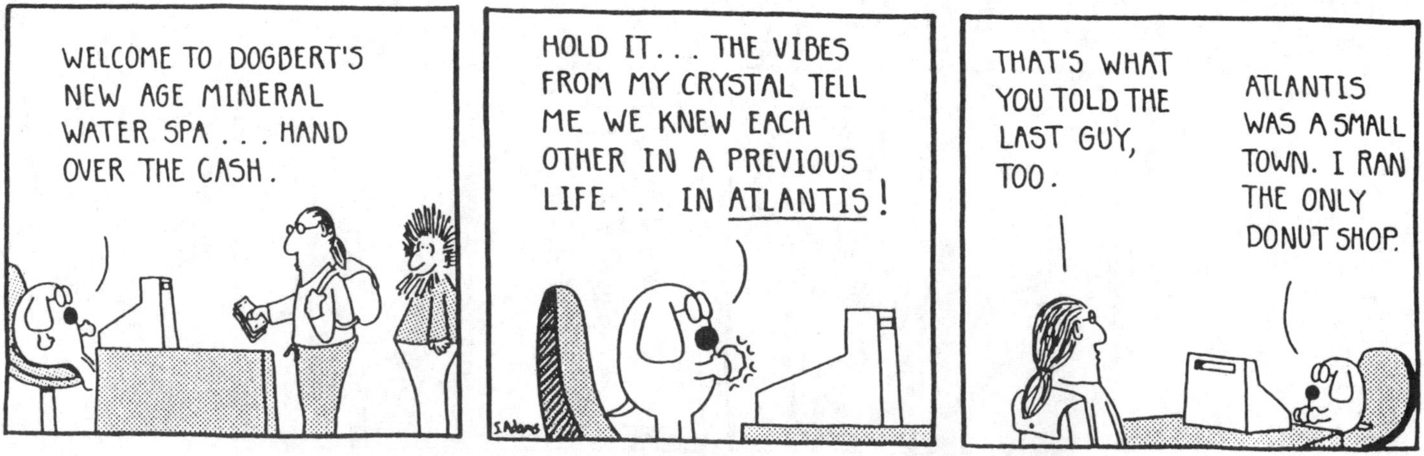
WELCOME TO DOGBERT'S NEW AGE MINERAL WATER SPA . . . HAND OVER THE CASH.
HOLD IT . . . THE VIBES FROM MY CRYSTAL TELL ME WE KNEW EACH OTHER IN A PREVIOUS LIFE . . . IN ATLANTIS!
S. Adams
THAT'S WHAT YOU TOLD THE LAST GUY, TOO.
ATLANTIS WAS A SMALL TOWN. I RAN THE ONLY DONUT SHOP.

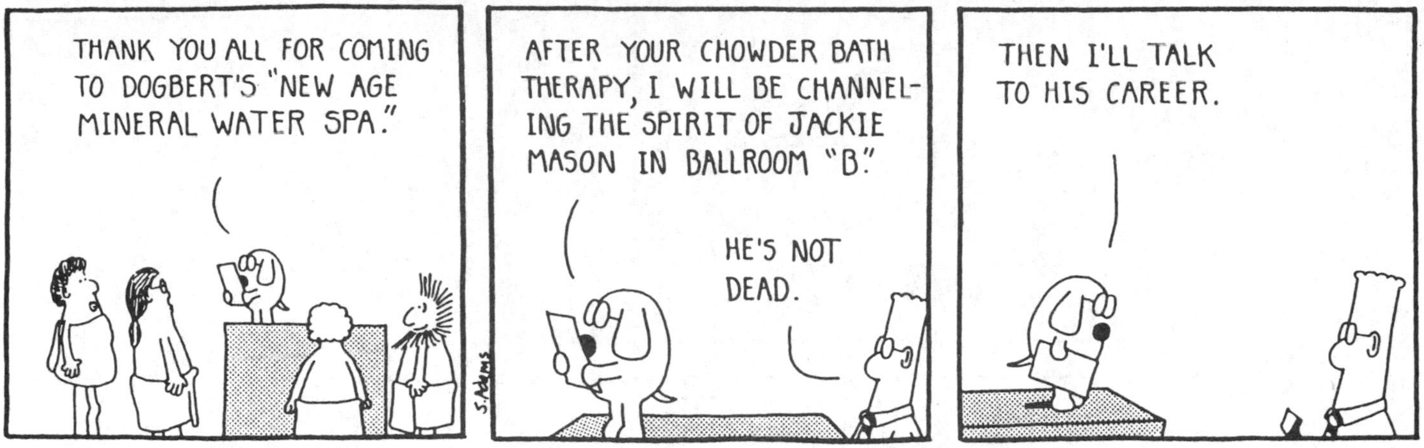
THANK YOU ALL FOR COMING TO DOGBERT'S "NEW AGE MINERAL WATER SPA."
S. Adams
AFTER YOUR CHOWDER BATH THERAPY, I WILL BE CHANNELING THE SPIRIT OF JACKIE MASON IN BALLROOM "B."
HE'S NOT DEAD.
THEN I'LL TALK TO HIS CAREER.

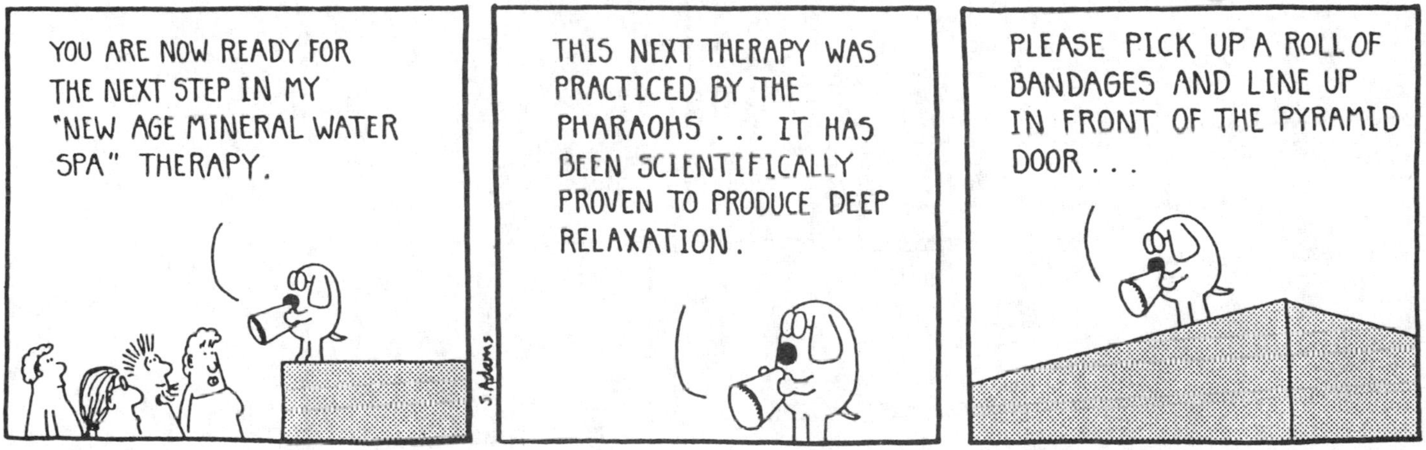
YOU ARE NOW READY FOR THE NEXT STEP IN MY "NEW AGE MINERAL WATER SPA" THERAPY.
S. Adams
THIS NEXT THERAPY WAS PRACTICED BY THE PHARAOHS . . . IT HAS BEEN SCIENTIFICALLY PROVEN TO PRODUCE DEEP RELAXATION.
PLEASE PICK UP A ROLL OF BANDAGES AND LINE UP IN FRONT OF THE PYRAMID DOOR . . .

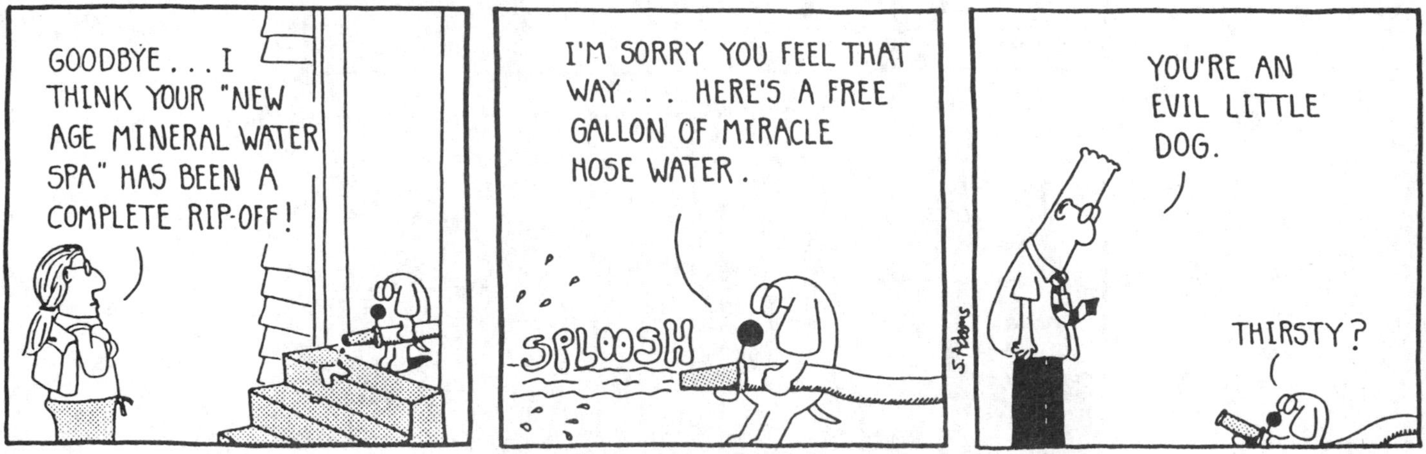
GOODBYE . . . I THINK YOUR "NEW AGE MINERAL WATER SPA" HAS BEEN A COMPLETE RIP-OFF!
I'M SORRY YOU FEEL THAT WAY . . . HERE'S A FREE GALLON OF MIRACLE HOSE WATER.
SPLOOSH
S. Adams
YOU'RE AN EVIL LITTLE DOG.
THIRSTY?

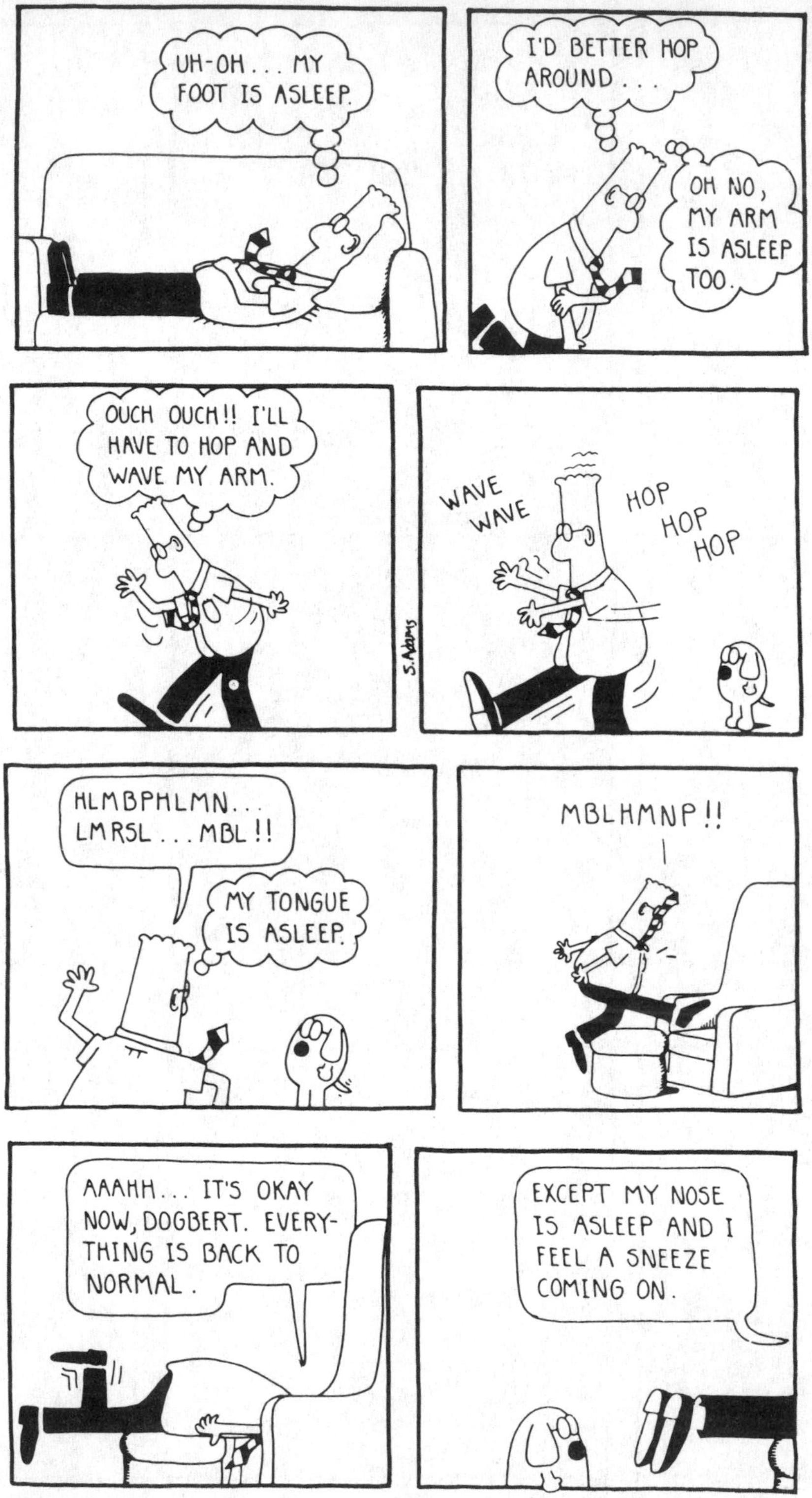
UH-OH... MY FOOT IS ASLEEP.
I'D BETTER HOP AROUND...
OH NO, MY ARM IS ASLEEP TOO.
OUCH OUCH!! I'LL HAVE TO HOP AND WAVE MY ARM.
S. Adams
WAVE WAVE
HOP HOP HOP
HLMBPHLMN... LMRSL...MBL!!
MY TONGUE IS ASLEEP.
MBLHMNP!!
AAAHH... IT'S OKAY NOW, DOGBERT. EVERY-THING IS BACK TO NORMAL.
EXCEPT MY NOSE IS ASLEEP AND I FEEL A SNEEZE COMING ON.

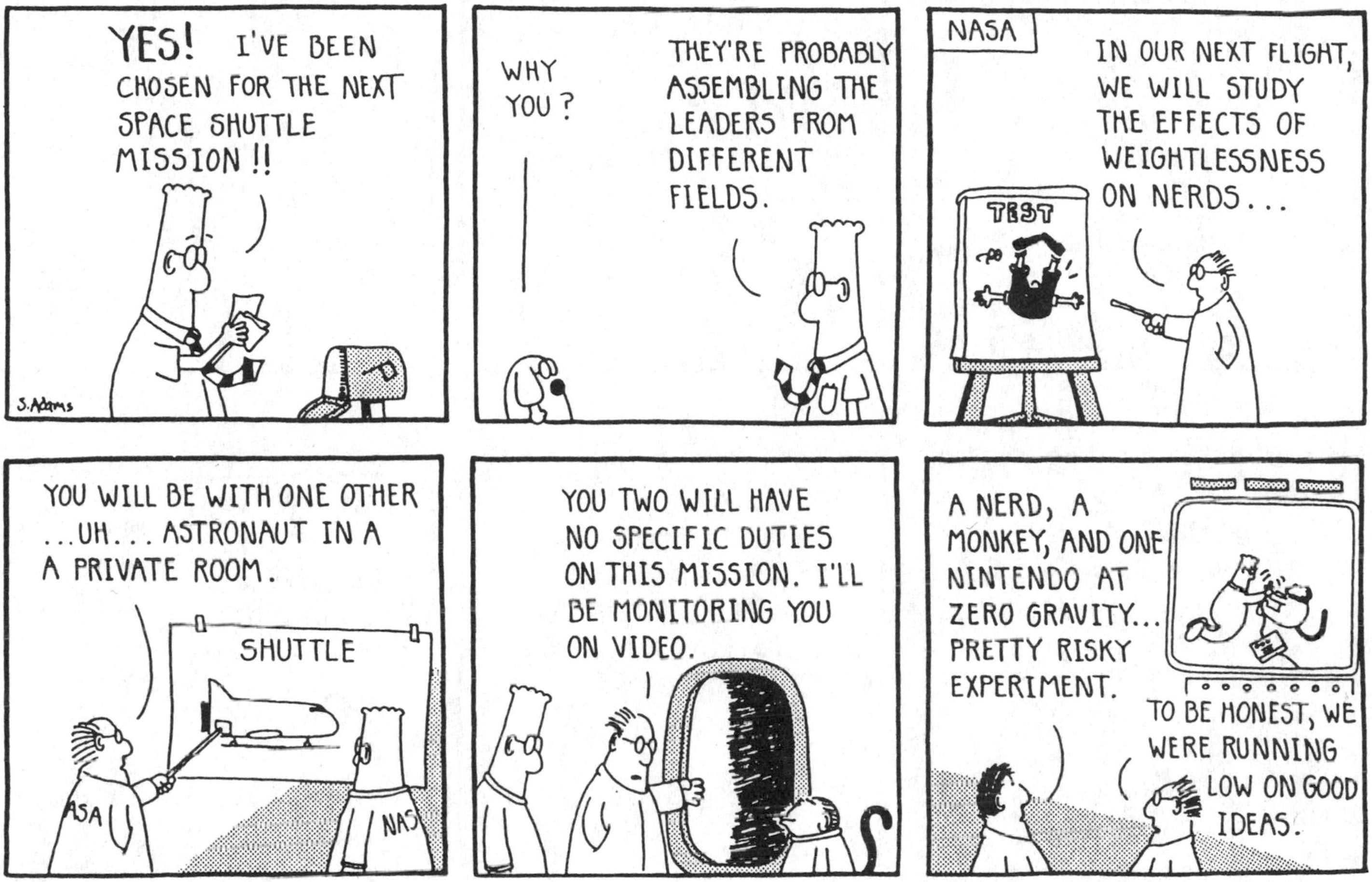
YES! I'VE BEEN CHOSEN FOR THE NEXT SPACE SHUTTLE MISSION !!
S. Adams
WHY YOU ?
THEY'RE PROBABLY ASSEMBLING THE LEADERS FROM DIFFERENT FIELDS.
NASA
IN OUR NEXT FLIGHT, WE WILL STUDY THE EFFECTS OF WEIGHTLESSNESS ON NERDS . . .
TEST
YOU WILL BE WITH ONE OTHER . . . UH . . . ASTRONAUT IN A A PRIVATE ROOM .
SHUTTLE
YOU TWO WILL HAVE NO SPECIFIC DUTIES ON THIS MISSION. I'LL BE MONITORING YOU ON VIDEO.
A NERD, A MONKEY, AND ONE NINTENDO AT ZERO GRAVITY... PRETTY RISKY EXPERIMENT.
TO BE HONEST, WE WERE RUNNING LOW ON GOOD IDEAS.

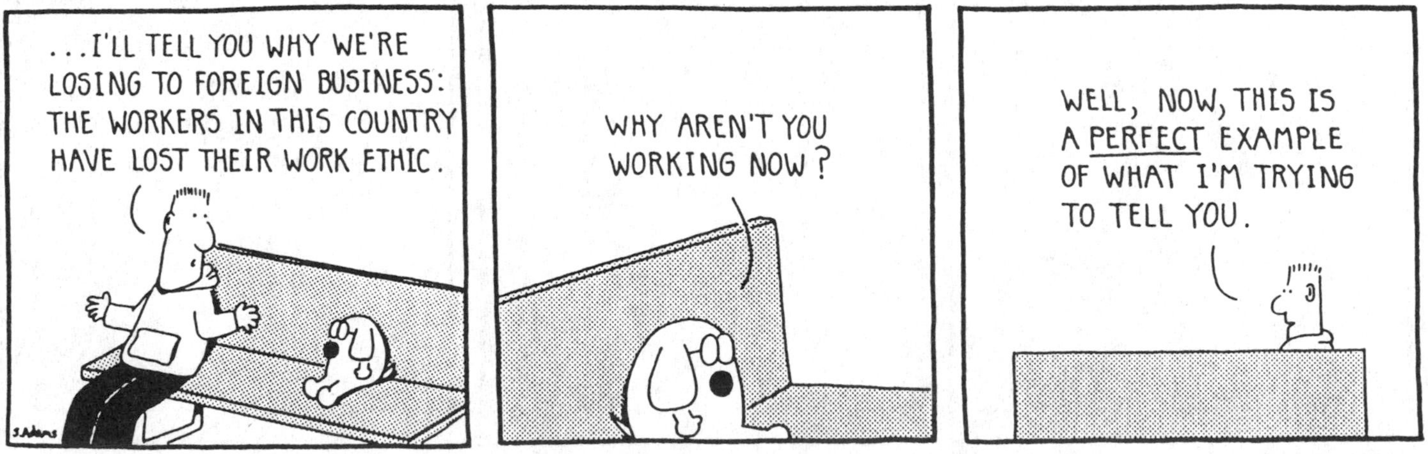
. . . I'LL TELL YOU WHY WE'RE LOSING TO FOREIGN BUSINESS: THE WORKERS IN THIS COUNTRY HAVE LOST THEIR WORK ETHIC .
S. Adams
WHY AREN'T YOU WORKING NOW ?
WELL, NOW, THIS IS A PERFECT EXAMPLE OF WHAT I'M TRYING TO TELL YOU .

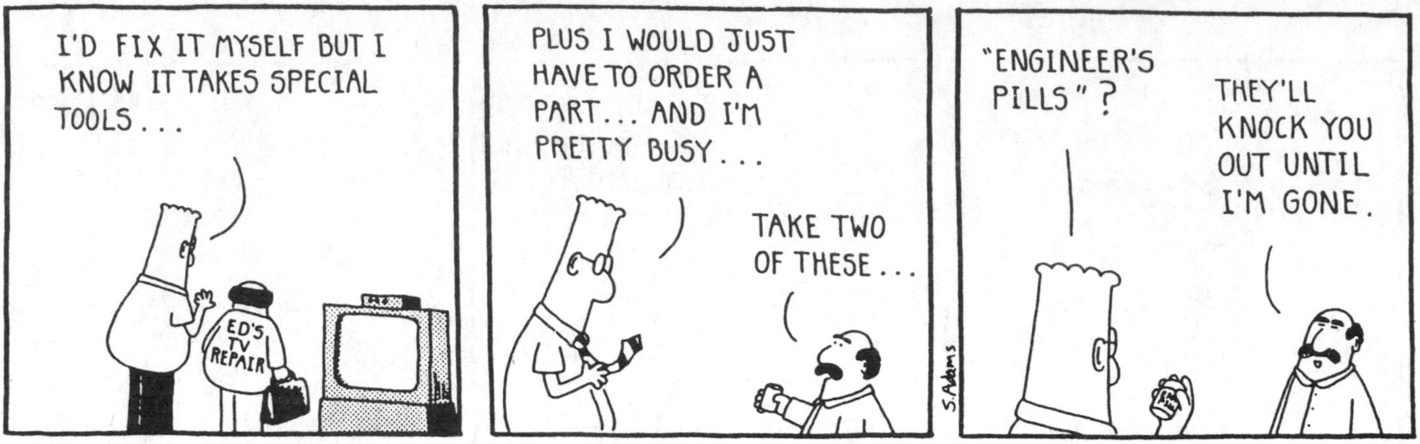
I'D FIX IT MYSELF BUT I KNOW IT TAKES SPECIAL TOOLS . . .
ED'S TV REPAIR
PLUS I WOULD JUST HAVE TO ORDER A PART . . . AND I'M PRETTY BUSY . . .
TAKE TWO OF THESE . . .
S. Adams
"ENGINEER'S PILLS" ?
THEY'LL KNOCK YOU OUT UNTIL I'M GONE .

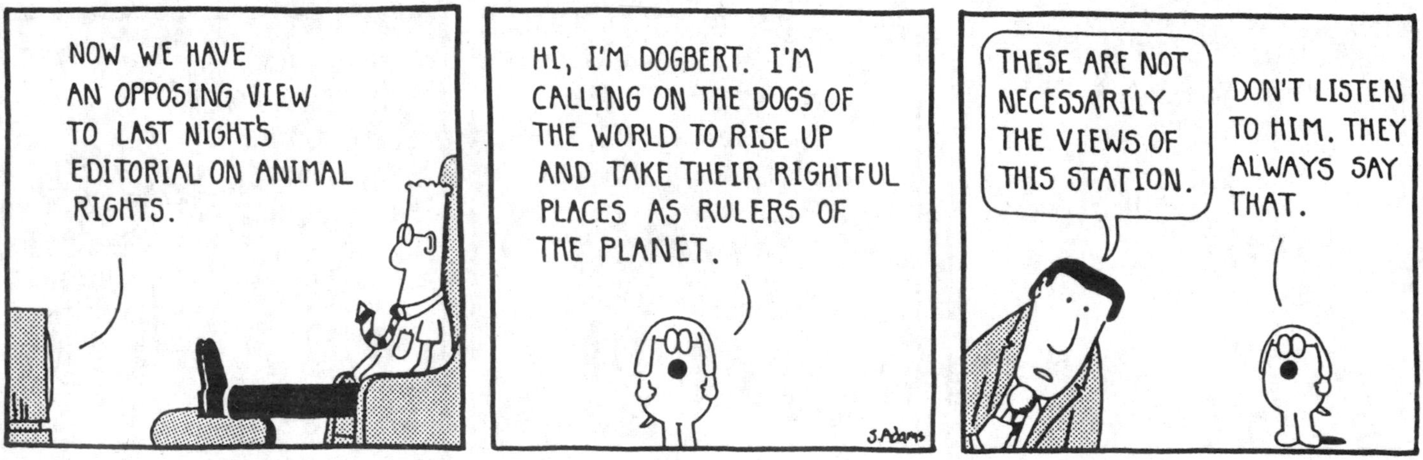
NOW WE HAVE AN OPPOSING VIEW TO LAST NIGHT'S EDITORIAL ON ANIMAL RIGHTS.
HI, I'M DOGBERT. I'M CALLING ON THE DOGS OF THE WORLD TO RISE UP AND TAKE THEIR RIGHTFUL PLACES AS RULERS OF THE PLANET.
S. Adams
THESE ARE NOT NECESSARILY THE VIEWS OF THIS STATION.
DON'T LISTEN TO HIM. THEY ALWAYS SAY THAT.

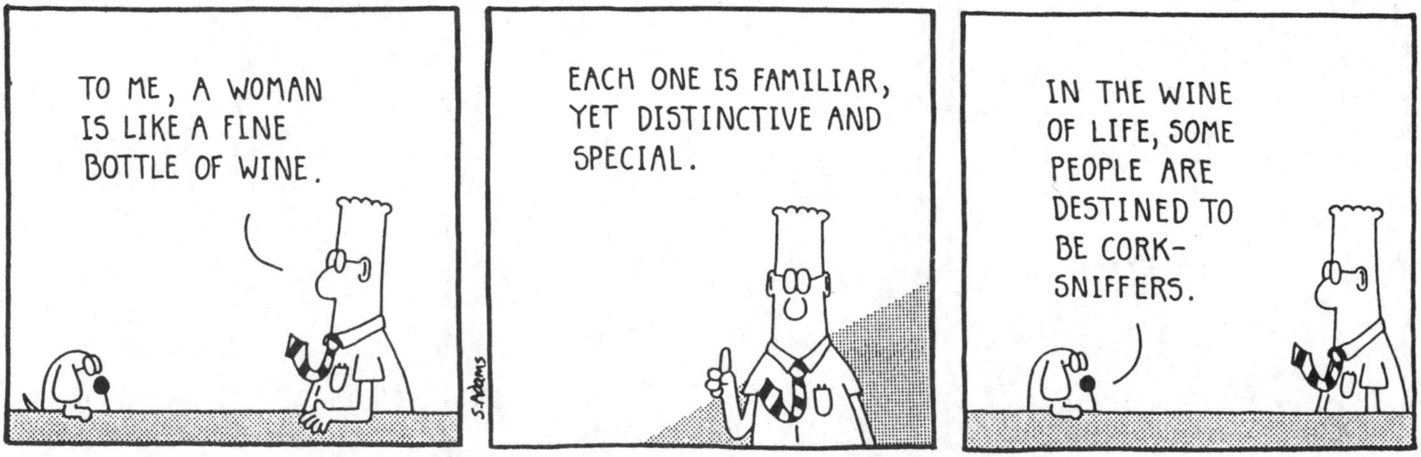
TO ME, A WOMAN IS LIKE A FINE BOTTLE OF WINE .
S. Adams
EACH ONE IS FAMILIAR, YET DISTINCTIVE AND SPECIAL .
IN THE WINE OF LIFE, SOME PEOPLE ARE DESTINED TO BE CORK-SNIFFERS .

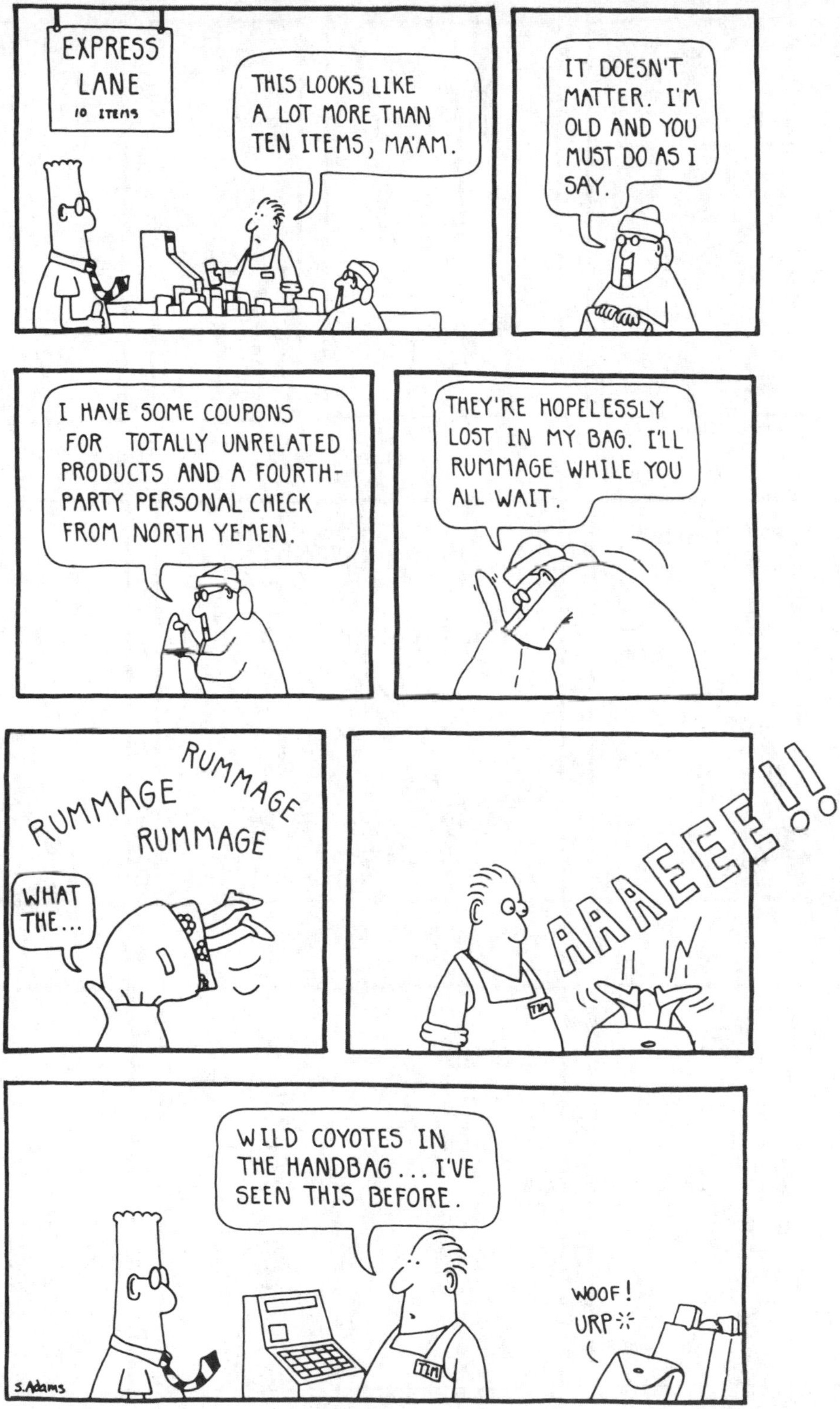

EXPRESS LANE
10 ITEMS
THIS LOOKS LIKE A LOT MORE THAN TEN ITEMS, MA'AM.
IT DOESN'T MATTER. I'M OLD AND YOU MUST DO AS I SAY.
I HAVE SOME COUPONS FOR TOTALLY UNRELATED PRODUCTS AND A FOURTH-PARTY PERSONAL CHECK FROM NORTH YEMEN.
THEY'RE HOPELESSLY LOST IN MY BAG. I'LL RUMMAGE WHILE YOU ALL WAIT.
RUMMAGE
RUMMAGE
RUMMAGE
WHAT THE...
AAAEEE!!
TIM
WILD COYOTES IN THE HANDBAG... I'VE SEEN THIS BEFORE.
WOOF!
URP
TIM
S.Adams

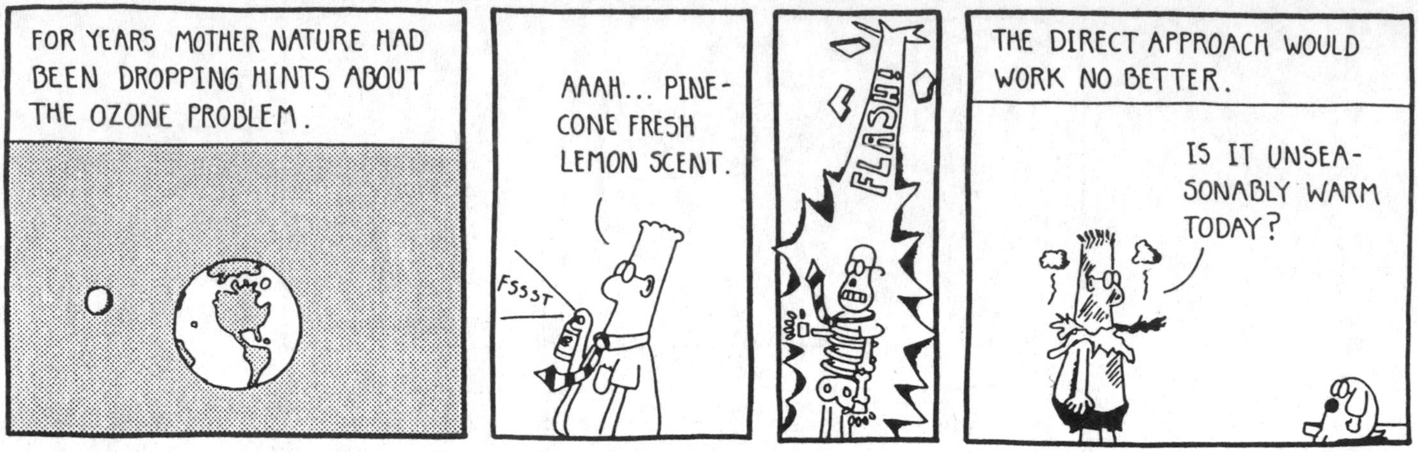
FOR YEARS MOTHER NATURE HAD BEEN DROPPING HINTS ABOUT THE OZONE PROBLEM.
AAAH... PINE-CONE FRESH LEMON SCENT.
FSSST
FLASH!
THE DIRECT APPROACH WOULD WORK NO BETTER.
IS IT UNSEA-SONABLY WARM TODAY?

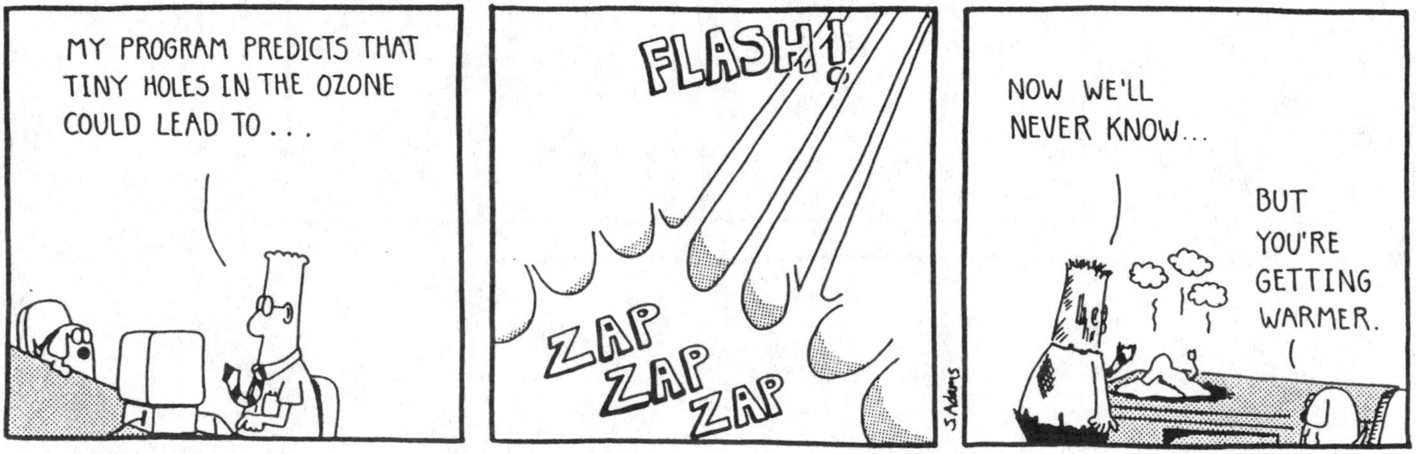
MY PROGRAM PREDICTS THAT TINY HOLES IN THE OZONE COULD LEAD TO...
FLASH!
ZAP
ZAP
ZAP
S. Adams
NOW WE'LL NEVER KNOW...
BUT YOU'RE GETTING WARMER.

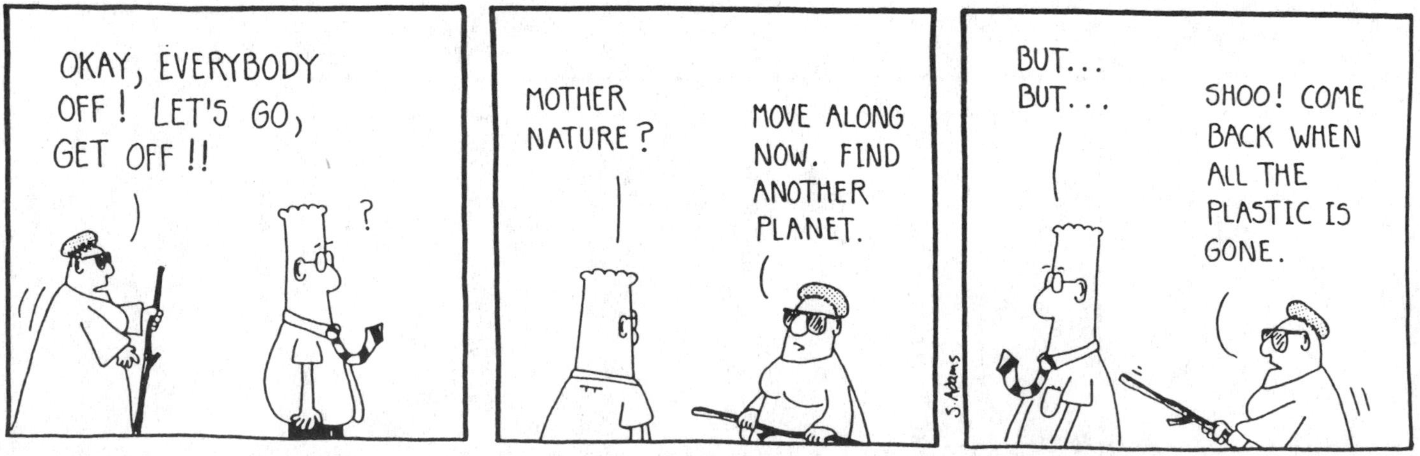
OKAY, EVERYBODY OFF! LET'S GO, GET OFF!!
?
MOTHER NATURE?
MOVE ALONG NOW. FIND ANOTHER PLANET.
S. Adams
BUT... BUT...
SHOO! COME BACK WHEN ALL THE PLASTIC IS GONE.

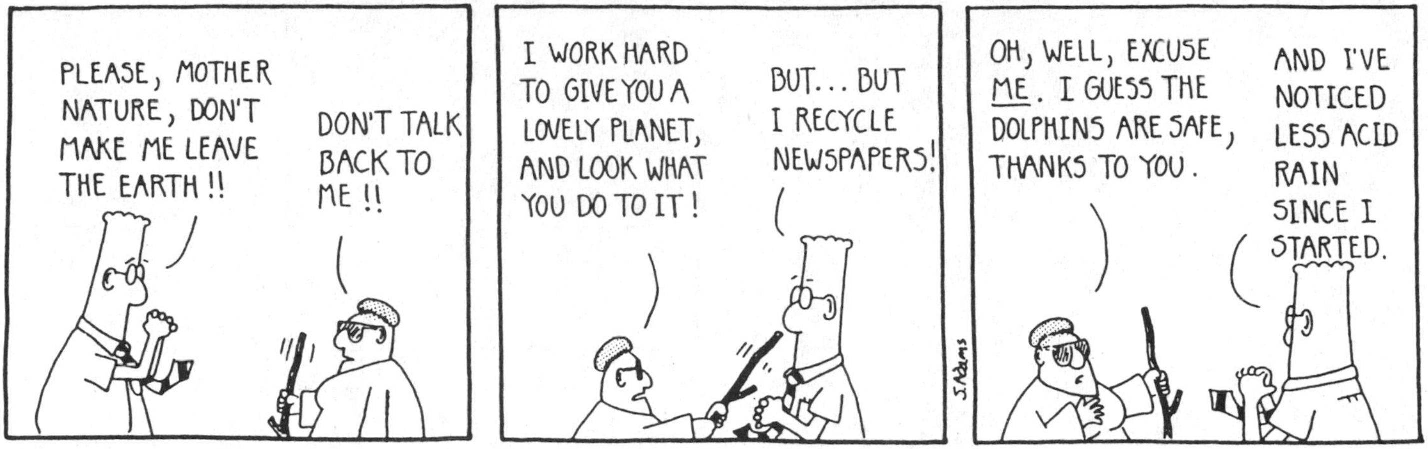
PLEASE, MOTHER NATURE, DON'T MAKE ME LEAVE THE EARTH !!
DON'T TALK BACK TO ME !!
I WORK HARD TO GIVE YOU A LOVELY PLANET, AND LOOK WHAT YOU DO TO IT !
BUT... BUT I RECYCLE NEWSPAPERS!
OH, WELL, EXCUSE ME. I GUESS THE DOLPHINS ARE SAFE, THANKS TO YOU.
AND I'VE NOTICED LESS ACID RAIN SINCE I STARTED.

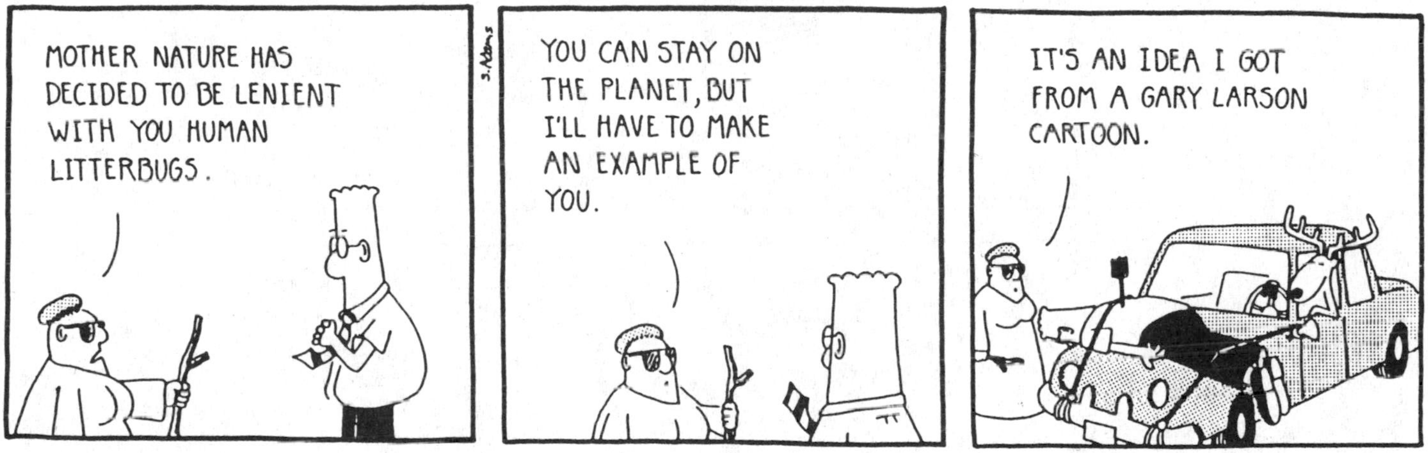
MOTHER NATURE HAS DECIDED TO BE LENIENT WITH YOU HUMAN LITTERBUGS.
YOU CAN STAY ON THE PLANET, BUT I'LL HAVE TO MAKE AN EXAMPLE OF YOU.
IT'S AN IDEA I GOT FROM A GARY LARSON CARTOON.

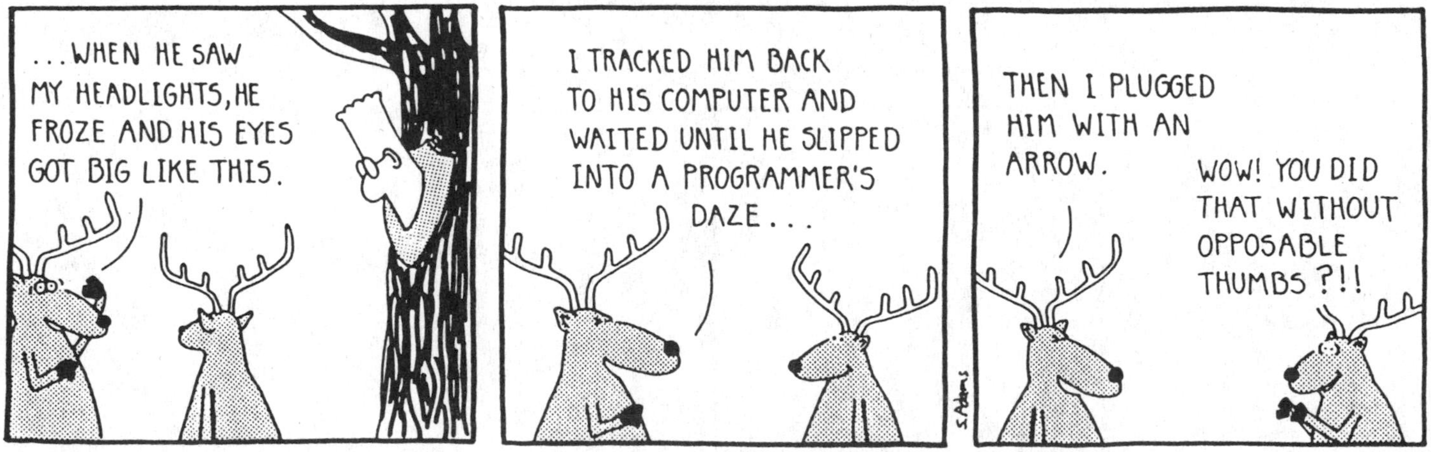
...WHEN HE SAW MY HEADLIGHTS, HE FROZE AND HIS EYES GOT BIG LIKE THIS.
I TRACKED HIM BACK TO HIS COMPUTER AND WAITED UNTIL HE SLIPPED INTO A PROGRAMMER'S DAZE...
THEN I PLUGGED HIM WITH AN ARROW.
WOW! YOU DID THAT WITHOUT OPPOSABLE THUMBS ?!!

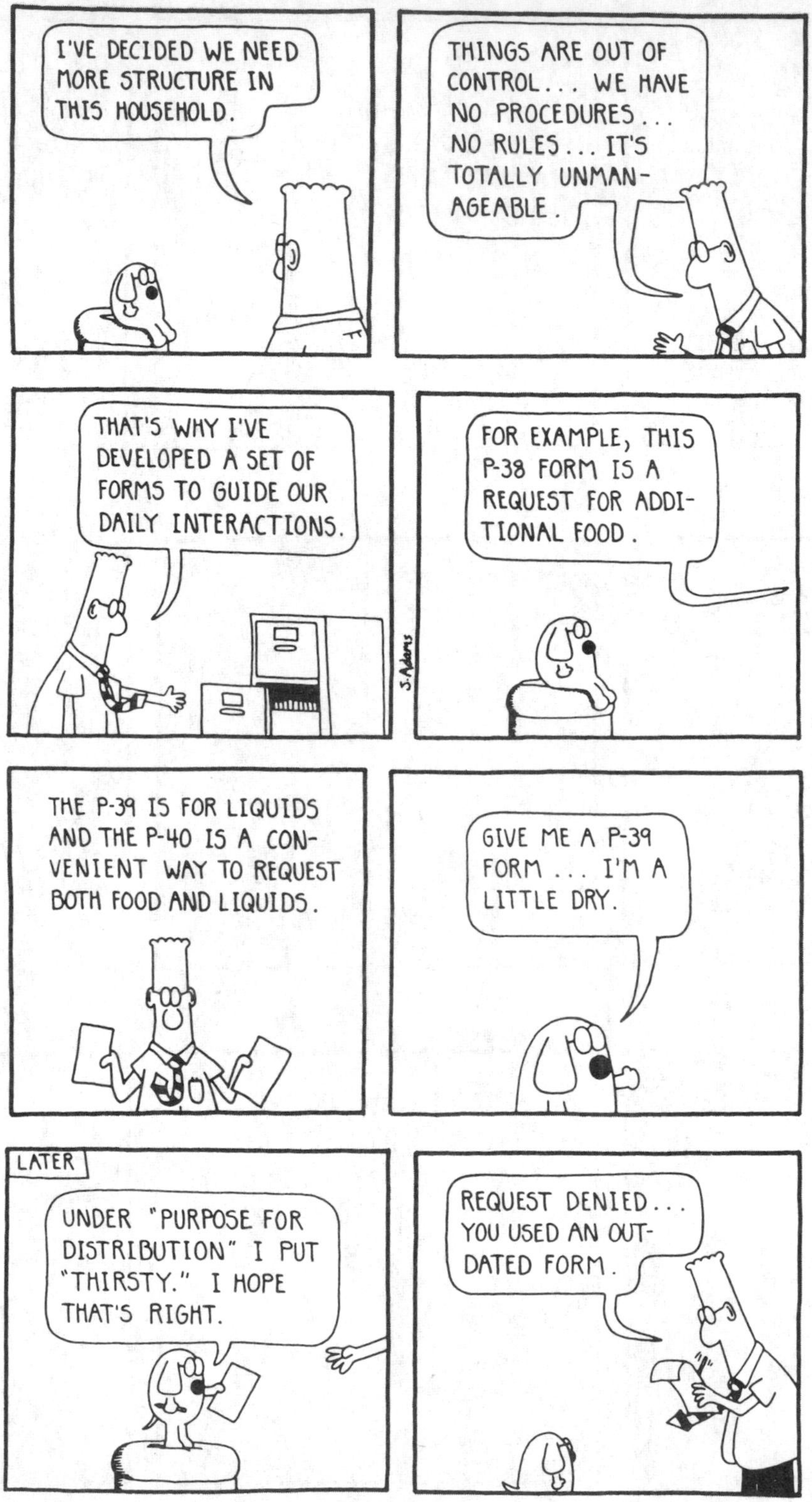
I'VE DECIDED WE NEED MORE STRUCTURE IN THIS HOUSEHOLD.
THINGS ARE OUT OF CONTROL... WE HAVE NO PROCEDURES... NO RULES... IT'S TOTALLY UNMAN-AGEABLE.
THAT'S WHY I'VE DEVELOPED A SET OF FORMS TO GUIDE OUR DAILY INTERACTIONS.
S. Adams
FOR EXAMPLE, THIS P-38 FORM IS A REQUEST FOR ADDI-TIONAL FOOD.
THE P-39 IS FOR LIQUIDS AND THE P-40 IS A CON-VENIENT WAY TO REQUEST BOTH FOOD AND LIQUIDS.
GIVE ME A P-39 FORM ... I'M A LITTLE DRY.
LATER
UNDER "PURPOSE FOR DISTRIBUTION" I PUT "THIRSTY." I HOPE THAT'S RIGHT.
REQUEST DENIED... YOU USED AN OUT-DATED FORM.

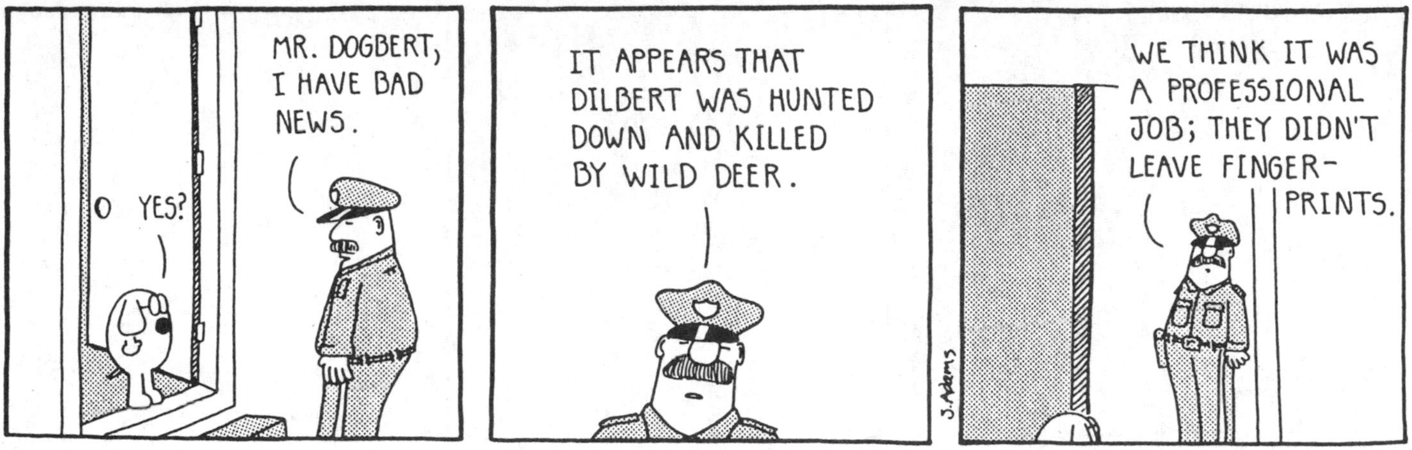
YES?
MR. DOGBERT, I HAVE BAD NEWS.
IT APPEARS THAT DILBERT WAS HUNTED DOWN AND KILLED BY WILD DEER.
WE THINK IT WAS A PROFESSIONAL JOB; THEY DIDN'T LEAVE FINGER-PRINTS.

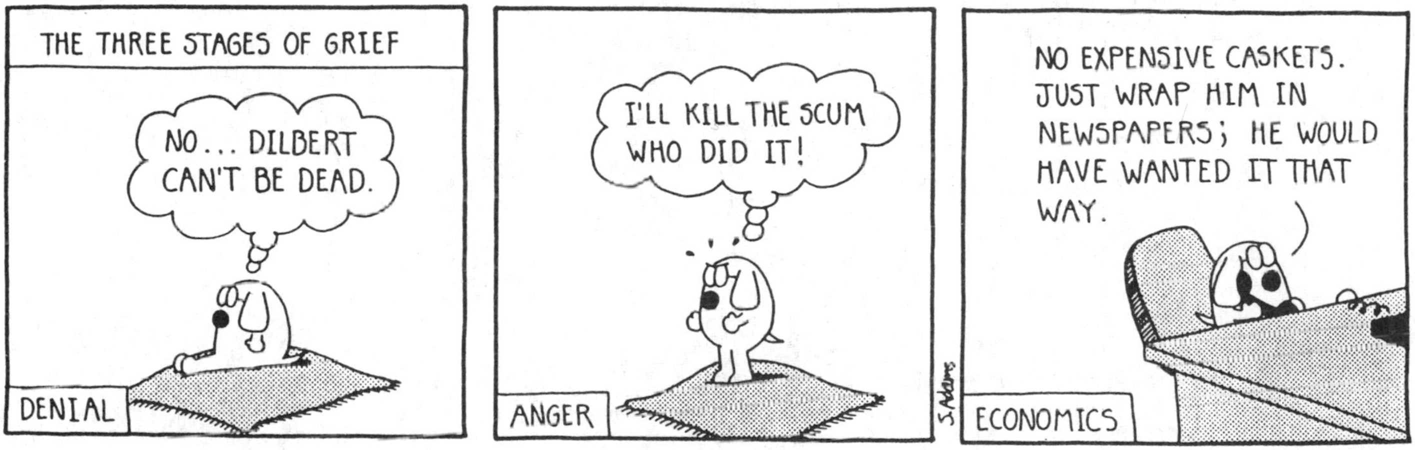
THE THREE STAGES OF GRIEF
NO... DILBERT CAN'T BE DEAD.
DENIAL
I'LL KILL THE SCUM WHO DID IT!
ANGER
NO EXPENSIVE CASKETS. JUST WRAP HIM IN NEWSPAPERS; HE WOULD HAVE WANTED IT THAT WAY.
ECONOMICS

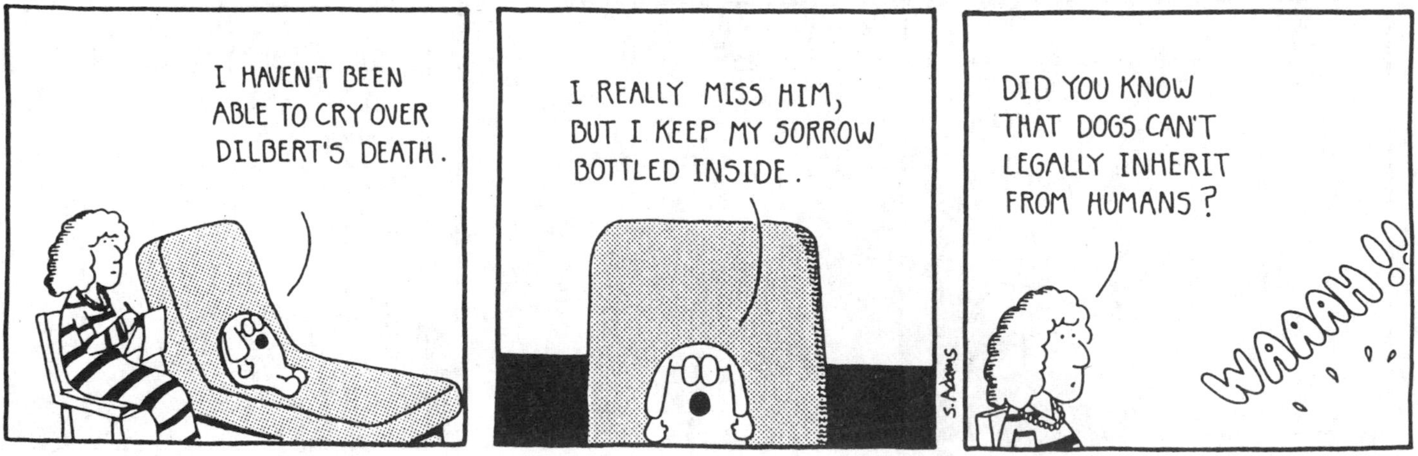
I HAVEN'T BEEN ABLE TO CRY OVER DILBERT'S DEATH.
I REALLY MISS HIM, BUT I KEEP MY SORROW BOTTLED INSIDE.
DID YOU KNOW THAT DOGS CAN'T LEGALLY INHERIT FROM HUMANS?
WAAAH!!

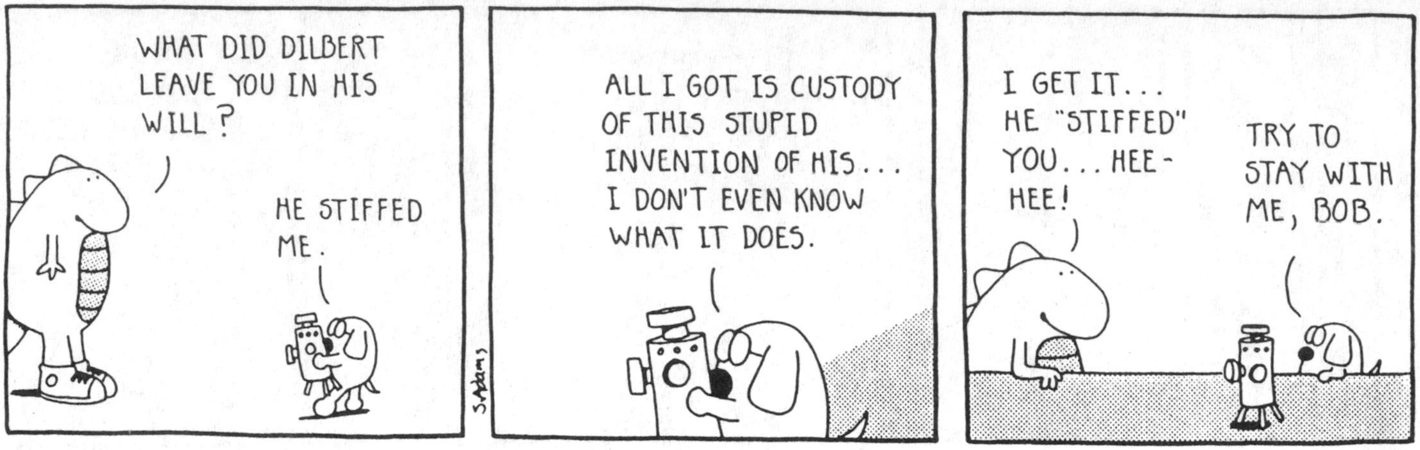
WHAT DID DILBERT LEAVE YOU IN HIS WILL?
HE STIFFED ME.
ALL I GOT IS CUSTODY OF THIS STUPID INVENTION OF HIS... I DON'T EVEN KNOW WHAT IT DOES.
I GET IT... HE "STIFFED" YOU... HEE-HEE!
TRY TO STAY WITH ME, BOB.
S. Adams

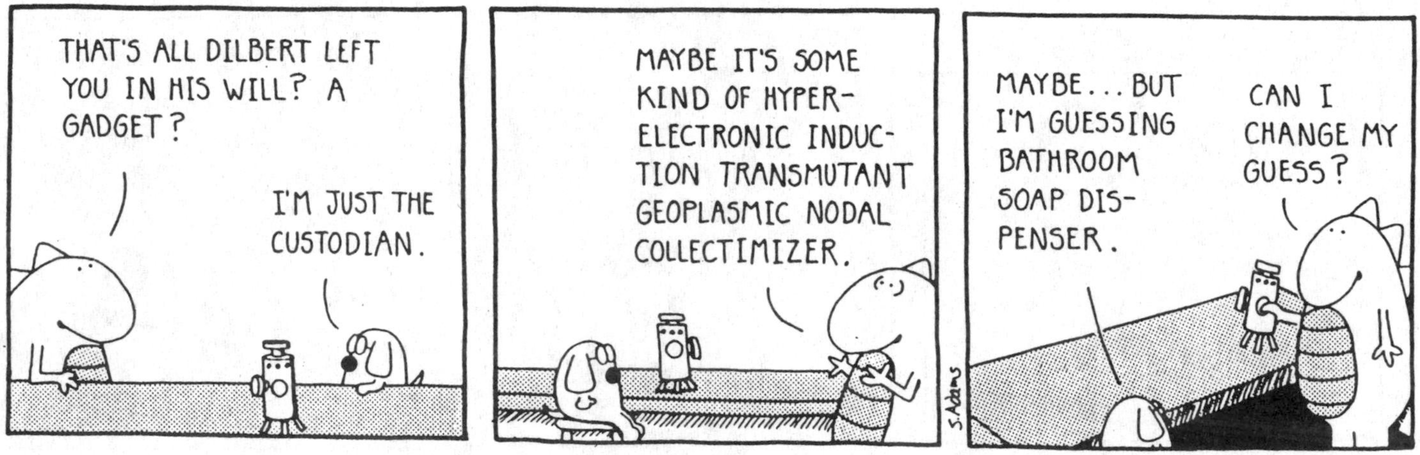
THAT'S ALL DILBERT LEFT YOU IN HIS WILL? A GADGET?
I'M JUST THE CUSTODIAN.
MAYBE IT'S SOME KIND OF HYPER-ELECTRONIC INDUCTION TRANSMUTANT GEOPLASMIC NODAL COLLECTIMIZER.
MAYBE... BUT I'M GUESSING BATHROOM SOAP DISPENSER.
CAN I CHANGE MY GUESS?
S. Adams

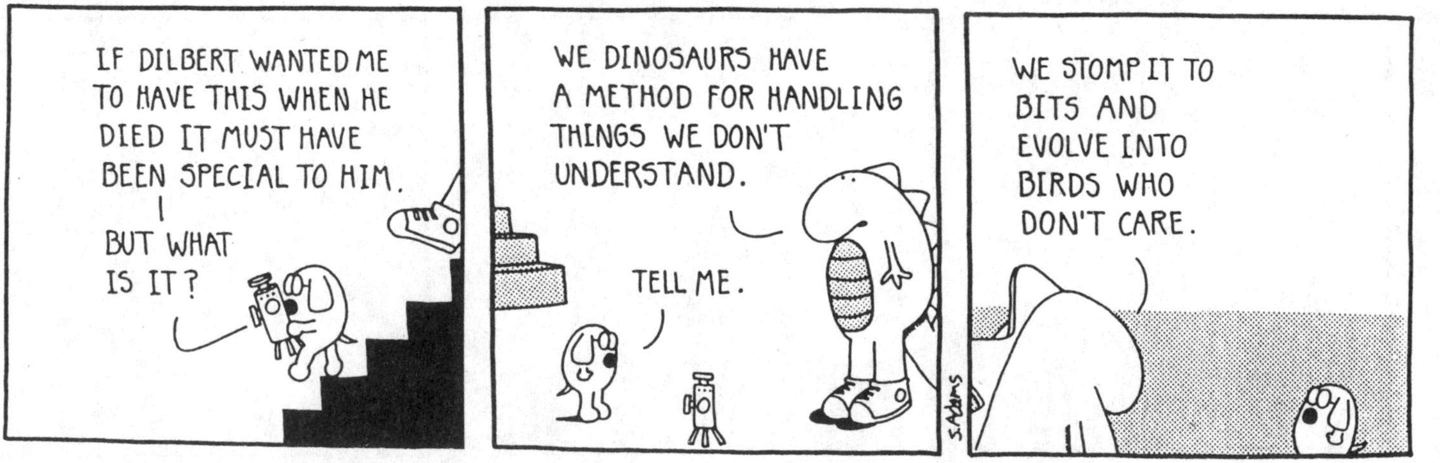
IF DILBERT WANTED ME TO HAVE THIS WHEN HE DIED IT MUST HAVE BEEN SPECIAL TO HIM.
BUT WHAT IS IT?
WE DINOSAURS HAVE A METHOD FOR HANDLING THINGS WE DON'T UNDERSTAND.
TELL ME.
WE STOMP IT TO BITS AND EVOLVE INTO BIRDS WHO DON'T CARE.
S. Adams

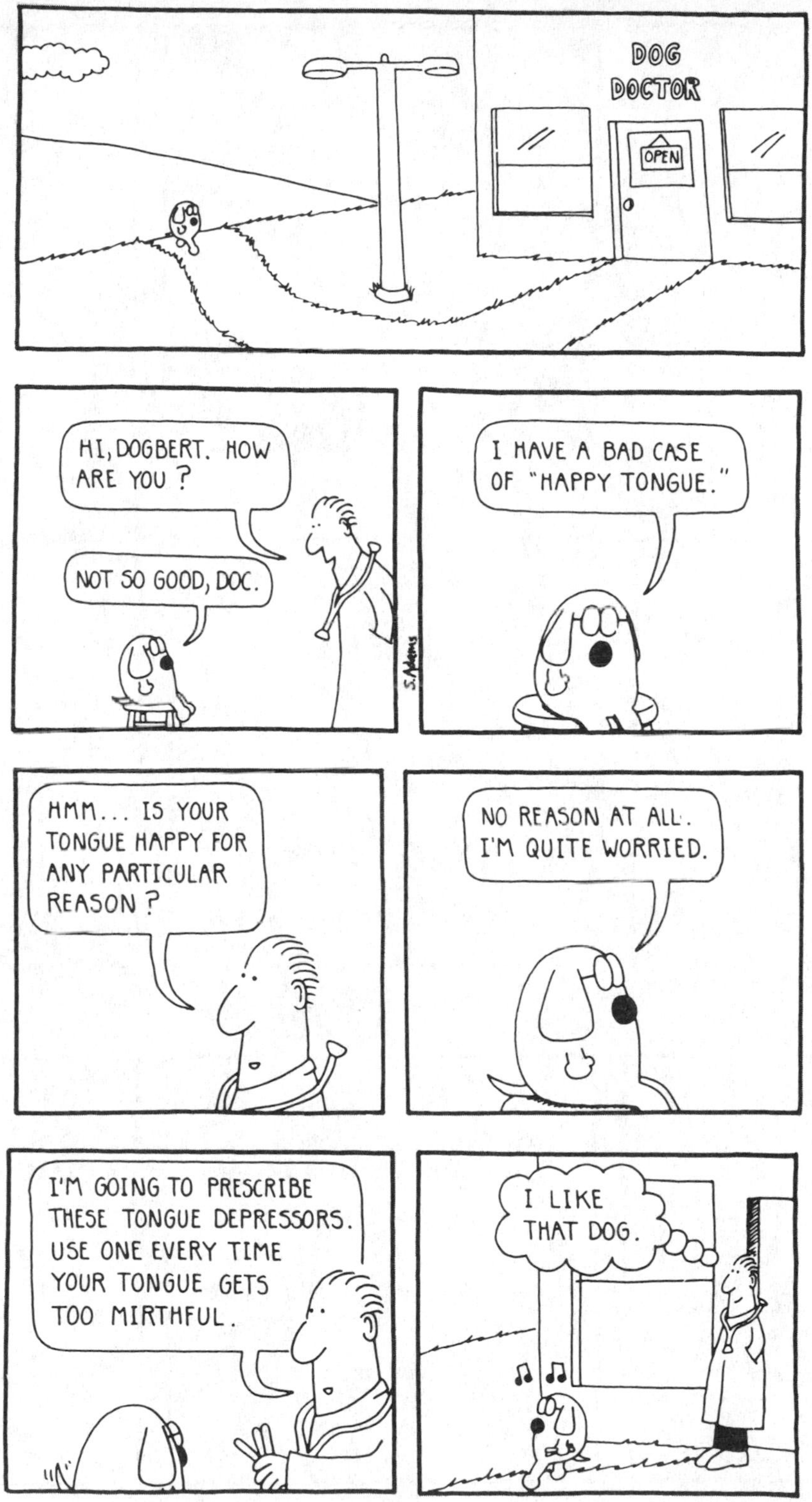
DOG DOCTOR
OPEN
HI, DOGBERT. HOW ARE YOU ?
NOT SO GOOD, DOC.
S. Adams
I HAVE A BAD CASE OF "HAPPY TONGUE."
HMM... IS YOUR TONGUE HAPPY FOR ANY PARTICULAR REASON ?
NO REASON AT ALL. I'M QUITE WORRIED.
I'M GOING TO PRESCRIBE THESE TONGUE DEPRESSORS. USE ONE EVERY TIME YOUR TONGUE GETS TOO MIRTHFUL.
I LIKE THAT DOG.

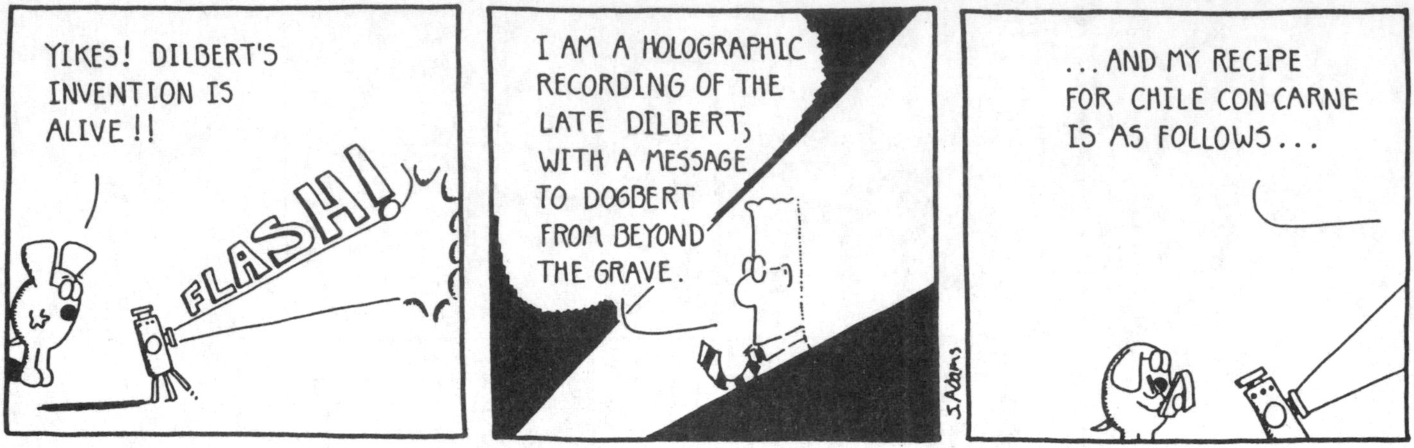
YIKES! DILBERT'S INVENTION IS ALIVE!!
FLASH!
I AM A HOLOGRAPHIC RECORDING OF THE LATE DILBERT, WITH A MESSAGE TO DOGBERT FROM BEYOND THE GRAVE.
...AND MY RECIPE FOR CHILE CON CARNE IS AS FOLLOWS...

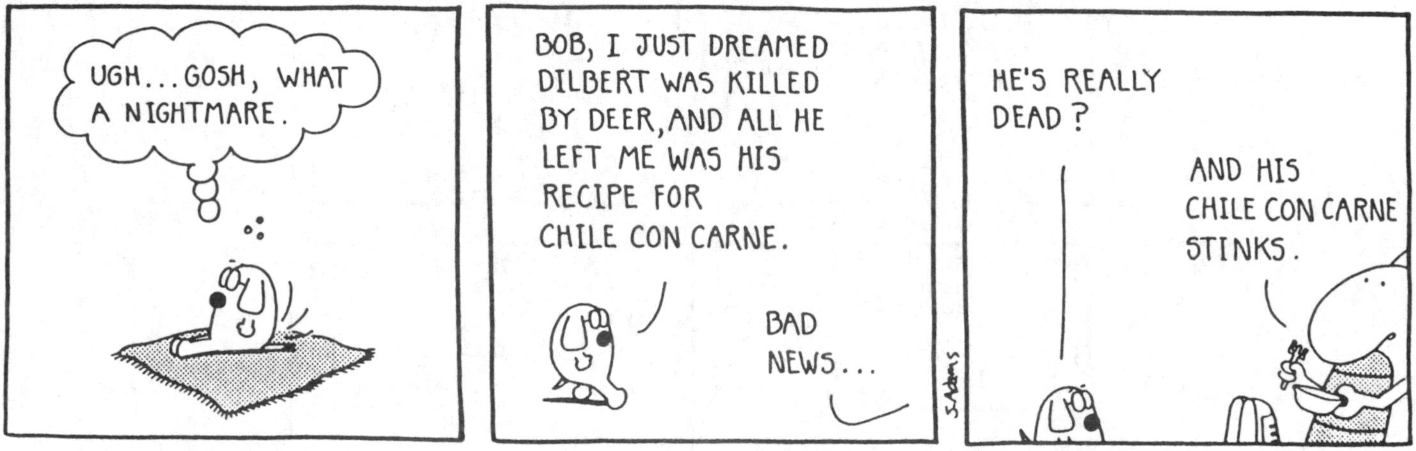
UGH...GOSH, WHAT A NIGHTMARE.
BOB, I JUST DREAMED DILBERT WAS KILLED BY DEER, AND ALL HE LEFT ME WAS HIS RECIPE FOR CHILE CON CARNE.
BAD NEWS...
HE'S REALLY DEAD?
AND HIS CHILE CON CARNE STINKS.

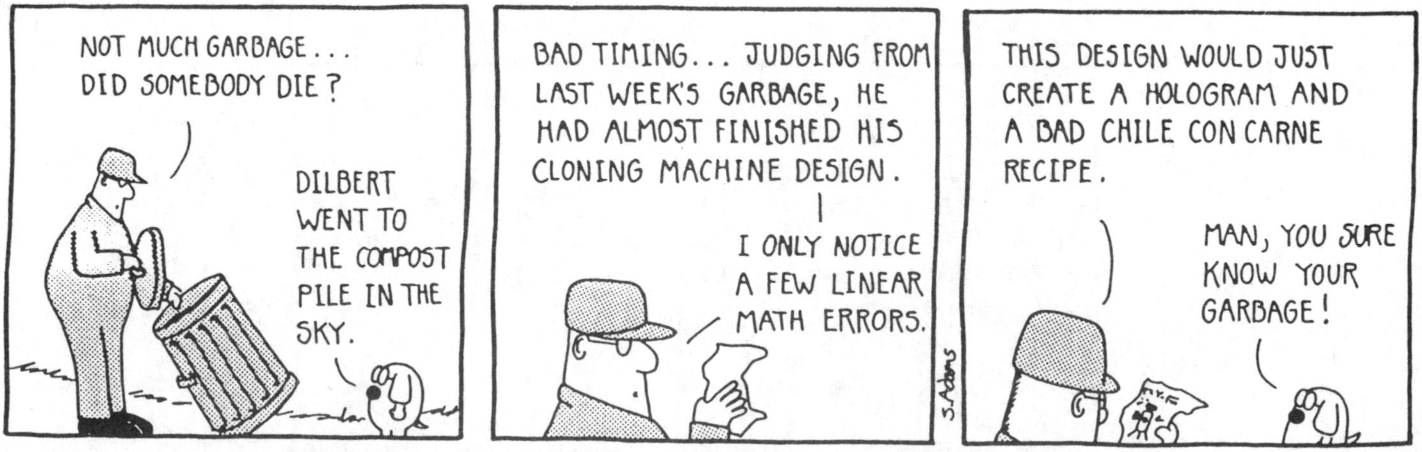
NOT MUCH GARBAGE... DID SOMEBODY DIE?
DILBERT WENT TO THE COMPOST PILE IN THE SKY.
BAD TIMING... JUDGING FROM LAST WEEK'S GARBAGE, HE HAD ALMOST FINISHED HIS CLONING MACHINE DESIGN.
I ONLY NOTICE A FEW LINEAR MATH ERRORS.
THIS DESIGN WOULD JUST CREATE A HOLOGRAM AND A BAD CHILE CON CARNE RECIPE.
MAN, YOU SURE KNOW YOUR GARBAGE!

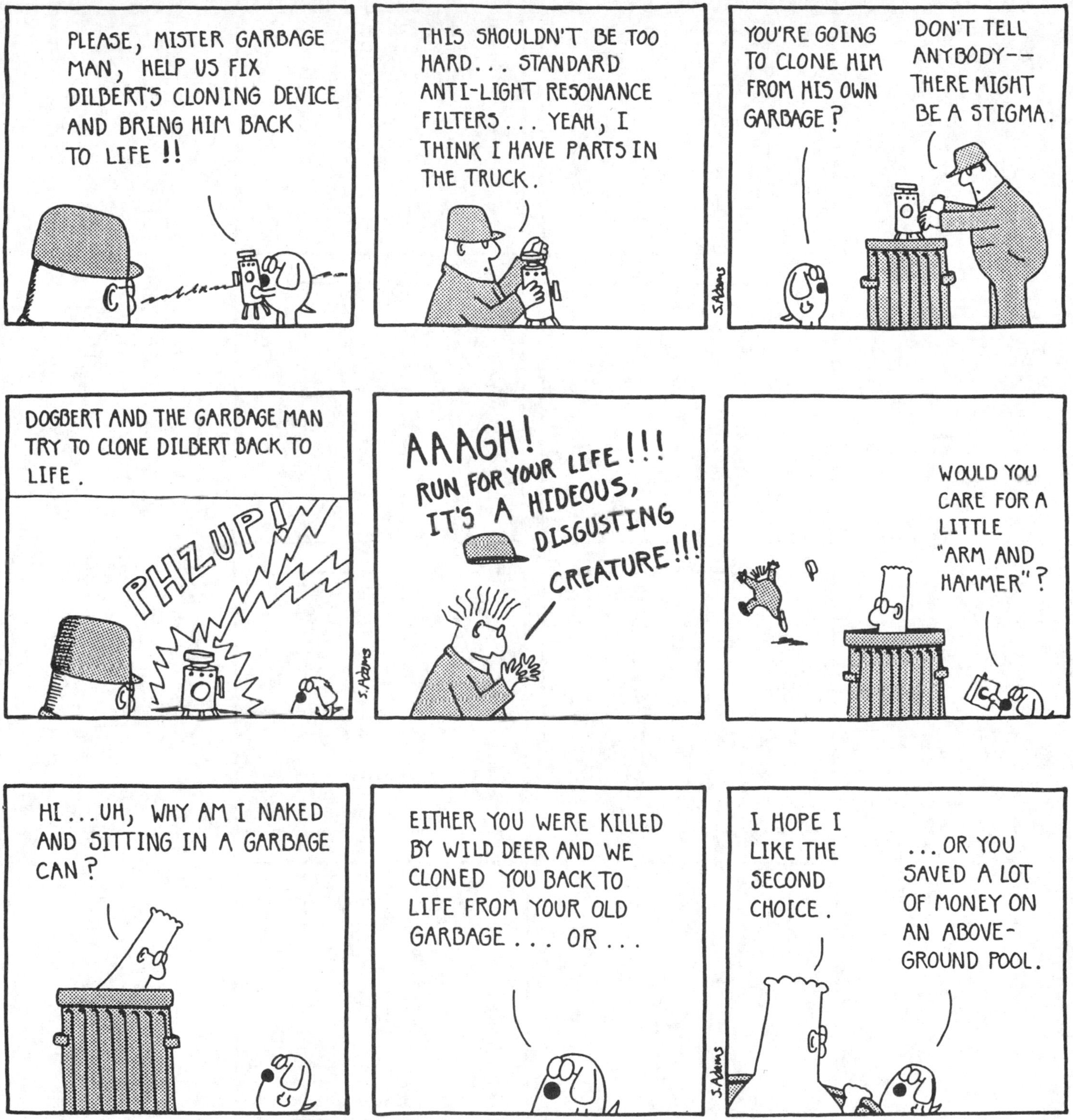
PLEASE, MISTER GARBAGE MAN, HELP US FIX DILBERT'S CLONING DEVICE AND BRING HIM BACK TO LIFE !!
THIS SHOULDN'T BE TOO HARD... STANDARD ANTI-LIGHT RESONANCE FILTERS... YEAH, I THINK I HAVE PARTS IN THE TRUCK.
YOU'RE GOING TO CLONE HIM FROM HIS OWN GARBAGE?
DON'T TELL ANYBODY-- THERE MIGHT BE A STIGMA.
S. Adams
DOGBERT AND THE GARBAGE MAN TRY TO CLONE DILBERT BACK TO LIFE.
PHZUP!
S. Adams
AAAGH!
RUN FOR YOUR LIFE!!!
IT'S A HIDEOUS, DISGUSTING CREATURE!!!
WOULD YOU CARE FOR A LITTLE "ARM AND HAMMER"?
HI... UH, WHY AM I NAKED AND SITTING IN A GARBAGE CAN?
EITHER YOU WERE KILLED BY WILD DEER AND WE CLONED YOU BACK TO LIFE FROM YOUR OLD GARBAGE... OR...
I HOPE I LIKE THE SECOND CHOICE.
...OR YOU SAVED A LOT OF MONEY ON AN ABOVE-GROUND POOL.
S. Adams

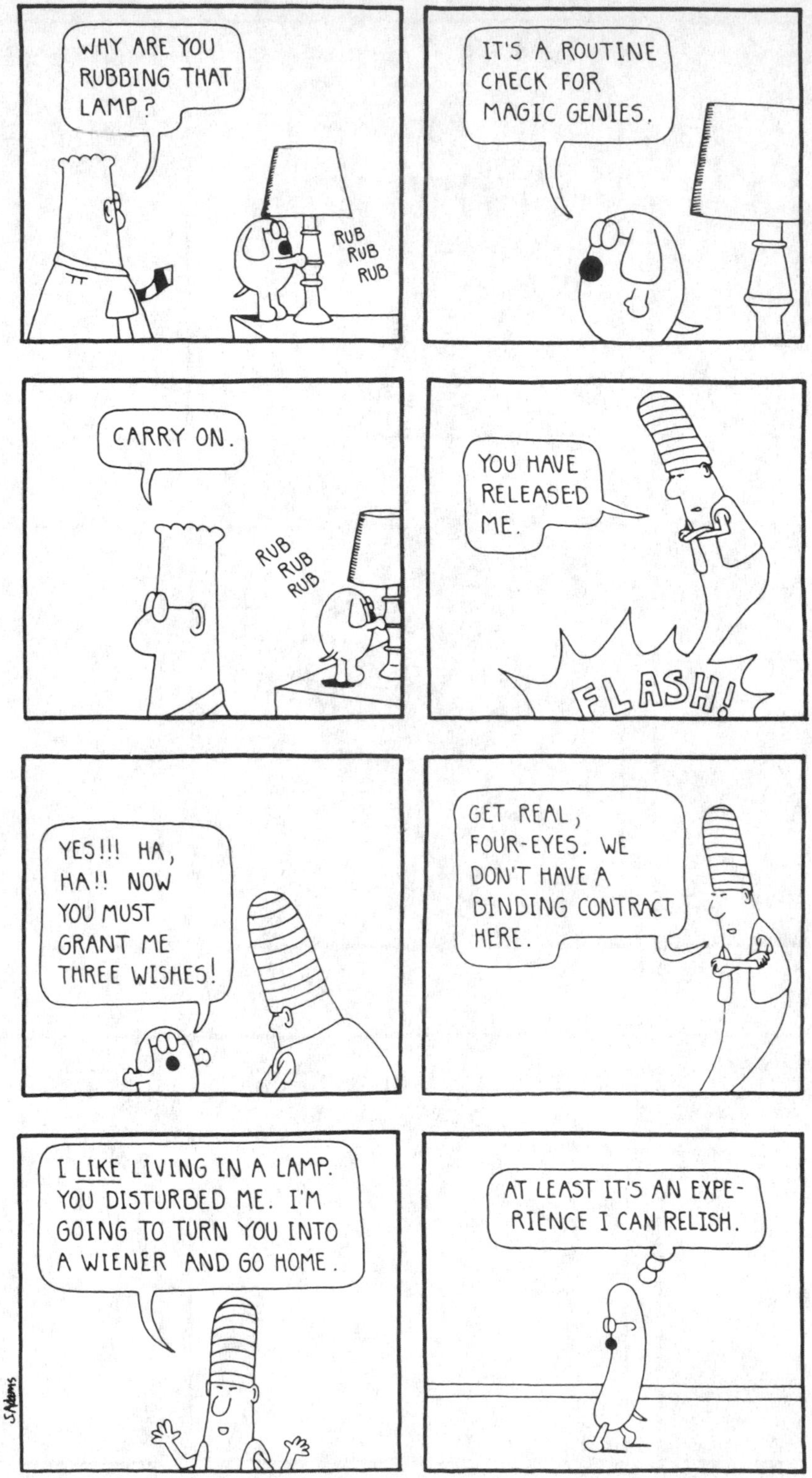
WHY ARE YOU RUBBING THAT LAMP?
RUB RUB RUB
IT'S A ROUTINE CHECK FOR MAGIC GENIES.
CARRY ON.
RUB RUB RUB
YOU HAVE RELEASED ME.
FLASH!
YES!!! HA, HA!! NOW YOU MUST GRANT ME THREE WISHES!
GET REAL, FOUR-EYES. WE DON'T HAVE A BINDING CONTRACT HERE.
I LIKE LIVING IN A LAMP. YOU DISTURBED ME. I'M GOING TO TURN YOU INTO A WIENER AND GO HOME.
AT LEAST IT'S AN EXPE-RIENCE I CAN RELISH.
S. Adams

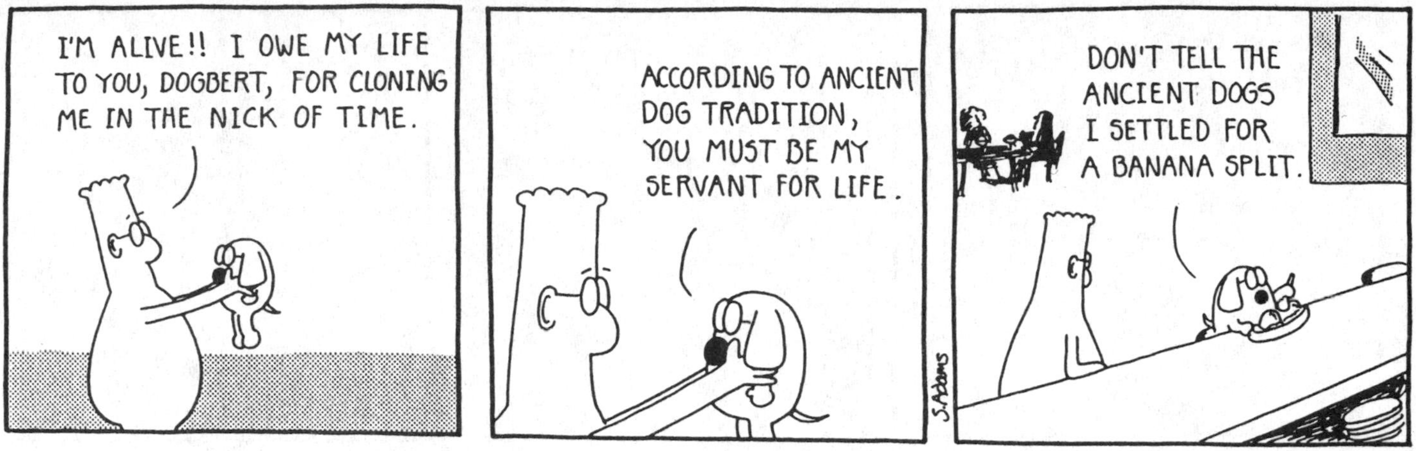
I'M ALIVE!! I OWE MY LIFE TO YOU, DOGBERT, FOR CLONING ME IN THE NICK OF TIME.
ACCORDING TO ANCIENT DOG TRADITION, YOU MUST BE MY SERVANT FOR LIFE.
DON'T TELL THE ANCIENT DOGS I SETTLED FOR A BANANA SPLIT.
S. Adams

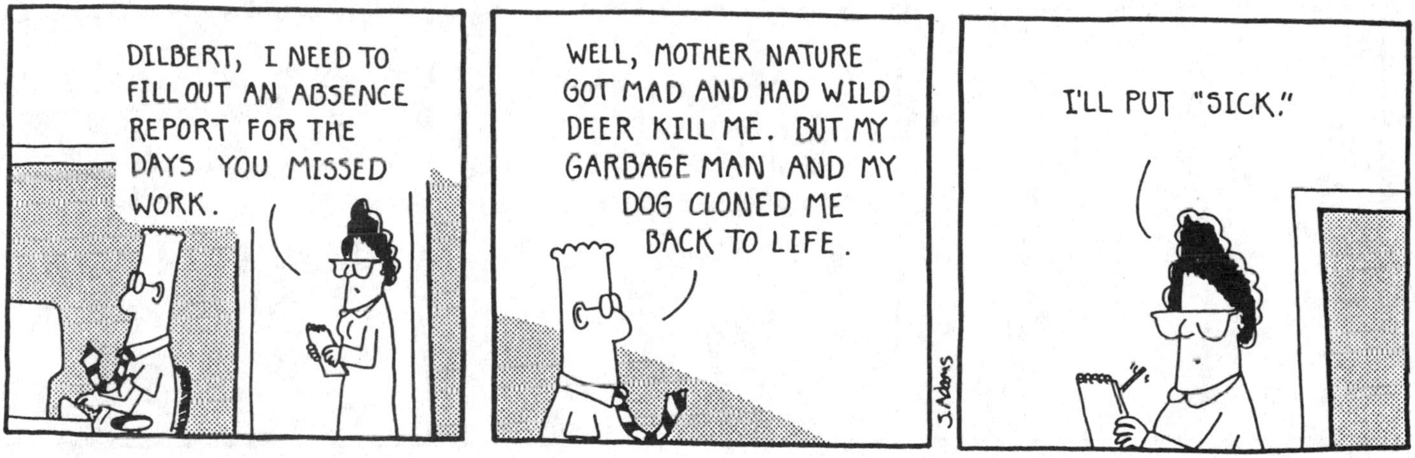
DILBERT, I NEED TO FILL OUT AN ABSENCE REPORT FOR THE DAYS YOU MISSED WORK.
WELL, MOTHER NATURE GOT MAD AND HAD WILD DEER KILL ME. BUT MY GARBAGE MAN AND MY DOG CLONED ME BACK TO LIFE.
I'LL PUT "SICK."
S. Adams

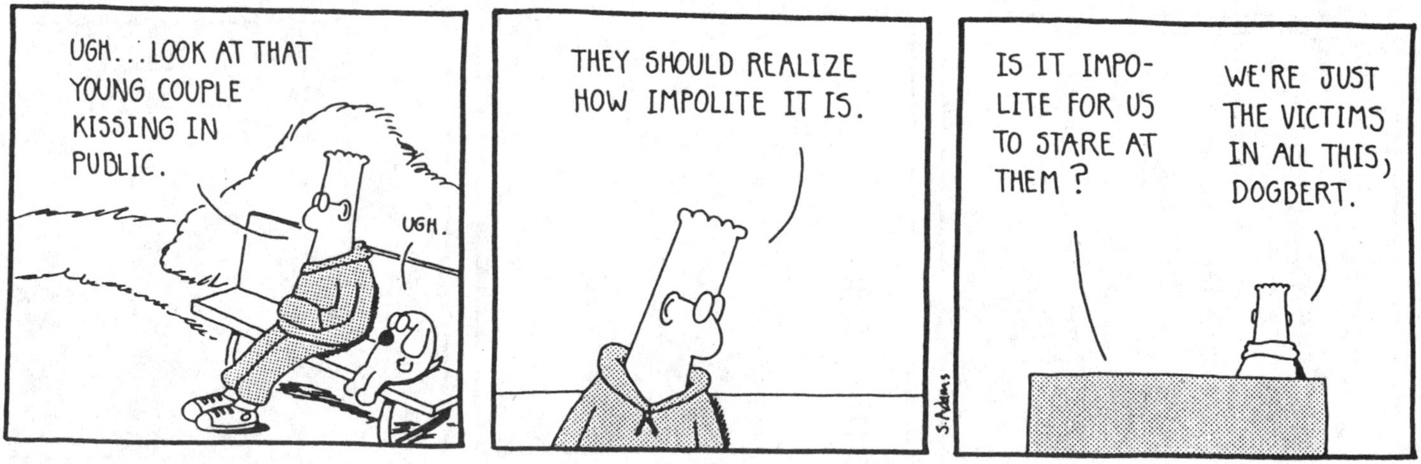
UGH... LOOK AT THAT YOUNG COUPLE KISSING IN PUBLIC.
UGH.
THEY SHOULD REALIZE HOW IMPOLITE IT IS.
IS IT IMPOLITE FOR US TO STARE AT THEM?
WE'RE JUST THE VICTIMS IN ALL THIS, DOGBERT.
S. Adams

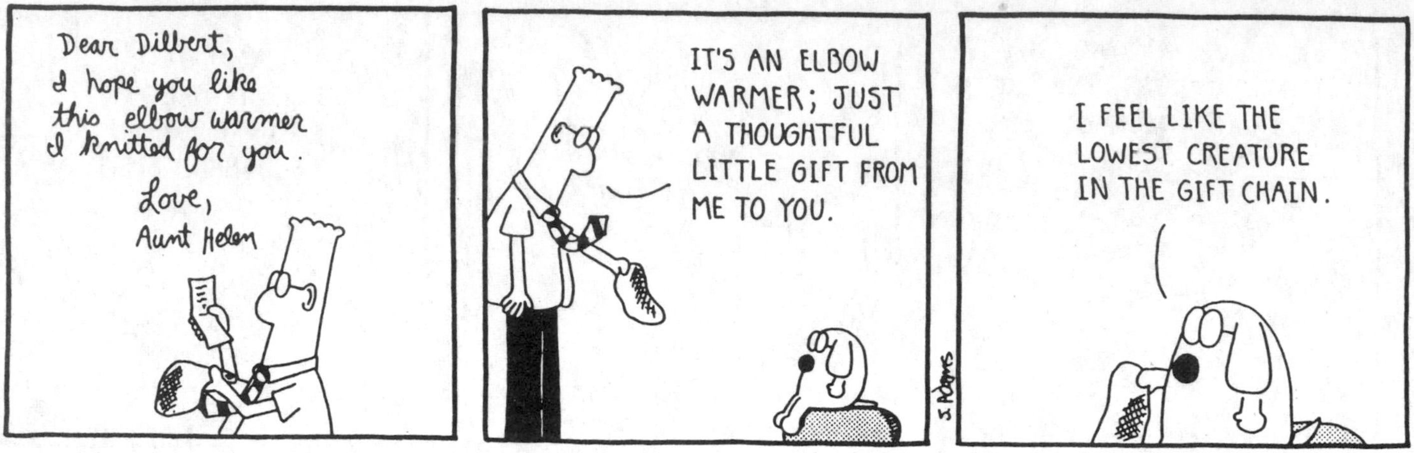
Dear Dilbert,
I hope you like this elbow warmer I knitted for you.
Love,
Aunt Helen
IT'S AN ELBOW WARMER; JUST A THOUGHTFUL LITTLE GIFT FROM ME TO YOU.
I FEEL LIKE THE LOWEST CREATURE IN THE GIFT CHAIN.

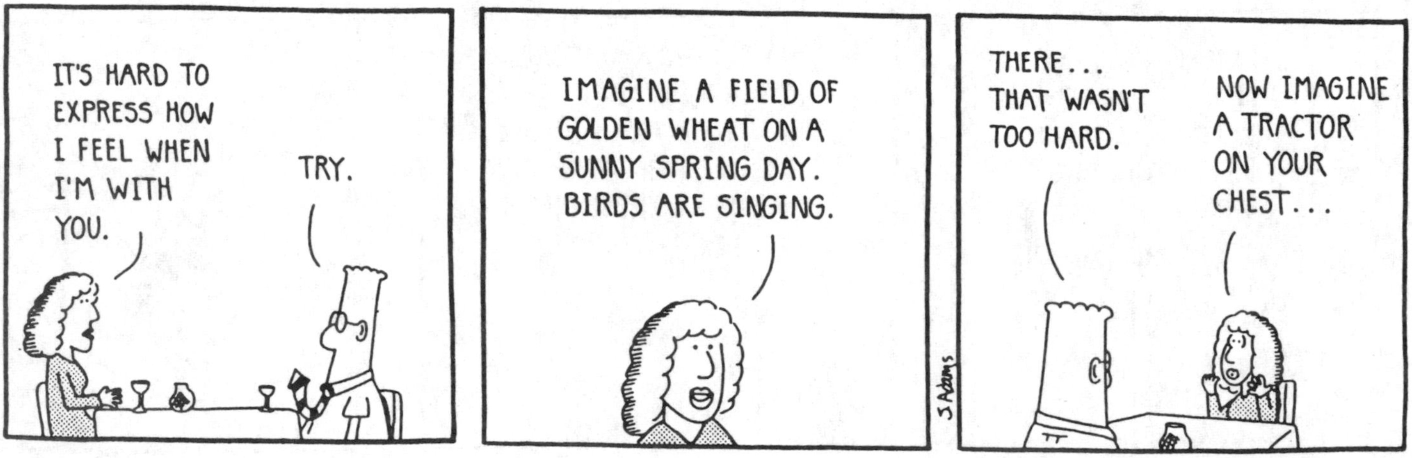
IT'S HARD TO EXPRESS HOW I FEEL WHEN I'M WITH YOU.
TRY.
IMAGINE A FIELD OF GOLDEN WHEAT ON A SUNNY SPRING DAY. BIRDS ARE SINGING.
THERE... THAT WASN'T TOO HARD.
NOW IMAGINE A TRACTOR ON YOUR CHEST...

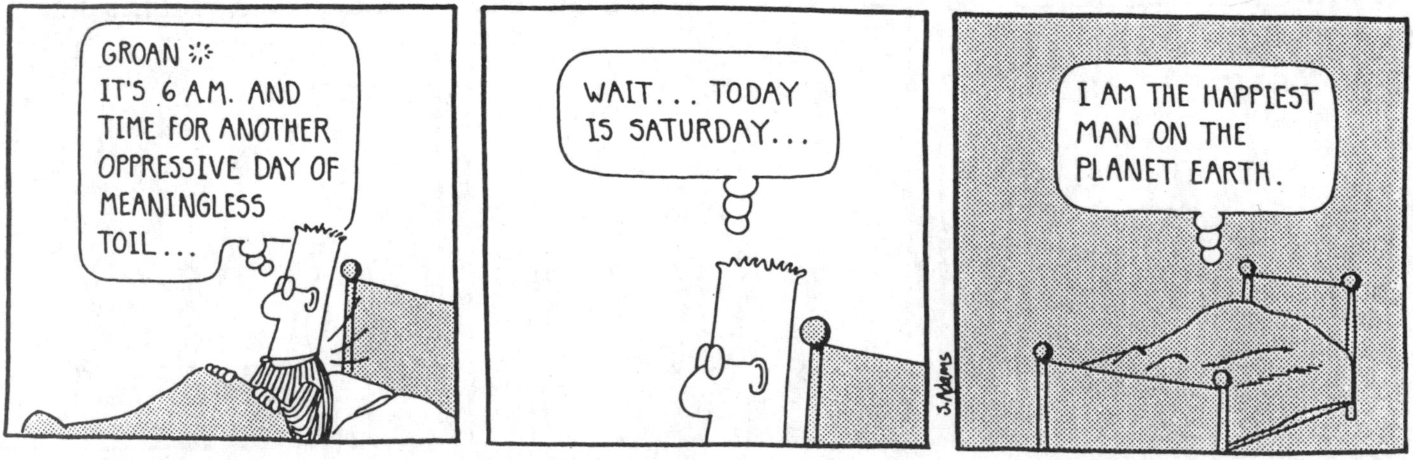
GROAN
IT'S 6 A.M. AND TIME FOR ANOTHER OPPRESSIVE DAY OF MEANINGLESS TOIL...
WAIT... TODAY IS SATURDAY...
I AM THE HAPPIEST MAN ON THE PLANET EARTH.

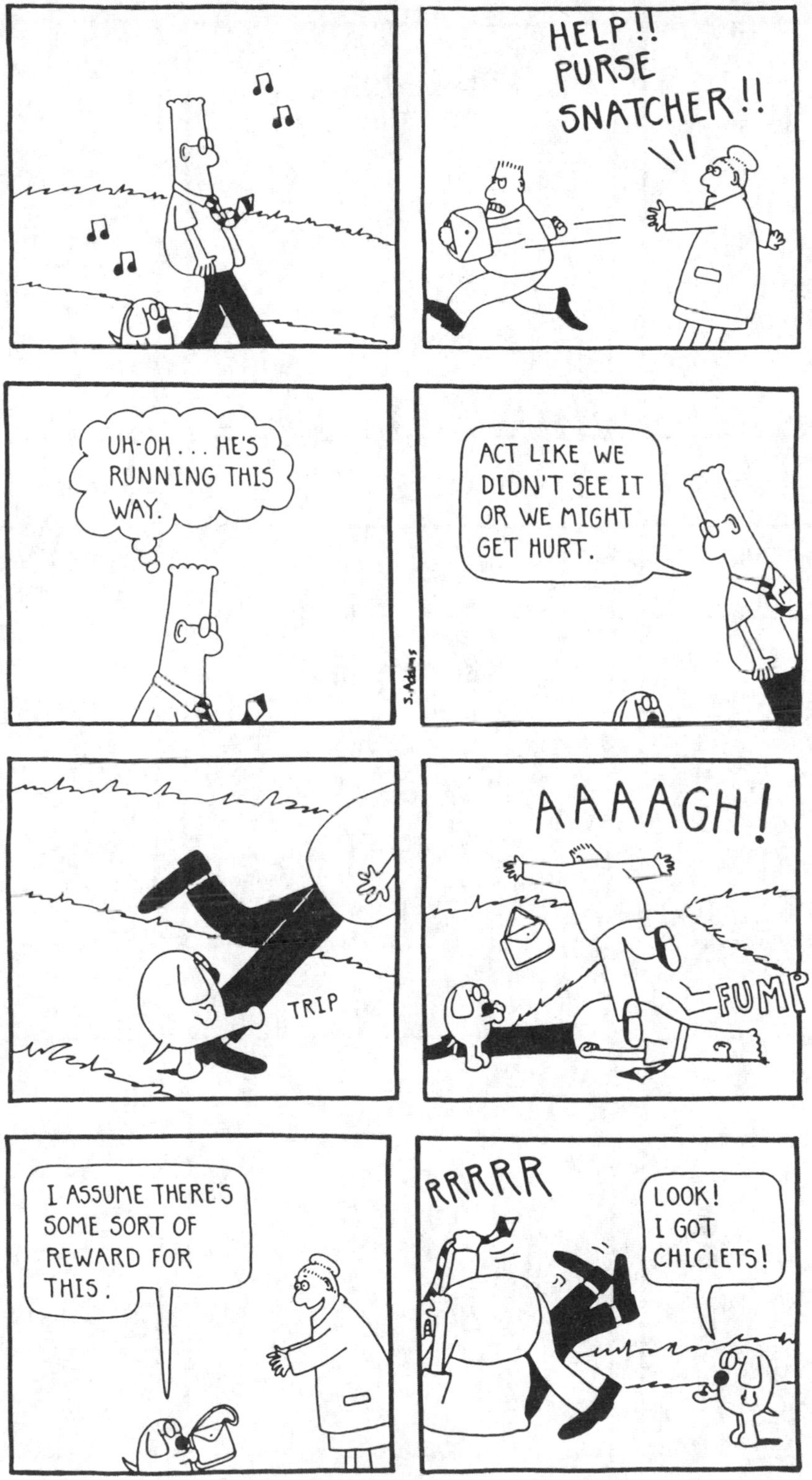
HELP!! PURSE SNATCHER!!
UH-OH . . . HE'S RUNNING THIS WAY.
S. Adams
ACT LIKE WE DIDN'T SEE IT OR WE MIGHT GET HURT.
TRIP
AAAAGH!
FUMP
I ASSUME THERE'S SOME SORT OF REWARD FOR THIS.
RRRRR
LOOK! I GOT CHICLETS!

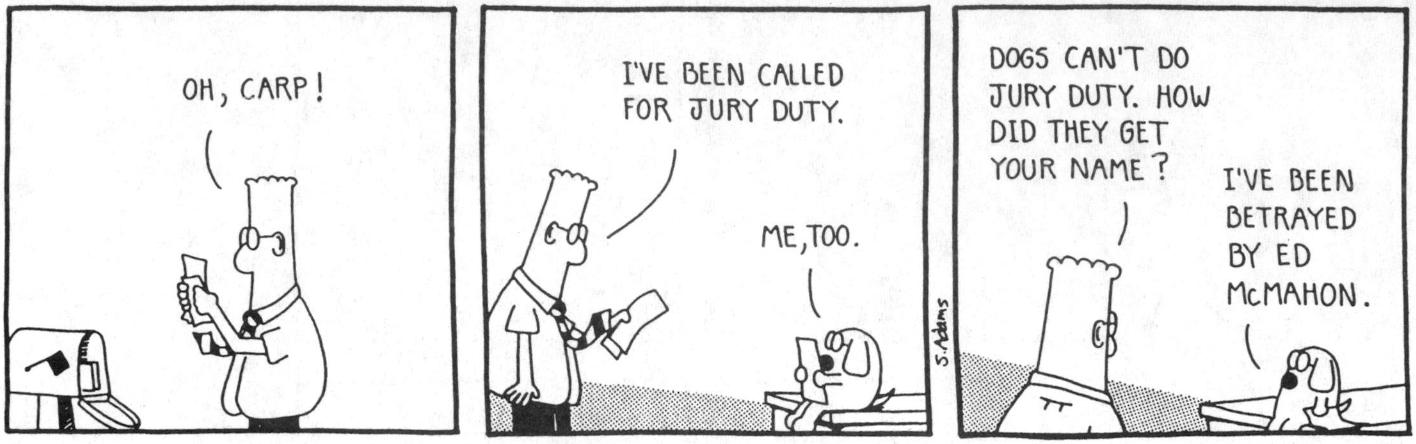
OH, CARP!
I'VE BEEN CALLED FOR JURY DUTY.
ME, TOO.
S. Adams
DOGS CAN'T DO JURY DUTY. HOW DID THEY GET YOUR NAME?
I'VE BEEN BETRAYED BY ED McMAHON.

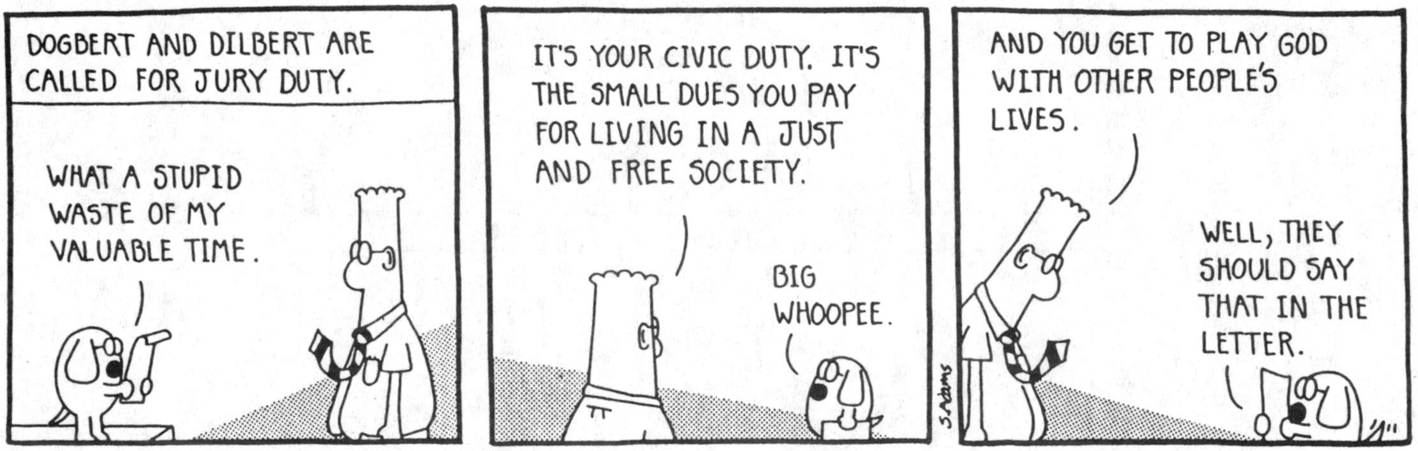
DOGBERT AND DILBERT ARE CALLED FOR JURY DUTY.
WHAT A STUPID WASTE OF MY VALUABLE TIME.
IT'S YOUR CIVIC DUTY. IT'S THE SMALL DUES YOU PAY FOR LIVING IN A JUST AND FREE SOCIETY.
BIG WHOOPEE.
S. Adams
AND YOU GET TO PLAY GOD WITH OTHER PEOPLE'S LIVES.
WELL, THEY SHOULD SAY THAT IN THE LETTER.

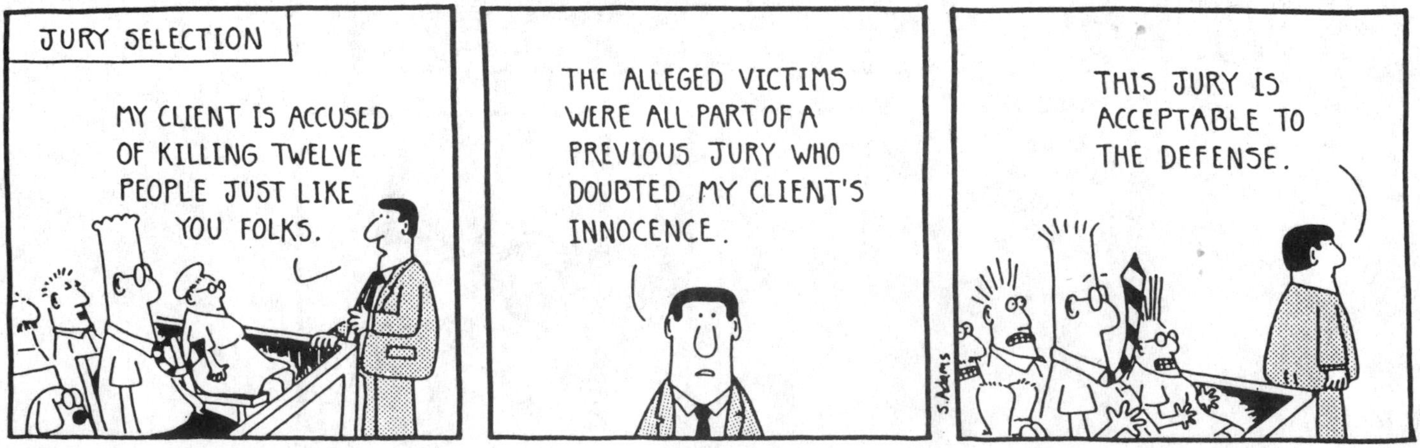
JURY SELECTION
MY CLIENT IS ACCUSED OF KILLING TWELVE PEOPLE JUST LIKE YOU FOLKS.
THE ALLEGED VICTIMS WERE ALL PART OF A PREVIOUS JURY WHO DOUBTED MY CLIENT'S INNOCENCE.
S. Adams
THIS JURY IS ACCEPTABLE TO THE DEFENSE.

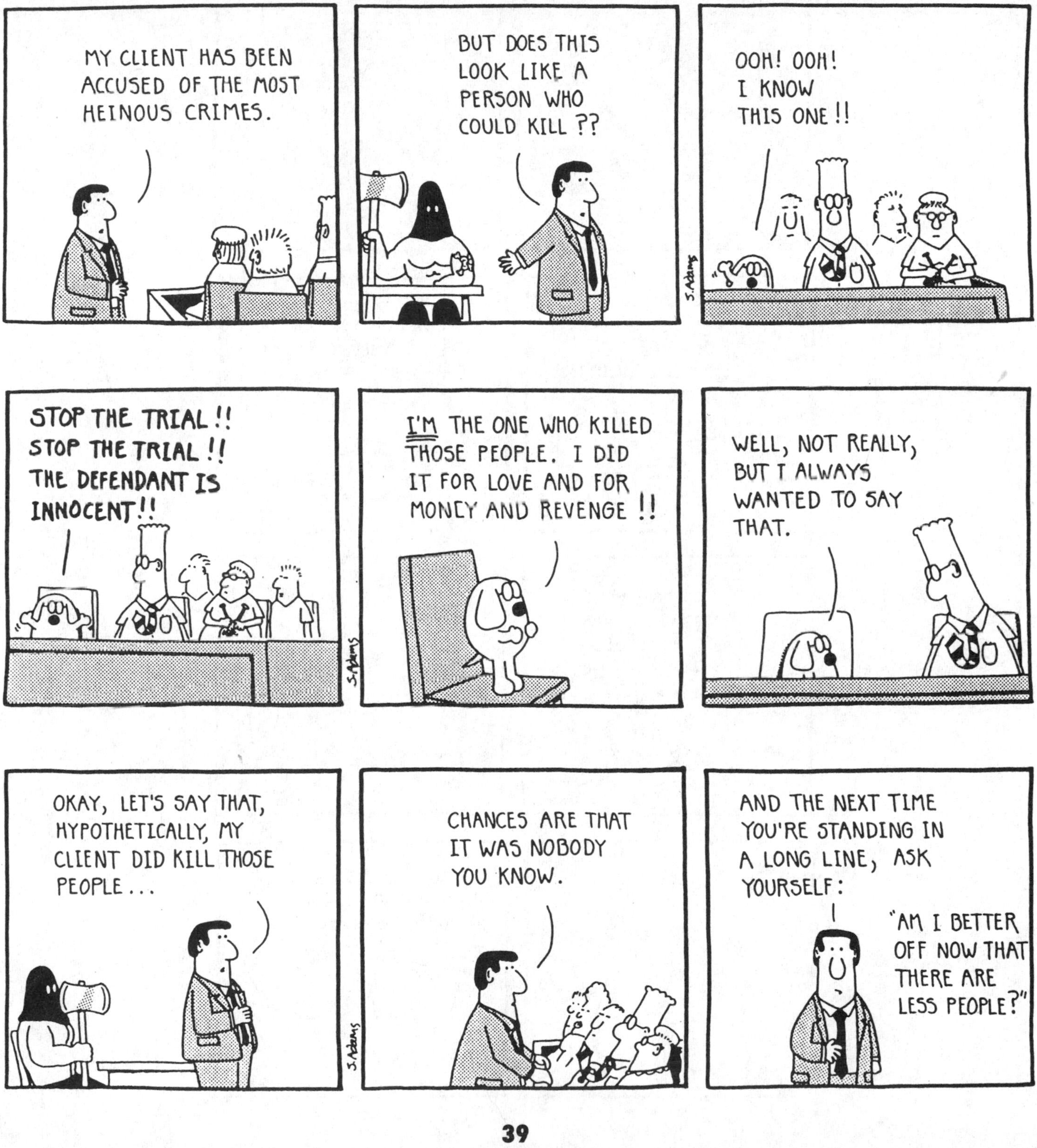
MY CLIENT HAS BEEN ACCUSED OF THE MOST HEINOUS CRIMES.
BUT DOES THIS LOOK LIKE A PERSON WHO COULD KILL ??
OOH! OOH! I KNOW THIS ONE !!
S. Adams
STOP THE TRIAL !! STOP THE TRIAL !! THE DEFENDANT IS INNOCENT !!
I'M THE ONE WHO KILLED THOSE PEOPLE. I DID IT FOR LOVE AND FOR MONEY AND REVENGE !!
S. Adams
WELL, NOT REALLY, BUT I ALWAYS WANTED TO SAY THAT.
OKAY, LET'S SAY THAT, HYPOTHETICALLY, MY CLIENT DID KILL THOSE PEOPLE...
S. Adams
CHANCES ARE THAT IT WAS NOBODY YOU KNOW.
AND THE NEXT TIME YOU'RE STANDING IN A LONG LINE, ASK YOURSELF:
"AM I BETTER OFF NOW THAT THERE ARE LESS PEOPLE?"

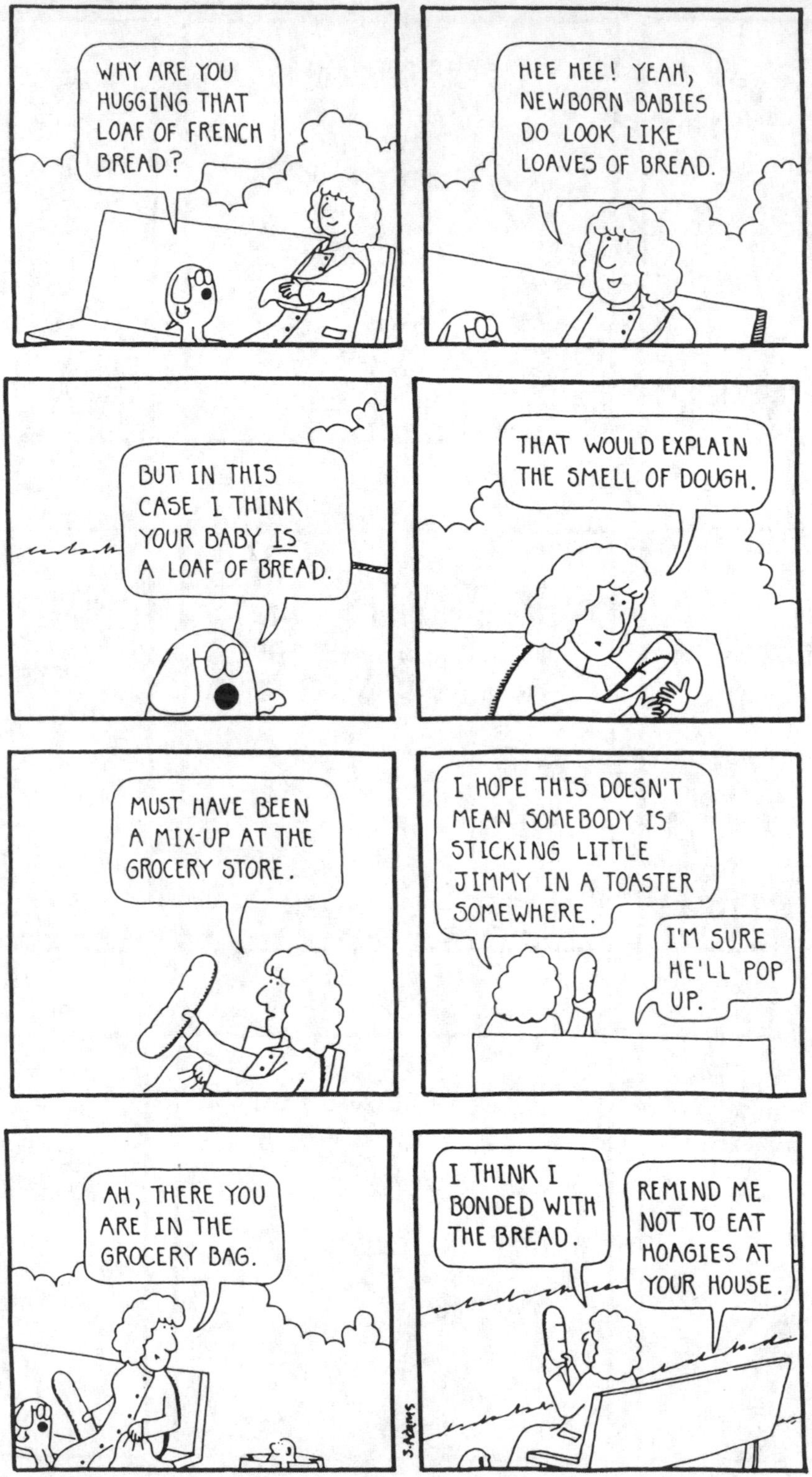
WHY ARE YOU HUGGING THAT LOAF OF FRENCH BREAD?
HEE HEE! YEAH, NEWBORN BABIES DO LOOK LIKE LOAVES OF BREAD.
BUT IN THIS CASE I THINK YOUR BABY IS A LOAF OF BREAD.
THAT WOULD EXPLAIN THE SMELL OF DOUGH.
MUST HAVE BEEN A MIX-UP AT THE GROCERY STORE.
I HOPE THIS DOESN'T MEAN SOMEBODY IS STICKING LITTLE JIMMY IN A TOASTER SOMEWHERE.
I'M SURE HE'LL POP UP.
AH, THERE YOU ARE IN THE GROCERY BAG.
I THINK I BONDED WITH THE BREAD.
REMIND ME NOT TO EAT HOAGIES AT YOUR HOUSE.
S. ADAMS

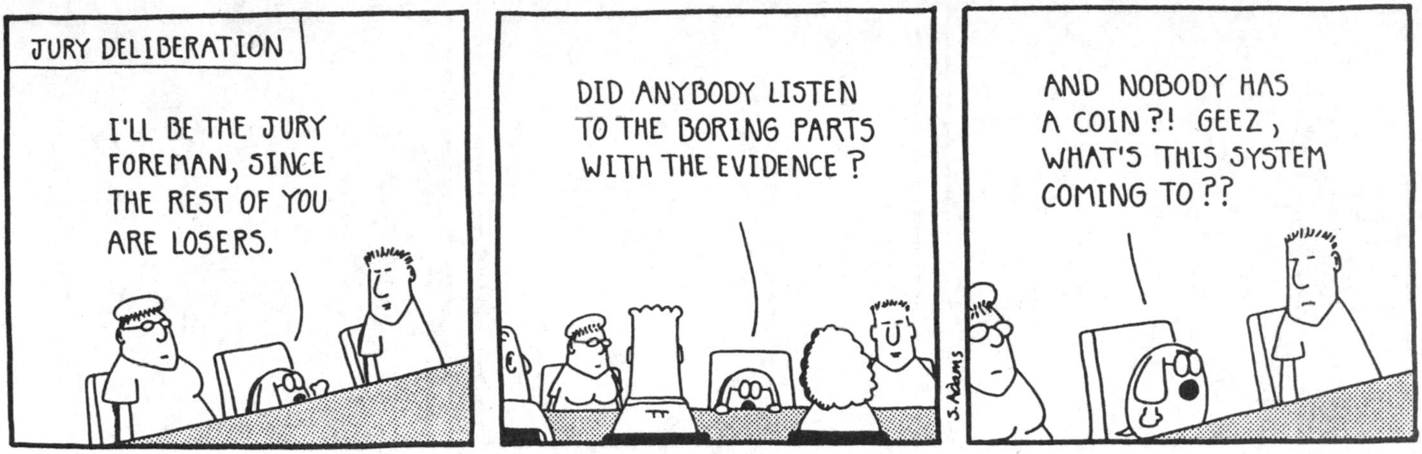
JURY DELIBERATION
I'LL BE THE JURY FOREMAN, SINCE THE REST OF YOU ARE LOSERS.
DID ANYBODY LISTEN TO THE BORING PARTS WITH THE EVIDENCE?
AND NOBODY HAS A COIN?! GEEZ, WHAT'S THIS SYSTEM COMING TO??

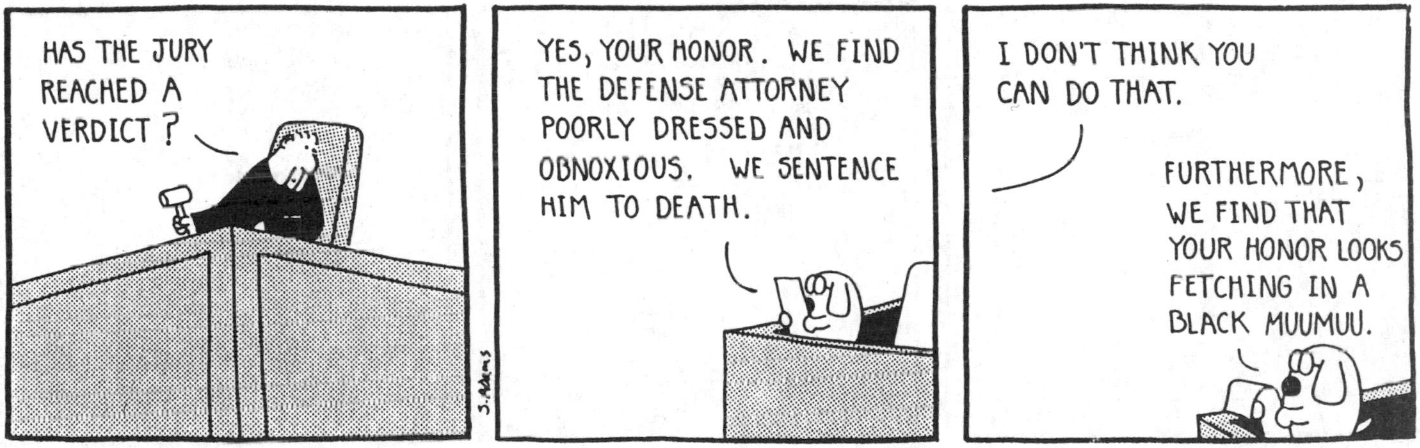
HAS THE JURY REACHED A VERDICT?
YES, YOUR HONOR. WE FIND THE DEFENSE ATTORNEY POORLY DRESSED AND OBNOXIOUS. WE SENTENCE HIM TO DEATH.
I DON'T THINK YOU CAN DO THAT.
FURTHERMORE, WE FIND THAT YOUR HONOR LOOKS FETCHING IN A BLACK MUUMUU.

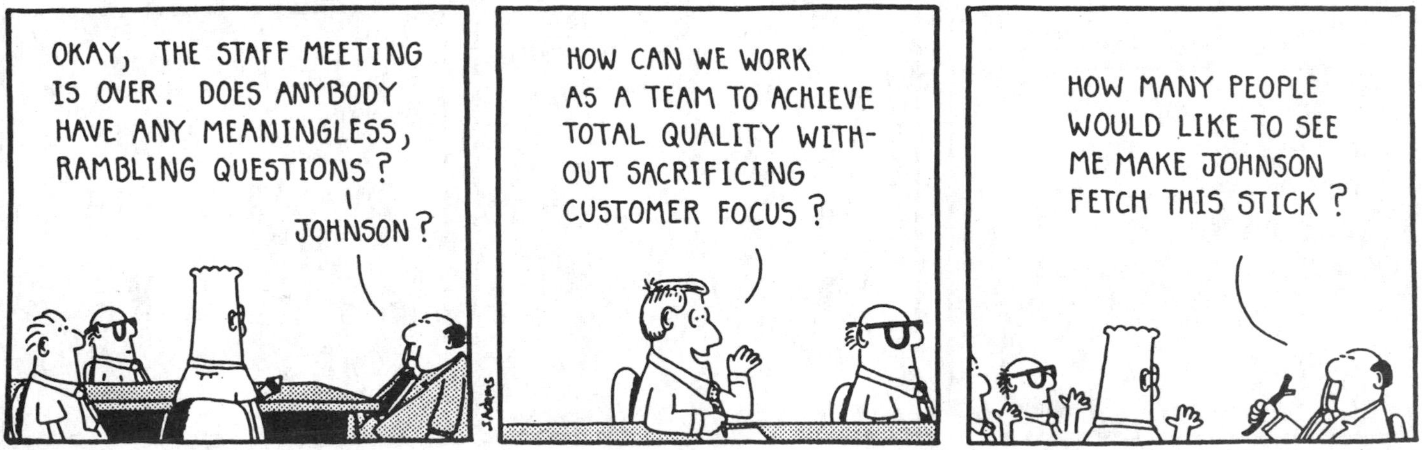
OKAY, THE STAFF MEETING IS OVER. DOES ANYBODY HAVE ANY MEANINGLESS, RAMBLING QUESTIONS?
JOHNSON?
HOW CAN WE WORK AS A TEAM TO ACHIEVE TOTAL QUALITY WITH-OUT SACRIFICING CUSTOMER FOCUS?
HOW MANY PEOPLE WOULD LIKE TO SEE ME MAKE JOHNSON FETCH THIS STICK?

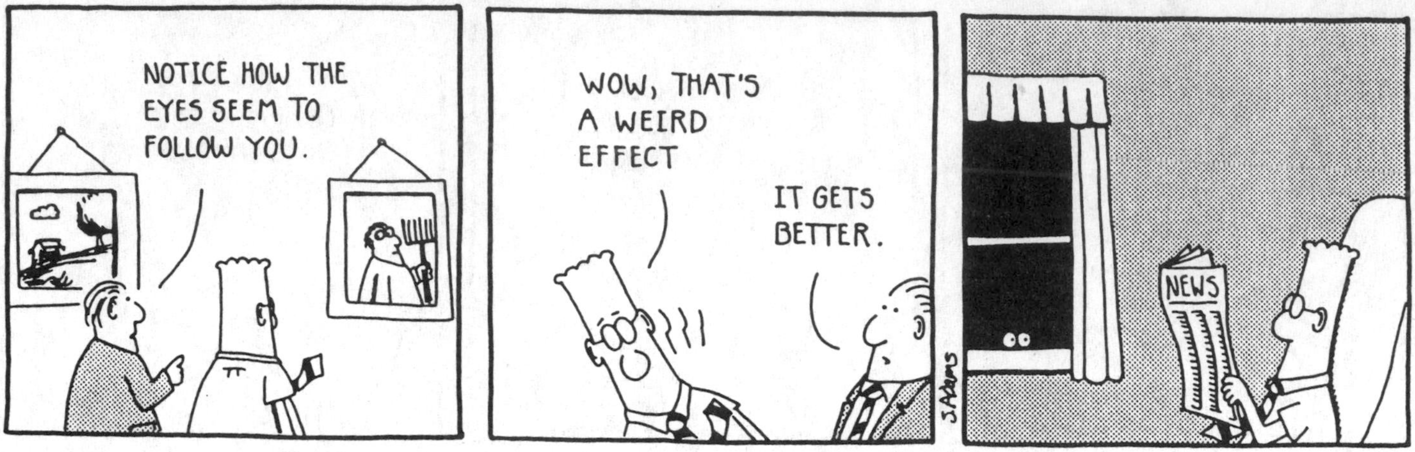
NOTICE HOW THE EYES SEEM TO FOLLOW YOU.
WOW, THAT'S A WEIRD EFFECT
IT GETS BETTER.
NEWS

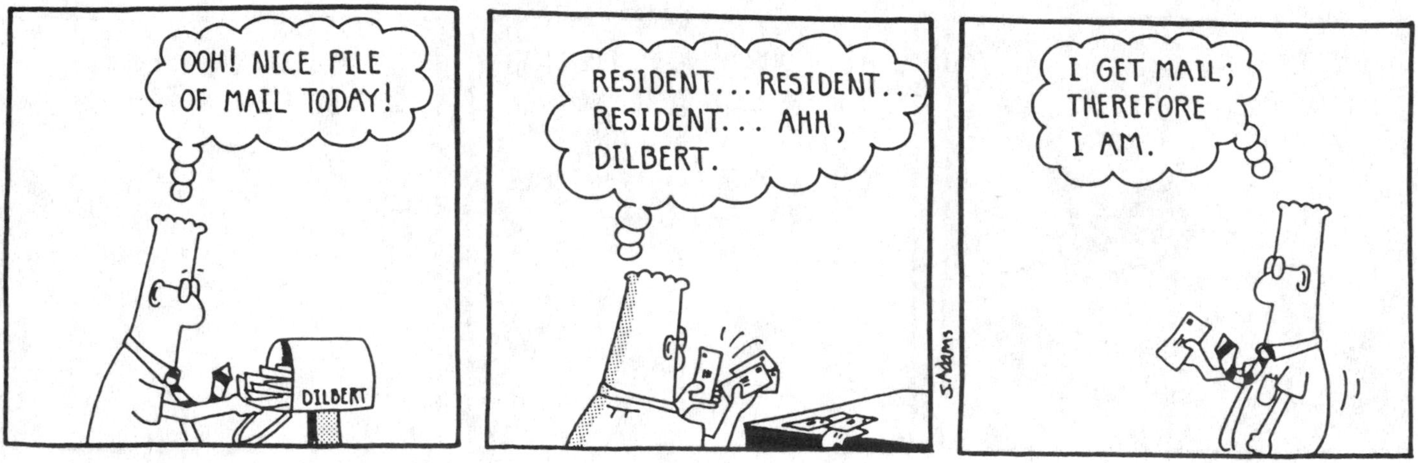
OOH! NICE PILE OF MAIL TODAY!
DILBERT
RESIDENT... RESIDENT... RESIDENT... AHH, DILBERT.
I GET MAIL; THEREFORE I AM.

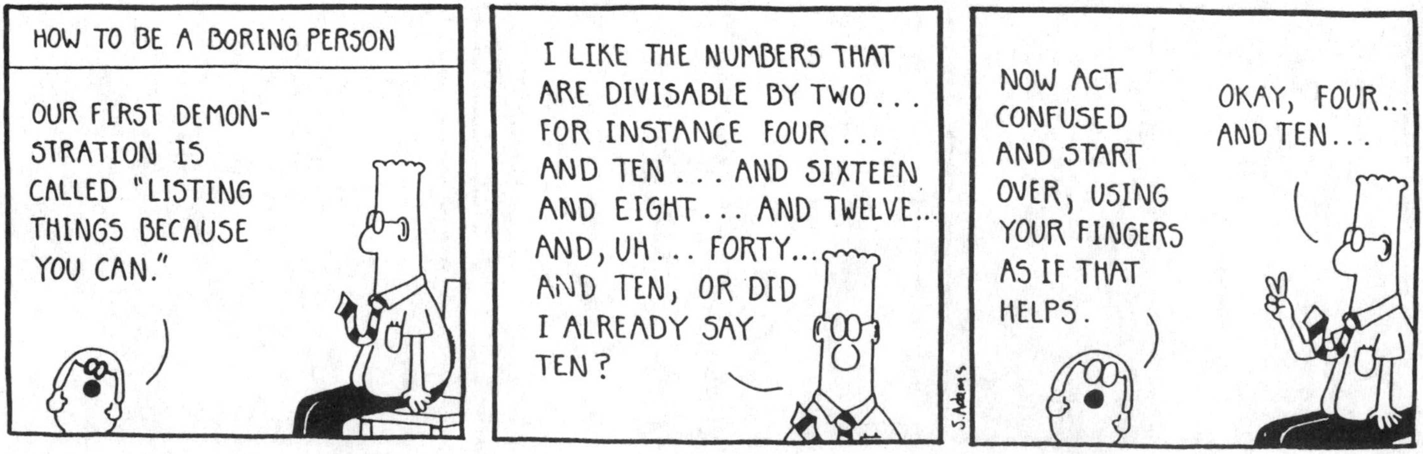
HOW TO BE A BORING PERSON
OUR FIRST DEMONSTRATION IS CALLED "LISTING THINGS BECAUSE YOU CAN."
I LIKE THE NUMBERS THAT ARE DIVISABLE BY TWO . . . FOR INSTANCE FOUR . . . AND TEN . . . AND SIXTEEN AND EIGHT . . . AND TWELVE... AND, UH . . . FORTY... AND TEN, OR DID I ALREADY SAY TEN?
NOW ACT CONFUSED AND START OVER, USING YOUR FINGERS AS IF THAT HELPS.
OKAY, FOUR... AND TEN . . .

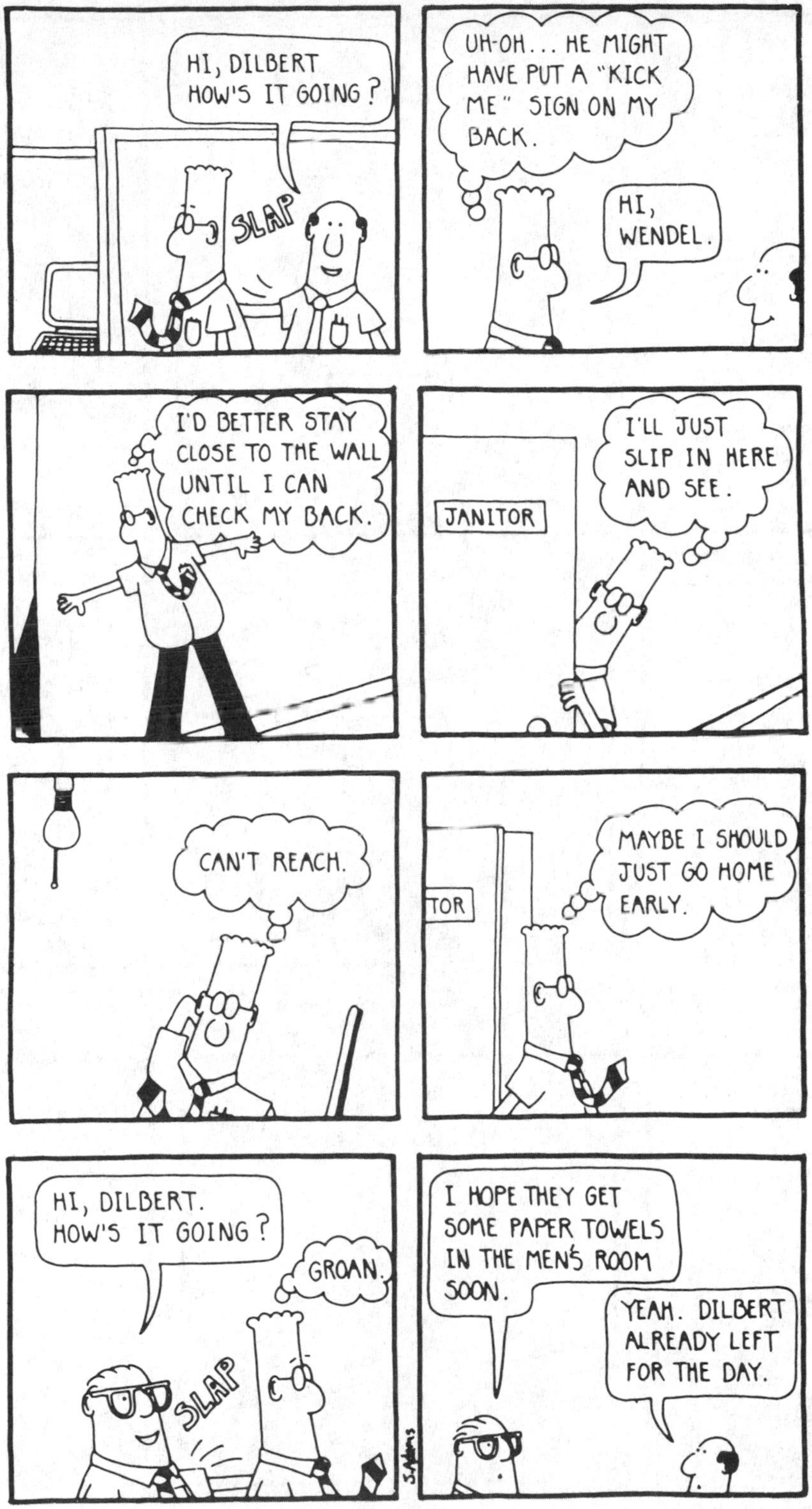
HI, DILBERT
HOW'S IT GOING?
SLAP
UH-OH... HE MIGHT HAVE PUT A "KICK ME" SIGN ON MY BACK.
HI, WENDEL.
I'D BETTER STAY CLOSE TO THE WALL UNTIL I CAN CHECK MY BACK.
JANITOR
I'LL JUST SLIP IN HERE AND SEE.
CAN'T REACH.
TOR
MAYBE I SHOULD JUST GO HOME EARLY.
HI, DILBERT.
HOW'S IT GOING?
GROAN.
SLAP
I HOPE THEY GET SOME PAPER TOWELS IN THE MEN'S ROOM SOON.
YEAH. DILBERT ALREADY LEFT FOR THE DAY.

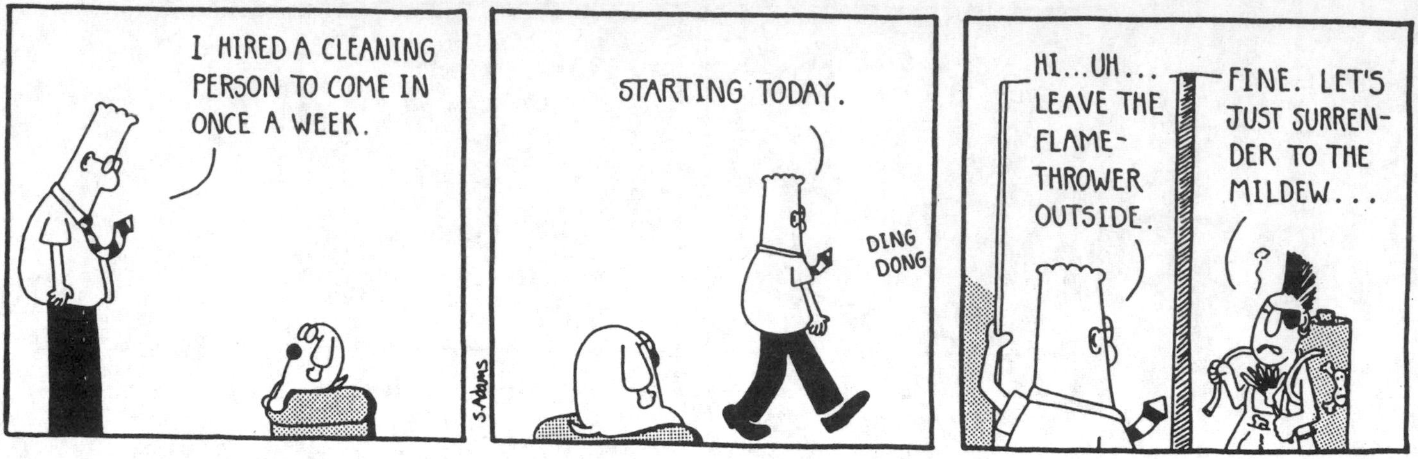
I HIRED A CLEANING PERSON TO COME IN ONCE A WEEK.
S. ADAMS
STARTING TODAY.
DING DONG
HI...UH... LEAVE THE FLAME-THROWER OUTSIDE.
FINE. LET'S JUST SURREN-DER TO THE MILDEW...

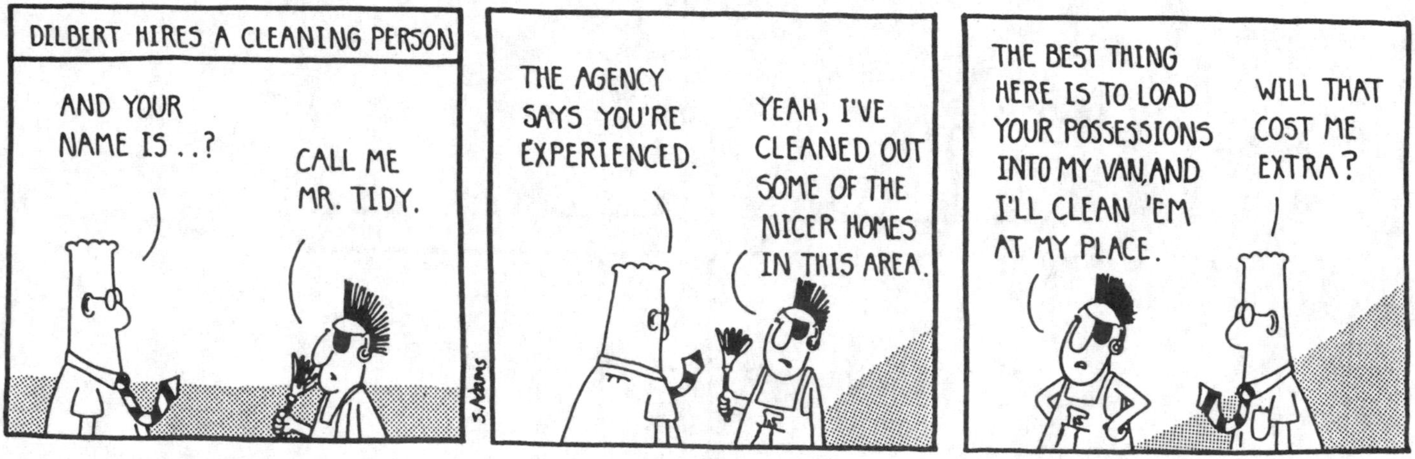
DILBERT HIRES A CLEANING PERSON
AND YOUR NAME IS..?
CALL ME MR. TIDY.
S. Adams
THE AGENCY SAYS YOU'RE EXPERIENCED.
YEAH, I'VE CLEANED OUT SOME OF THE NICER HOMES IN THIS AREA.
THE BEST THING HERE IS TO LOAD YOUR POSSESSIONS INTO MY VAN, AND I'LL CLEAN 'EM AT MY PLACE.
WILL THAT COST ME EXTRA?

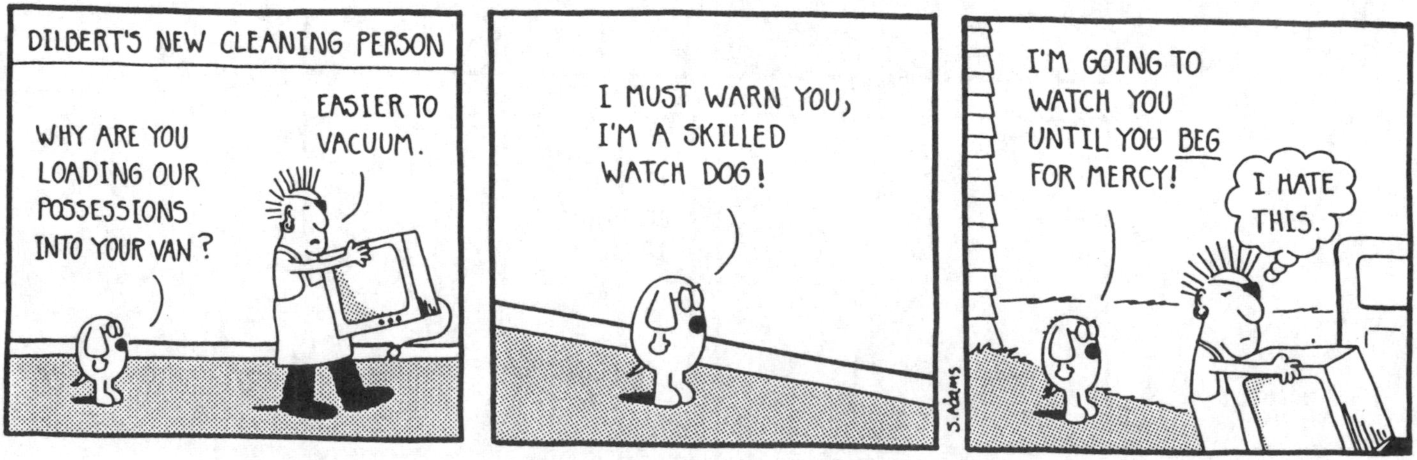
DILBERT'S NEW CLEANING PERSON
WHY ARE YOU LOADING OUR POSSESSIONS INTO YOUR VAN?
EASIER TO VACUUM.
I MUST WARN YOU, I'M A SKILLED WATCH DOG!
S. Adams
I'M GOING TO WATCH YOU UNTIL YOU BEG FOR MERCY!
I HATE THIS.

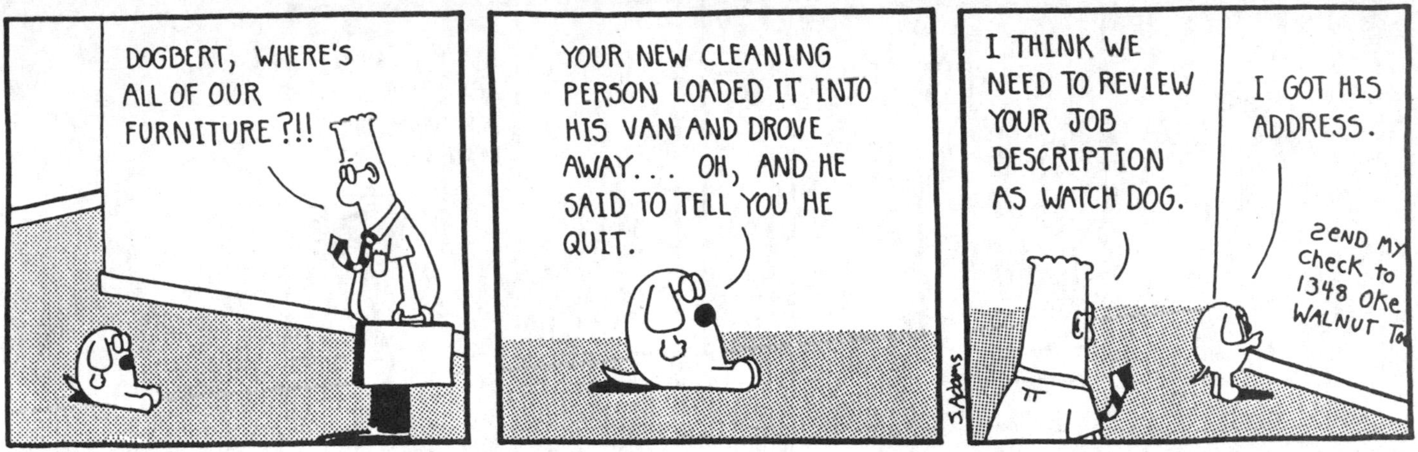
DOGBERT, WHERE'S ALL OF OUR FURNITURE?!!
YOUR NEW CLEANING PERSON LOADED IT INTO HIS VAN AND DROVE AWAY... OH, AND HE SAID TO TELL YOU HE QUIT.
I THINK WE NEED TO REVIEW YOUR JOB DESCRIPTION AS WATCH DOG.
I GOT HIS ADDRESS.
SEND MY Check to 1348 Oke WALNUT
S. Adams

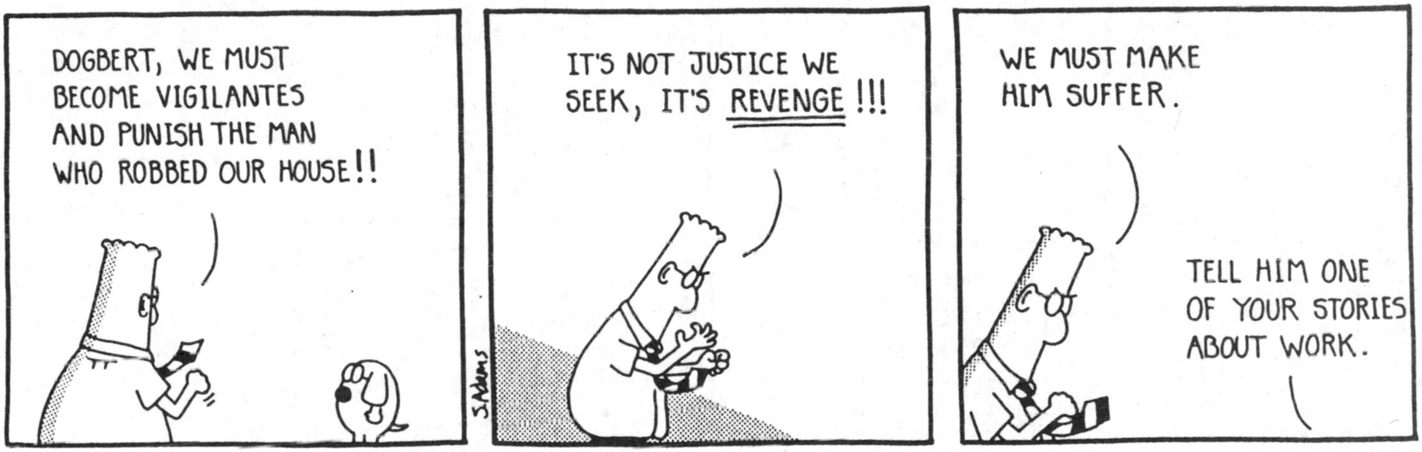
DOGBERT, WE MUST BECOME VIGILANTES AND PUNISH THE MAN WHO ROBBED OUR HOUSE!!
S. Adams
IT'S NOT JUSTICE WE SEEK, IT'S REVENGE!!!
WE MUST MAKE HIM SUFFER.
TELL HIM ONE OF YOUR STORIES ABOUT WORK.

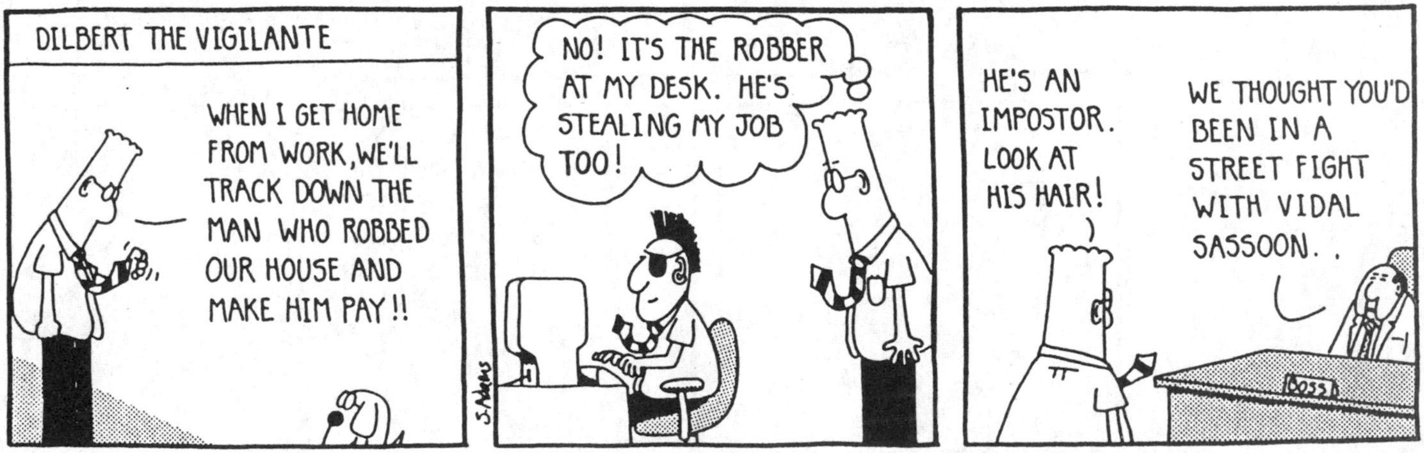
DILBERT THE VIGILANTE
WHEN I GET HOME FROM WORK, WE'LL TRACK DOWN THE MAN WHO ROBBED OUR HOUSE AND MAKE HIM PAY!!
S. Adams
NO! IT'S THE ROBBER AT MY DESK. HE'S STEALING MY JOB TOO!
HE'S AN IMPOSTOR. LOOK AT HIS HAIR!
WE THOUGHT YOU'D BEEN IN A STREET FIGHT WITH VIDAL SASSOON..
BOSS

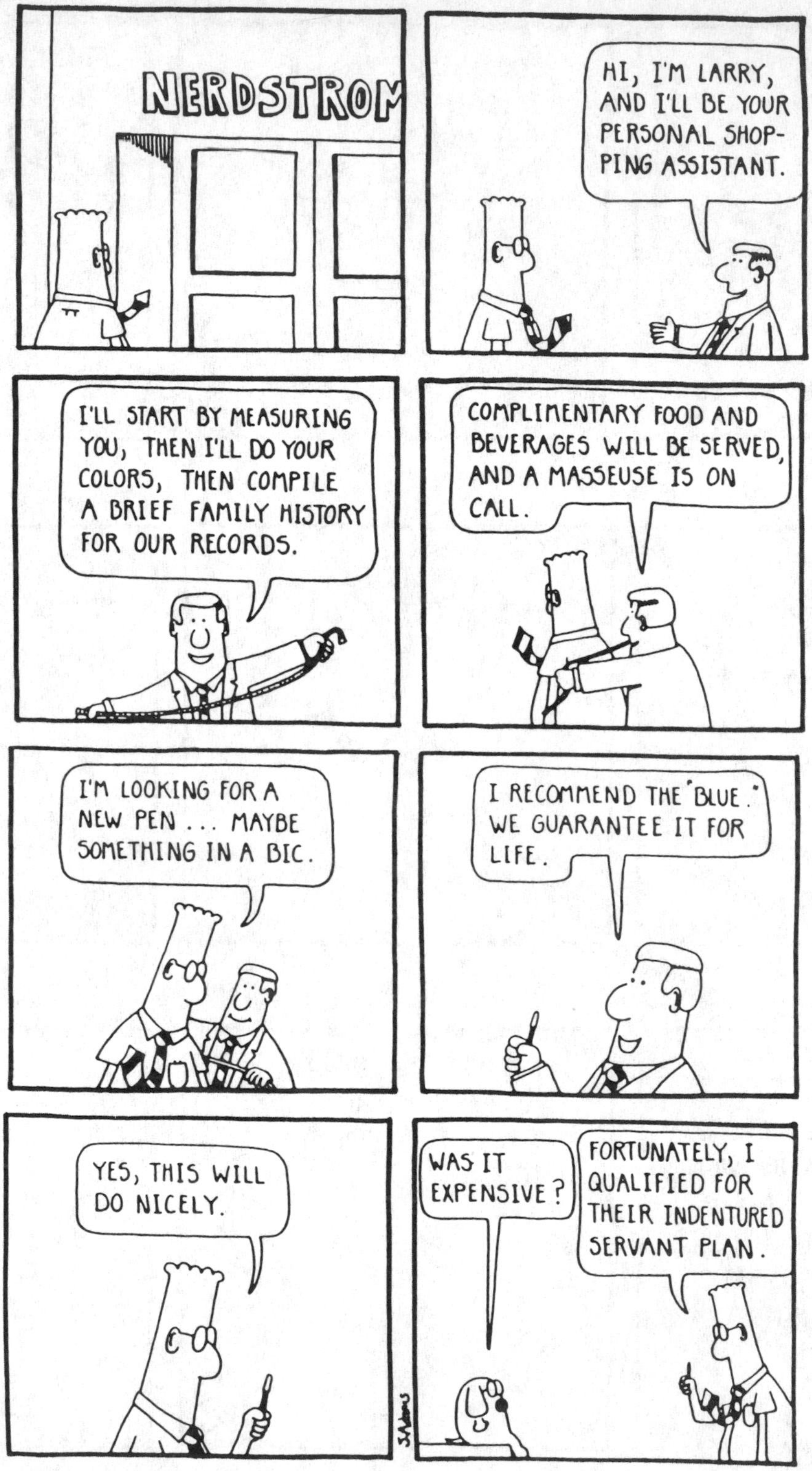
NERDSTROM
HI, I'M LARRY, AND I'LL BE YOUR PERSONAL SHOPPING ASSISTANT.
I'LL START BY MEASURING YOU, THEN I'LL DO YOUR COLORS, THEN COMPILE A BRIEF FAMILY HISTORY FOR OUR RECORDS.
COMPLIMENTARY FOOD AND BEVERAGES WILL BE SERVED, AND A MASSEUSE IS ON CALL.
I'M LOOKING FOR A NEW PEN ... MAYBE SOMETHING IN A BIC.
I RECOMMEND THE "BLUE." WE GUARANTEE IT FOR LIFE.
YES, THIS WILL DO NICELY.
WAS IT EXPENSIVE?
FORTUNATELY, I QUALIFIED FOR THEIR INDENTURED SERVANT PLAN.

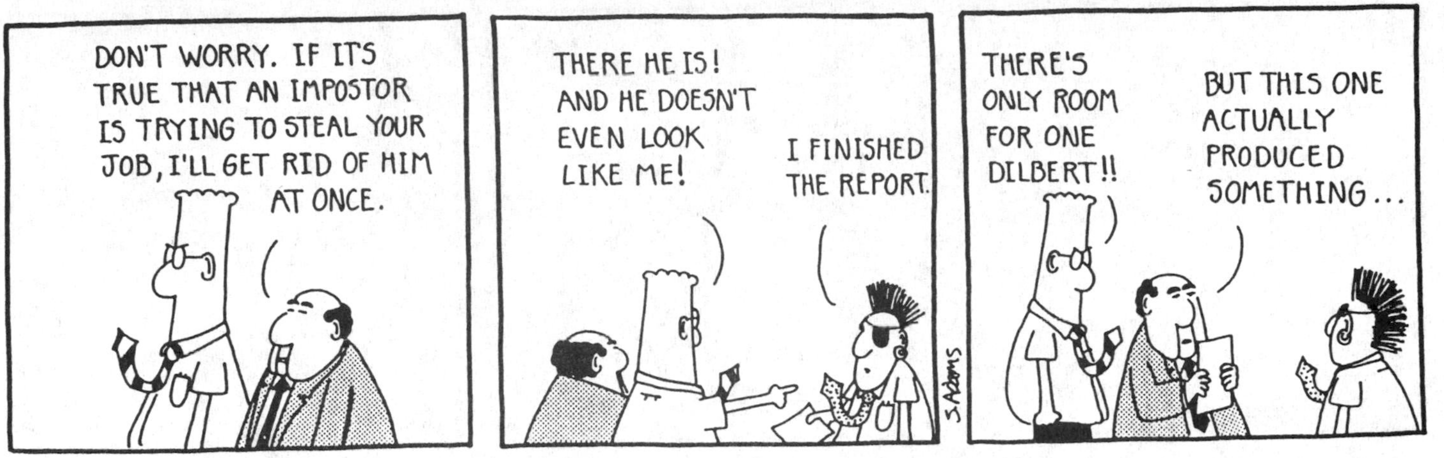
DON'T WORRY. IF IT'S TRUE THAT AN IMPOSTOR IS TRYING TO STEAL YOUR JOB, I'LL GET RID OF HIM AT ONCE.
THERE HE IS! AND HE DOESN'T EVEN LOOK LIKE ME!
I FINISHED THE REPORT.
THERE'S ONLY ROOM FOR ONE DILBERT!!
BUT THIS ONE ACTUALLY PRODUCED SOMETHING...

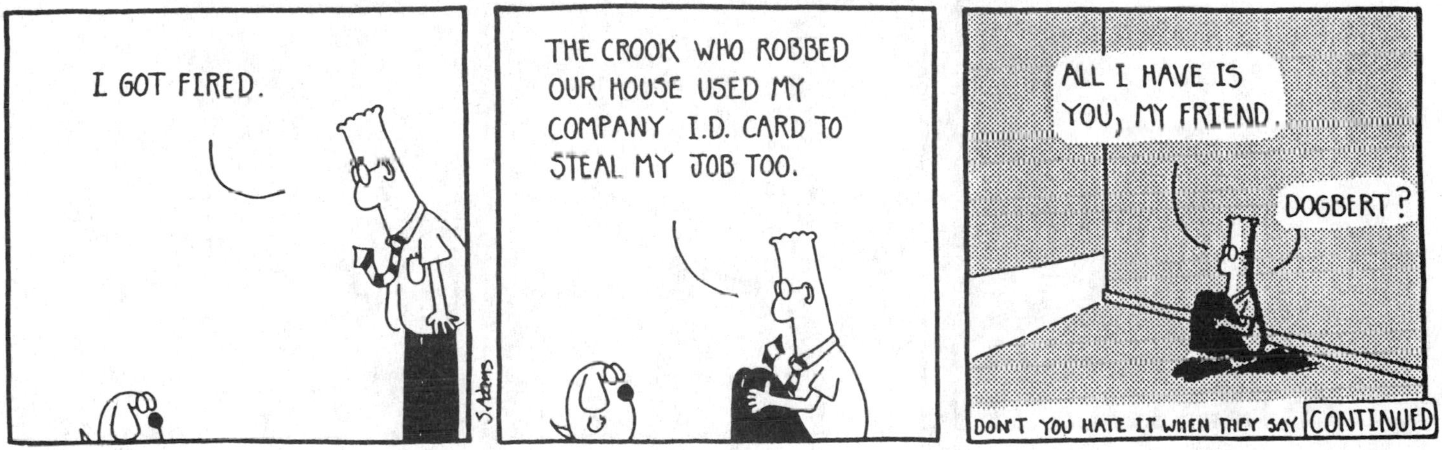
I GOT FIRED.
THE CROOK WHO ROBBED OUR HOUSE USED MY COMPANY I.D. CARD TO STEAL MY JOB TOO.
ALL I HAVE IS YOU, MY FRIEND.
DOGBERT?
DON'T YOU HATE IT WHEN THEY SAY CONTINUED

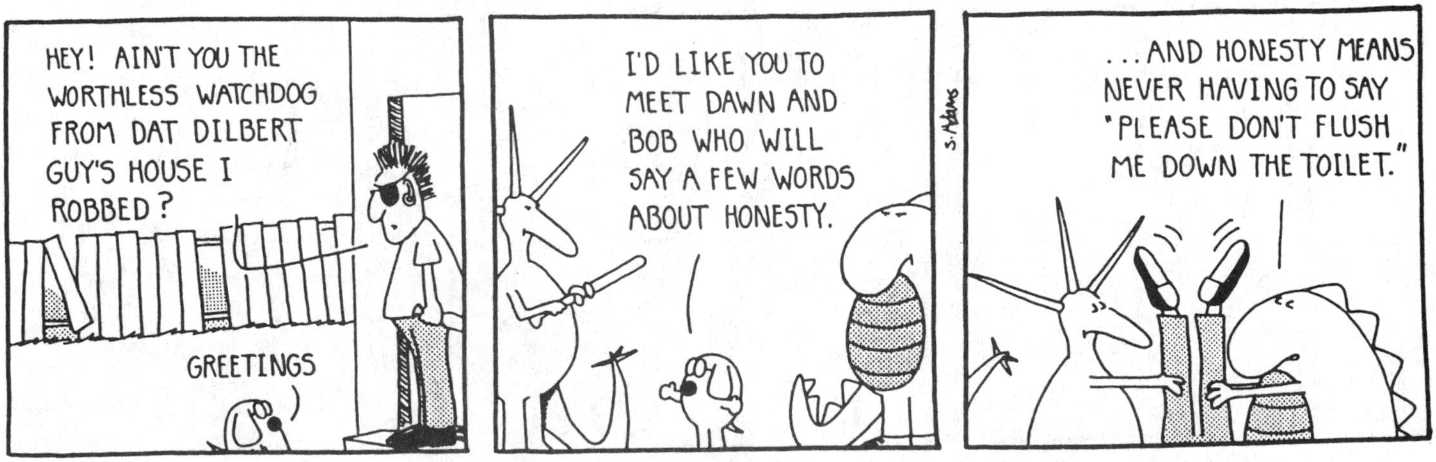
HEY! AIN'T YOU THE WORTHLESS WATCHDOG FROM DAT DILBERT GUY'S HOUSE I ROBBED?
GREETINGS
I'D LIKE YOU TO MEET DAWN AND BOB WHO WILL SAY A FEW WORDS ABOUT HONESTY.
...AND HONESTY MEANS NEVER HAVING TO SAY "PLEASE DON'T FLUSH ME DOWN THE TOILET."

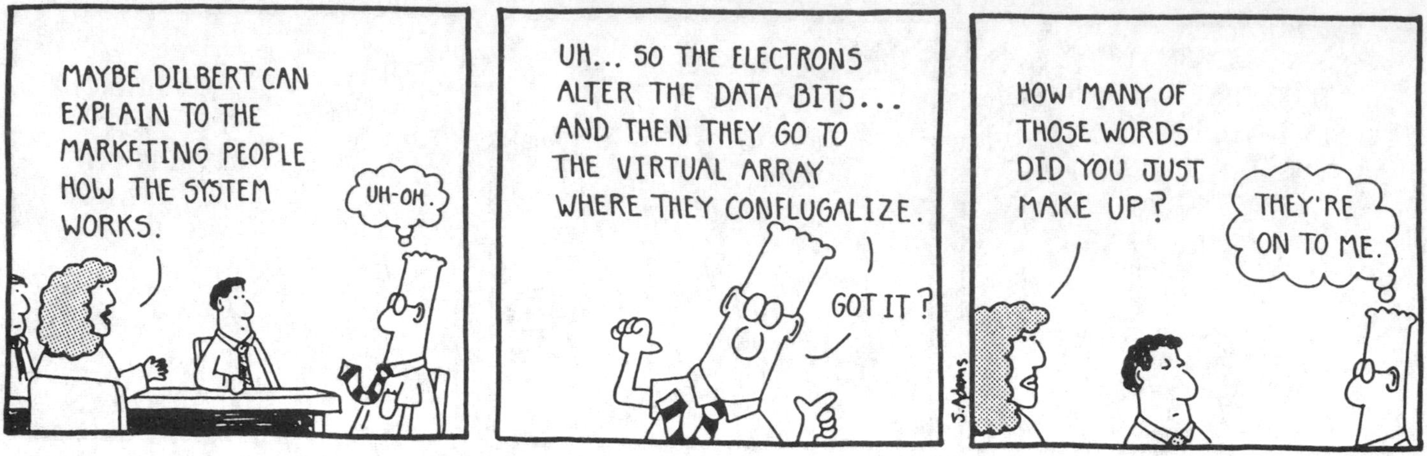
MAYBE DILBERT CAN EXPLAIN TO THE MARKETING PEOPLE HOW THE SYSTEM WORKS.
UH-OH.
UH... SO THE ELECTRONS ALTER THE DATA BITS... AND THEN THEY GO TO THE VIRTUAL ARRAY WHERE THEY CONFLUGALIZE.
GOT IT?
HOW MANY OF THOSE WORDS DID YOU JUST MAKE UP?
THEY'RE ON TO ME.

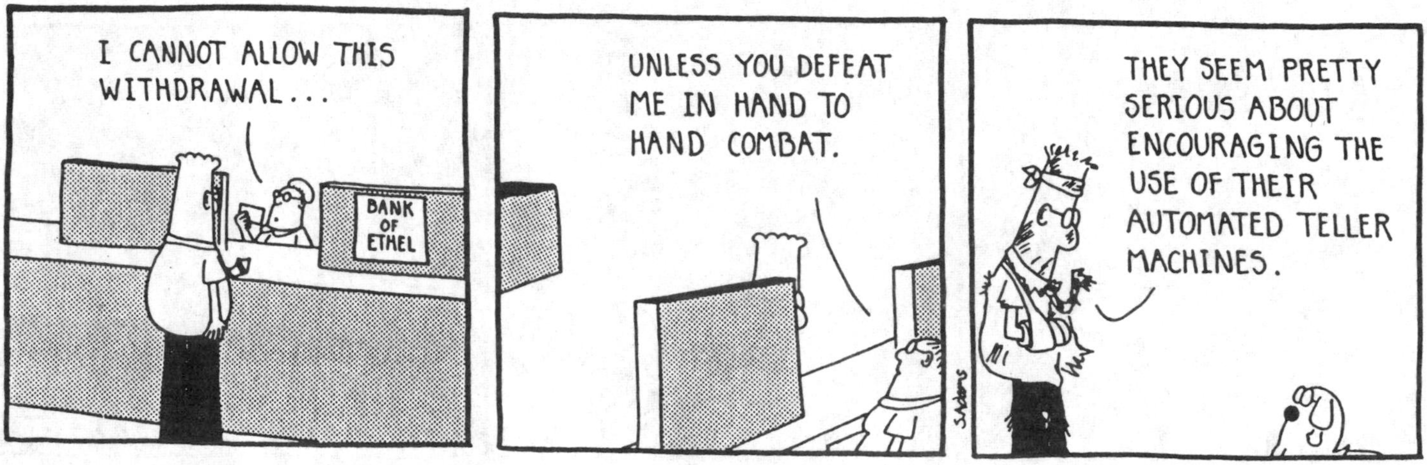
I CANNOT ALLOW THIS WITHDRAWAL...
BANK OF ETHEL
UNLESS YOU DEFEAT ME IN HAND TO HAND COMBAT.
THEY SEEM PRETTY SERIOUS ABOUT ENCOURAGING THE USE OF THEIR AUTOMATED TELLER MACHINES.

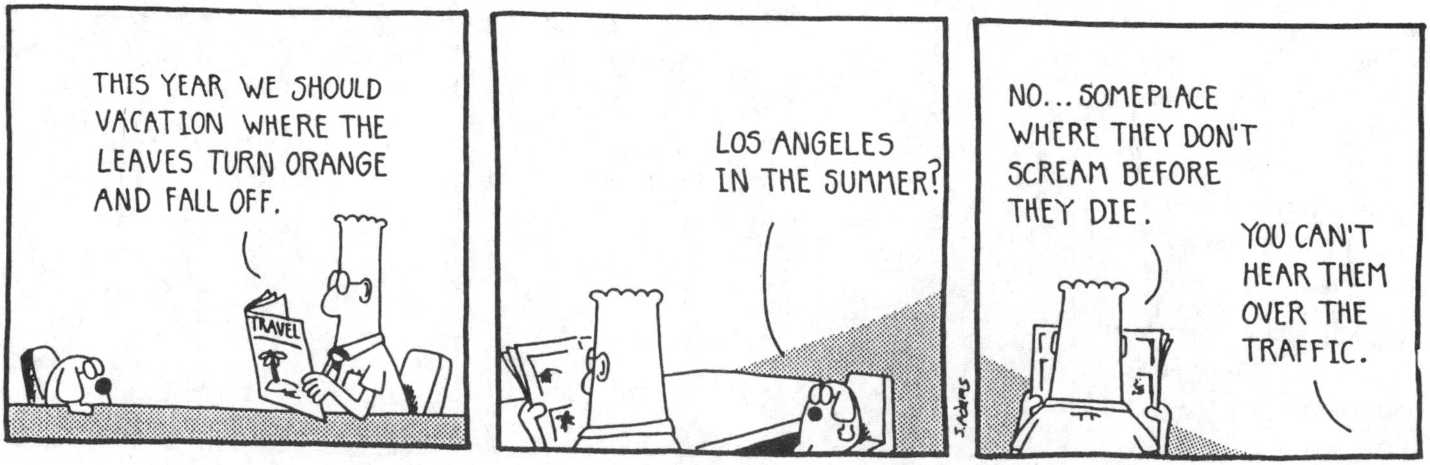
THIS YEAR WE SHOULD VACATION WHERE THE LEAVES TURN ORANGE AND FALL OFF.
TRAVEL
LOS ANGELES IN THE SUMMER?
NO... SOMEPLACE WHERE THEY DON'T SCREAM BEFORE THEY DIE.
YOU CAN'T HEAR THEM OVER THE TRAFFIC.

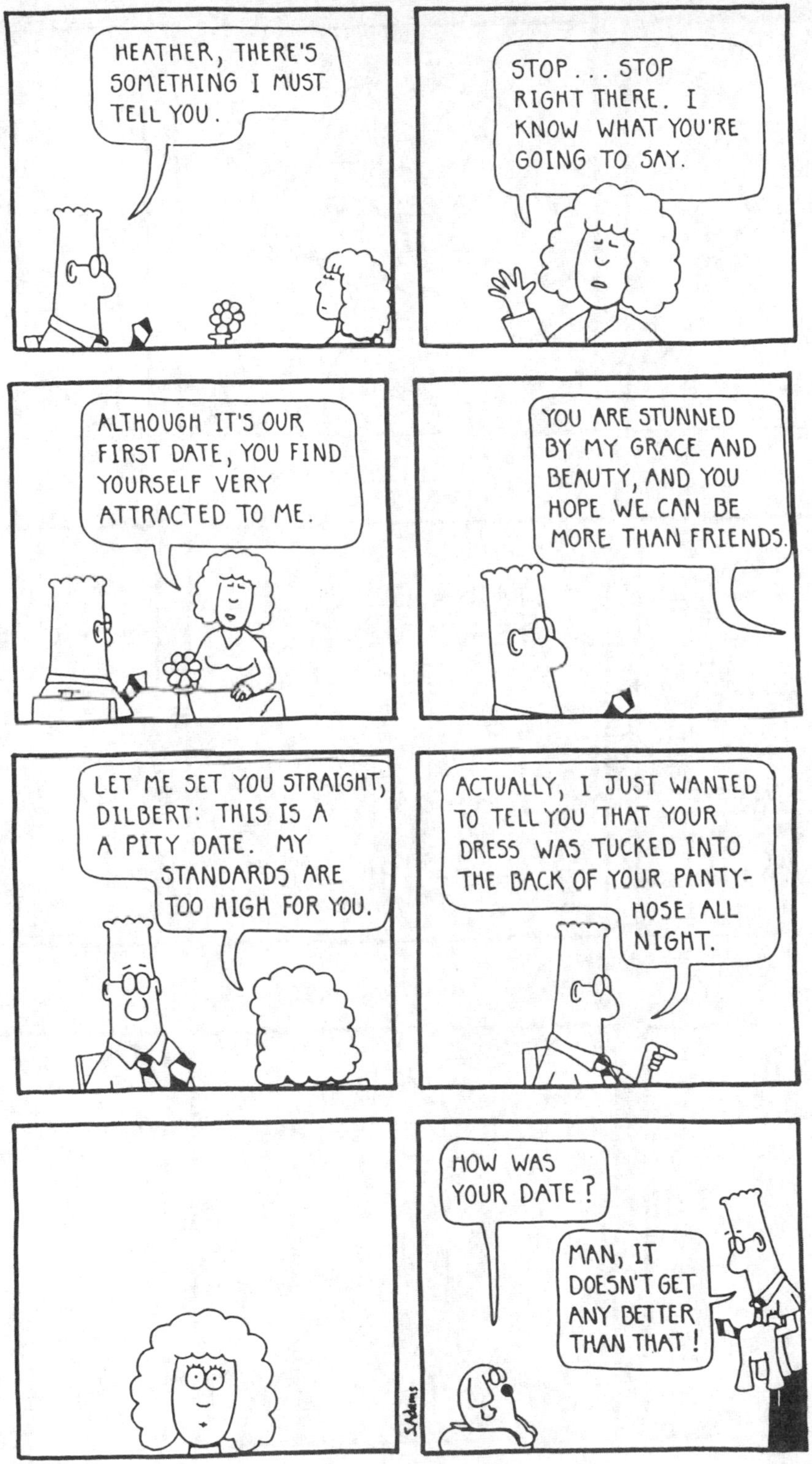
HEATHER, THERE'S SOMETHING I MUST TELL YOU.
STOP... STOP RIGHT THERE. I KNOW WHAT YOU'RE GOING TO SAY.
ALTHOUGH IT'S OUR FIRST DATE, YOU FIND YOURSELF VERY ATTRACTED TO ME.
YOU ARE STUNNED BY MY GRACE AND BEAUTY, AND YOU HOPE WE CAN BE MORE THAN FRIENDS.
LET ME SET YOU STRAIGHT, DILBERT: THIS IS A PITY DATE. MY STANDARDS ARE TOO HIGH FOR YOU.
ACTUALLY, I JUST WANTED TO TELL YOU THAT YOUR DRESS WAS TUCKED INTO THE BACK OF YOUR PANTY-HOSE ALL NIGHT.
S.Adams
HOW WAS YOUR DATE?
MAN, IT DOESN'T GET ANY BETTER THAN THAT!

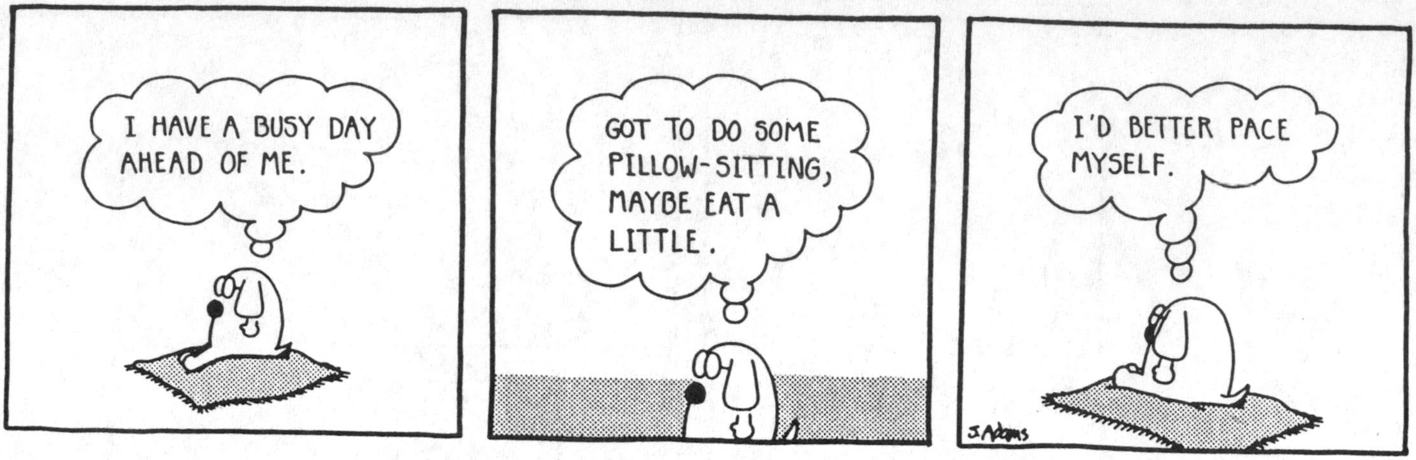
I HAVE A BUSY DAY AHEAD OF ME.
GOT TO DO SOME PILLOW-SITTING, MAYBE EAT A LITTLE.
I'D BETTER PACE MYSELF.
S. Adams

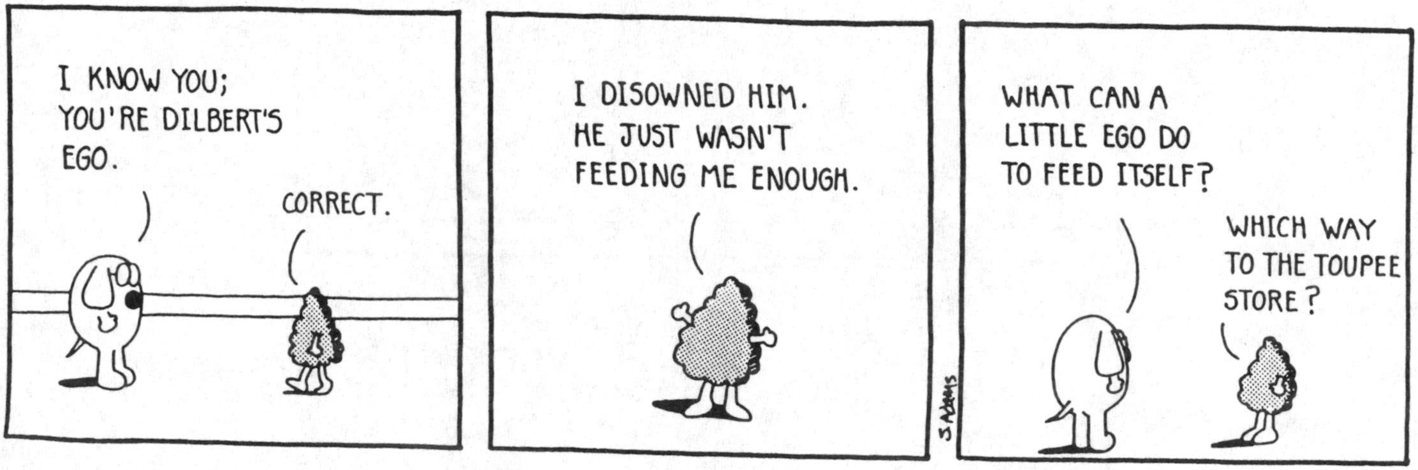
I KNOW YOU; YOU'RE DILBERT'S EGO.
CORRECT.
I DISOWNED HIM. HE JUST WASN'T FEEDING ME ENOUGH.
WHAT CAN A LITTLE EGO DO TO FEED ITSELF?
WHICH WAY TO THE TOUPEE STORE?
S. Adams

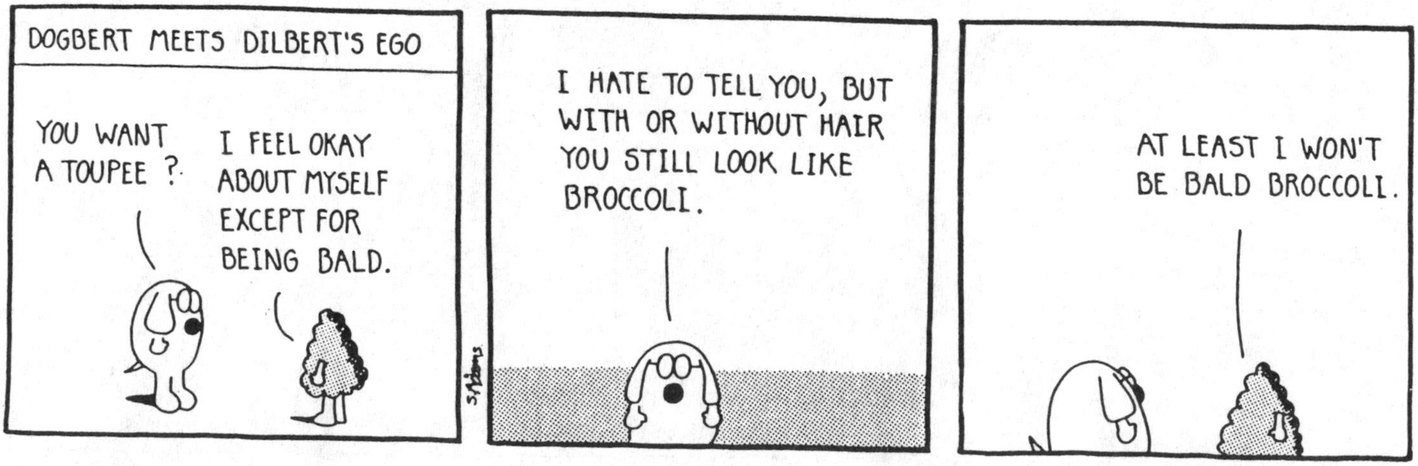
DOGBERT MEETS DILBERT'S EGO
YOU WANT A TOUPEE ?
I FEEL OKAY ABOUT MYSELF EXCEPT FOR BEING BALD.
I HATE TO TELL YOU, BUT WITH OR WITHOUT HAIR YOU STILL LOOK LIKE BROCCOLI.
AT LEAST I WON'T BE BALD BROCCOLI.
S. Adams

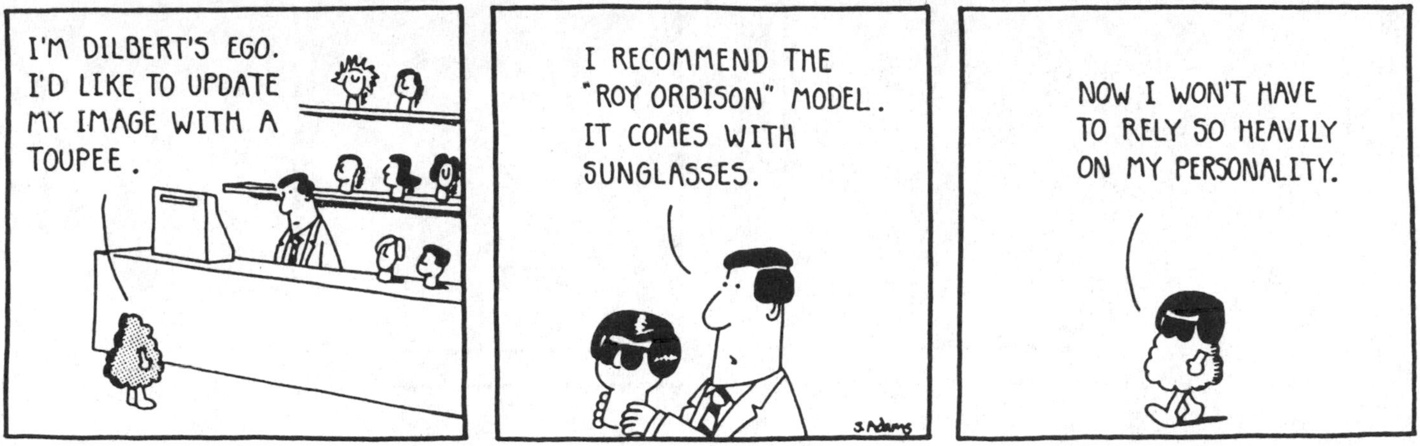
I'M DILBERT'S EGO. I'D LIKE TO UPDATE MY IMAGE WITH A TOUPEE.
I RECOMMEND THE "ROY ORBISON" MODEL. IT COMES WITH SUNGLASSES.
NOW I WON'T HAVE TO RELY SO HEAVILY ON MY PERSONALITY.

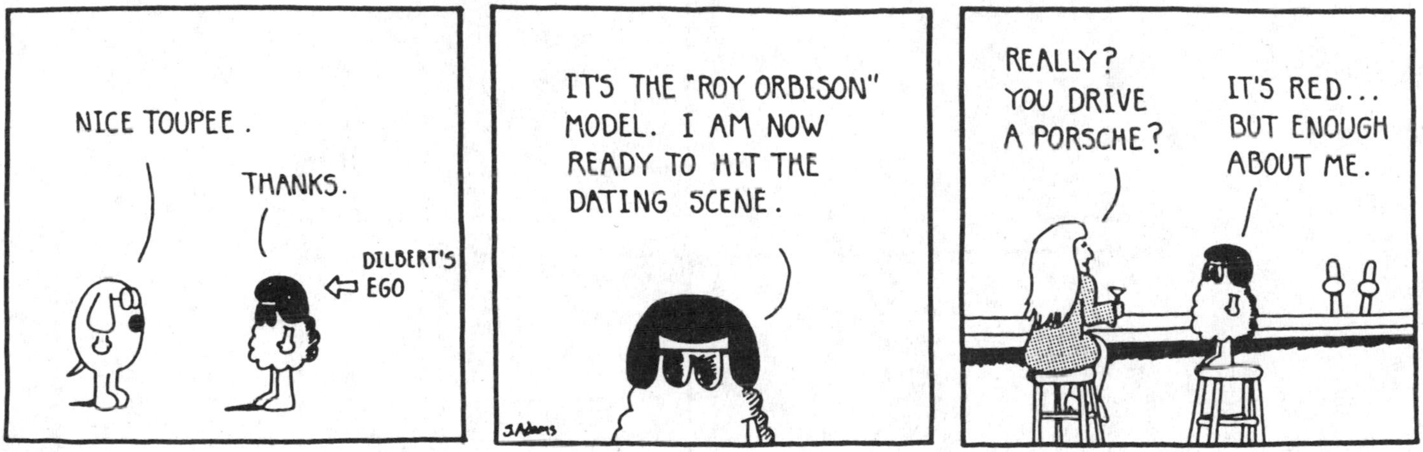
NICE TOUPEE.
THANKS.
DILBERT'S EGO
IT'S THE "ROY ORBISON" MODEL. I AM NOW READY TO HIT THE DATING SCENE.
REALLY? YOU DRIVE A PORSCHE?
IT'S RED... BUT ENOUGH ABOUT ME.

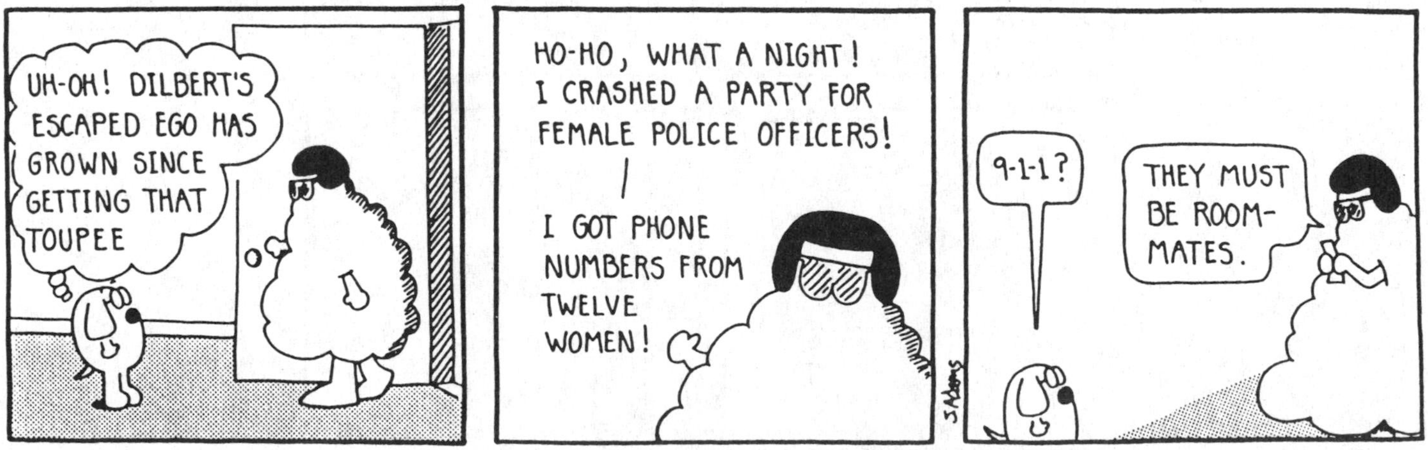
UH-OH! DILBERT'S ESCAPED EGO HAS GROWN SINCE GETTING THAT TOUPEE
HO-HO, WHAT A NIGHT! I CRASHED A PARTY FOR FEMALE POLICE OFFICERS!
I GOT PHONE NUMBERS FROM TWELVE WOMEN!
9-1-1?
THEY MUST BE ROOM-MATES.

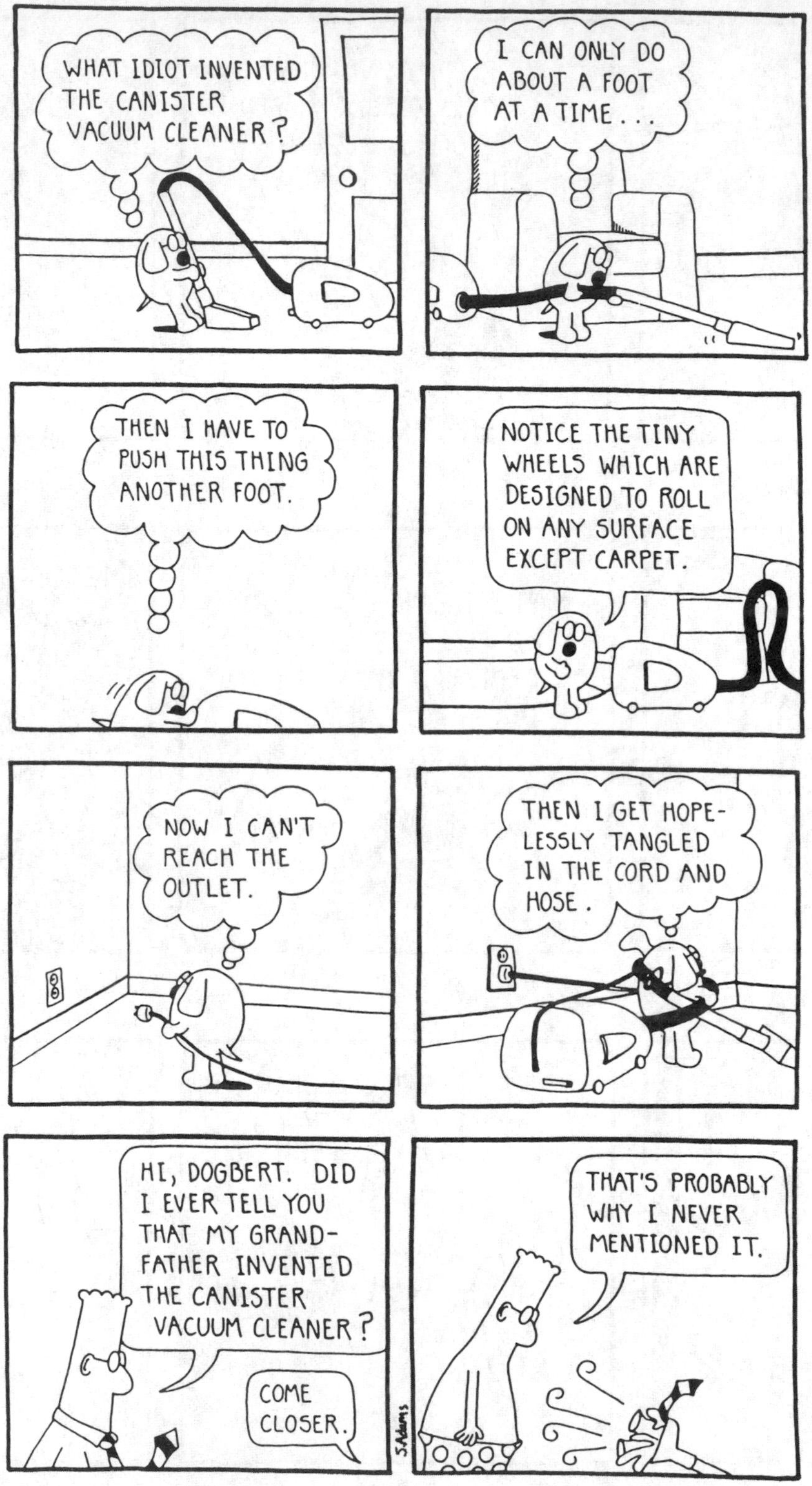
WHAT IDIOT INVENTED THE CANISTER VACUUM CLEANER?
I CAN ONLY DO ABOUT A FOOT AT A TIME . . .
THEN I HAVE TO PUSH THIS THING ANOTHER FOOT.
NOTICE THE TINY WHEELS WHICH ARE DESIGNED TO ROLL ON ANY SURFACE EXCEPT CARPET.
NOW I CAN'T REACH THE OUTLET.
THEN I GET HOPE-LESSLY TANGLED IN THE CORD AND HOSE.
HI, DOGBERT. DID I EVER TELL YOU THAT MY GRAND-FATHER INVENTED THE CANISTER VACUUM CLEANER?
COME CLOSER.
S.Adams
THAT'S PROBABLY WHY I NEVER MENTIONED IT.

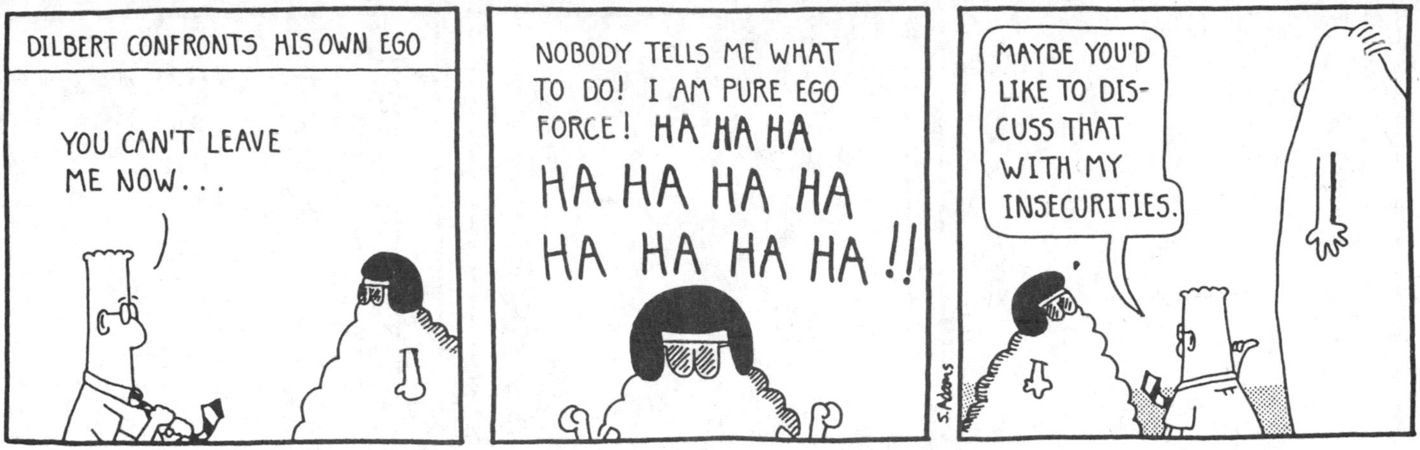
DILBERT CONFRONTS HIS OWN EGO
YOU CAN'T LEAVE ME NOW...
NOBODY TELLS ME WHAT TO DO! I AM PURE EGO FORCE! HA HA HA HA HA HA HA HA HA HA HA!!
MAYBE YOU'D LIKE TO DISCUSS THAT WITH MY INSECURITIES.

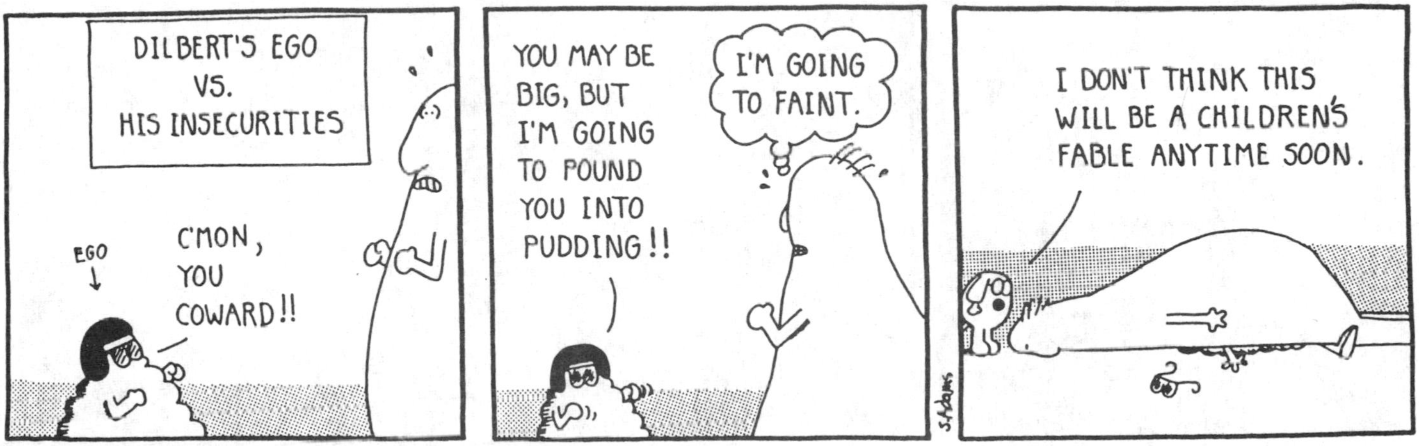
DILBERT'S EGO VS. HIS INSECURITIES
EGO
C'MON, YOU COWARD!!
YOU MAY BE BIG, BUT I'M GOING TO POUND YOU INTO PUDDING!!
I'M GOING TO FAINT.
I DON'T THINK THIS WILL BE A CHILDREN'S FABLE ANYTIME SOON.

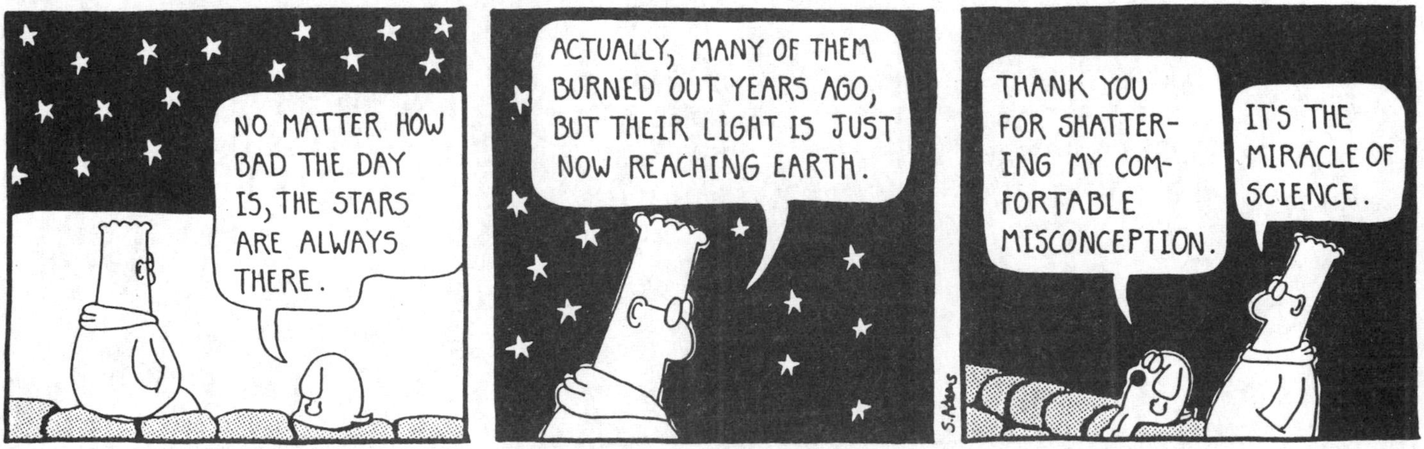
NO MATTER HOW BAD THE DAY IS, THE STARS ARE ALWAYS THERE.
ACTUALLY, MANY OF THEM BURNED OUT YEARS AGO, BUT THEIR LIGHT IS JUST NOW REACHING EARTH.
THANK YOU FOR SHATTERING MY COMFORTABLE MISCONCEPTION.
IT'S THE MIRACLE OF SCIENCE.

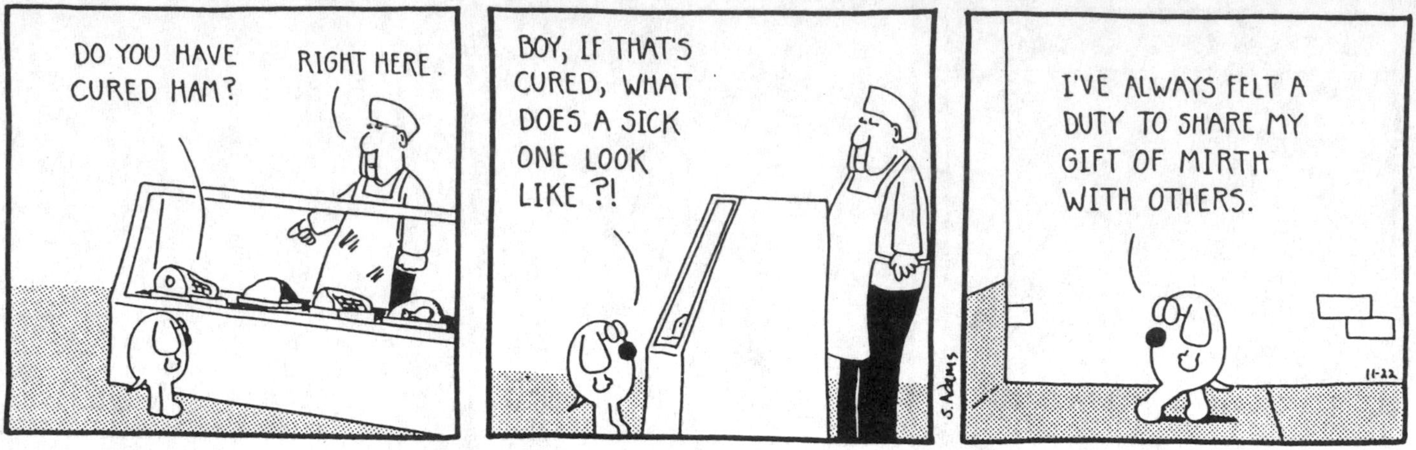
DO YOU HAVE CURED HAM?
RIGHT HERE.
BOY, IF THAT'S CURED, WHAT DOES A SICK ONE LOOK LIKE ?!
S. Adams
I'VE ALWAYS FELT A DUTY TO SHARE MY GIFT OF MIRTH WITH OTHERS.
11-22

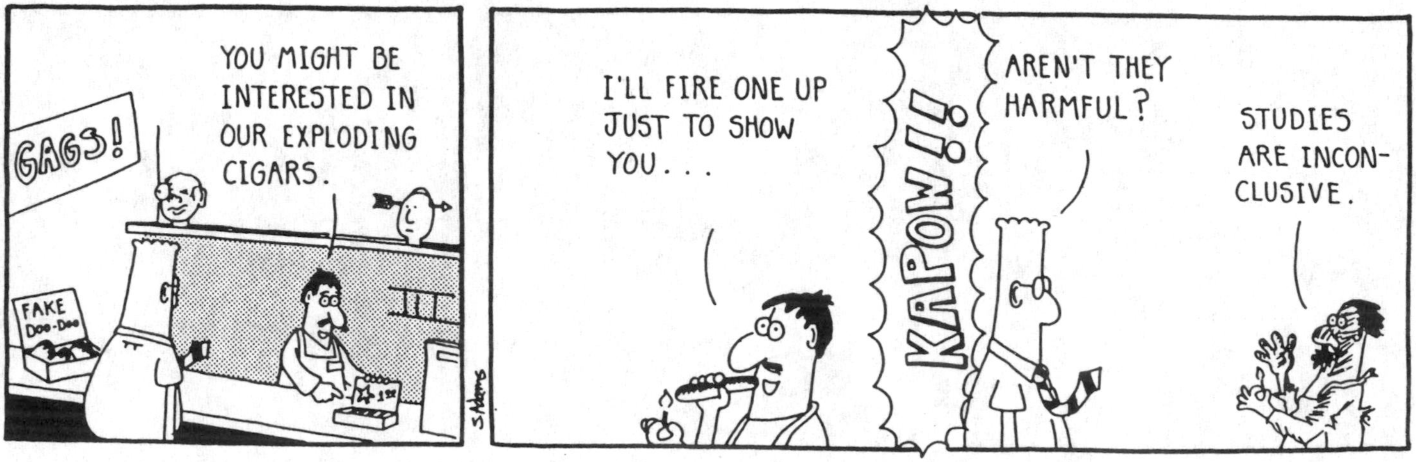
GAGS!
YOU MIGHT BE INTERESTED IN OUR EXPLODING CIGARS.
FAKE Doo-Doo
S. Adams
I'LL FIRE ONE UP JUST TO SHOW YOU . . .
KAPOW!!
AREN'T THEY HARMFUL?
STUDIES ARE INCON-CLUSIVE.

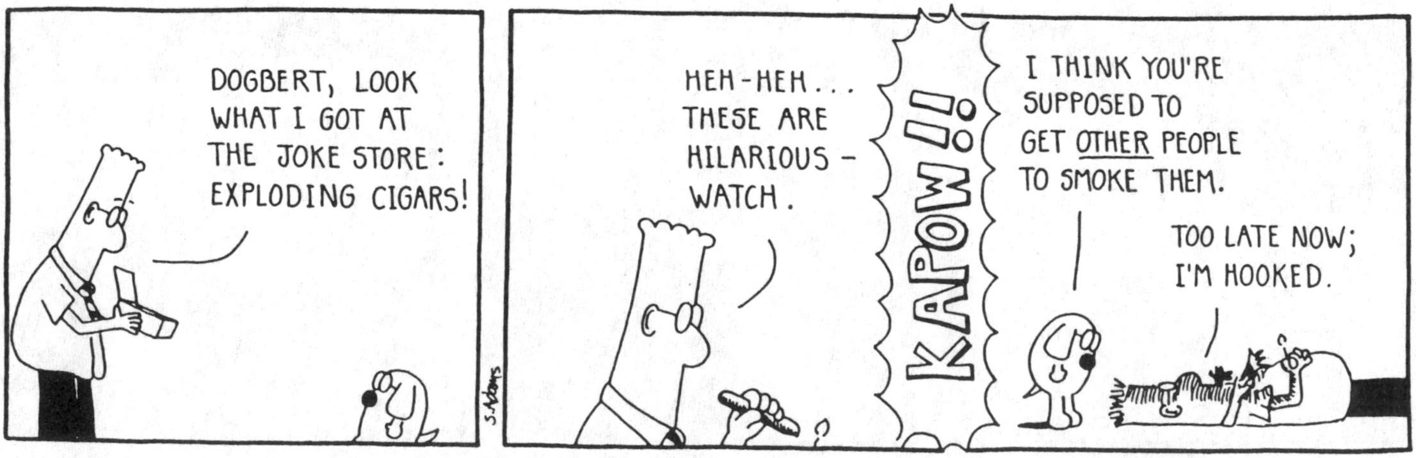
DOGBERT, LOOK WHAT I GOT AT THE JOKE STORE: EXPLODING CIGARS!
S. Adams
HEH-HEH . . . THESE ARE HILARIOUS - WATCH.
KAPOW!!
I THINK YOU'RE SUPPOSED TO GET OTHER PEOPLE TO SMOKE THEM.
TOO LATE NOW; I'M HOOKED.

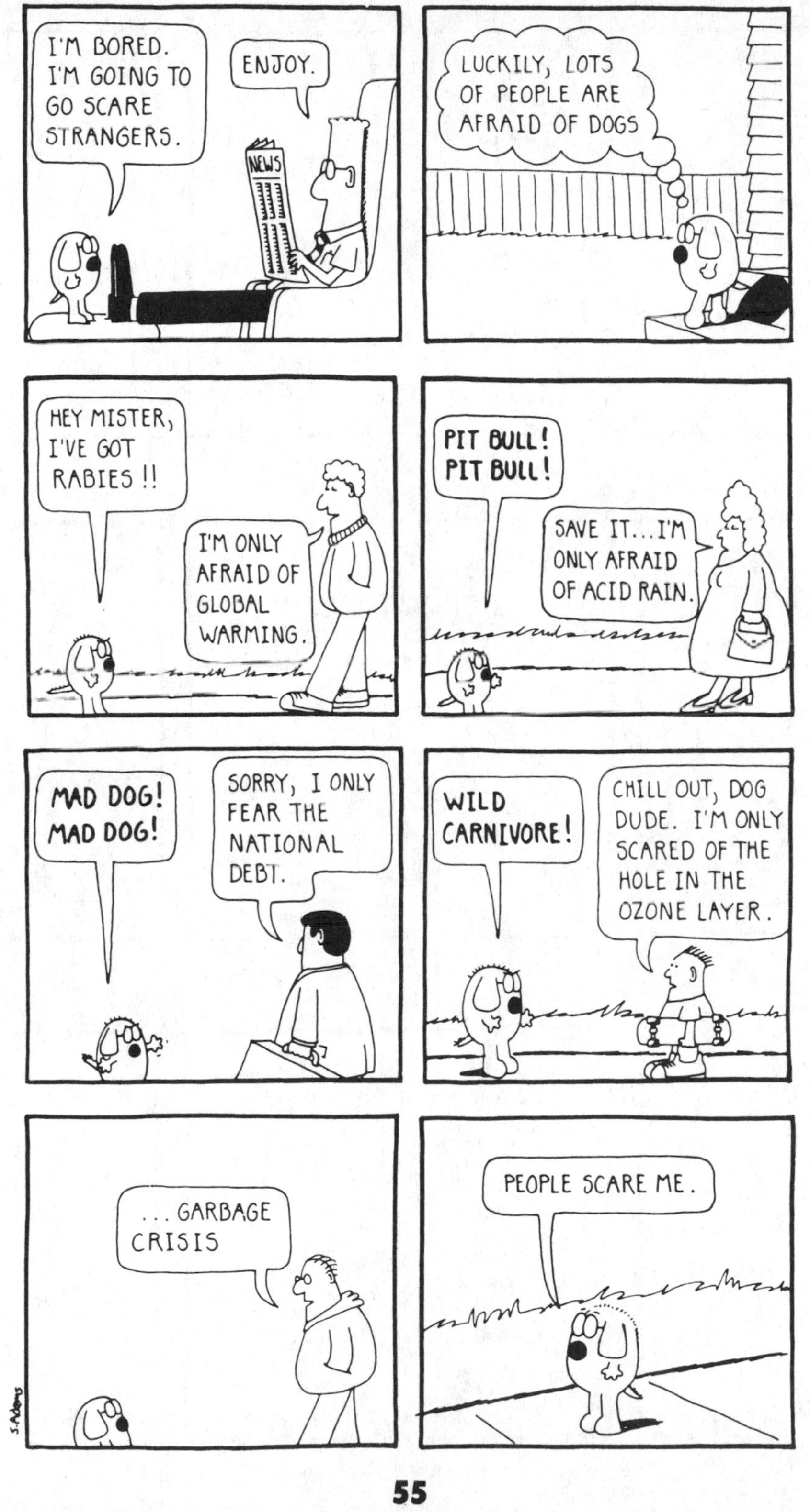
I'M BORED. I'M GOING TO GO SCARE STRANGERS.
ENJOY.
LUCKILY, LOTS OF PEOPLE ARE AFRAID OF DOGS
NEWS
HEY MISTER, I'VE GOT RABIES !!
I'M ONLY AFRAID OF GLOBAL WARMING.
PIT BULL! PIT BULL!
SAVE IT...I'M ONLY AFRAID OF ACID RAIN.
MAD DOG! MAD DOG!
SORRY, I ONLY FEAR THE NATIONAL DEBT.
WILD CARNIVORE!
CHILL OUT, DOG DUDE. I'M ONLY SCARED OF THE HOLE IN THE OZONE LAYER.
... GARBAGE CRISIS
PEOPLE SCARE ME.
S. Adams

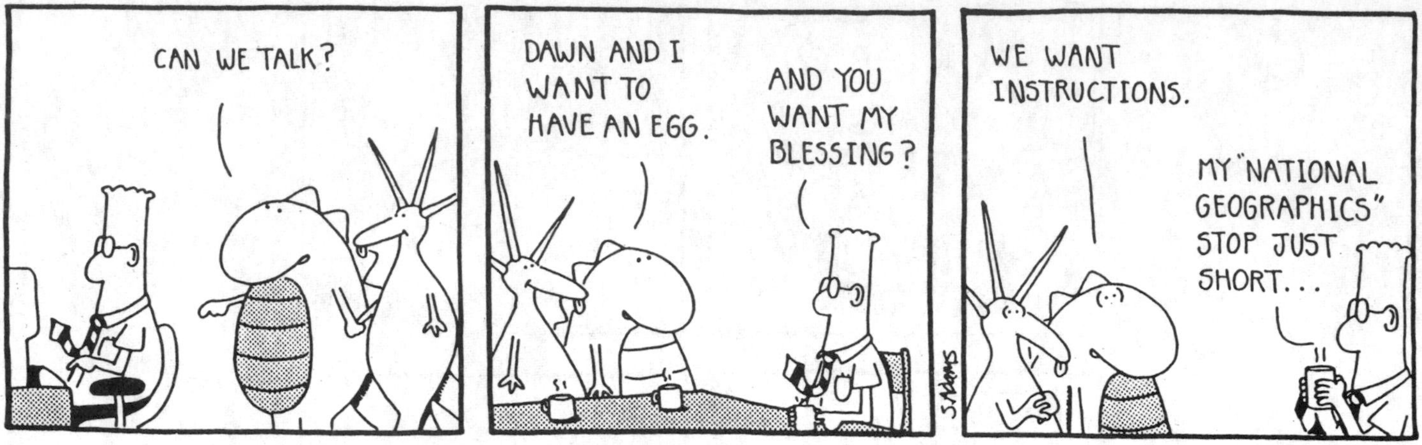
CAN WE TALK?
DAWN AND I WANT TO HAVE AN EGG.
AND YOU WANT MY BLESSING?
WE WANT INSTRUCTIONS.
MY "NATIONAL GEOGRAPHICS" STOP JUST SHORT...
S.Adams

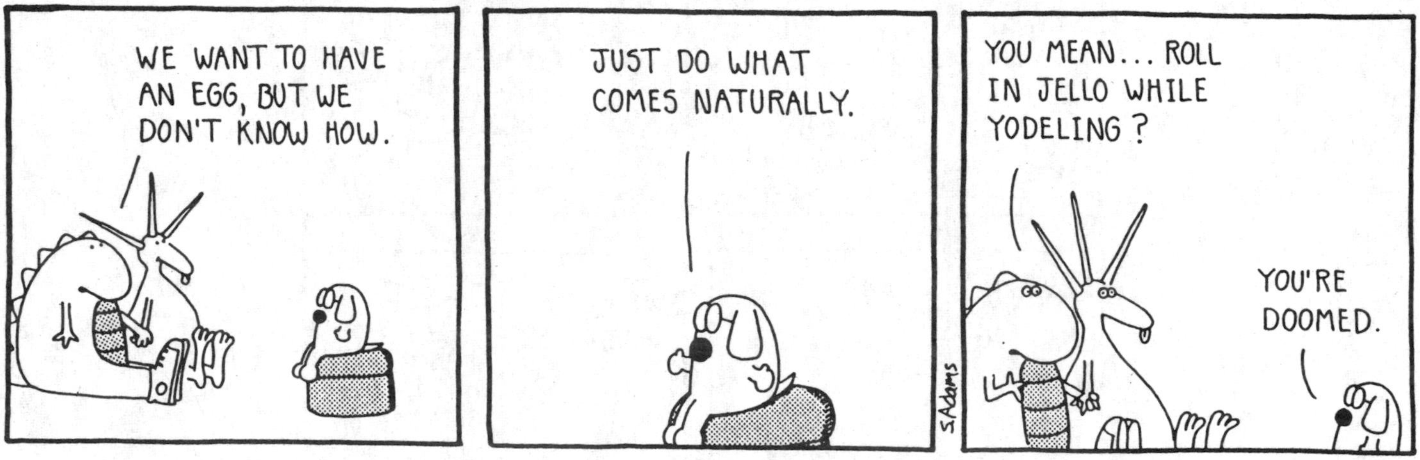
WE WANT TO HAVE AN EGG, BUT WE DON'T KNOW HOW.
JUST DO WHAT COMES NATURALLY.
YOU MEAN... ROLL IN JELLO WHILE YODELING?
YOU'RE DOOMED.
S.Adams

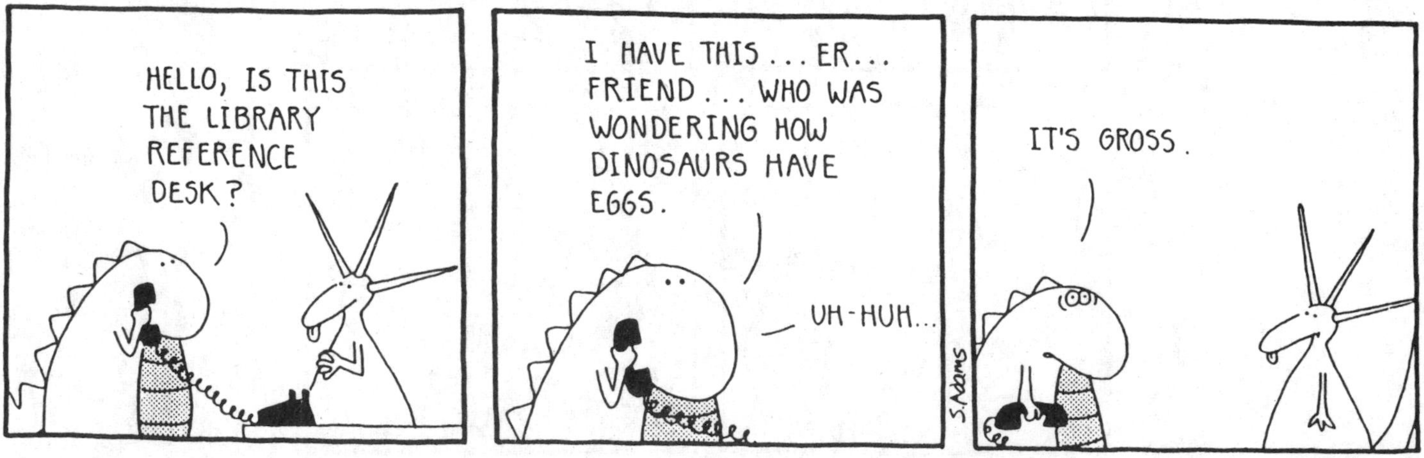
HELLO, IS THIS THE LIBRARY REFERENCE DESK?
I HAVE THIS... ER... FRIEND... WHO WAS WONDERING HOW DINOSAURS HAVE EGGS.
UH-HUH...
IT'S GROSS.
S.Adams

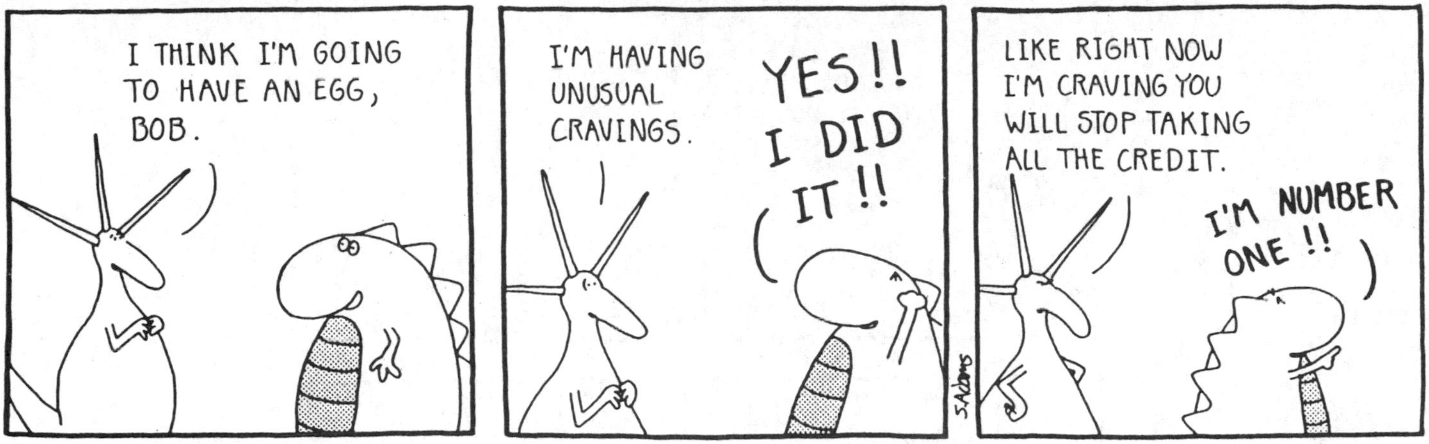
I THINK I'M GOING TO HAVE AN EGG, BOB.
I'M HAVING UNUSUAL CRAVINGS.
YES!! I DID IT!!
LIKE RIGHT NOW I'M CRAVING YOU WILL STOP TAKING ALL THE CREDIT.
I'M NUMBER ONE!!

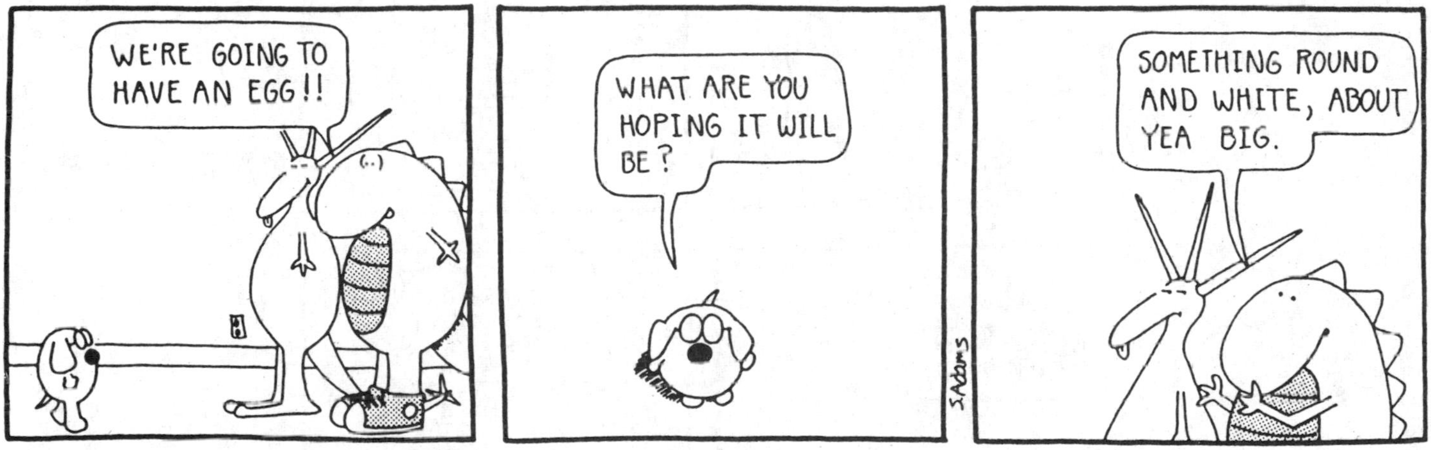
WE'RE GOING TO HAVE AN EGG!!
WHAT ARE YOU HOPING IT WILL BE?
SOMETHING ROUND AND WHITE, ABOUT YEA BIG.

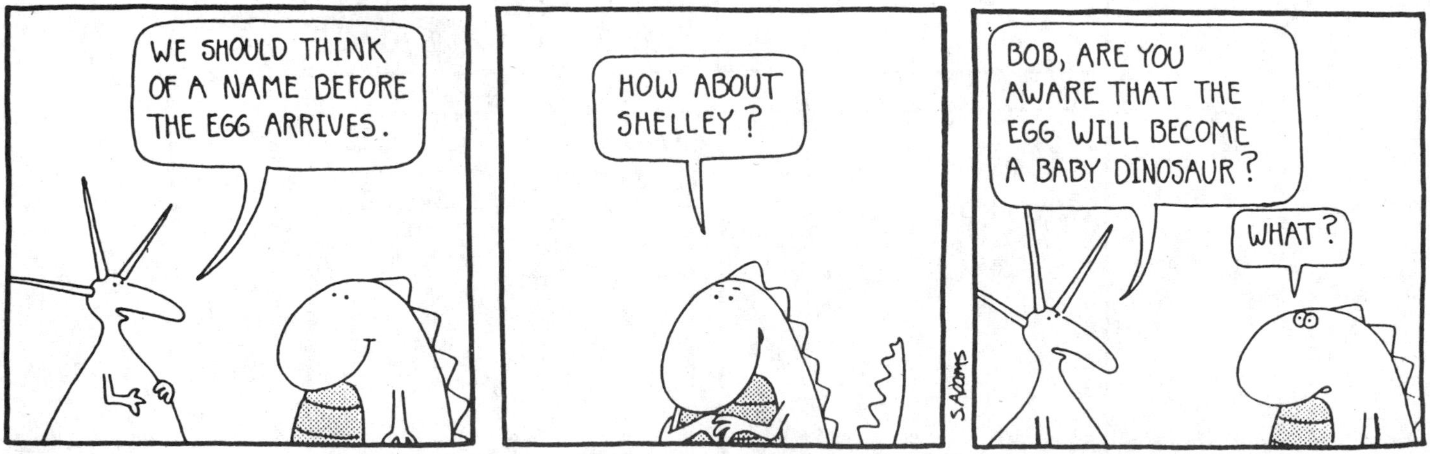
WE SHOULD THINK OF A NAME BEFORE THE EGG ARRIVES.
HOW ABOUT SHELLEY?
BOB, ARE YOU AWARE THAT THE EGG WILL BECOME A BABY DINOSAUR?
WHAT?

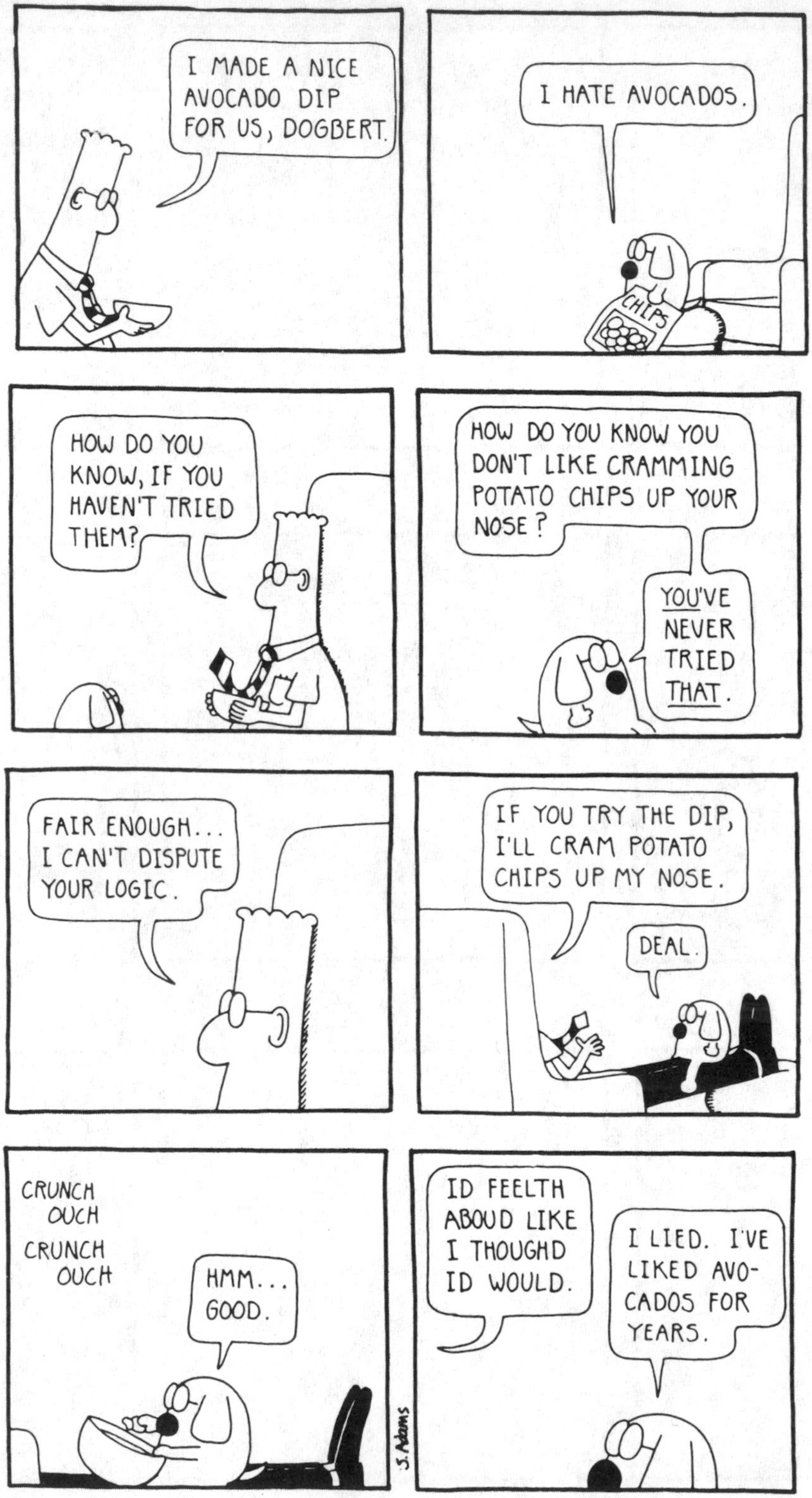
I MADE A NICE AVOCADO DIP FOR US, DOGBERT.
I HATE AVOCADOS.
CHIPS
HOW DO YOU KNOW, IF YOU HAVEN'T TRIED THEM?
HOW DO YOU KNOW YOU DON'T LIKE CRAMMING POTATO CHIPS UP YOUR NOSE?
YOU'VE NEVER TRIED THAT.
FAIR ENOUGH... I CAN'T DISPUTE YOUR LOGIC.
IF YOU TRY THE DIP, I'LL CRAM POTATO CHIPS UP MY NOSE.
DEAL.
CRUNCH
OUCH
CRUNCH
OUCH
HMM... GOOD.
S. Adams
ID FEELTH ABOUD LIKE I THOUGHD ID WOULD.
I LIED. I'VE LIKED AVOCADOS FOR YEARS.

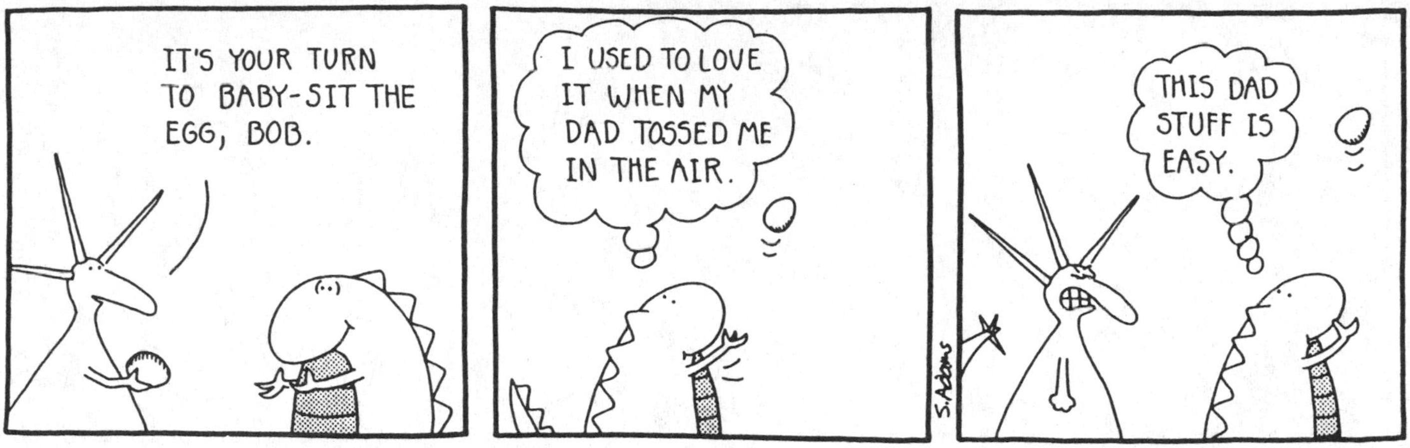
IT'S YOUR TURN TO BABY-SIT THE EGG, BOB.
I USED TO LOVE IT WHEN MY DAD TOSSED ME IN THE AIR.
THIS DAD STUFF IS EASY.
S. Adams

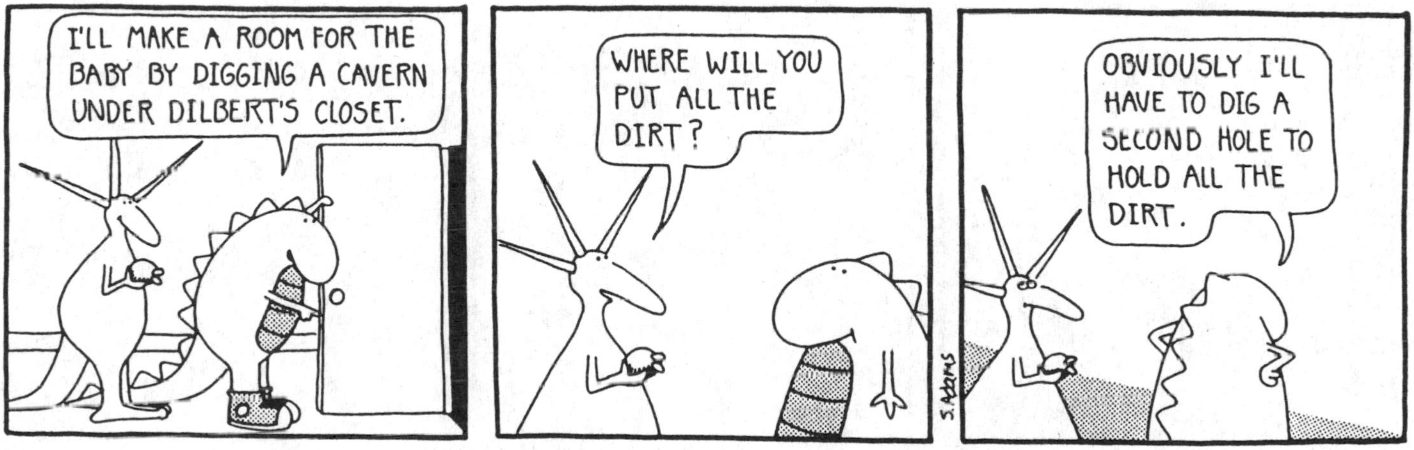
I'LL MAKE A ROOM FOR THE BABY BY DIGGING A CAVERN UNDER DILBERT'S CLOSET.
WHERE WILL YOU PUT ALL THE DIRT?
OBVIOUSLY I'LL HAVE TO DIG A SECOND HOLE TO HOLD ALL THE DIRT.
S. Adams

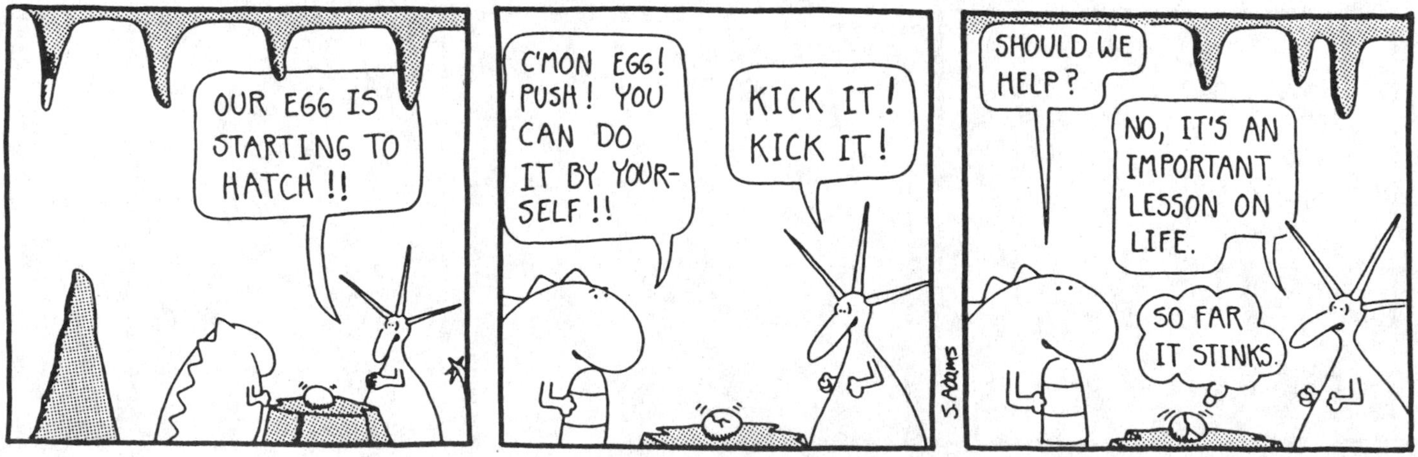
OUR EGG IS STARTING TO HATCH !!
C'MON EGG! PUSH! YOU CAN DO IT BY YOURSELF !!
KICK IT! KICK IT!
S. Adams
SHOULD WE HELP?
NO, IT'S AN IMPORTANT LESSON ON LIFE.
SO FAR IT STINKS.

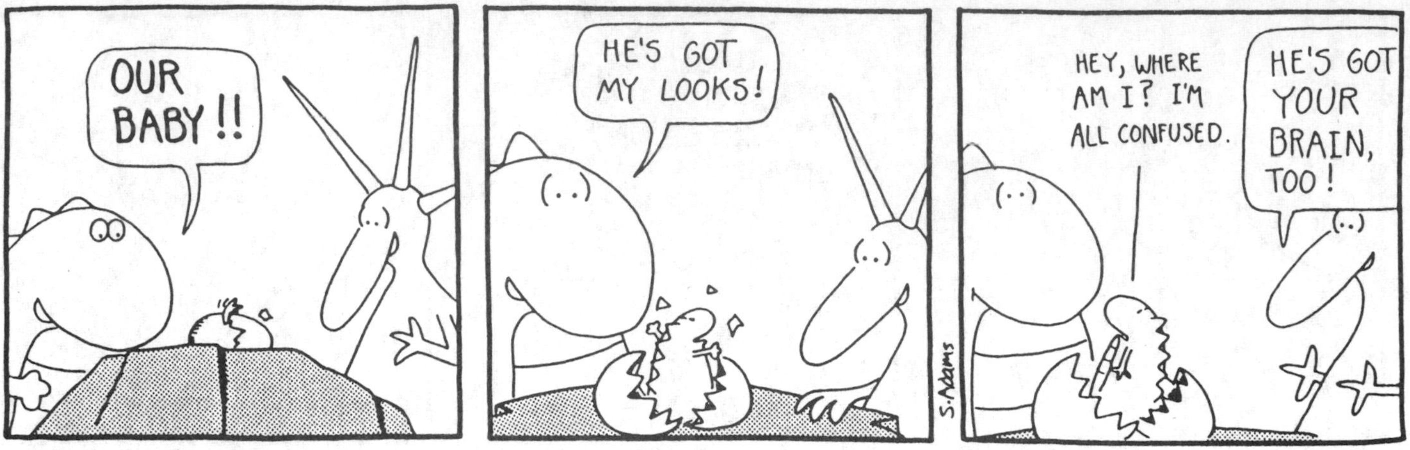
OUR BABY!!
HE'S GOT MY LOOKS!
HEY, WHERE AM I? I'M ALL CONFUSED.
HE'S GOT YOUR BRAIN, TOO!
S. Adams

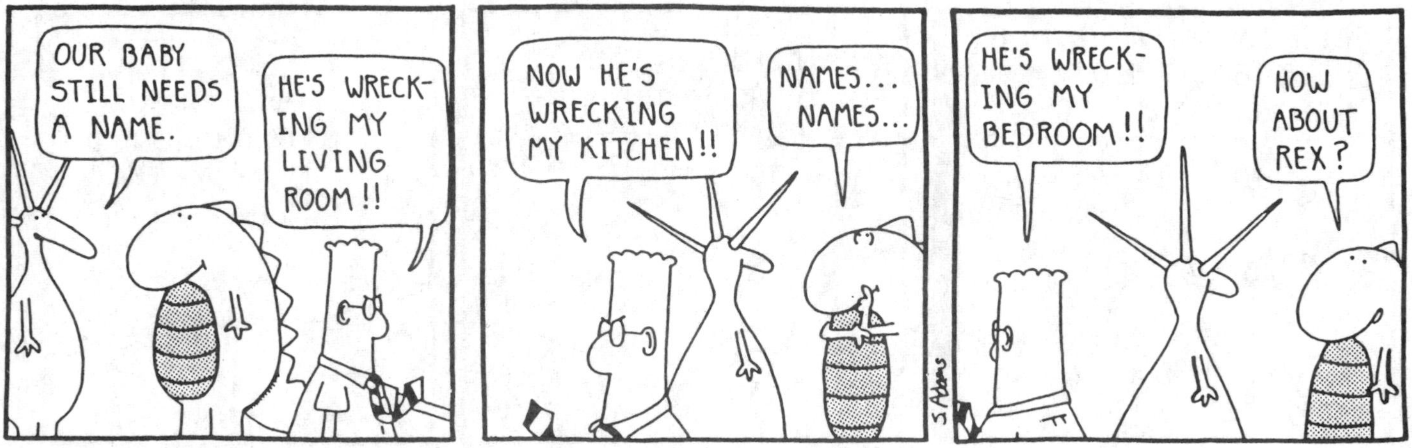
OUR BABY STILL NEEDS A NAME.
HE'S WRECK-ING MY LIVING ROOM!!
NOW HE'S WRECKING MY KITCHEN!!
NAMES... NAMES...
HE'S WRECK-ING MY BEDROOM!!
HOW ABOUT REX?
S. Adams

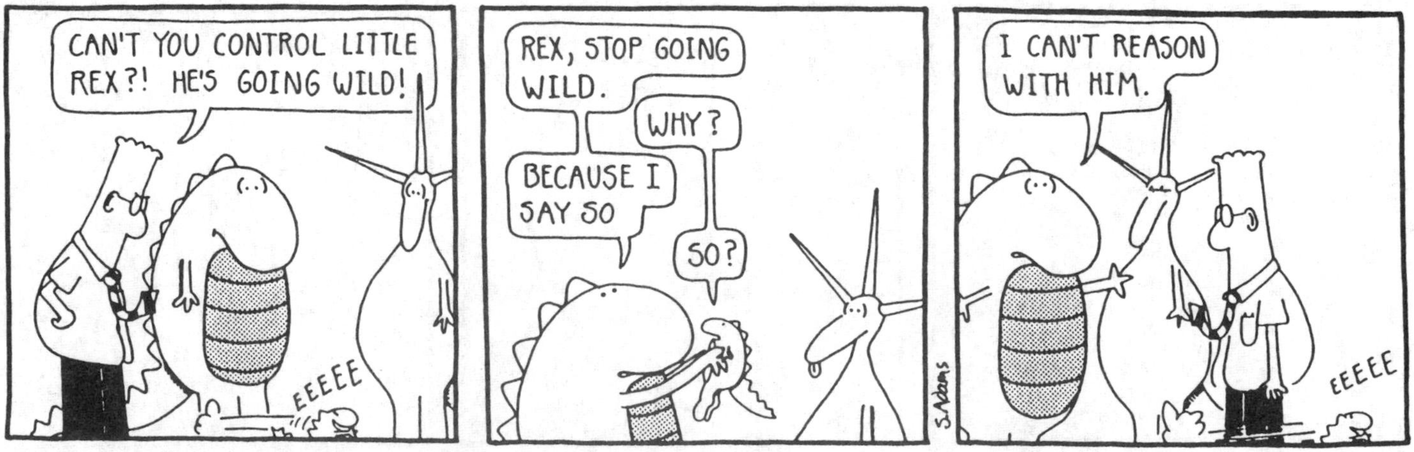
CAN'T YOU CONTROL LITTLE REX?! HE'S GOING WILD!
EEEEE
REX, STOP GOING WILD.
WHY?
BECAUSE I SAY SO
SO?
I CAN'T REASON WITH HIM.
EEEEE
S. Adams

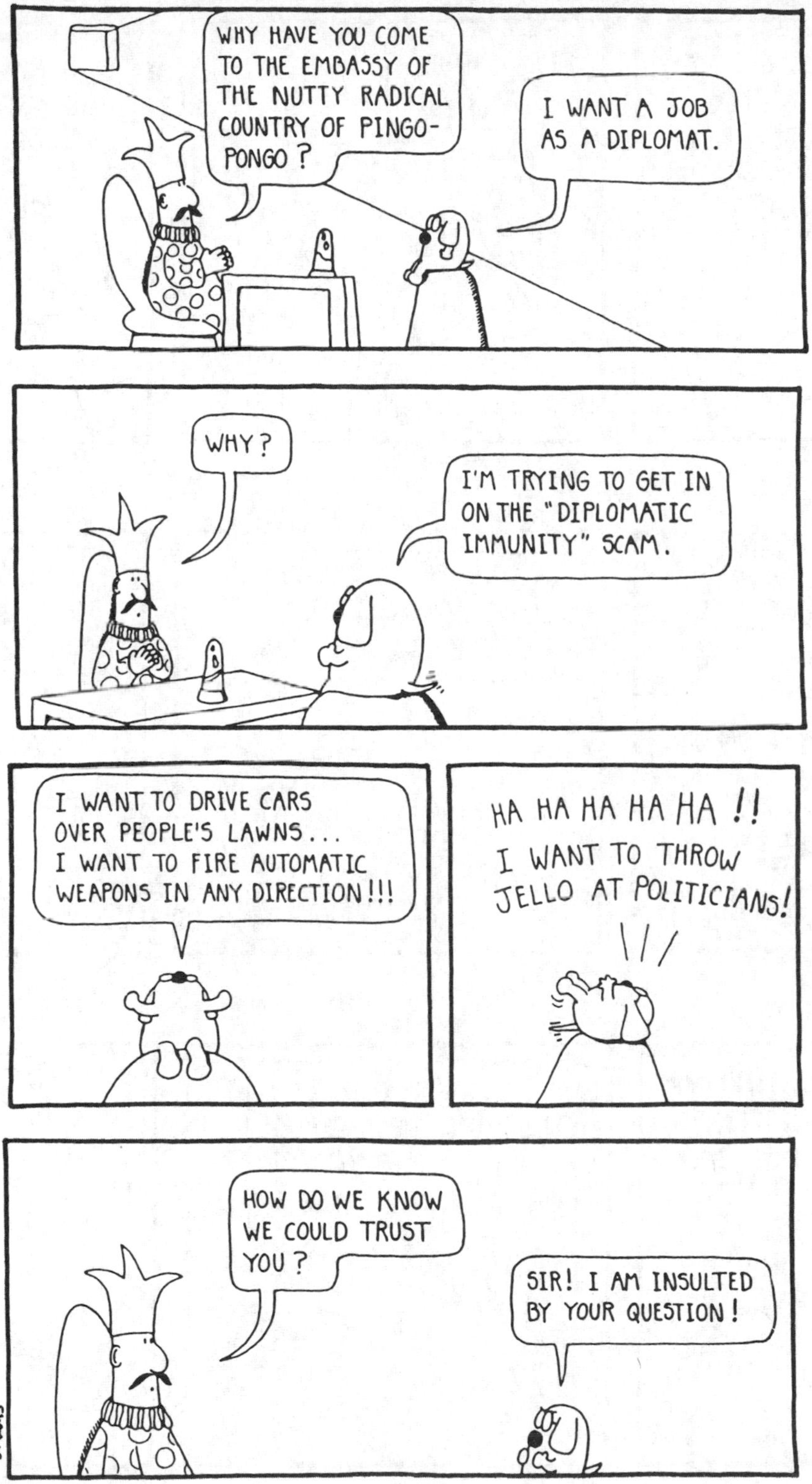
WHY HAVE YOU COME TO THE EMBASSY OF THE NUTTY RADICAL COUNTRY OF PINGO-PONGO ?
I WANT A JOB AS A DIPLOMAT.
WHY ?
I'M TRYING TO GET IN ON THE "DIPLOMATIC IMMUNITY" SCAM.
I WANT TO DRIVE CARS OVER PEOPLE'S LAWNS... I WANT TO FIRE AUTOMATIC WEAPONS IN ANY DIRECTION!!!
HA HA HA HA HA !!
I WANT TO THROW JELLO AT POLITICIANS!
HOW DO WE KNOW WE COULD TRUST YOU ?
SIR! I AM INSULTED BY YOUR QUESTION!
S.Adams

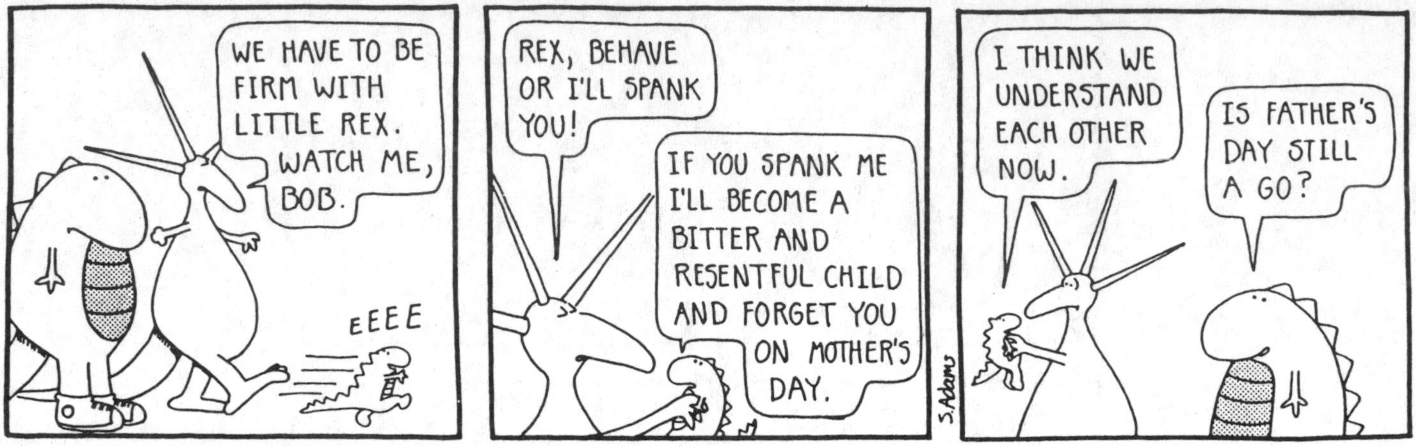
WE HAVE TO BE FIRM WITH LITTLE REX. WATCH ME, BOB.
EEEE
REX, BEHAVE OR I'LL SPANK YOU!
IF YOU SPANK ME I'LL BECOME A BITTER AND RESENTFUL CHILD AND FORGET YOU ON MOTHER'S DAY.
I THINK WE UNDERSTAND EACH OTHER NOW.
IS FATHER'S DAY STILL A GO?
S. Adams

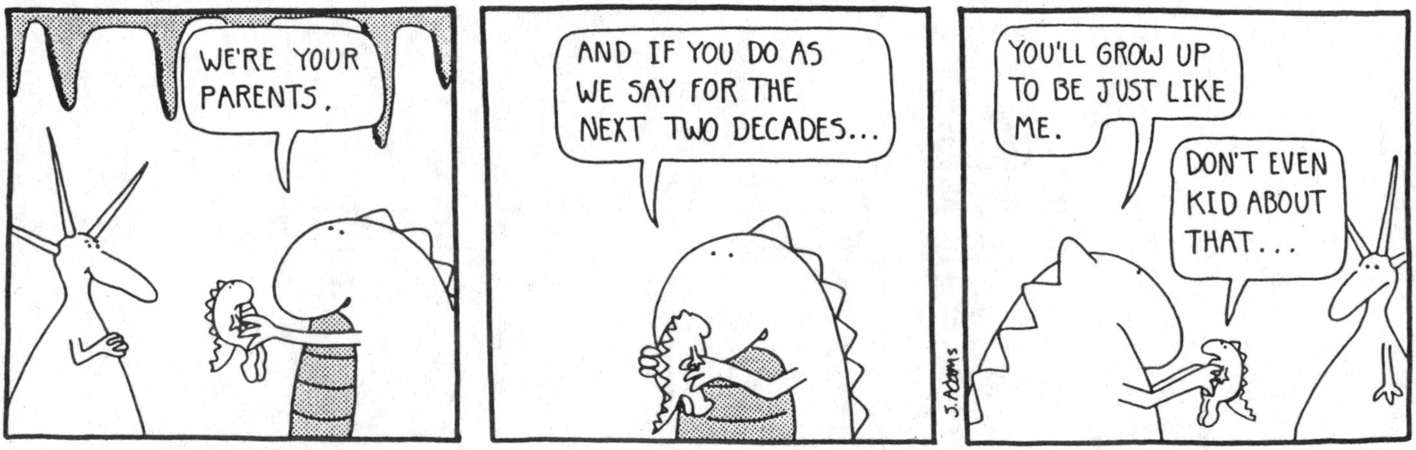
WE'RE YOUR PARENTS.
AND IF YOU DO AS WE SAY FOR THE NEXT TWO DECADES...
YOU'LL GROW UP TO BE JUST LIKE ME.
DON'T EVEN KID ABOUT THAT...
S. Adams

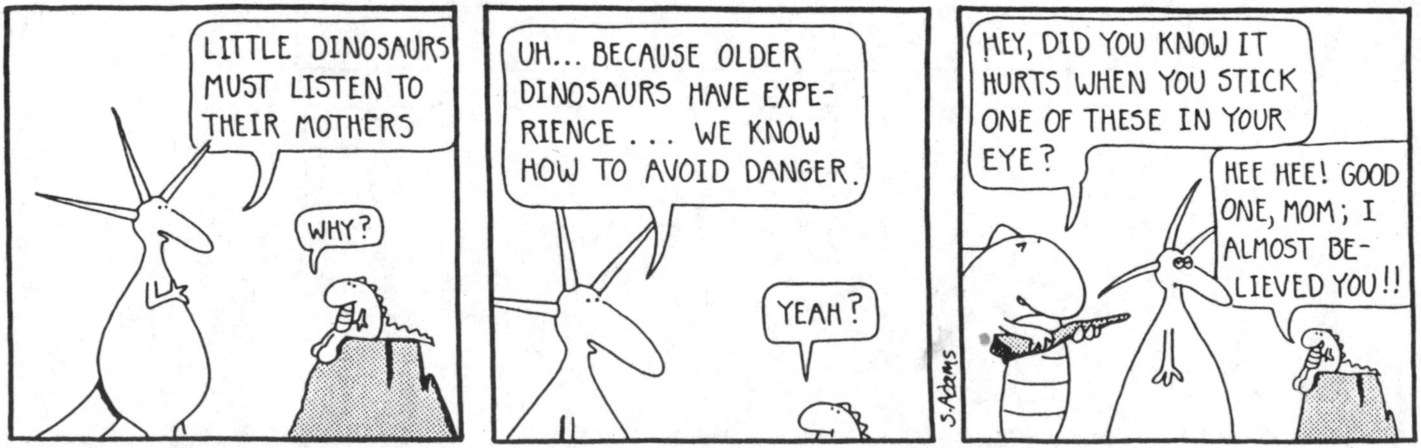
LITTLE DINOSAURS MUST LISTEN TO THEIR MOTHERS
WHY?
UH... BECAUSE OLDER DINOSAURS HAVE EXPE- RIENCE . . . WE KNOW HOW TO AVOID DANGER.
YEAH?
HEY, DID YOU KNOW IT HURTS WHEN YOU STICK ONE OF THESE IN YOUR EYE?
HEE HEE! GOOD ONE, MOM; I ALMOST BE- LIEVED YOU!!
S. Adams

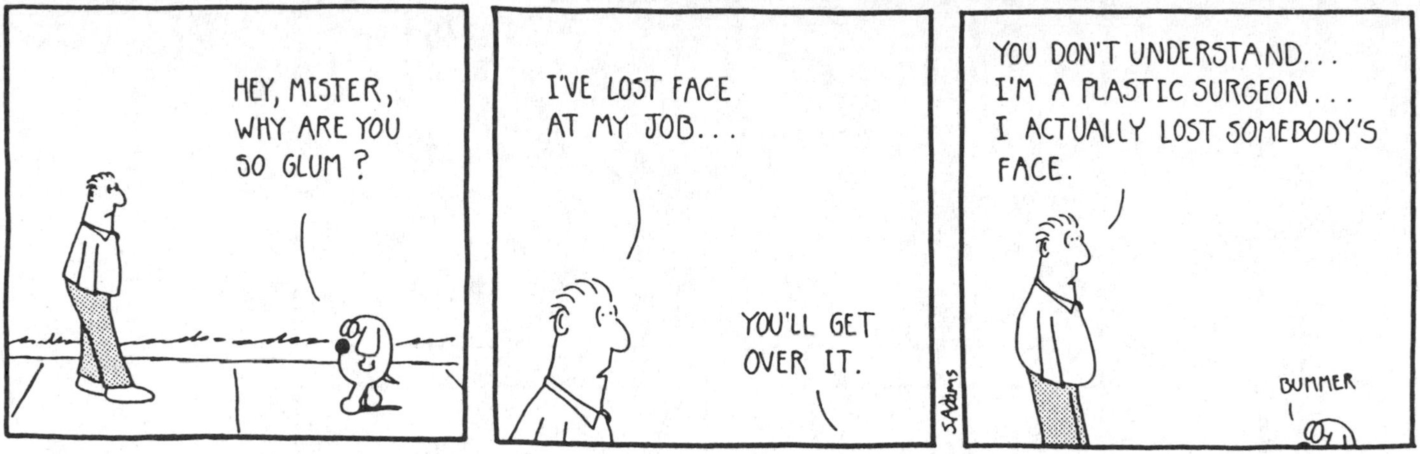
HEY, MISTER, WHY ARE YOU SO GLUM?
I'VE LOST FACE AT MY JOB...
YOU'LL GET OVER IT.
S.Adams
YOU DON'T UNDERSTAND... I'M A PLASTIC SURGEON... I ACTUALLY LOST SOMEBODY'S FACE.
BUMMER

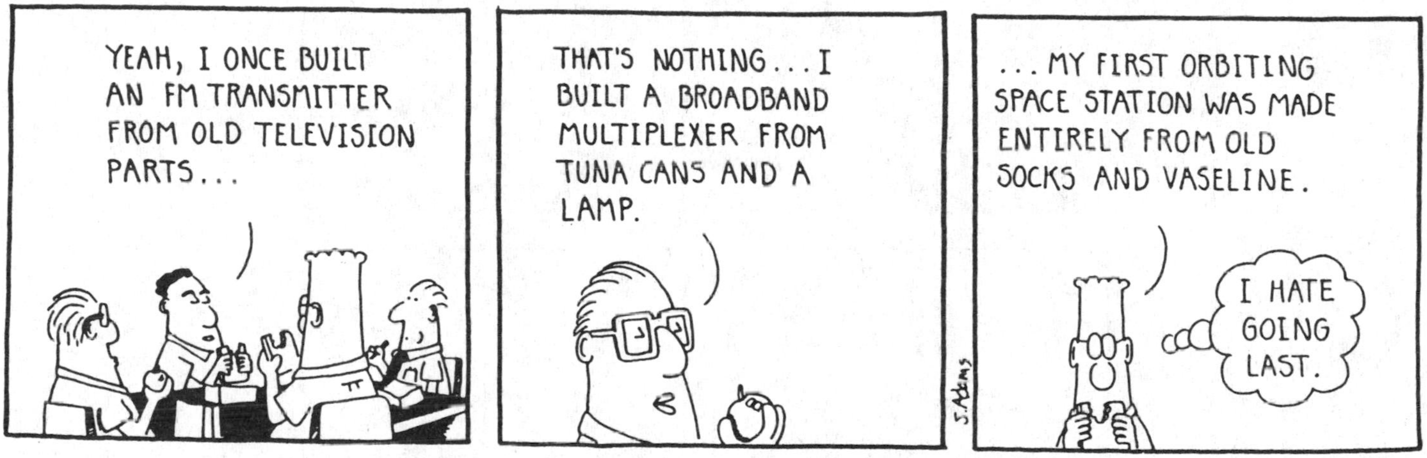
YEAH, I ONCE BUILT AN FM TRANSMITTER FROM OLD TELEVISION PARTS...
THAT'S NOTHING... I BUILT A BROADBAND MULTIPLEXER FROM TUNA CANS AND A LAMP.
S.Adams
... MY FIRST ORBITING SPACE STATION WAS MADE ENTIRELY FROM OLD SOCKS AND VASELINE.
I HATE GOING LAST.

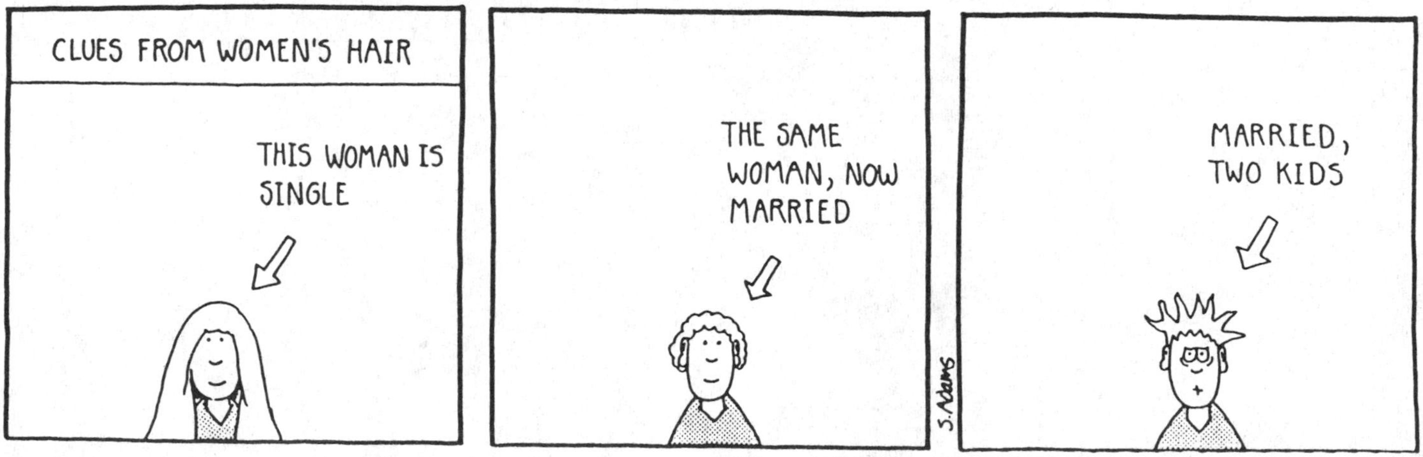
CLUES FROM WOMEN'S HAIR
THIS WOMAN IS SINGLE
THE SAME WOMAN, NOW MARRIED
S.Adams
MARRIED, TWO KIDS

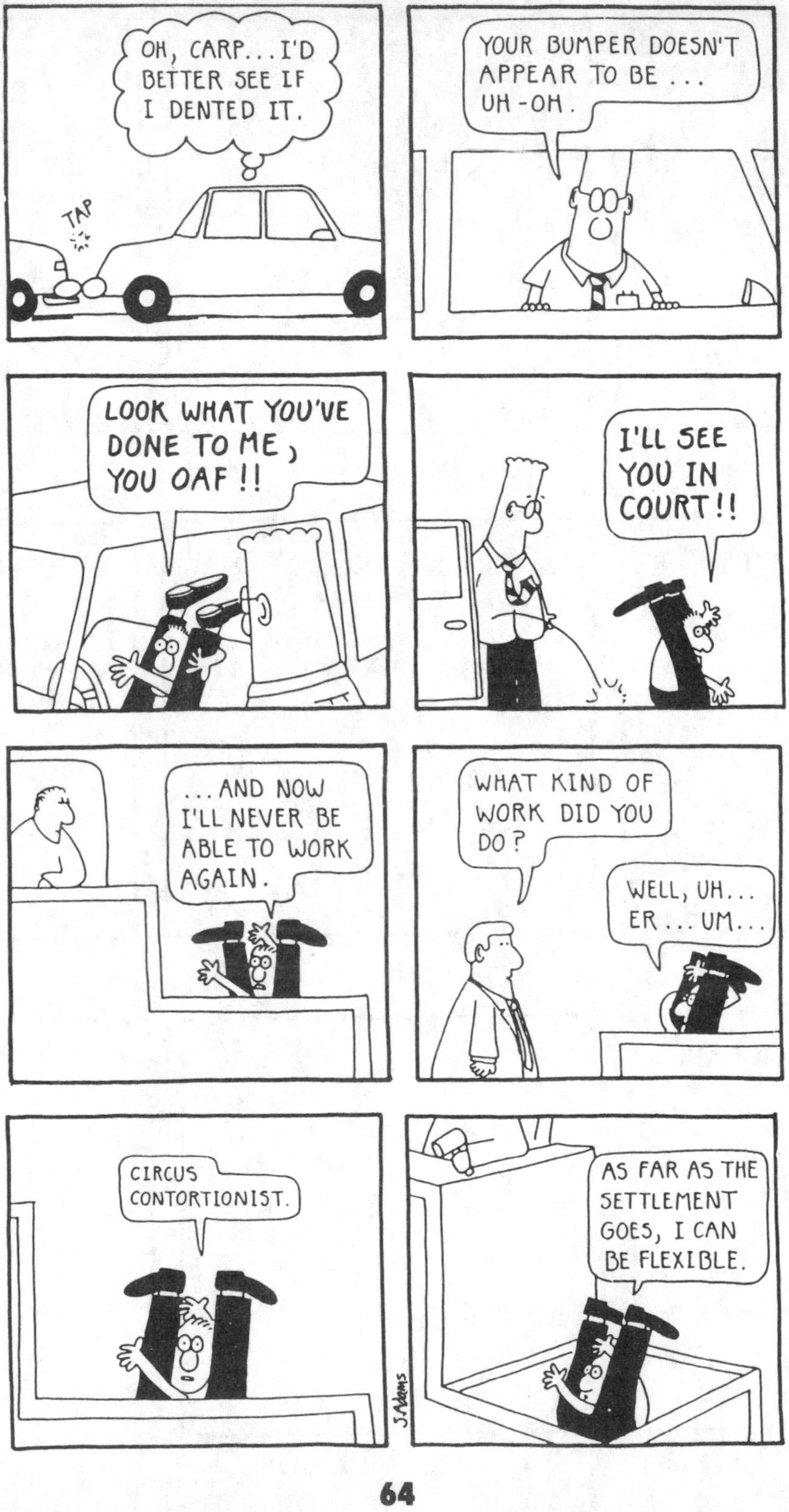
TAP
OH, CARP... I'D BETTER SEE IF I DENTED IT.
YOUR BUMPER DOESN'T APPEAR TO BE ... UH-OH.
LOOK WHAT YOU'VE DONE TO ME, YOU OAF!!
I'LL SEE YOU IN COURT!!
... AND NOW I'LL NEVER BE ABLE TO WORK AGAIN.
WHAT KIND OF WORK DID YOU DO?
WELL, UH... ER... UM...
CIRCUS CONTORTIONIST.
AS FAR AS THE SETTLEMENT GOES, I CAN BE FLEXIBLE.
S.Adams

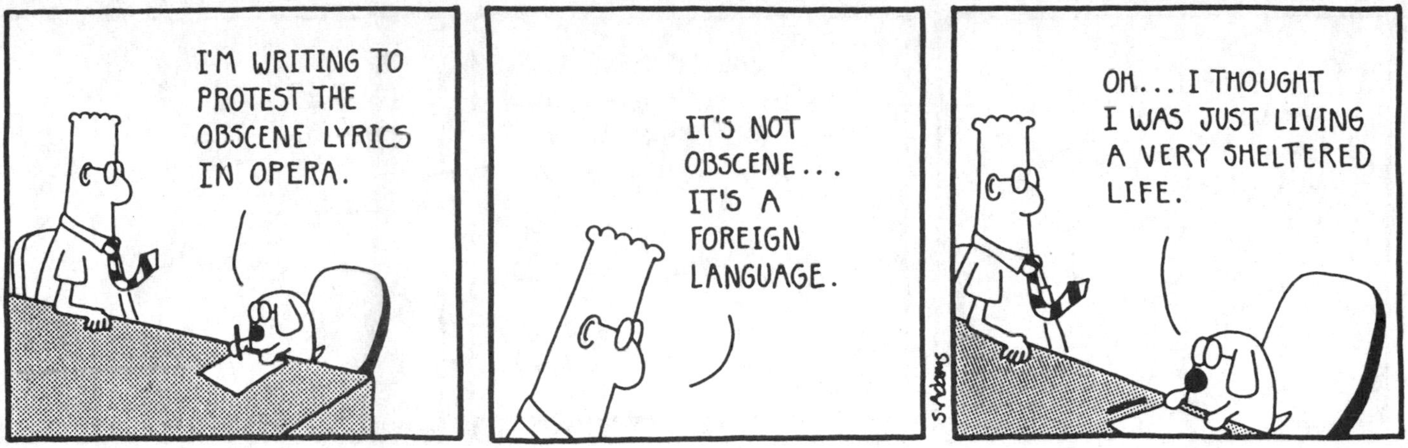
I'M WRITING TO PROTEST THE OBSCENE LYRICS IN OPERA.
IT'S NOT OBSCENE... IT'S A FOREIGN LANGUAGE.
OH... I THOUGHT I WAS JUST LIVING A VERY SHELTERED LIFE.
S. Adams

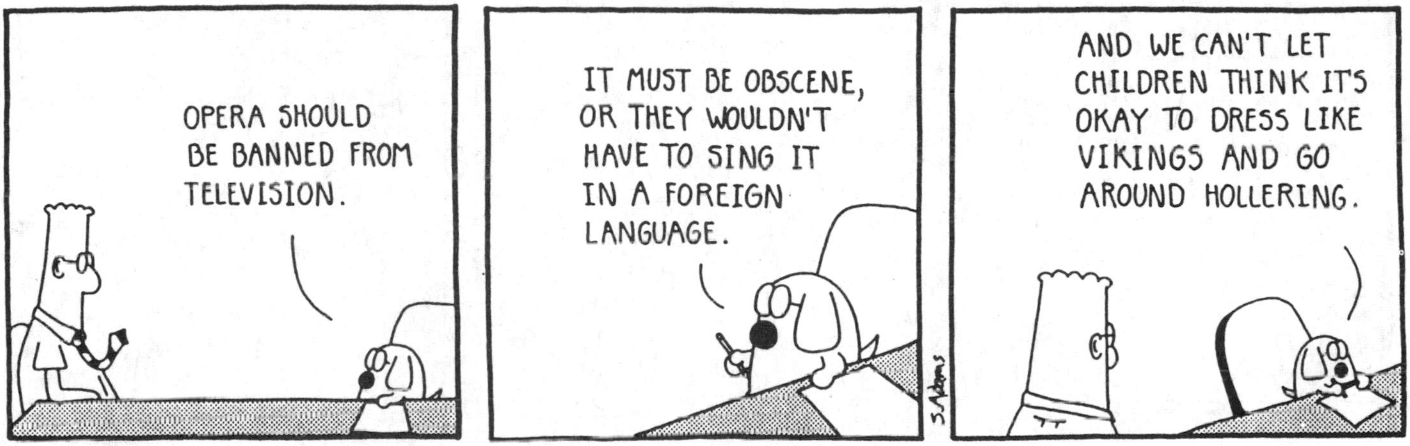
OPERA SHOULD BE BANNED FROM TELEVISION.
IT MUST BE OBSCENE, OR THEY WOULDN'T HAVE TO SING IT IN A FOREIGN LANGUAGE.
AND WE CAN'T LET CHILDREN THINK IT'S OKAY TO DRESS LIKE VIKINGS AND GO AROUND HOLLERING.
S. Adams

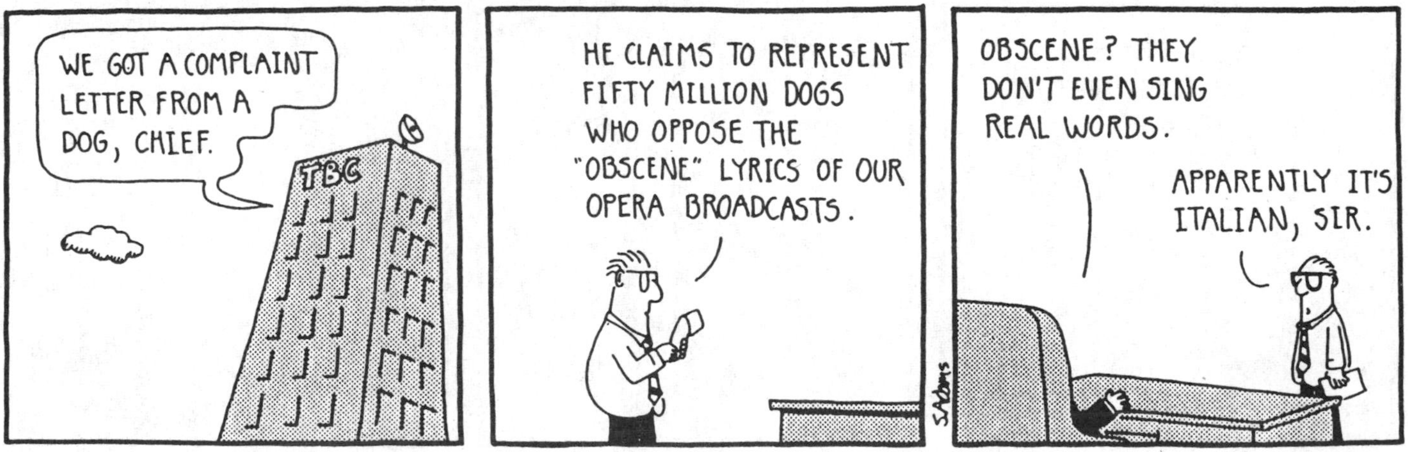
WE GOT A COMPLAINT LETTER FROM A DOG, CHIEF.
TBC
HE CLAIMS TO REPRESENT FIFTY MILLION DOGS WHO OPPOSE THE "OBSCENE" LYRICS OF OUR OPERA BROADCASTS.
OBSCENE? THEY DON'T EVEN SING REAL WORDS.
APPARENTLY IT'S ITALIAN, SIR.
S. Adams

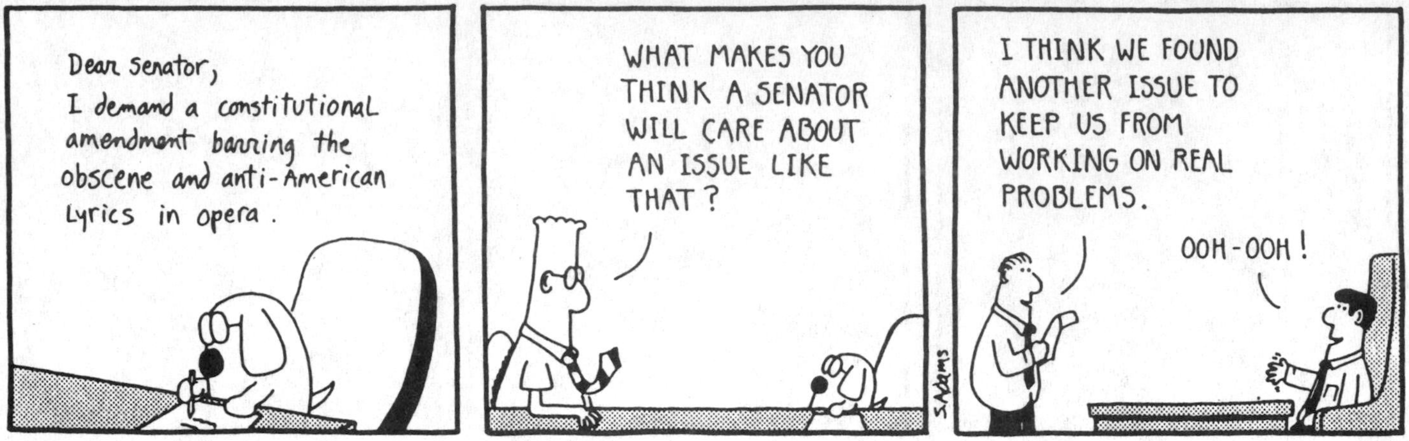
Dear Senator,
I demand a constitutional amendment barring the obscene and anti-American lyrics in opera.
WHAT MAKES YOU THINK A SENATOR WILL CARE ABOUT AN ISSUE LIKE THAT?
I THINK WE FOUND ANOTHER ISSUE TO KEEP US FROM WORKING ON REAL PROBLEMS.
OOH-OOH!

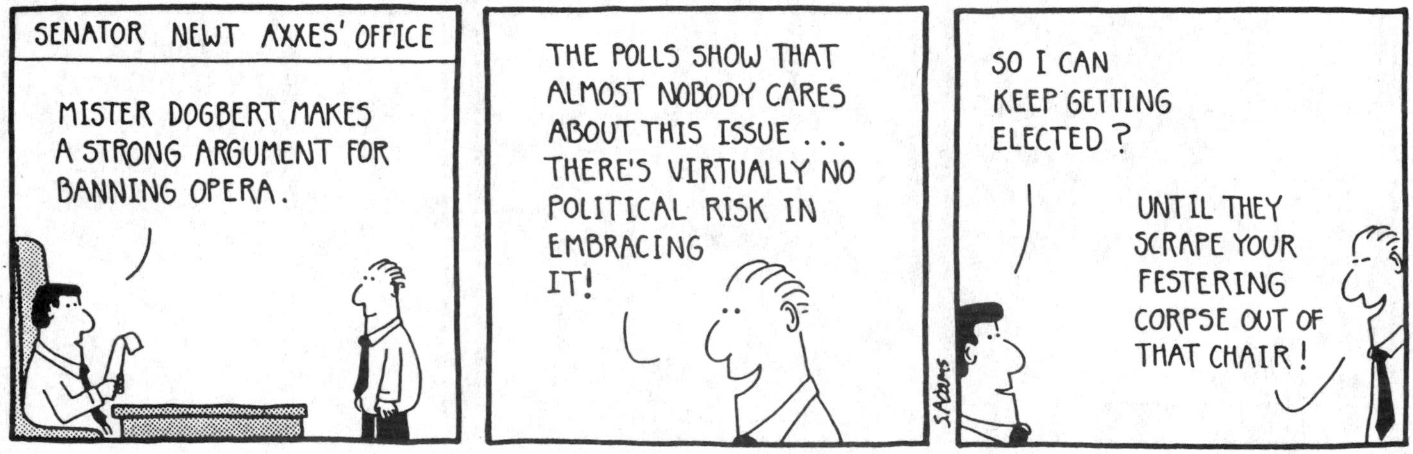
SENATOR NEWT AXXES' OFFICE
MISTER DOGBERT MAKES A STRONG ARGUMENT FOR BANNING OPERA.
THE POLLS SHOW THAT ALMOST NOBODY CARES ABOUT THIS ISSUE... THERE'S VIRTUALLY NO POLITICAL RISK IN EMBRACING IT!
SO I CAN KEEP GETTING ELECTED?
UNTIL THEY SCRAPE YOUR FESTERING CORPSE OUT OF THAT CHAIR!

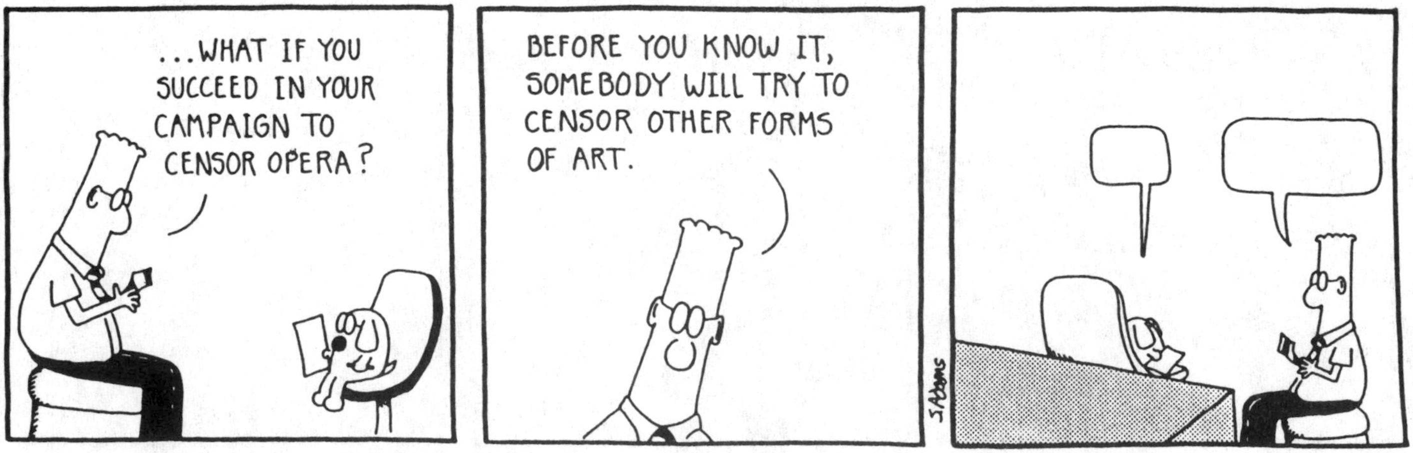
...WHAT IF YOU SUCCEED IN YOUR CAMPAIGN TO CENSOR OPERA?
BEFORE YOU KNOW IT, SOMEBODY WILL TRY TO CENSOR OTHER FORMS OF ART.

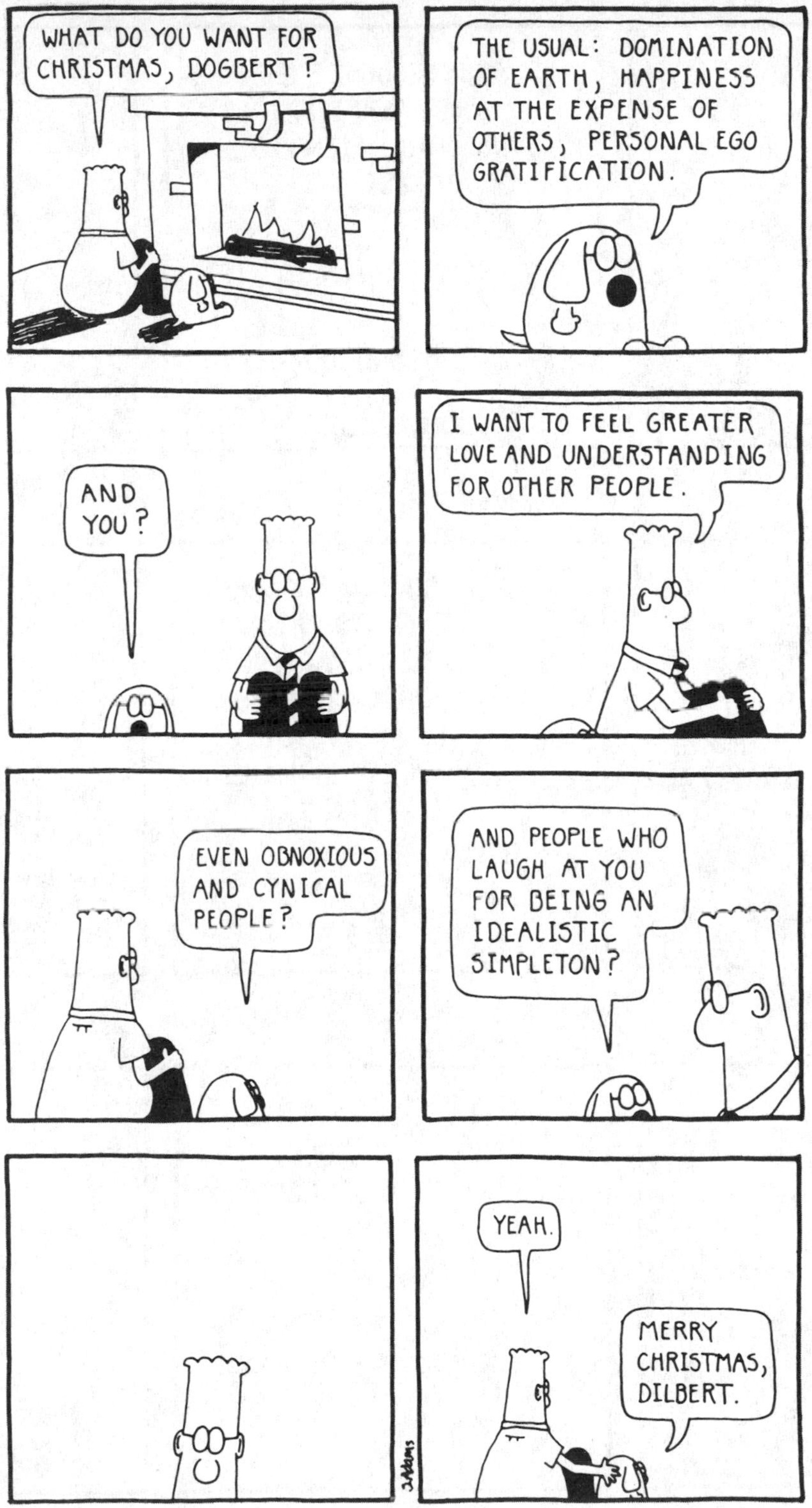
WHAT DO YOU WANT FOR CHRISTMAS, DOGBERT?
THE USUAL: DOMINATION OF EARTH, HAPPINESS AT THE EXPENSE OF OTHERS, PERSONAL EGO GRATIFICATION.
AND YOU?
I WANT TO FEEL GREATER LOVE AND UNDERSTANDING FOR OTHER PEOPLE.
EVEN OBNOXIOUS AND CYNICAL PEOPLE?
AND PEOPLE WHO LAUGH AT YOU FOR BEING AN IDEALISTIC SIMPLETON?
YEAH.
MERRY CHRISTMAS, DILBERT.

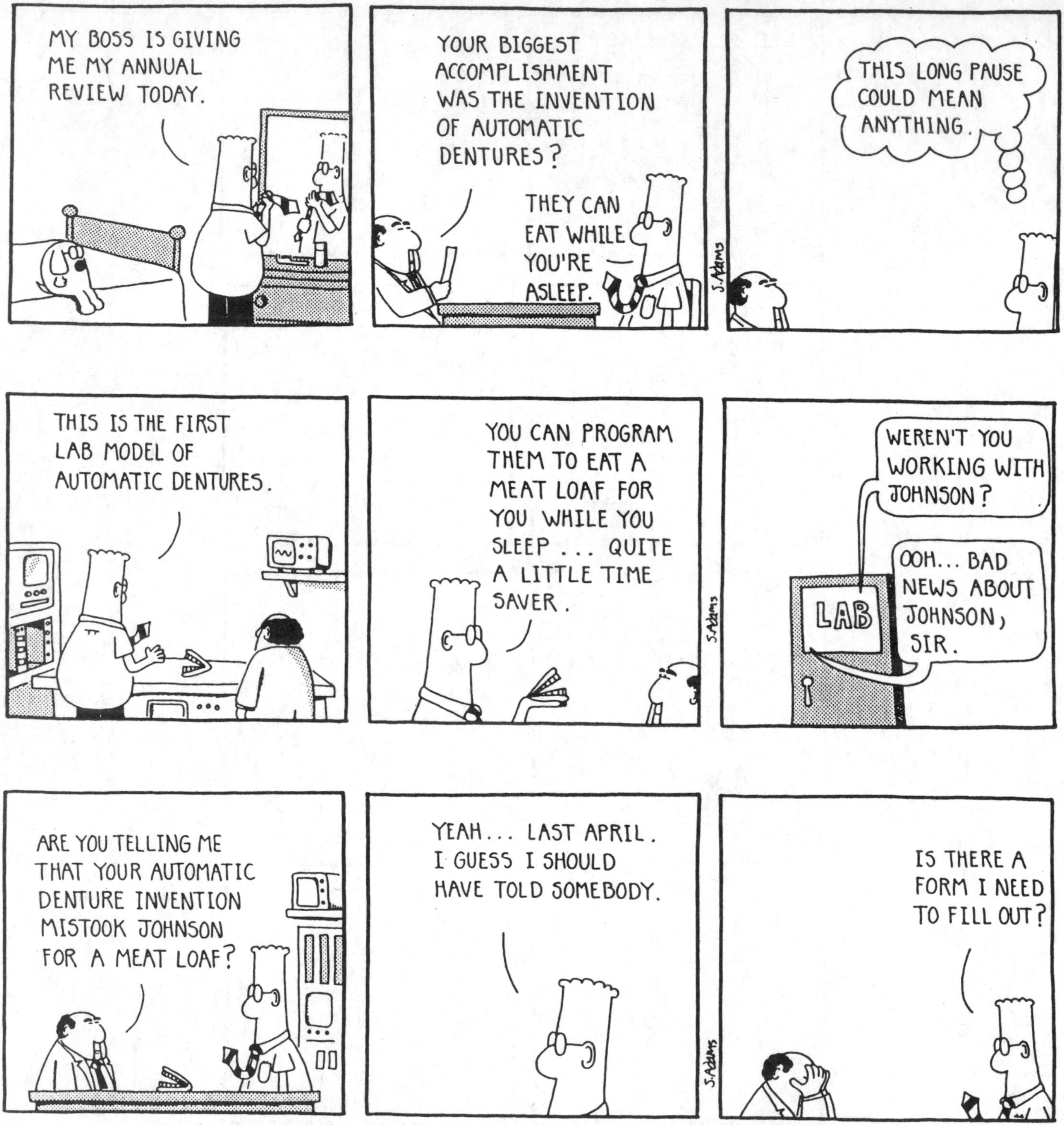
MY BOSS IS GIVING ME MY ANNUAL REVIEW TODAY.
YOUR BIGGEST ACCOMPLISHMENT WAS THE INVENTION OF AUTOMATIC DENTURES?
THEY CAN EAT WHILE YOU'RE ASLEEP.
THIS LONG PAUSE COULD MEAN ANYTHING.
S. Adams
THIS IS THE FIRST LAB MODEL OF AUTOMATIC DENTURES.
YOU CAN PROGRAM THEM TO EAT A MEAT LOAF FOR YOU WHILE YOU SLEEP . . . QUITE A LITTLE TIME SAVER.
WEREN'T YOU WORKING WITH JOHNSON?
LAB
OOH... BAD NEWS ABOUT JOHNSON, SIR.
S. Adams
ARE YOU TELLING ME THAT YOUR AUTOMATIC DENTURE INVENTION MISTOOK JOHNSON FOR A MEAT LOAF?
YEAH... LAST APRIL. I GUESS I SHOULD HAVE TOLD SOMEBODY.
IS THERE A FORM I NEED TO FILL OUT?
S. Adams

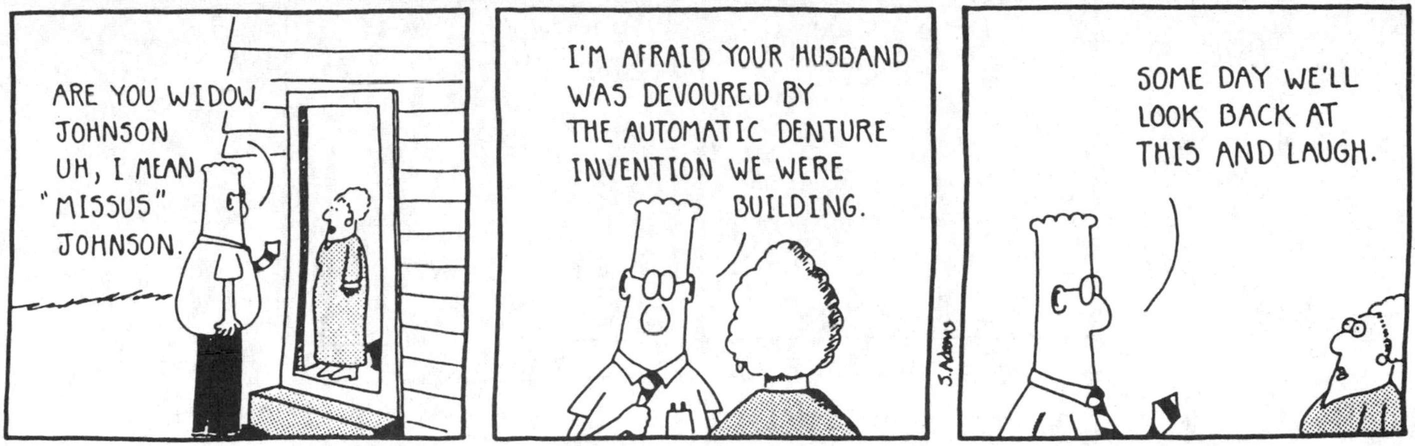
ARE YOU WIDOW JOHNSON UH, I MEAN "MISSUS" JOHNSON.
I'M AFRAID YOUR HUSBAND WAS DEVOURED BY THE AUTOMATIC DENTURE INVENTION WE WERE BUILDING.
S.Adams
SOME DAY WE'LL LOOK BACK AT THIS AND LAUGH.

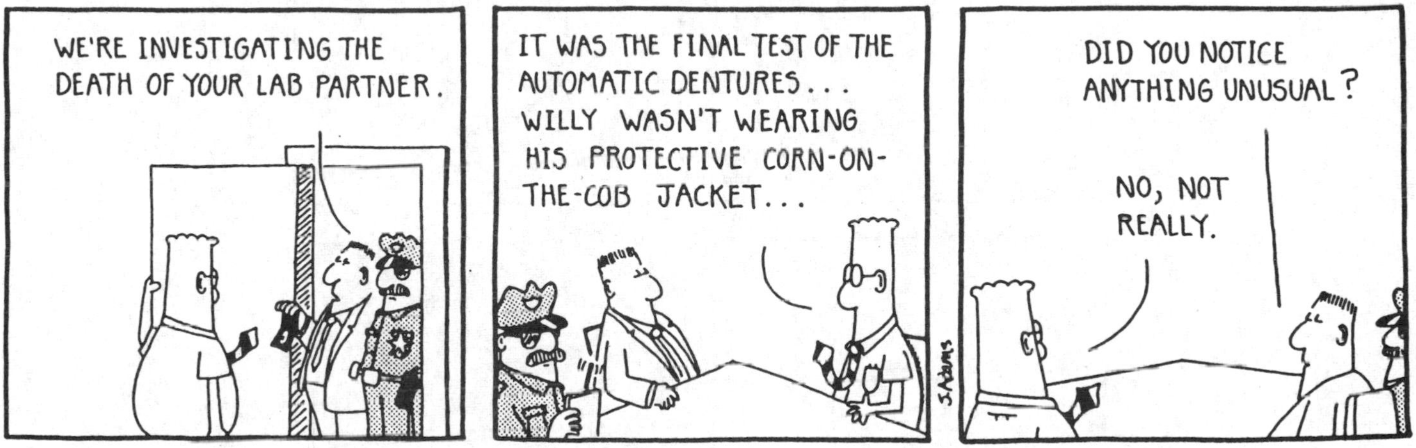
WE'RE INVESTIGATING THE DEATH OF YOUR LAB PARTNER.
IT WAS THE FINAL TEST OF THE AUTOMATIC DENTURES... WILLY WASN'T WEARING HIS PROTECTIVE CORN-ON-THE-COB JACKET...
S.Adams
DID YOU NOTICE ANYTHING UNUSUAL?
NO, NOT REALLY.

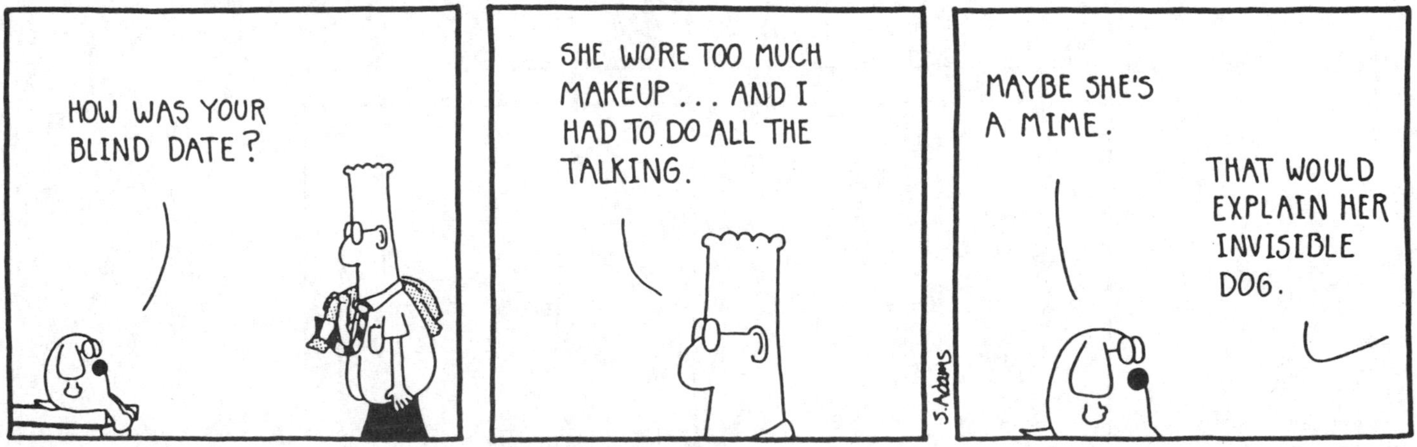
HOW WAS YOUR BLIND DATE?
SHE WORE TOO MUCH MAKEUP... AND I HAD TO DO ALL THE TALKING.
S.Adams
MAYBE SHE'S A MIME.
THAT WOULD EXPLAIN HER INVISIBLE DOG.

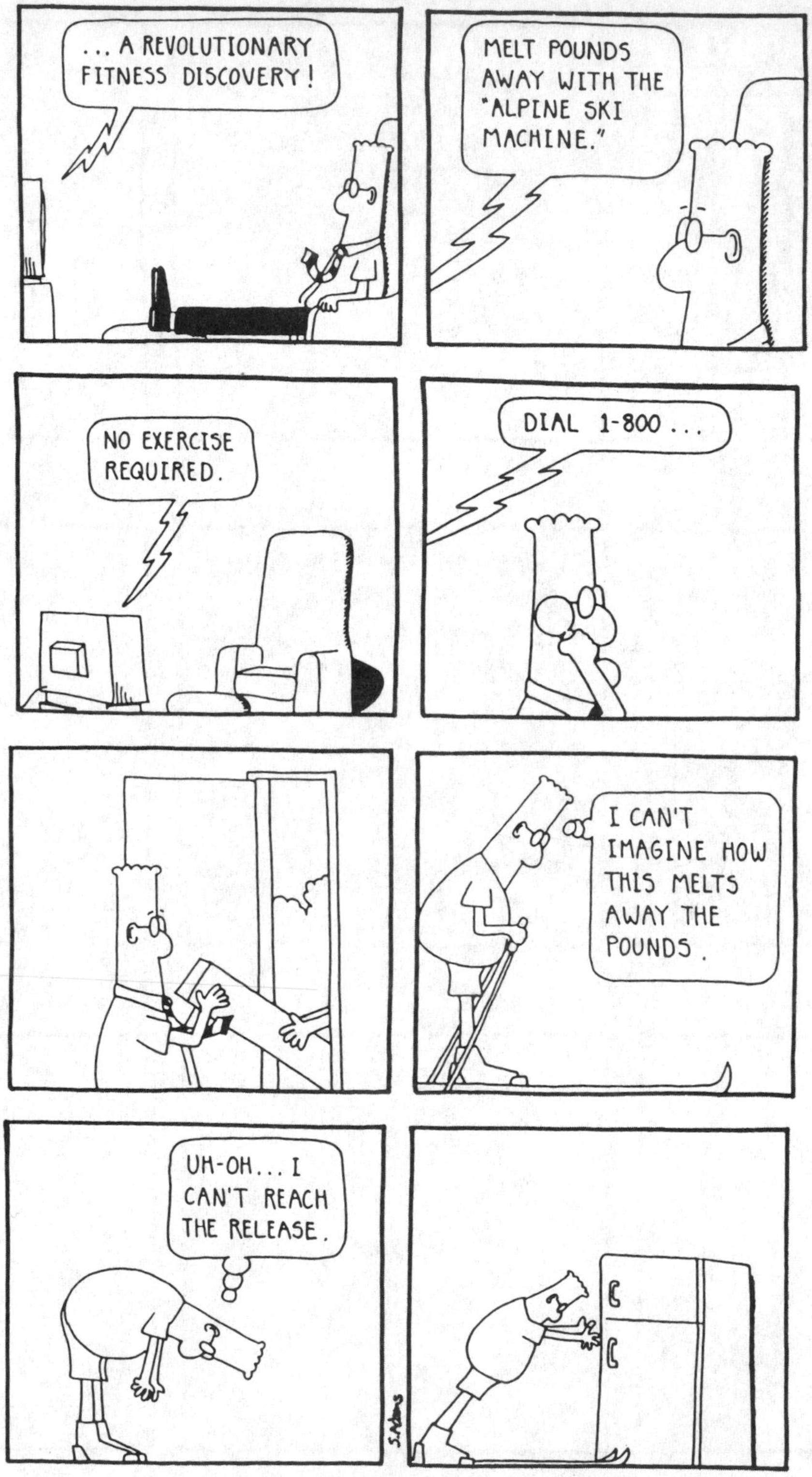
... A REVOLUTIONARY FITNESS DISCOVERY!
MELT POUNDS AWAY WITH THE "ALPINE SKI MACHINE."
NO EXERCISE REQUIRED.
DIAL 1-800 ...
I CAN'T IMAGINE HOW THIS MELTS AWAY THE POUNDS.
UH-OH... I CAN'T REACH THE RELEASE.
S.Adams

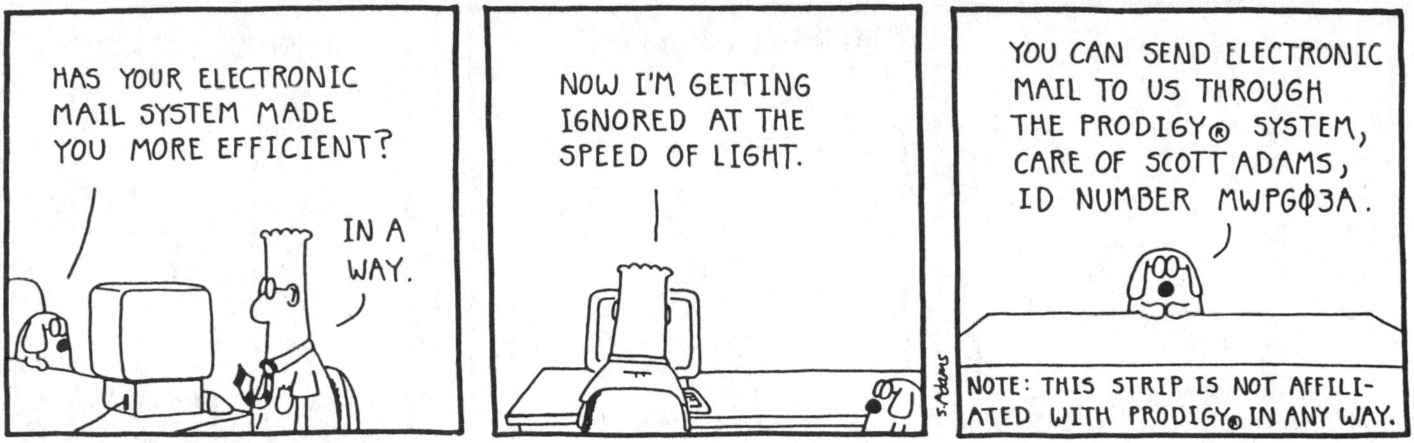
HAS YOUR ELECTRONIC MAIL SYSTEM MADE YOU MORE EFFICIENT?
IN A WAY.
NOW I'M GETTING IGNORED AT THE SPEED OF LIGHT.
YOU CAN SEND ELECTRONIC MAIL TO US THROUGH THE PRODIGY® SYSTEM, CARE OF SCOTT ADAMS, ID NUMBER MWPGØ3A.
NOTE: THIS STRIP IS NOT AFFILIATED WITH PRODIGY® IN ANY WAY.

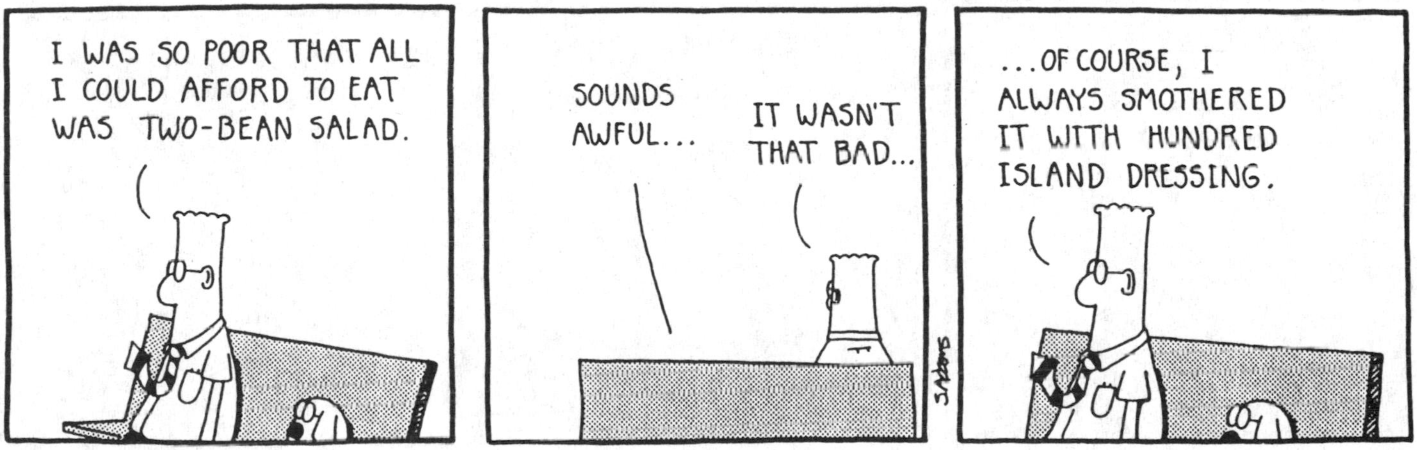
I WAS SO POOR THAT ALL I COULD AFFORD TO EAT WAS TWO-BEAN SALAD.
SOUNDS AWFUL...
IT WASN'T THAT BAD...
...OF COURSE, I ALWAYS SMOTHERED IT WITH HUNDRED ISLAND DRESSING.

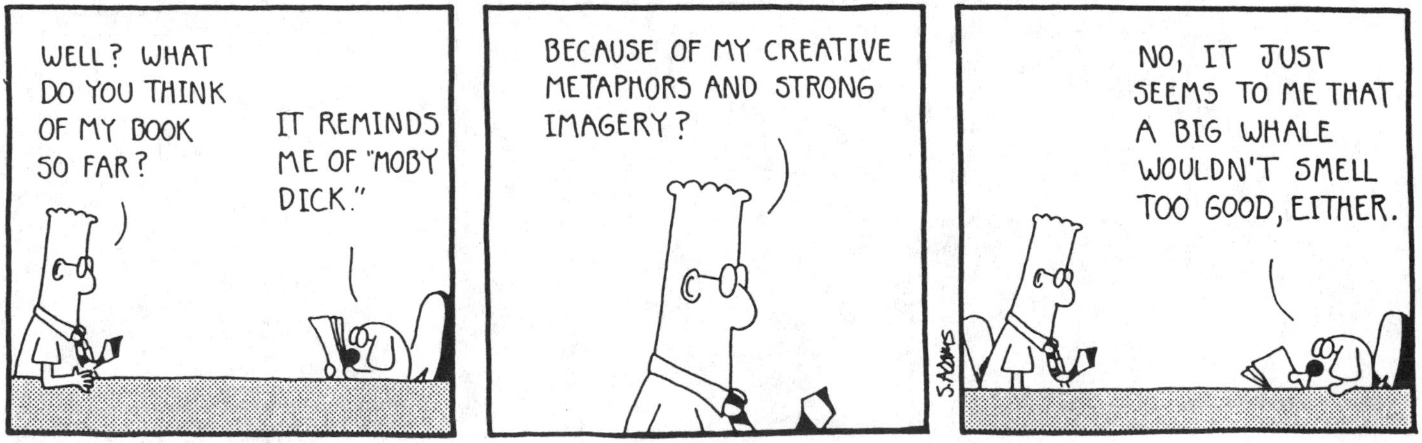
WELL? WHAT DO YOU THINK OF MY BOOK SO FAR?
IT REMINDS ME OF "MOBY DICK."
BECAUSE OF MY CREATIVE METAPHORS AND STRONG IMAGERY?
NO, IT JUST SEEMS TO ME THAT A BIG WHALE WOULDN'T SMELL TOO GOOD, EITHER.

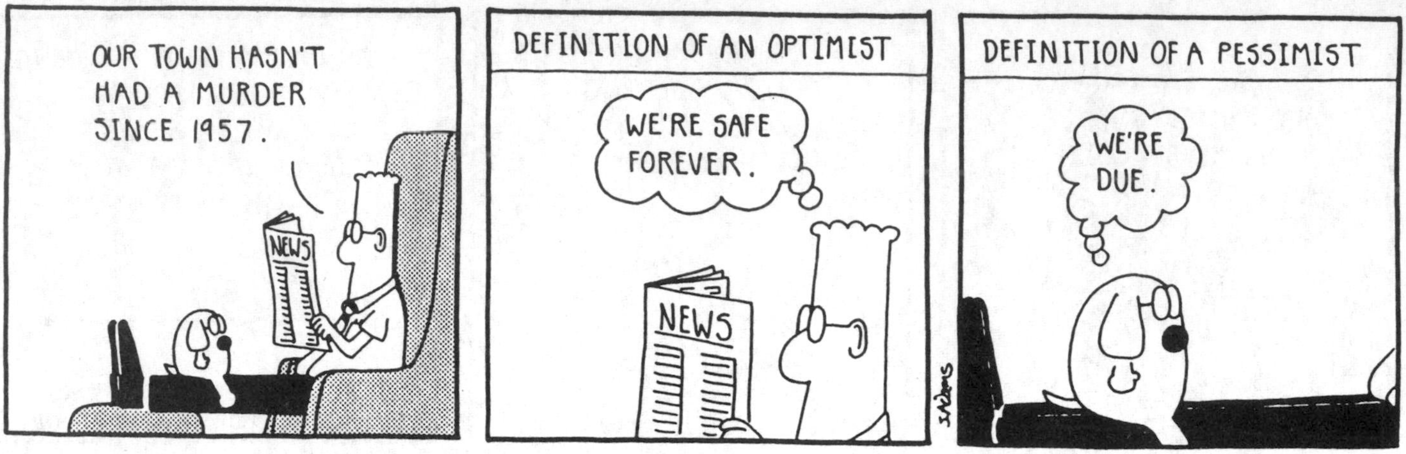
OUR TOWN HASN'T HAD A MURDER SINCE 1957.
NEWS
DEFINITION OF AN OPTIMIST
WE'RE SAFE FOREVER.
NEWS
DEFINITION OF A PESSIMIST
WE'RE DUE.

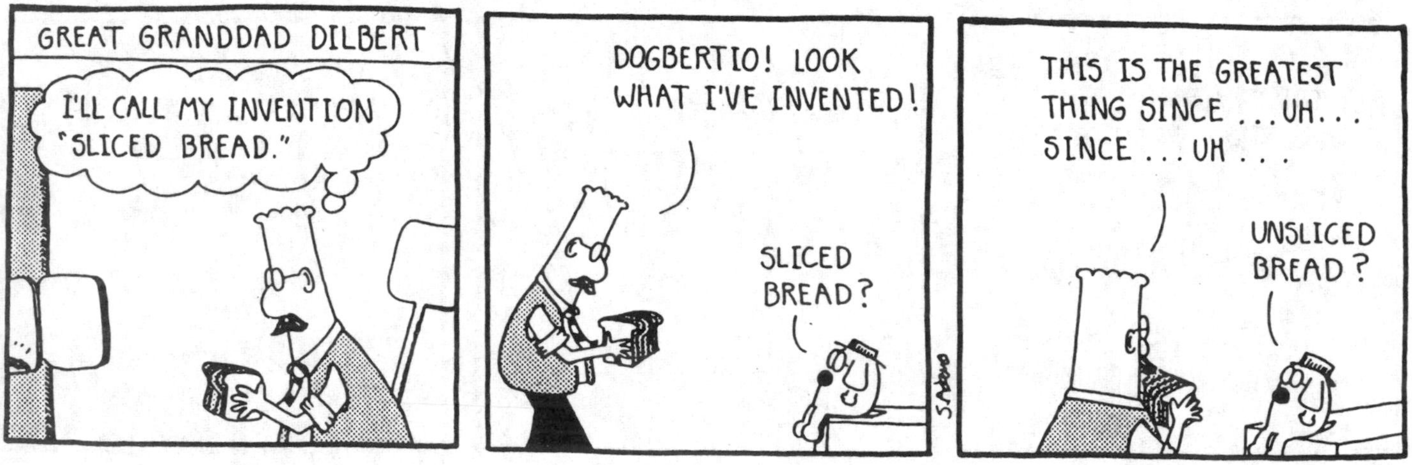
GREAT GRANDDAD DILBERT
I'LL CALL MY INVENTION "SLICED BREAD."
DOGBERTIO! LOOK WHAT I'VE INVENTED!
SLICED BREAD?
THIS IS THE GREATEST THING SINCE ...UH... SINCE ... UH . . .
UNSLICED BREAD?

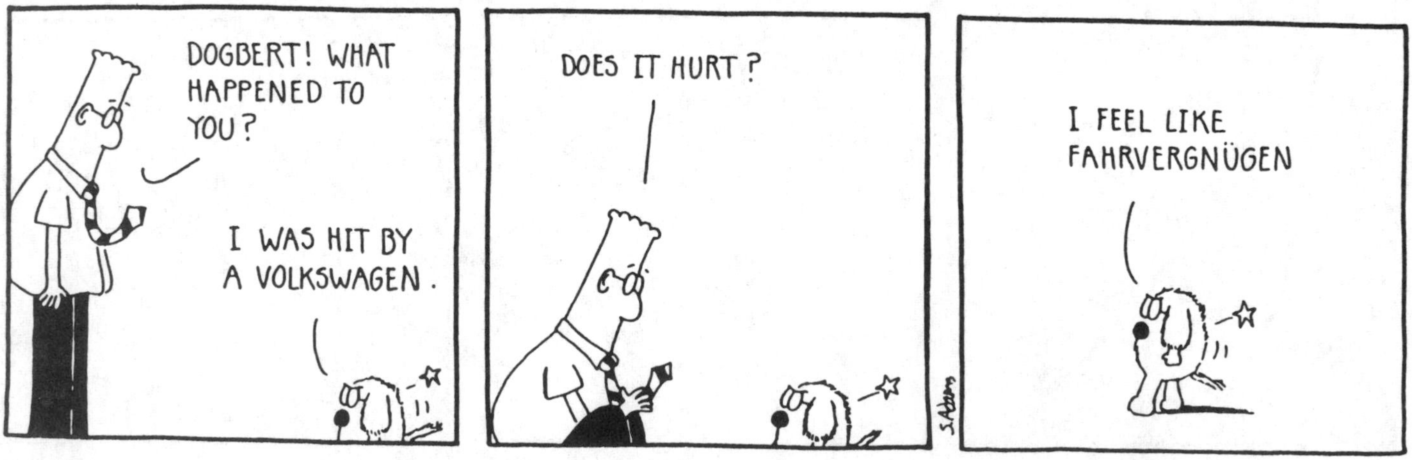
DOGBERT! WHAT HAPPENED TO YOU?
I WAS HIT BY A VOLKSWAGEN.
DOES IT HURT?
I FEEL LIKE FAHRVERGNÜGEN

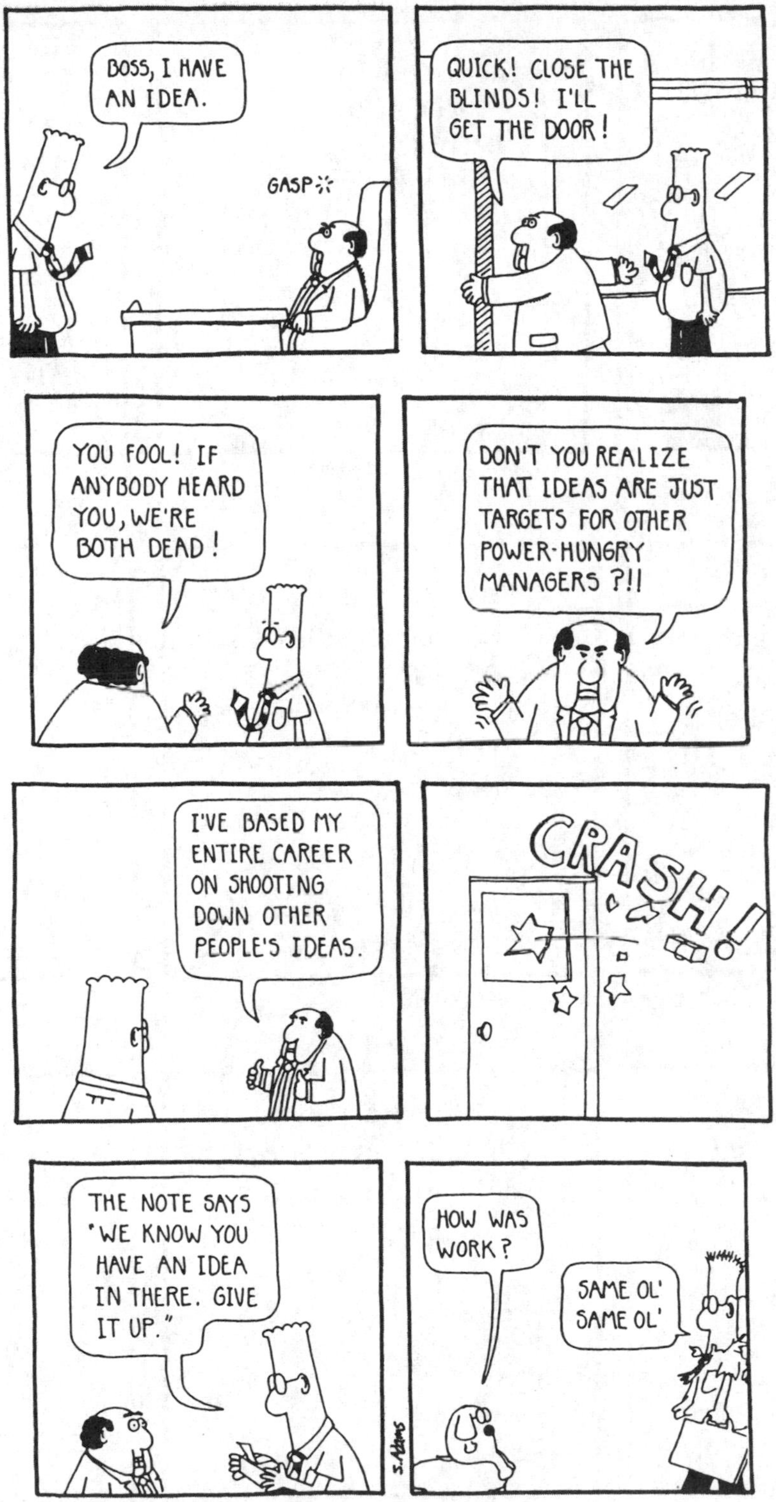
BOSS, I HAVE AN IDEA.
GASP
QUICK! CLOSE THE BLINDS! I'LL GET THE DOOR!
YOU FOOL! IF ANYBODY HEARD YOU, WE'RE BOTH DEAD!
DON'T YOU REALIZE THAT IDEAS ARE JUST TARGETS FOR OTHER POWER-HUNGRY MANAGERS ?!!
I'VE BASED MY ENTIRE CAREER ON SHOOTING DOWN OTHER PEOPLE'S IDEAS.
CRASH!
THE NOTE SAYS "WE KNOW YOU HAVE AN IDEA IN THERE. GIVE IT UP."
HOW WAS WORK?
SAME OL' SAME OL'

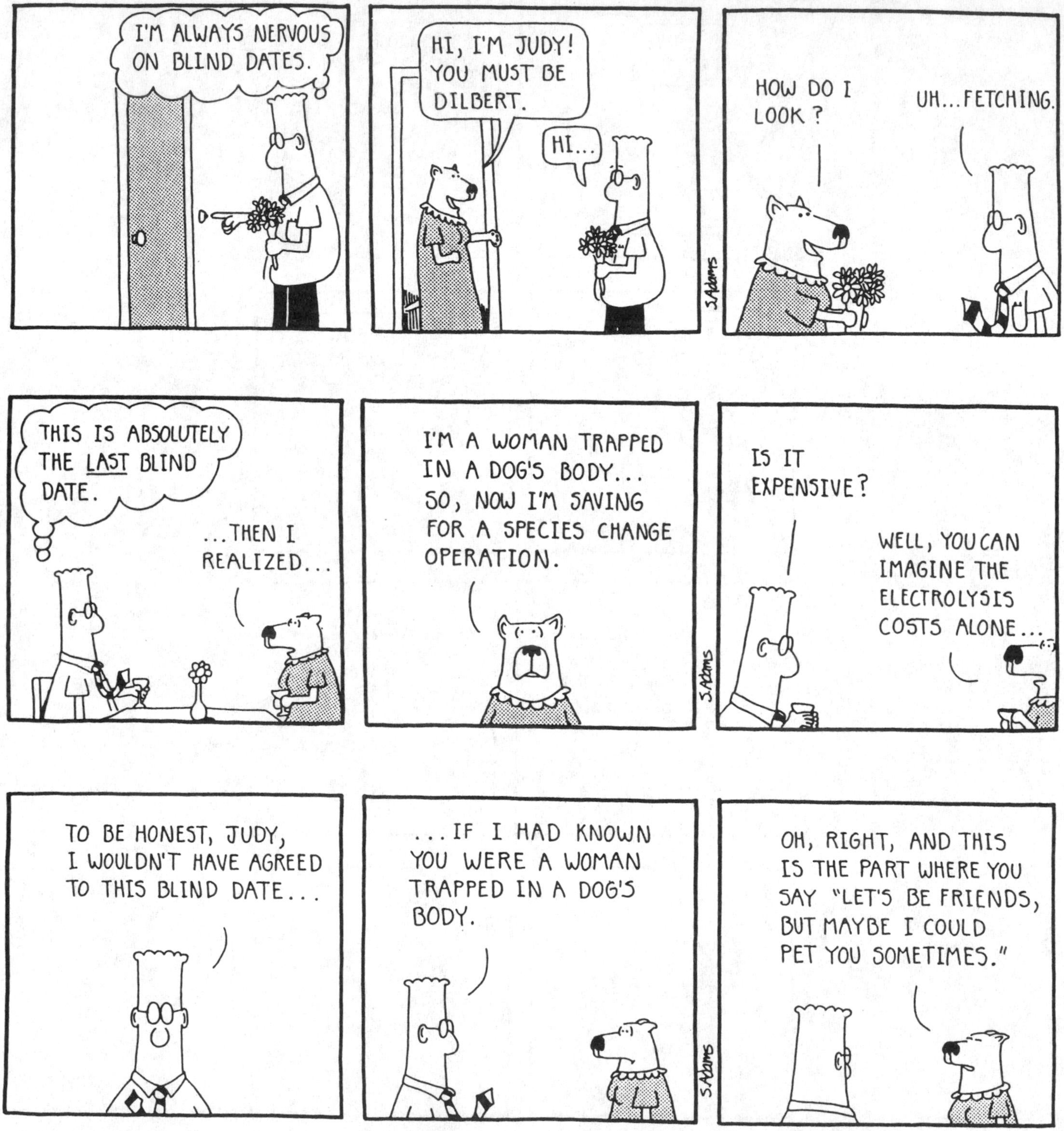
I'M ALWAYS NERVOUS ON BLIND DATES.
HI, I'M JUDY! YOU MUST BE DILBERT.
HI...
S.Adams
HOW DO I LOOK ?
UH...FETCHING.
THIS IS ABSOLUTELY THE LAST BLIND DATE.
...THEN I REALIZED...
I'M A WOMAN TRAPPED IN A DOG'S BODY... SO, NOW I'M SAVING FOR A SPECIES CHANGE OPERATION.
S.Adams
IS IT EXPENSIVE?
WELL, YOU CAN IMAGINE THE ELECTROLYSIS COSTS ALONE...
TO BE HONEST, JUDY, I WOULDN'T HAVE AGREED TO THIS BLIND DATE...
...IF I HAD KNOWN YOU WERE A WOMAN TRAPPED IN A DOG'S BODY.
S.Adams
OH, RIGHT, AND THIS IS THE PART WHERE YOU SAY "LET'S BE FRIENDS, BUT MAYBE I COULD PET YOU SOMETIMES."

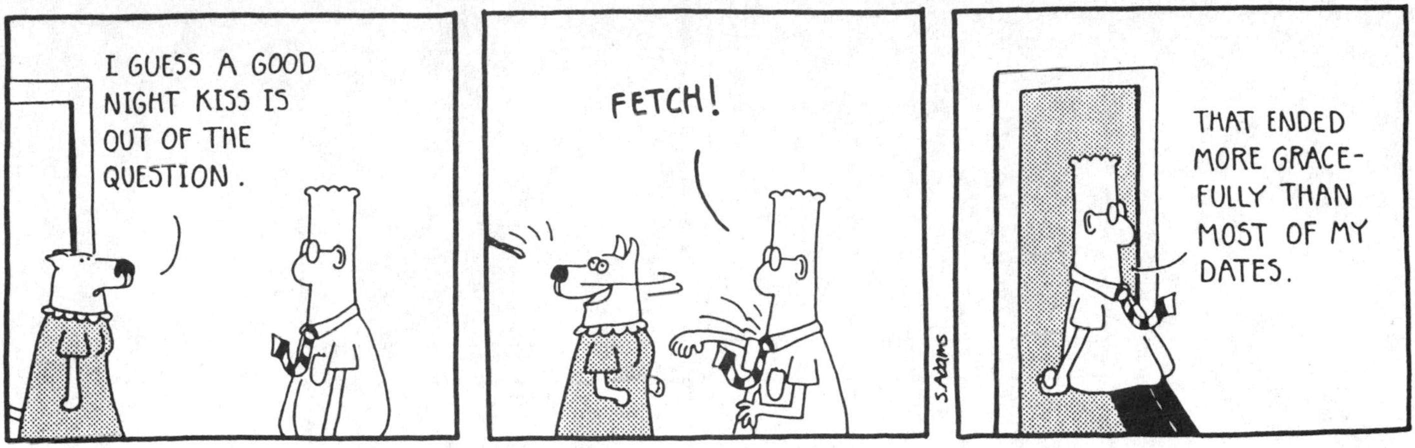
I GUESS A GOOD NIGHT KISS IS OUT OF THE QUESTION.
FETCH!
THAT ENDED MORE GRACEFULLY THAN MOST OF MY DATES.
S. Adams

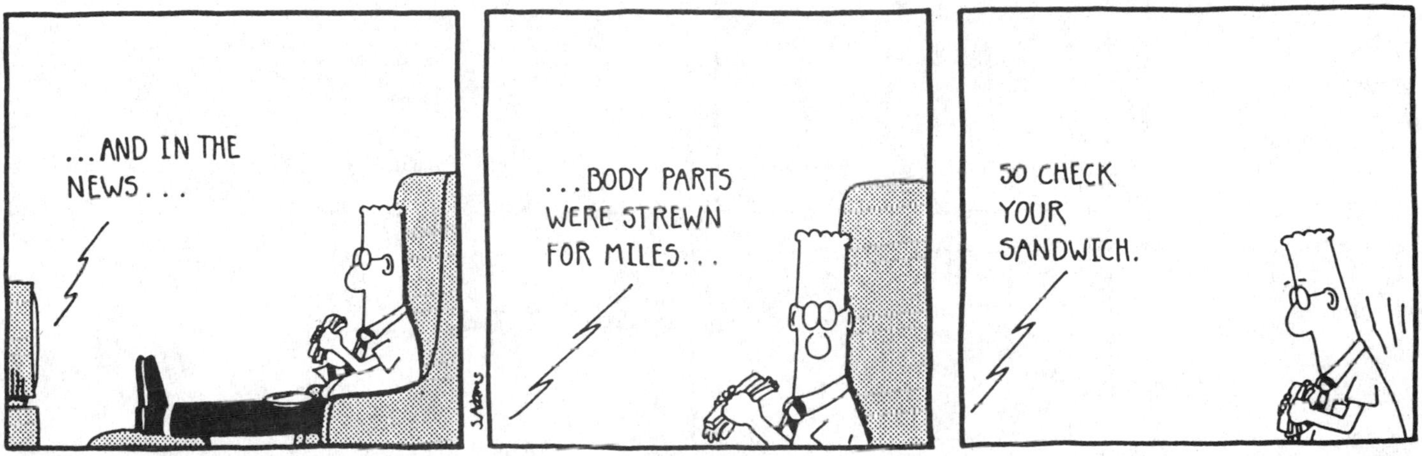
...AND IN THE NEWS...
S. Adams
...BODY PARTS WERE STREWN FOR MILES...
SO CHECK YOUR SANDWICH.

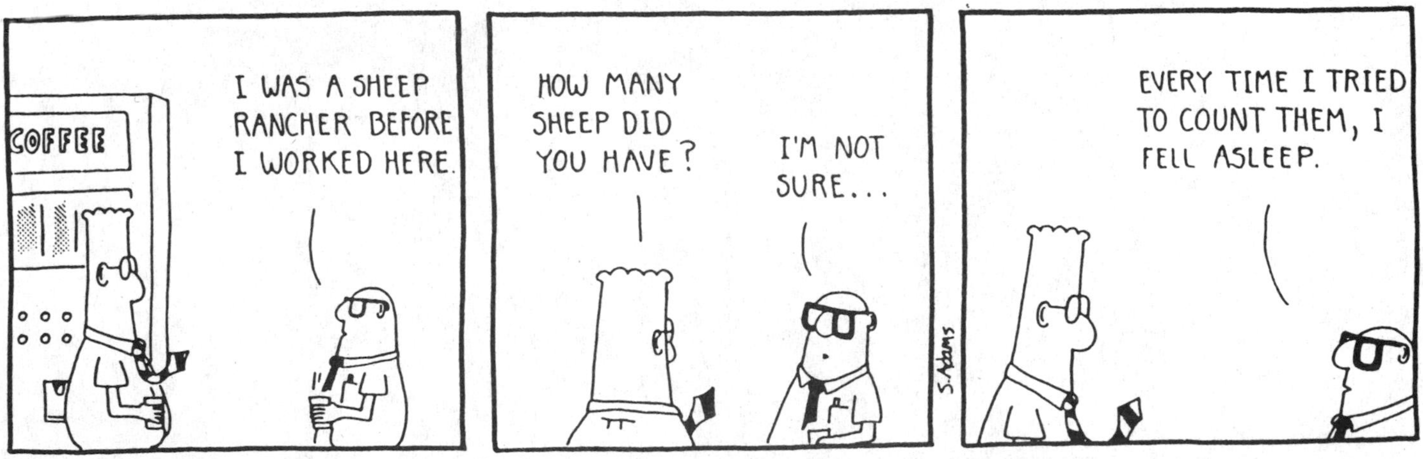
COFFEE
I WAS A SHEEP RANCHER BEFORE I WORKED HERE.
HOW MANY SHEEP DID YOU HAVE?
I'M NOT SURE...
S. Adams
EVERY TIME I TRIED TO COUNT THEM, I FELL ASLEEP.

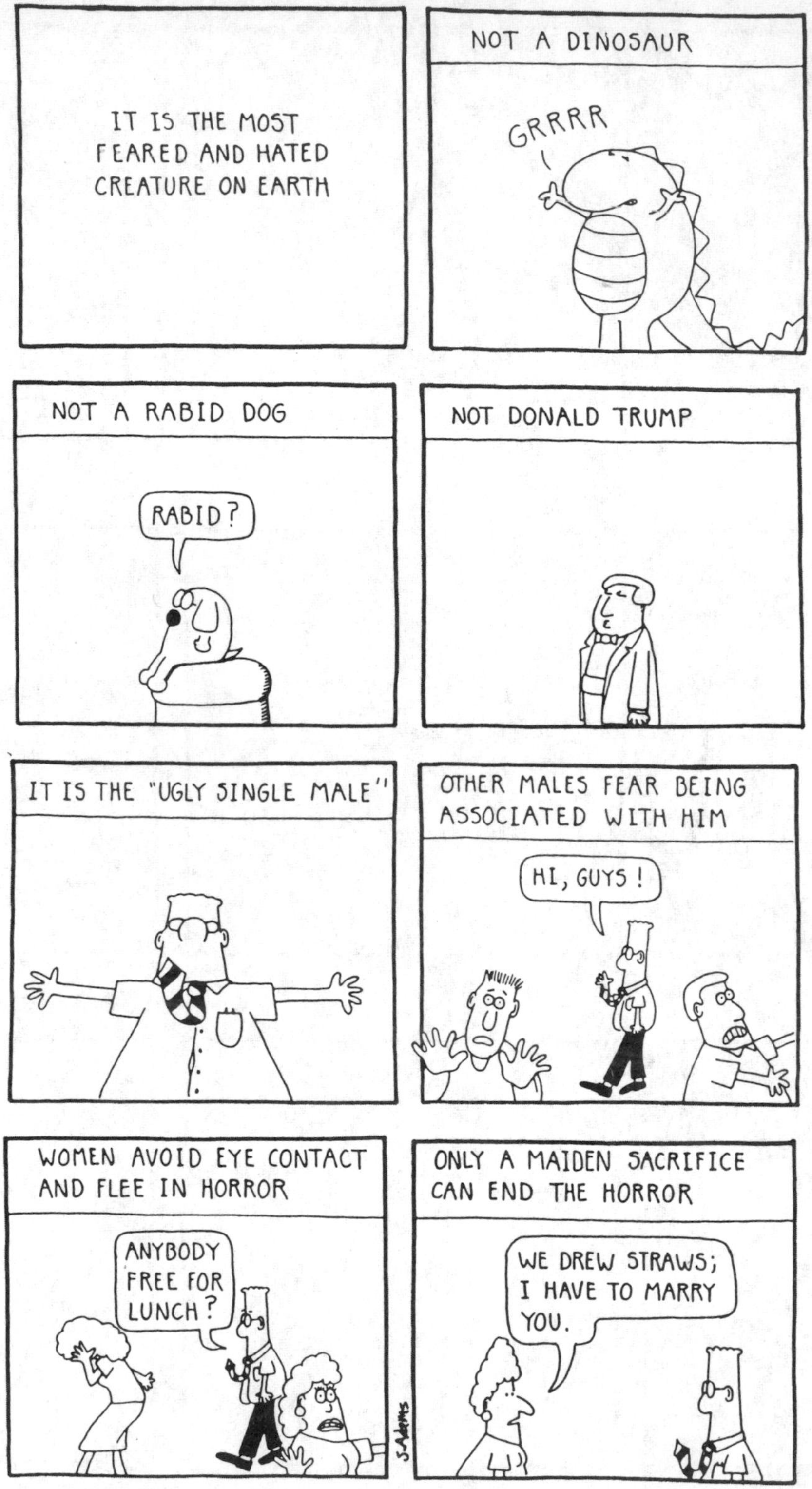
IT IS THE MOST FEARED AND HATED CREATURE ON EARTH
NOT A DINOSAUR
GRRRR
NOT A RABID DOG
RABID?
NOT DONALD TRUMP
IT IS THE "UGLY SINGLE MALE"
OTHER MALES FEAR BEING ASSOCIATED WITH HIM
HI, GUYS!
WOMEN AVOID EYE CONTACT AND FLEE IN HORROR
ANYBODY FREE FOR LUNCH?
S.Adams
ONLY A MAIDEN SACRIFICE CAN END THE HORROR
WE DREW STRAWS; I HAVE TO MARRY YOU.

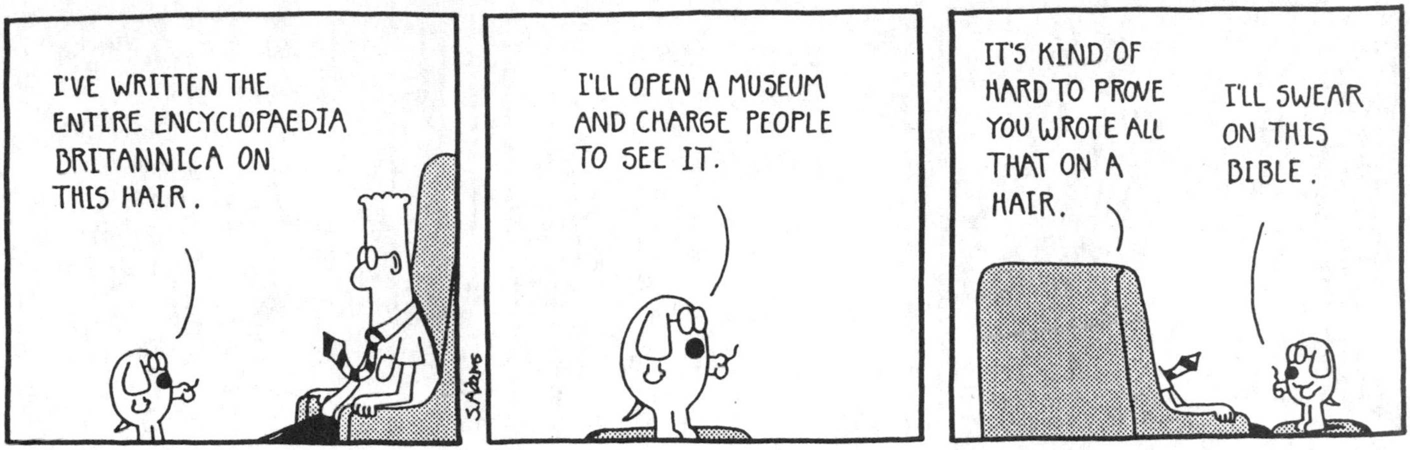
I'VE WRITTEN THE ENTIRE ENCYCLOPAEDIA BRITANNICA ON THIS HAIR.
I'LL OPEN A MUSEUM AND CHARGE PEOPLE TO SEE IT.
IT'S KIND OF HARD TO PROVE YOU WROTE ALL THAT ON A HAIR.
I'LL SWEAR ON THIS BIBLE.

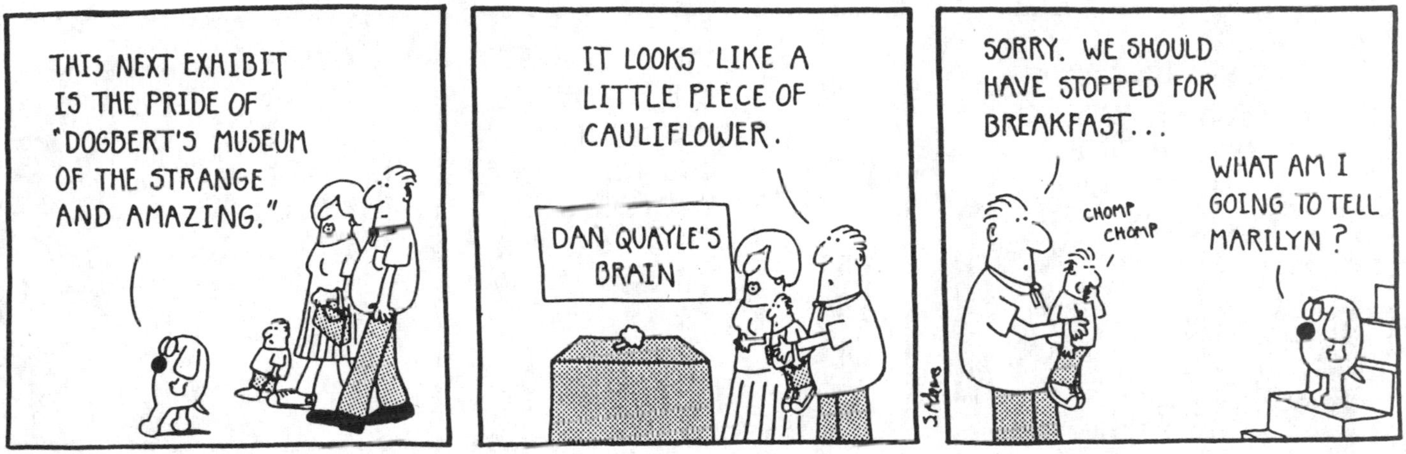
THIS NEXT EXHIBIT IS THE PRIDE OF "DOGBERT'S MUSEUM OF THE STRANGE AND AMAZING."
IT LOOKS LIKE A LITTLE PIECE OF CAULIFLOWER.
DAN QUAYLE'S BRAIN
SORRY. WE SHOULD HAVE STOPPED FOR BREAKFAST...
CHOMP CHOMP
WHAT AM I GOING TO TELL MARILYN?

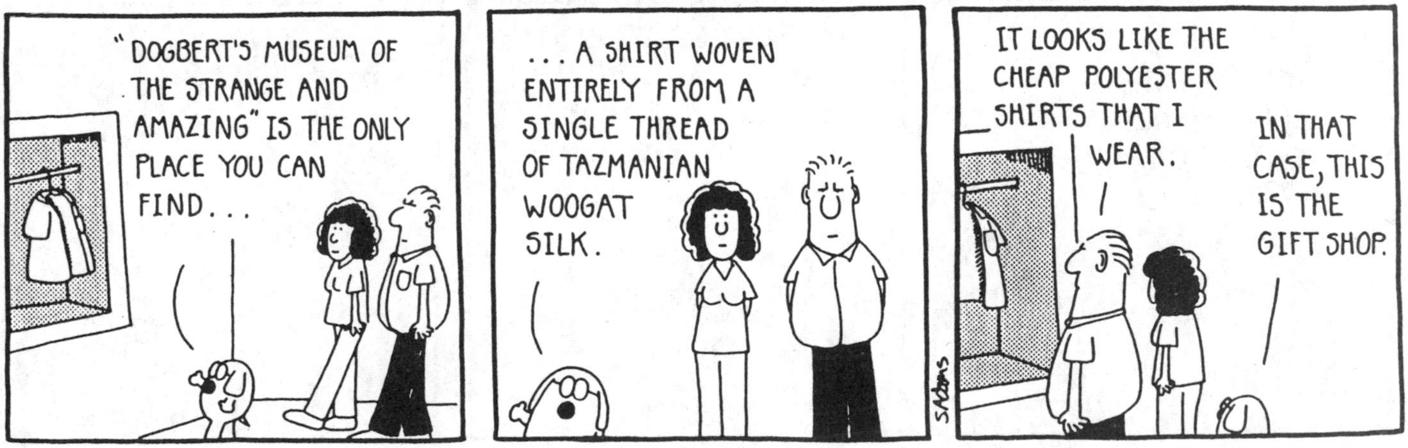
"DOGBERT'S MUSEUM OF THE STRANGE AND AMAZING" IS THE ONLY PLACE YOU CAN FIND...
... A SHIRT WOVEN ENTIRELY FROM A SINGLE THREAD OF TAZMANIAN WOOGAT SILK.
IT LOOKS LIKE THE CHEAP POLYESTER SHIRTS THAT I WEAR.
IN THAT CASE, THIS IS THE GIFT SHOP.

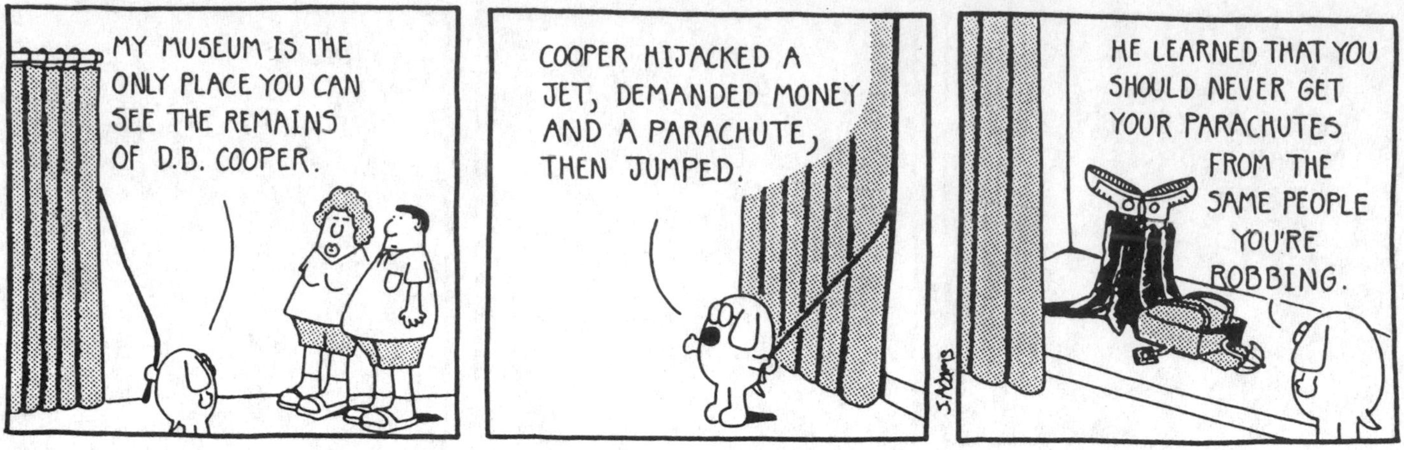
MY MUSEUM IS THE ONLY PLACE YOU CAN SEE THE REMAINS OF D.B. COOPER.
COOPER HIJACKED A JET, DEMANDED MONEY AND A PARACHUTE, THEN JUMPED.
HE LEARNED THAT YOU SHOULD NEVER GET YOUR PARACHUTES FROM THE SAME PEOPLE YOU'RE ROBBING.

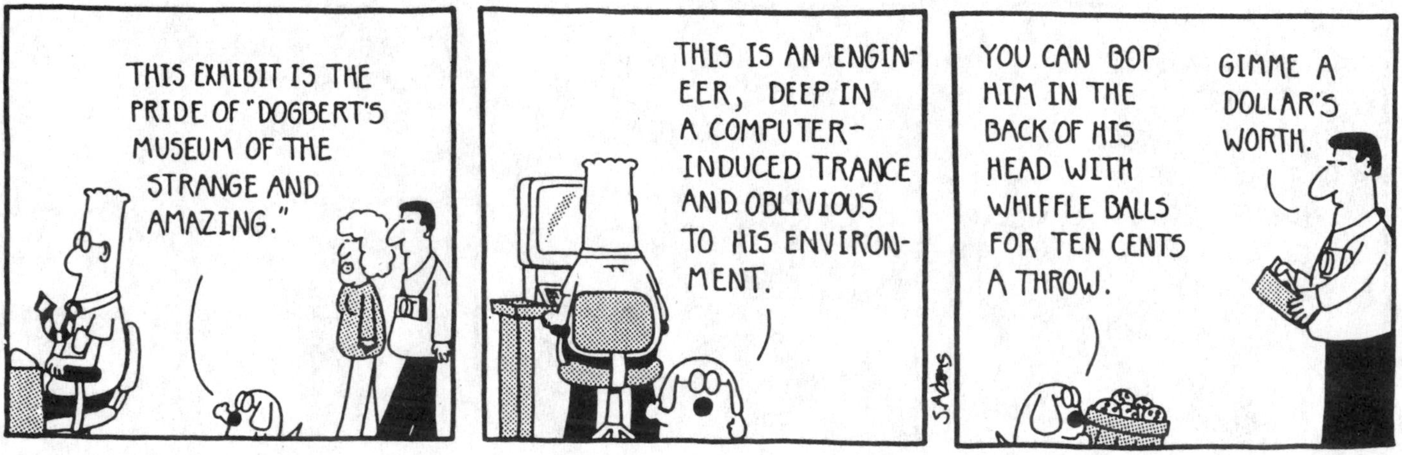
THIS EXHIBIT IS THE PRIDE OF "DOGBERT'S MUSEUM OF THE STRANGE AND AMAZING."
THIS IS AN ENGINEER, DEEP IN A COMPUTER-INDUCED TRANCE AND OBLIVIOUS TO HIS ENVIRONMENT.
YOU CAN BOP HIM IN THE BACK OF HIS HEAD WITH WHIFFLE BALLS FOR TEN CENTS A THROW.
GIMME A DOLLAR'S WORTH.

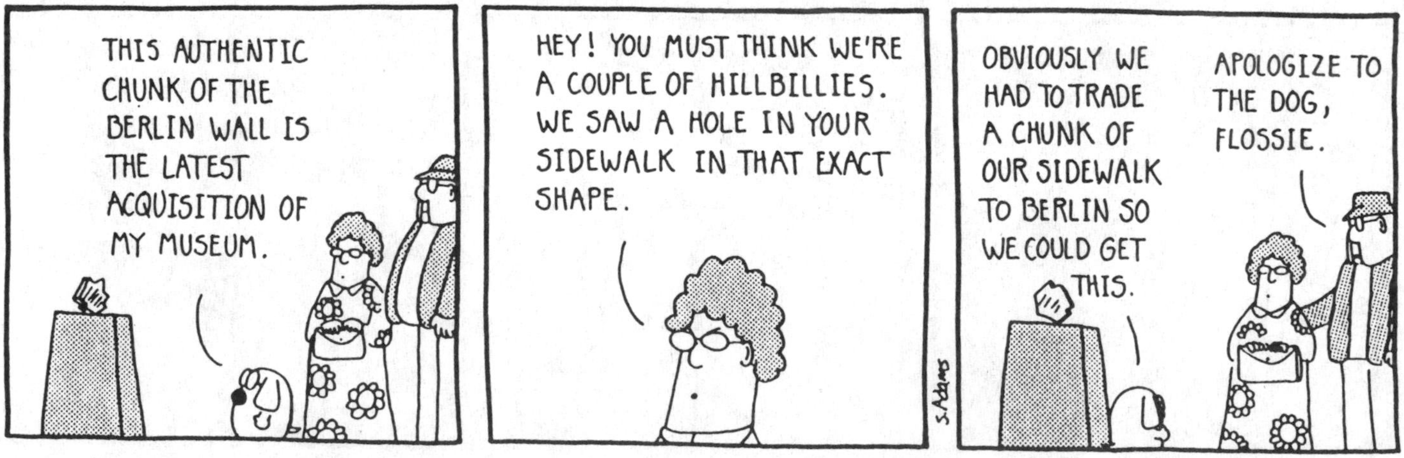
THIS AUTHENTIC CHUNK OF THE BERLIN WALL IS THE LATEST ACQUISITION OF MY MUSEUM.
HEY! YOU MUST THINK WE'RE A COUPLE OF HILLBILLIES. WE SAW A HOLE IN YOUR SIDEWALK IN THAT EXACT SHAPE.
OBVIOUSLY WE HAD TO TRADE A CHUNK OF OUR SIDEWALK TO BERLIN SO WE COULD GET THIS.
APOLOGIZE TO THE DOG, FLOSSIE.

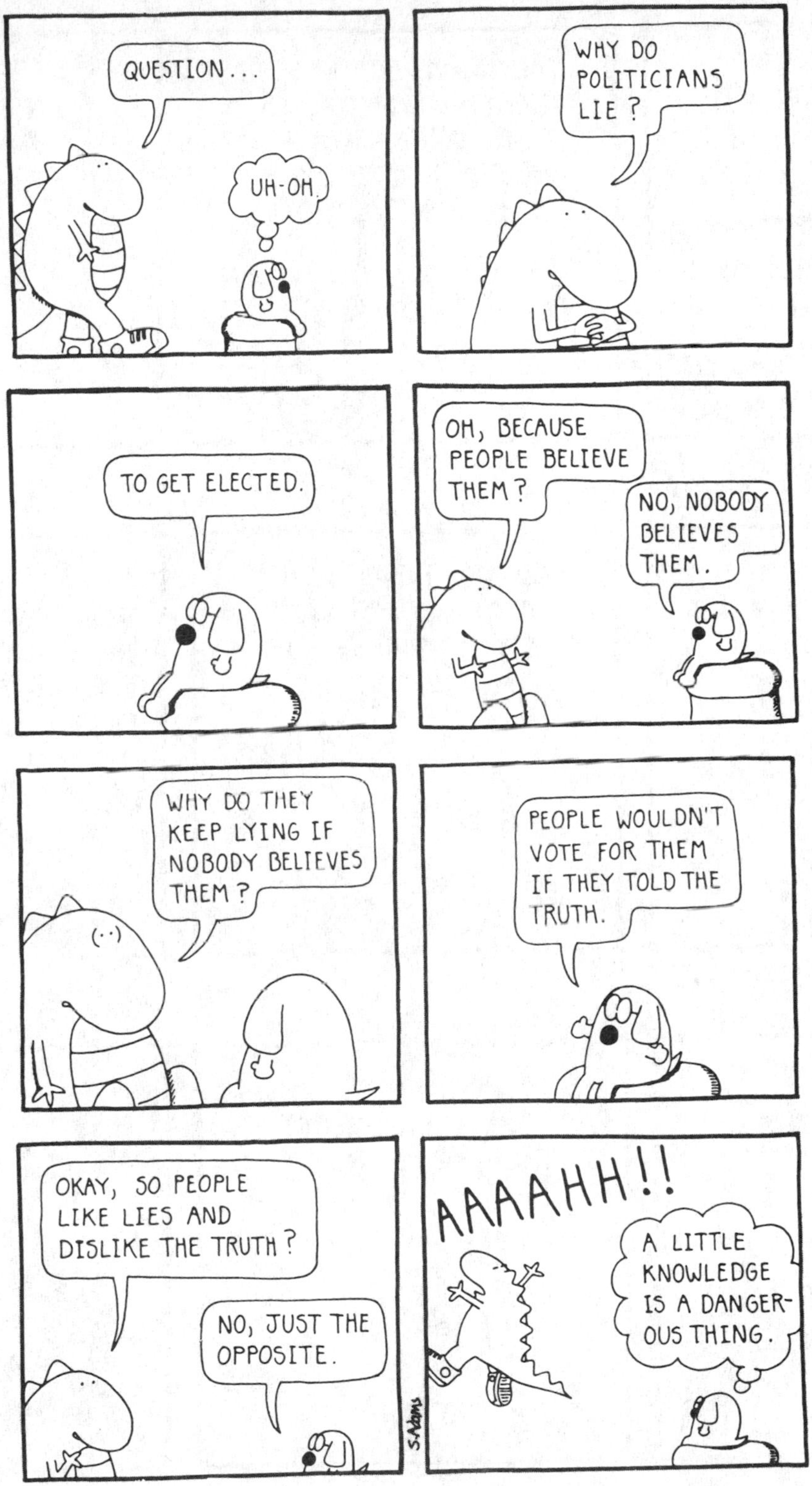
QUESTION...
UH-OH.
WHY DO POLITICIANS LIE?
TO GET ELECTED.
OH, BECAUSE PEOPLE BELIEVE THEM?
NO, NOBODY BELIEVES THEM.
WHY DO THEY KEEP LYING IF NOBODY BELIEVES THEM?
PEOPLE WOULDN'T VOTE FOR THEM IF THEY TOLD THE TRUTH.
OKAY, SO PEOPLE LIKE LIES AND DISLIKE THE TRUTH?
NO, JUST THE OPPOSITE.
S.Adams
AAAAHH!!
A LITTLE KNOWLEDGE IS A DANGEROUS THING.

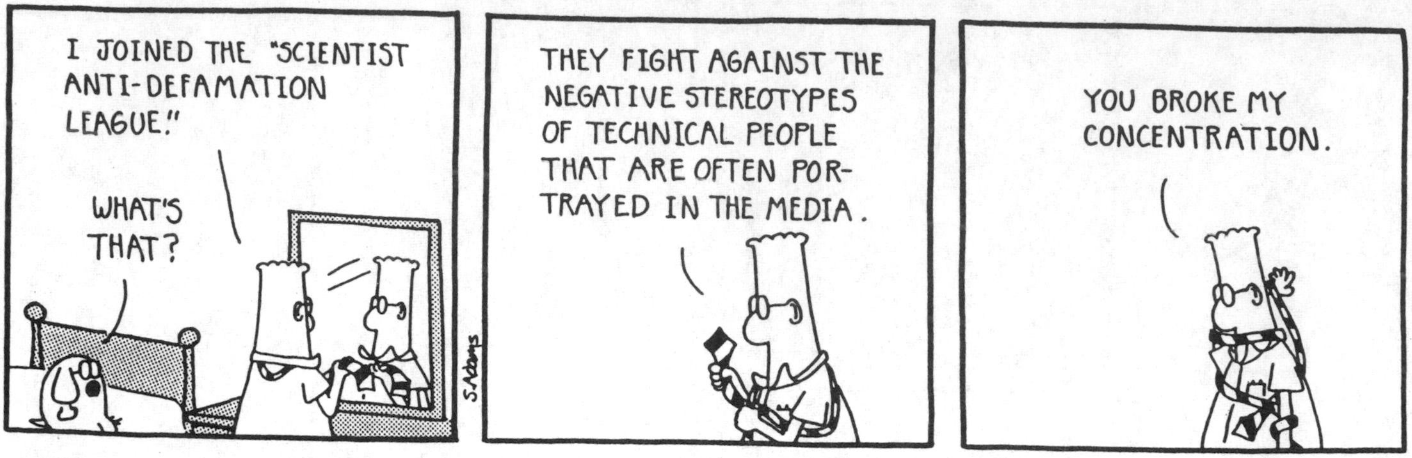
I JOINED THE "SCIENTIST ANTI-DEFAMATION LEAGUE."
WHAT'S THAT?
THEY FIGHT AGAINST THE NEGATIVE STEREOTYPES OF TECHNICAL PEOPLE THAT ARE OFTEN POR-TRAYED IN THE MEDIA.
YOU BROKE MY CONCENTRATION.

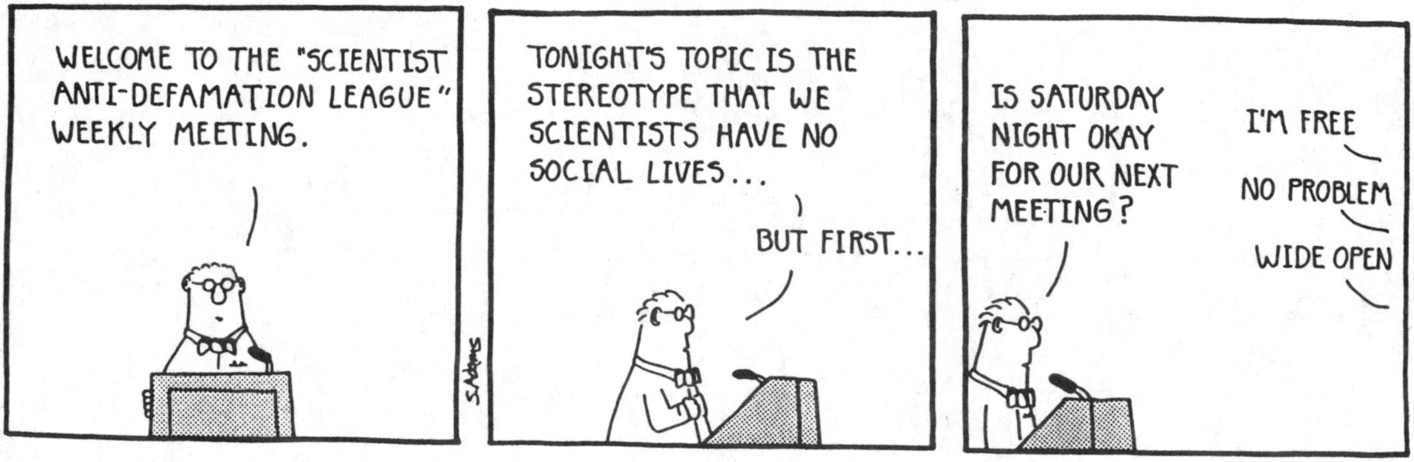
WELCOME TO THE "SCIENTIST ANTI-DEFAMATION LEAGUE" WEEKLY MEETING.
TONIGHT'S TOPIC IS THE STEREOTYPE THAT WE SCIENTISTS HAVE NO SOCIAL LIVES...
BUT FIRST...
IS SATURDAY NIGHT OKAY FOR OUR NEXT MEETING?
I'M FREE
NO PROBLEM
WIDE OPEN

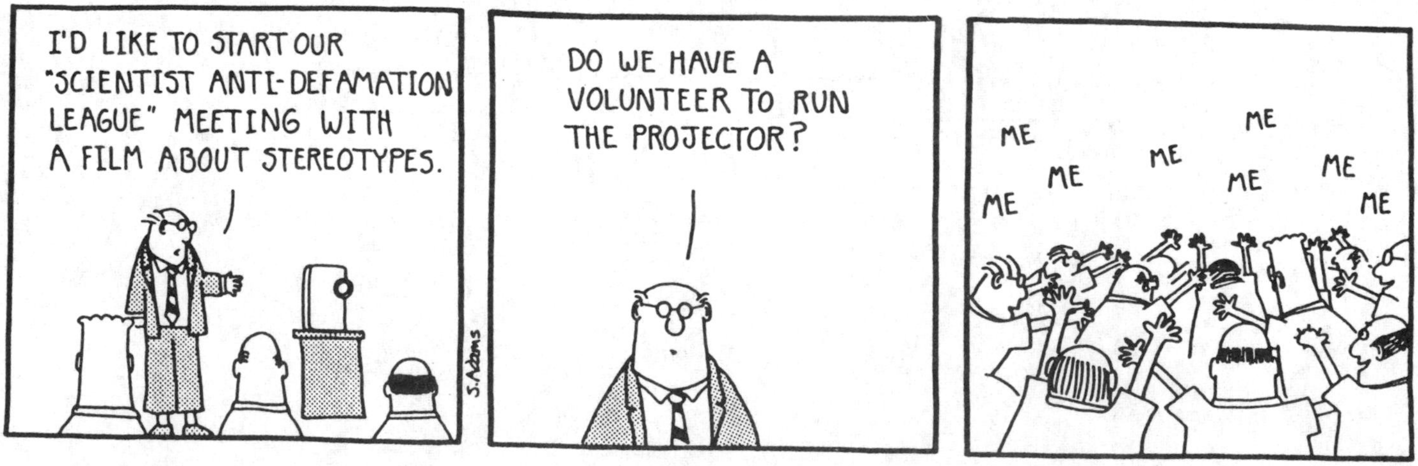
I'D LIKE TO START OUR "SCIENTIST ANTI-DEFAMATION LEAGUE" MEETING WITH A FILM ABOUT STEREOTYPES.
DO WE HAVE A VOLUNTEER TO RUN THE PROJECTOR?
ME
ME
ME
ME
ME
ME
ME
ME

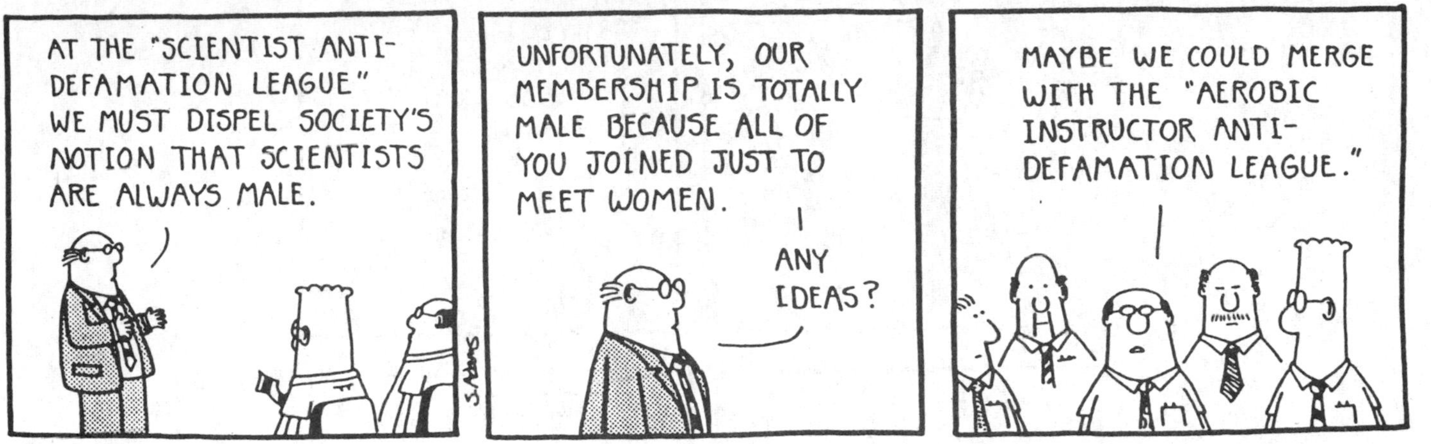
AT THE "SCIENTIST ANTI-DEFAMATION LEAGUE" WE MUST DISPEL SOCIETY'S NOTION THAT SCIENTISTS ARE ALWAYS MALE.
UNFORTUNATELY, OUR MEMBERSHIP IS TOTALLY MALE BECAUSE ALL OF YOU JOINED JUST TO MEET WOMEN.
ANY IDEAS?
MAYBE WE COULD MERGE WITH THE "AEROBIC INSTRUCTOR ANTI-DEFAMATION LEAGUE."

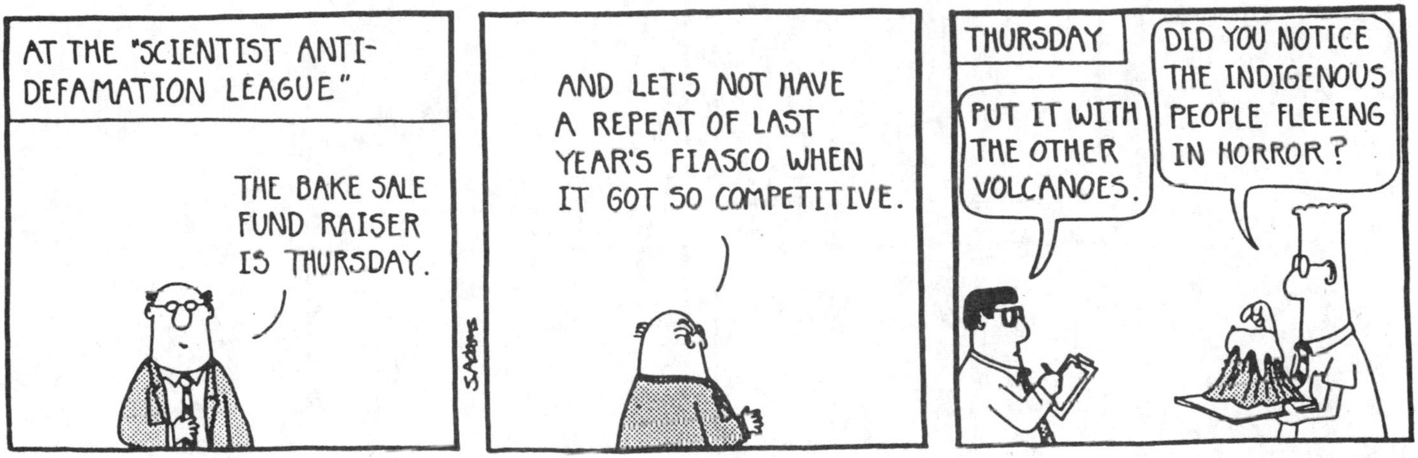
AT THE "SCIENTIST ANTI-DEFAMATION LEAGUE"
THE BAKE SALE FUND RAISER IS THURSDAY.
AND LET'S NOT HAVE A REPEAT OF LAST YEAR'S FIASCO WHEN IT GOT SO COMPETITIVE.
THURSDAY
DID YOU NOTICE THE INDIGENOUS PEOPLE FLEEING IN HORROR?
PUT IT WITH THE OTHER VOLCANOES.

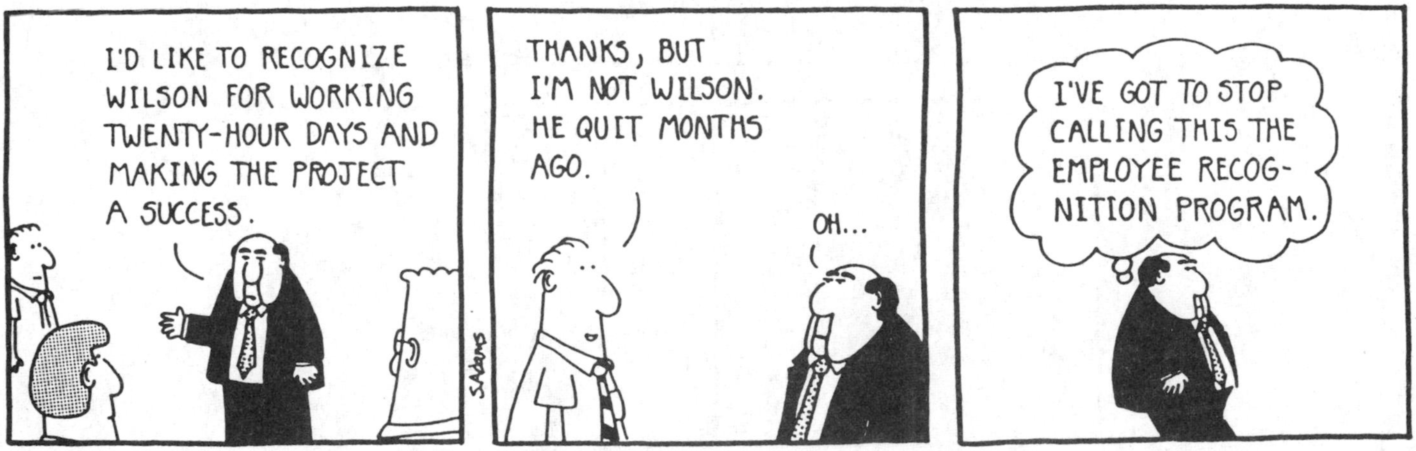
I'D LIKE TO RECOGNIZE WILSON FOR WORKING TWENTY-HOUR DAYS AND MAKING THE PROJECT A SUCCESS.
THANKS, BUT I'M NOT WILSON. HE QUIT MONTHS AGO.
OH...
I'VE GOT TO STOP CALLING THIS THE EMPLOYEE RECOGNITION PROGRAM.

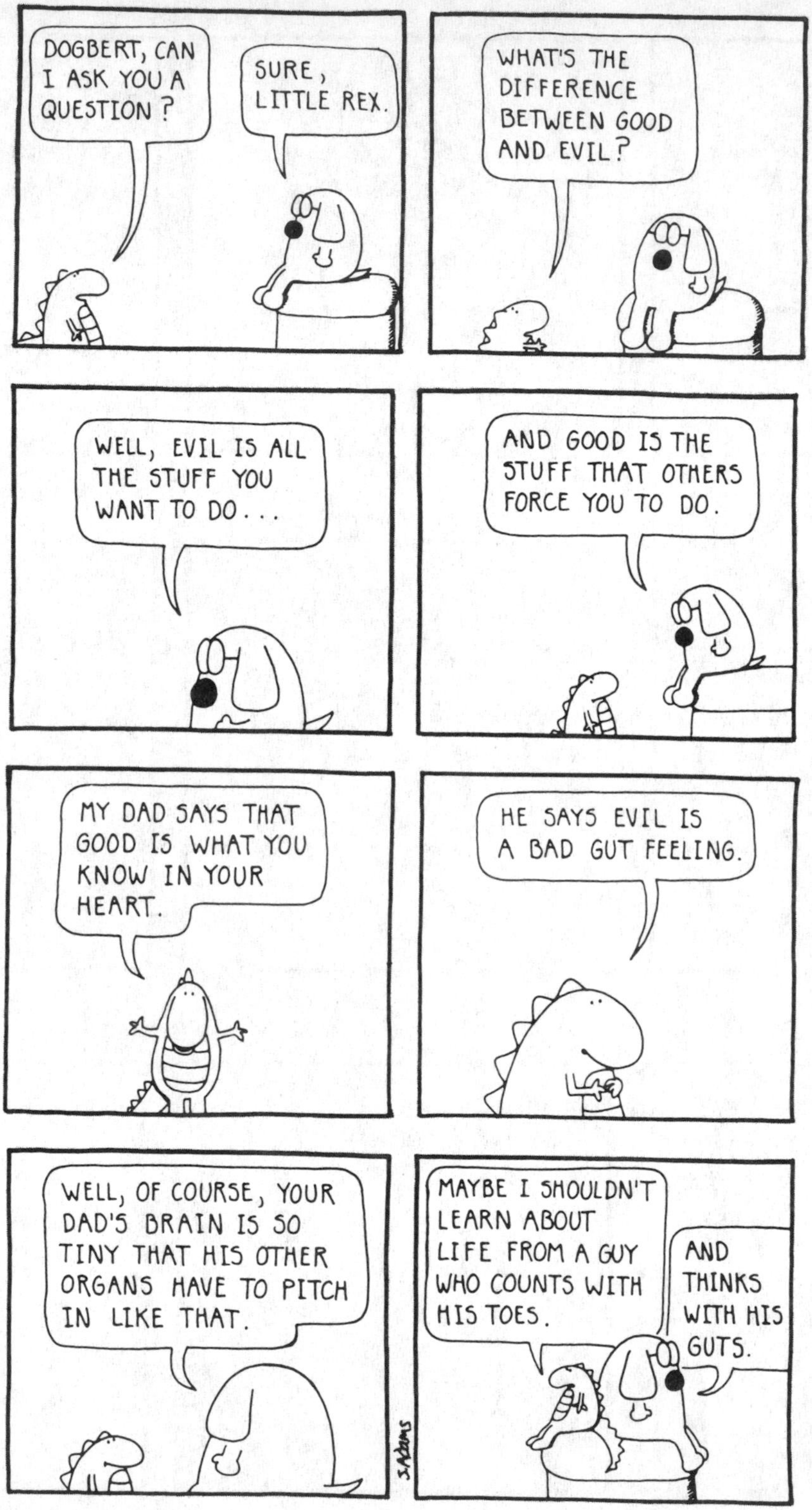
DOGBERT, CAN I ASK YOU A QUESTION?
SURE, LITTLE REX.
WHAT'S THE DIFFERENCE BETWEEN GOOD AND EVIL?
WELL, EVIL IS ALL THE STUFF YOU WANT TO DO...
AND GOOD IS THE STUFF THAT OTHERS FORCE YOU TO DO.
MY DAD SAYS THAT GOOD IS WHAT YOU KNOW IN YOUR HEART.
HE SAYS EVIL IS A BAD GUT FEELING.
WELL, OF COURSE, YOUR DAD'S BRAIN IS SO TINY THAT HIS OTHER ORGANS HAVE TO PITCH IN LIKE THAT.
S.ADAMS
MAYBE I SHOULDN'T LEARN ABOUT LIFE FROM A GUY WHO COUNTS WITH HIS TOES.
AND THINKS WITH HIS GUTS.

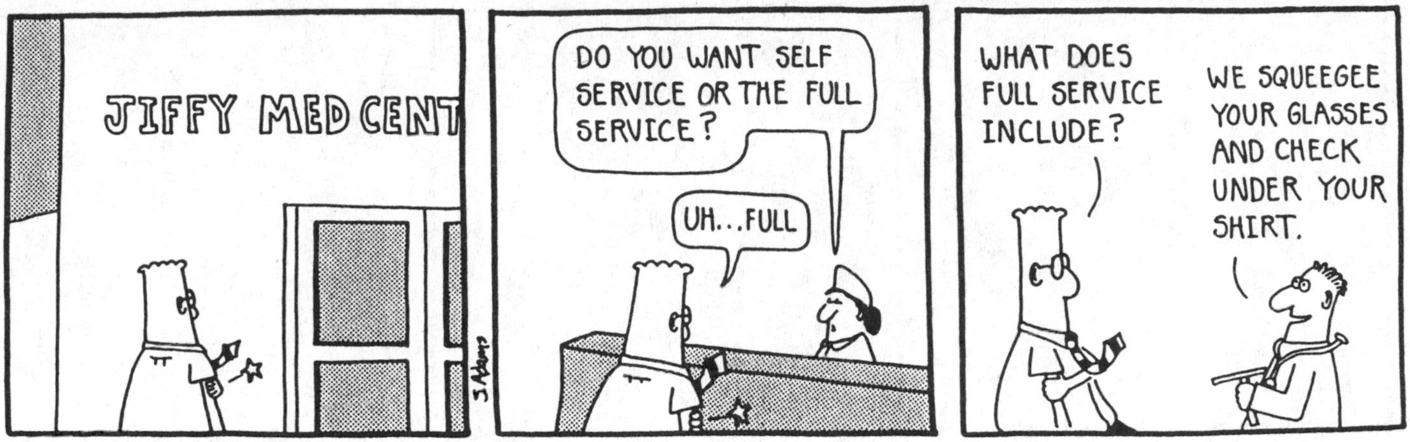
JIFFY MED CENT
DO YOU WANT SELF SERVICE OR THE FULL SERVICE?
UH...FULL
WHAT DOES FULL SERVICE INCLUDE?
WE SQUEEGEE YOUR GLASSES AND CHECK UNDER YOUR SHIRT.

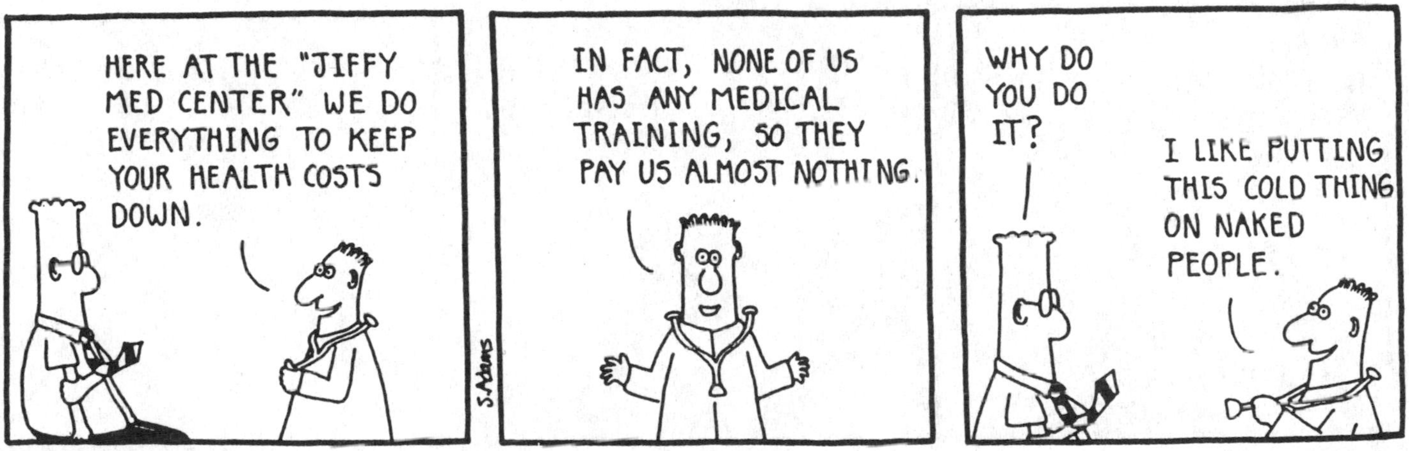
HERE AT THE "JIFFY MED CENTER" WE DO EVERYTHING TO KEEP YOUR HEALTH COSTS DOWN.
IN FACT, NONE OF US HAS ANY MEDICAL TRAINING, SO THEY PAY US ALMOST NOTHING.
WHY DO YOU DO IT?
I LIKE PUTTING THIS COLD THING ON NAKED PEOPLE.

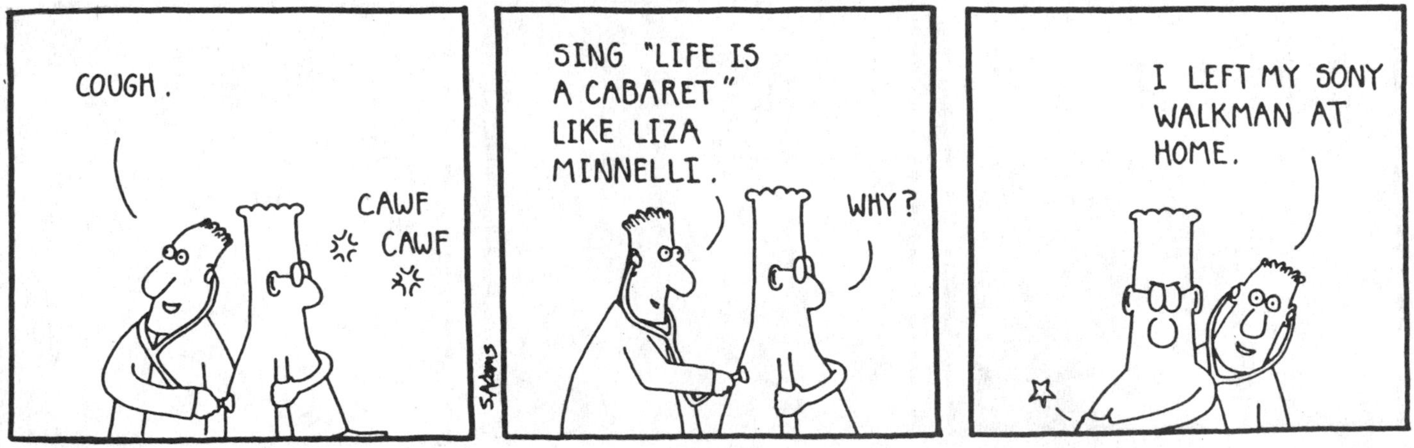
COUGH.
CAWF CAWF
SING "LIFE IS A CABARET" LIKE LIZA MINNELLI.
WHY?
I LEFT MY SONY WALKMAN AT HOME.

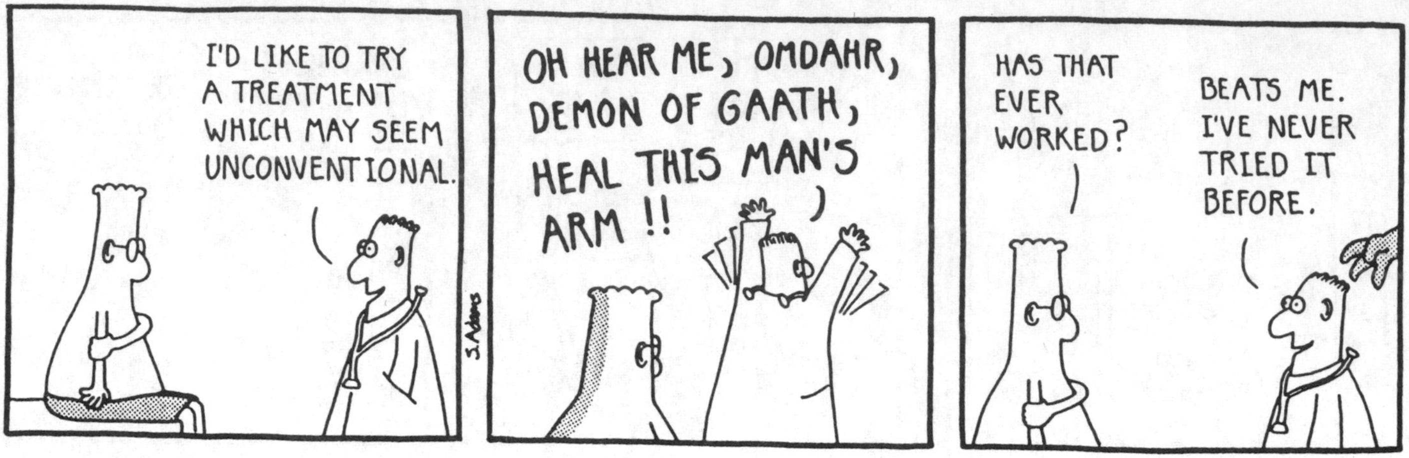
I'D LIKE TO TRY A TREATMENT WHICH MAY SEEM UNCONVENTIONAL.
OH HEAR ME, OMDAHR, DEMON OF GAATH, HEAL THIS MAN'S ARM !!
HAS THAT EVER WORKED?
BEATS ME. I'VE NEVER TRIED IT BEFORE.

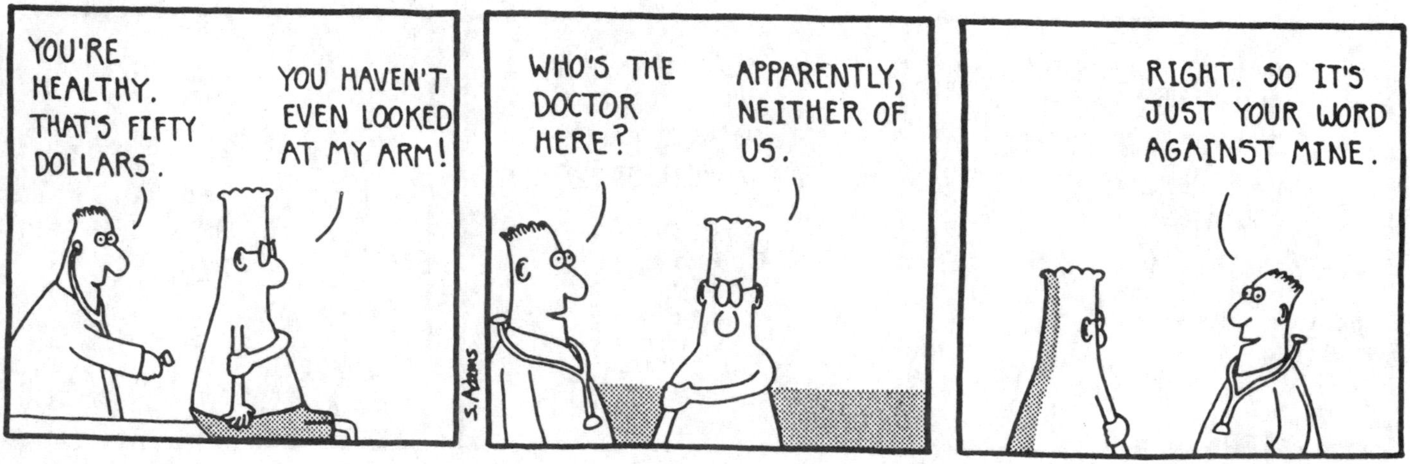
YOU'RE HEALTHY. THAT'S FIFTY DOLLARS.
YOU HAVEN'T EVEN LOOKED AT MY ARM!
WHO'S THE DOCTOR HERE?
APPARENTLY, NEITHER OF US.
RIGHT. SO IT'S JUST YOUR WORD AGAINST MINE.

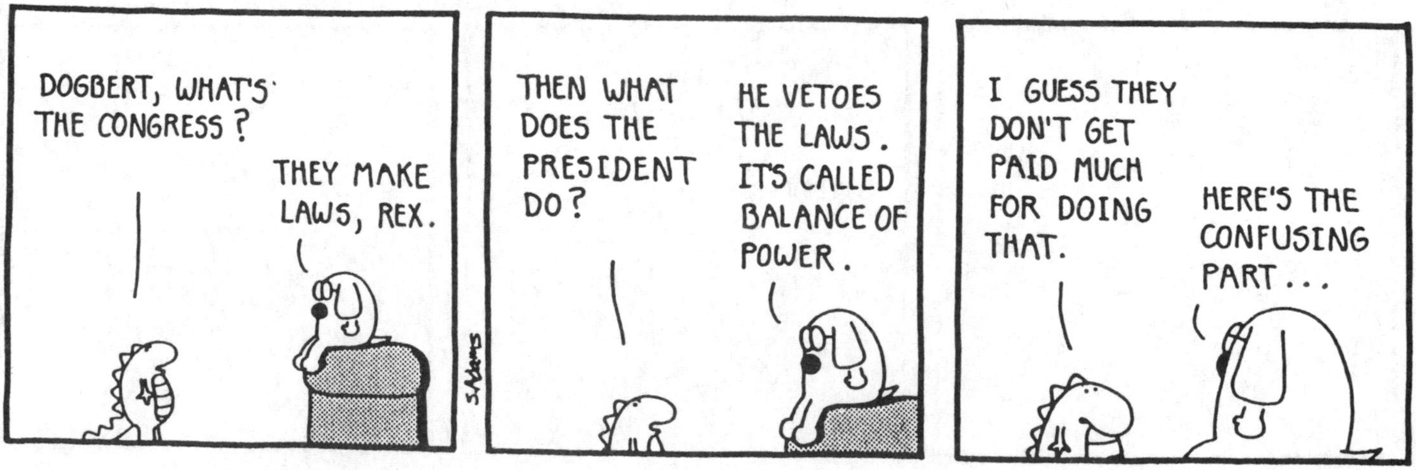
DOGBERT, WHAT'S THE CONGRESS?
THEY MAKE LAWS, REX.
THEN WHAT DOES THE PRESIDENT DO?
HE VETOES THE LAWS. IT'S CALLED BALANCE OF POWER.
I GUESS THEY DON'T GET PAID MUCH FOR DOING THAT.
HERE'S THE CONFUSING PART...

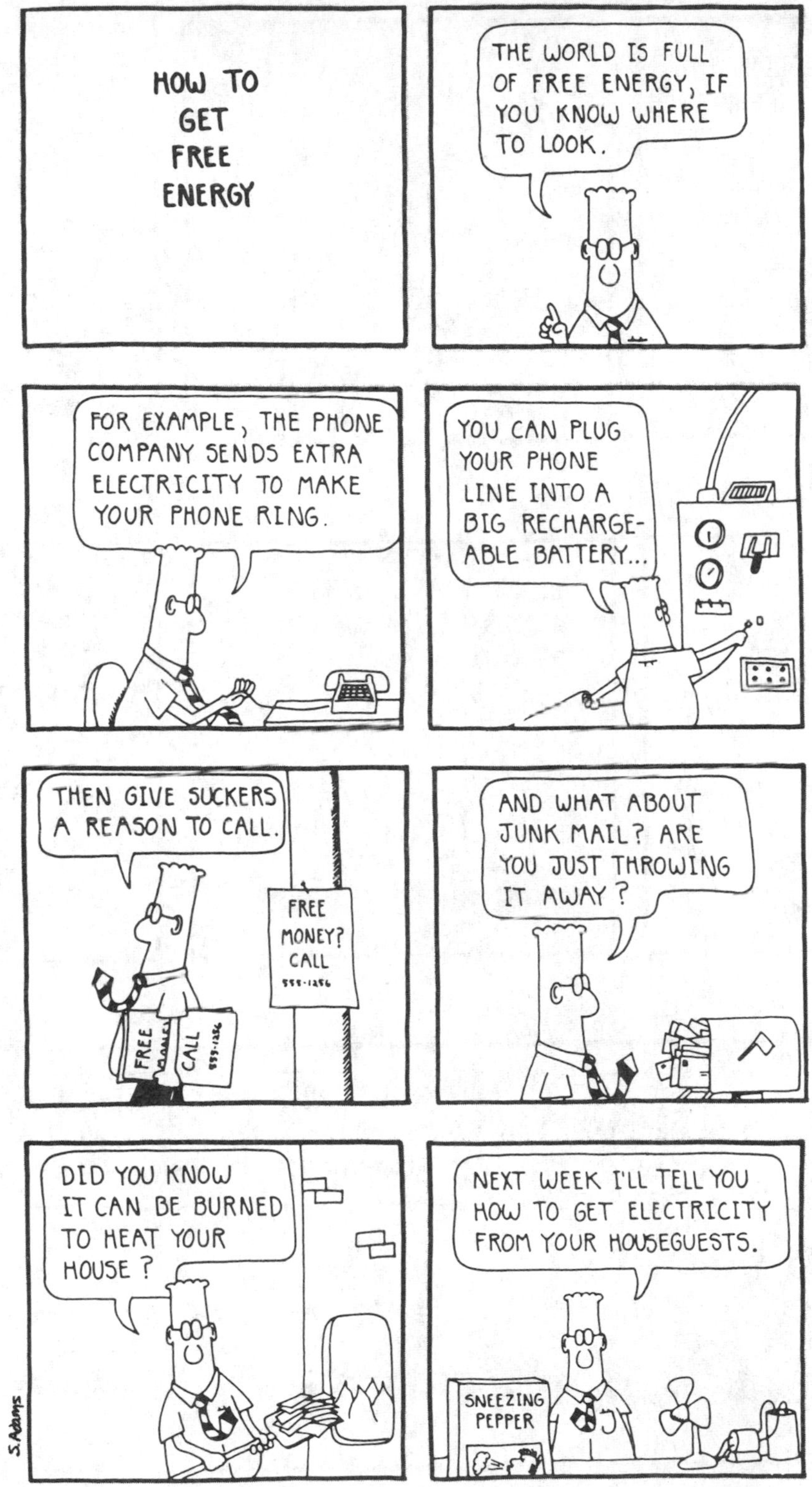
HOW TO GET FREE ENERGY
THE WORLD IS FULL OF FREE ENERGY, IF YOU KNOW WHERE TO LOOK.
FOR EXAMPLE, THE PHONE COMPANY SENDS EXTRA ELECTRICITY TO MAKE YOUR PHONE RING.
YOU CAN PLUG YOUR PHONE LINE INTO A BIG RECHARGE-ABLE BATTERY...
THEN GIVE SUCKERS A REASON TO CALL.
FREE MONEY? CALL 555-1256
AND WHAT ABOUT JUNK MAIL? ARE YOU JUST THROWING IT AWAY?
DID YOU KNOW IT CAN BE BURNED TO HEAT YOUR HOUSE?
S. Adams
NEXT WEEK I'LL TELL YOU HOW TO GET ELECTRICITY FROM YOUR HOUSEGUESTS.
SNEEZING PEPPER

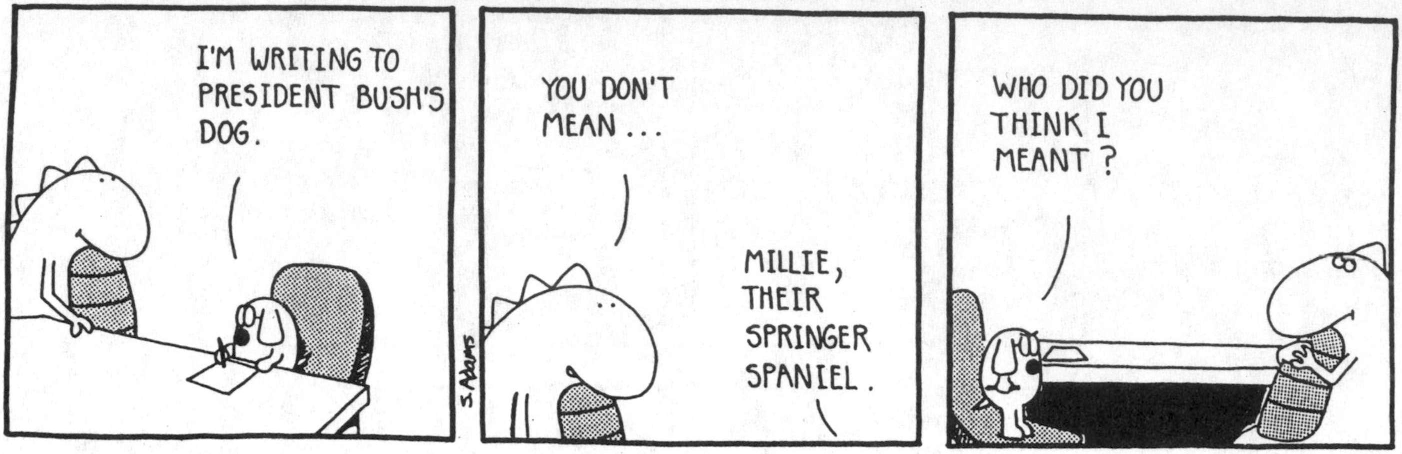
I'M WRITING TO PRESIDENT BUSH'S DOG.
YOU DON'T MEAN . . .
MILLIE, THEIR SPRINGER SPANIEL.
WHO DID YOU THINK I MEANT ?
S. Adams

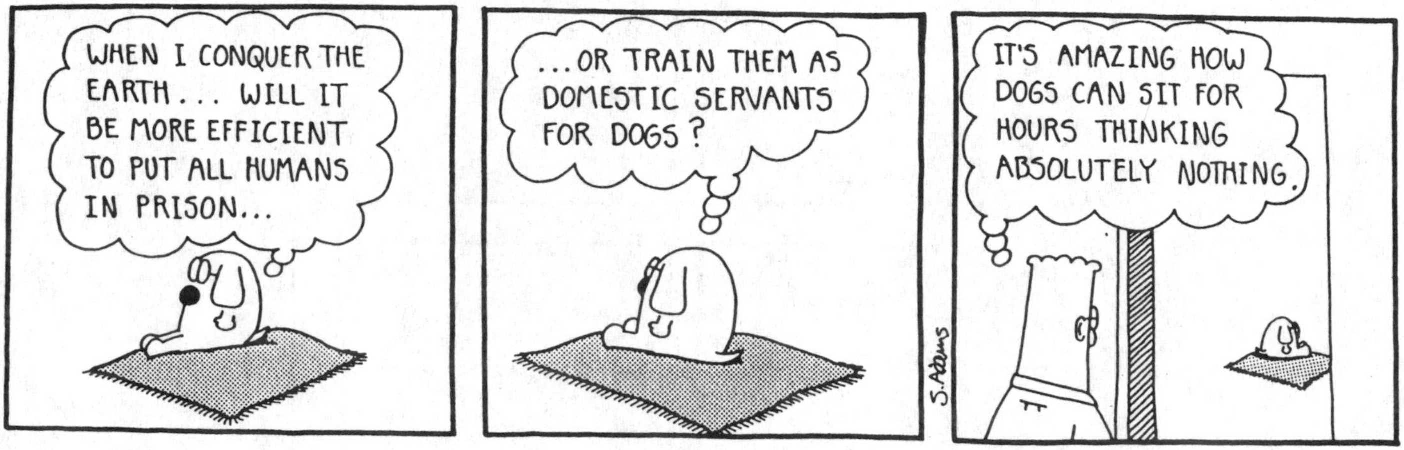
WHEN I CONQUER THE EARTH . . . WILL IT BE MORE EFFICIENT TO PUT ALL HUMANS IN PRISON . . .
. . . OR TRAIN THEM AS DOMESTIC SERVANTS FOR DOGS ?
IT'S AMAZING HOW DOGS CAN SIT FOR HOURS THINKING ABSOLUTELY NOTHING.
S. Adams

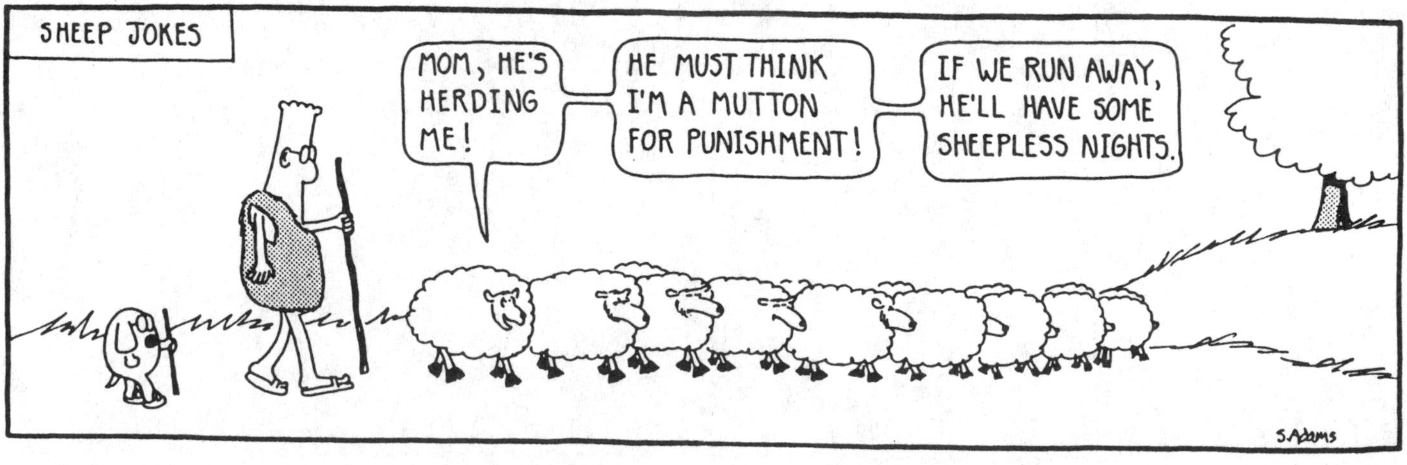
SHEEP JOKES
MOM, HE'S HERDING ME!
HE MUST THINK I'M A MUTTON FOR PUNISHMENT!
IF WE RUN AWAY, HE'LL HAVE SOME SHEEPLESS NIGHTS.
S. Adams

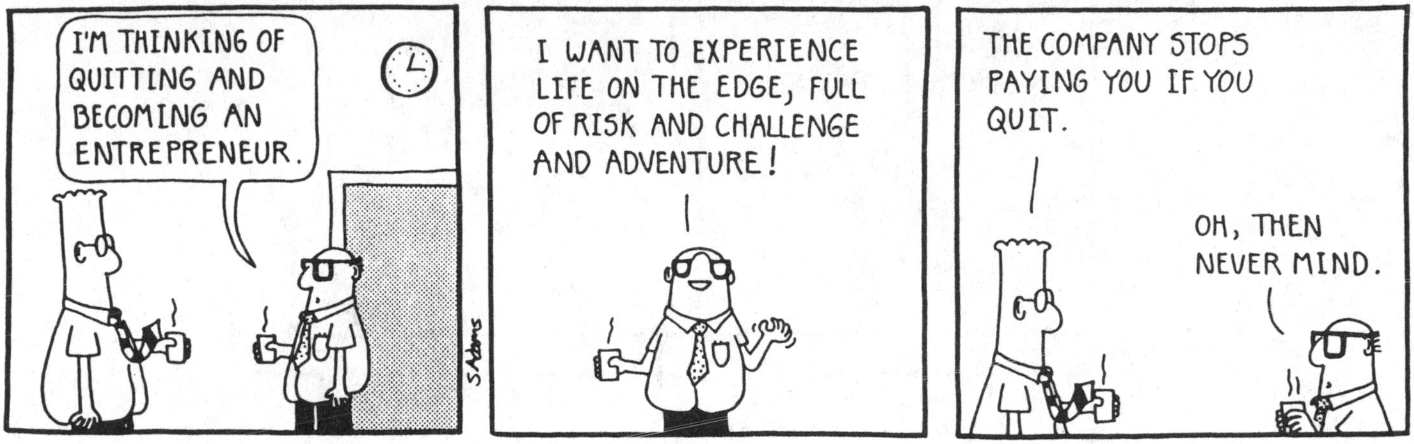
I'M THINKING OF QUITTING AND BECOMING AN ENTREPRENEUR.
I WANT TO EXPERIENCE LIFE ON THE EDGE, FULL OF RISK AND CHALLENGE AND ADVENTURE!
THE COMPANY STOPS PAYING YOU IF YOU QUIT.
OH, THEN NEVER MIND.

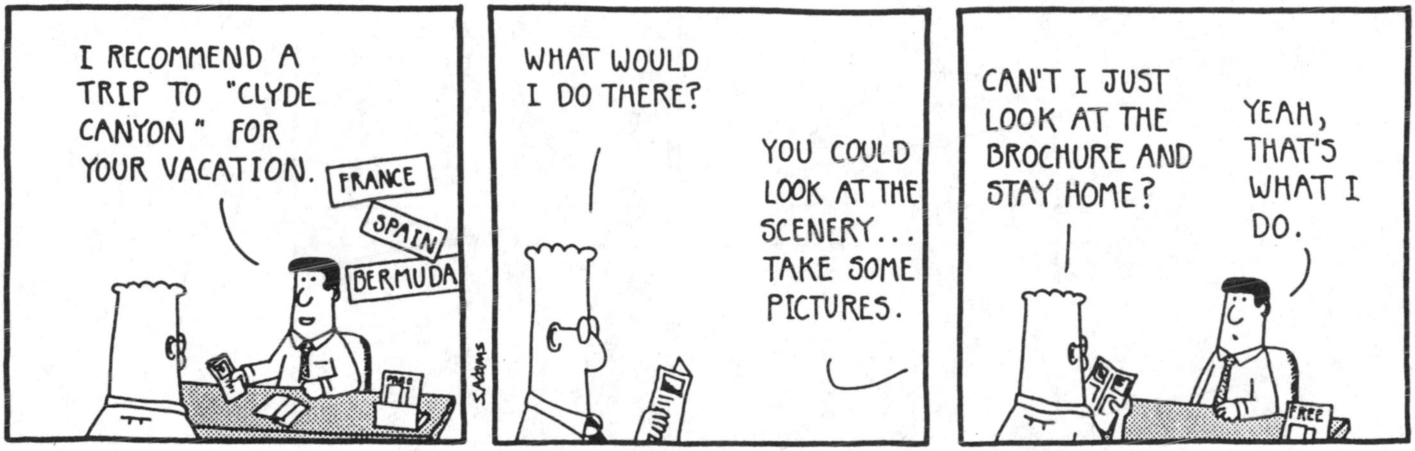
I RECOMMEND A TRIP TO "CLYDE CANYON" FOR YOUR VACATION.
FRANCE
SPAIN
BERMUDA
WHAT WOULD I DO THERE?
YOU COULD LOOK AT THE SCENERY... TAKE SOME PICTURES.
CAN'T I JUST LOOK AT THE BROCHURE AND STAY HOME?
YEAH, THAT'S WHAT I DO.
FREE

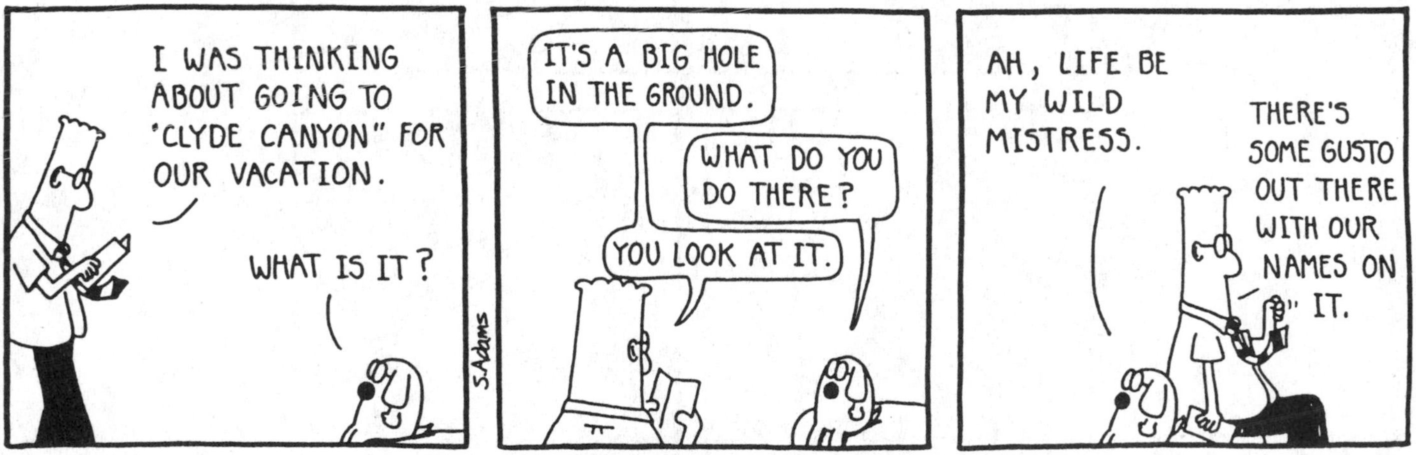
I WAS THINKING ABOUT GOING TO "CLYDE CANYON" FOR OUR VACATION.
WHAT IS IT?
IT'S A BIG HOLE IN THE GROUND.
WHAT DO YOU DO THERE?
YOU LOOK AT IT.
AH, LIFE BE MY WILD MISTRESS.
THERE'S SOME GUSTO OUT THERE WITH OUR NAMES ON IT.

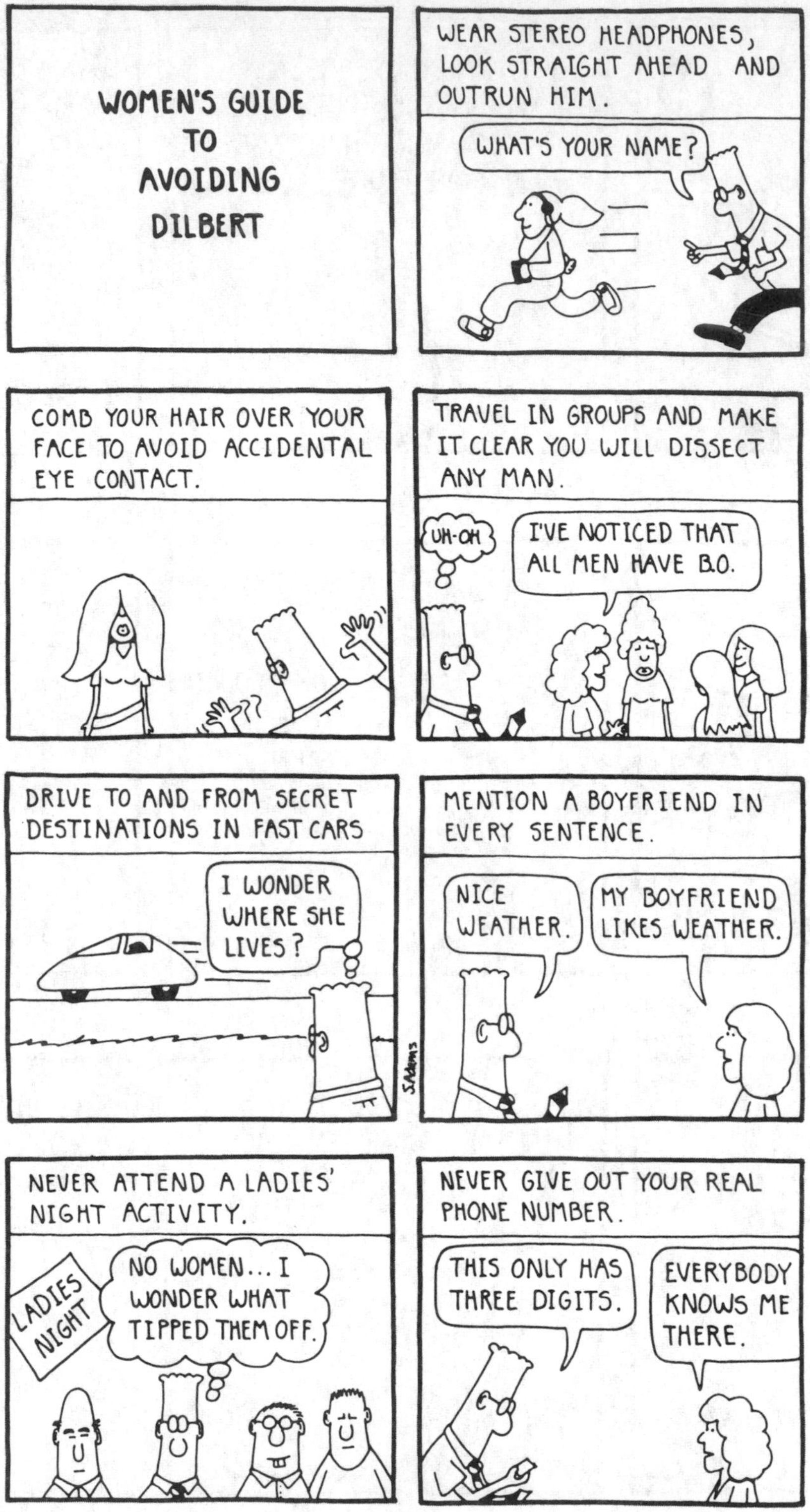
WOMEN'S GUIDE TO AVOIDING DILBERT
WEAR STEREO HEADPHONES, LOOK STRAIGHT AHEAD AND OUTRUN HIM.
WHAT'S YOUR NAME?
COMB YOUR HAIR OVER YOUR FACE TO AVOID ACCIDENTAL EYE CONTACT.
TRAVEL IN GROUPS AND MAKE IT CLEAR YOU WILL DISSECT ANY MAN.
UH-OH
I'VE NOTICED THAT ALL MEN HAVE B.O.
DRIVE TO AND FROM SECRET DESTINATIONS IN FAST CARS
I WONDER WHERE SHE LIVES?
MENTION A BOYFRIEND IN EVERY SENTENCE.
NICE WEATHER.
MY BOYFRIEND LIKES WEATHER.
NEVER ATTEND A LADIES' NIGHT ACTIVITY.
LADIES NIGHT
NO WOMEN... I WONDER WHAT TIPPED THEM OFF.
NEVER GIVE OUT YOUR REAL PHONE NUMBER.
THIS ONLY HAS THREE DIGITS.
EVERYBODY KNOWS ME THERE.

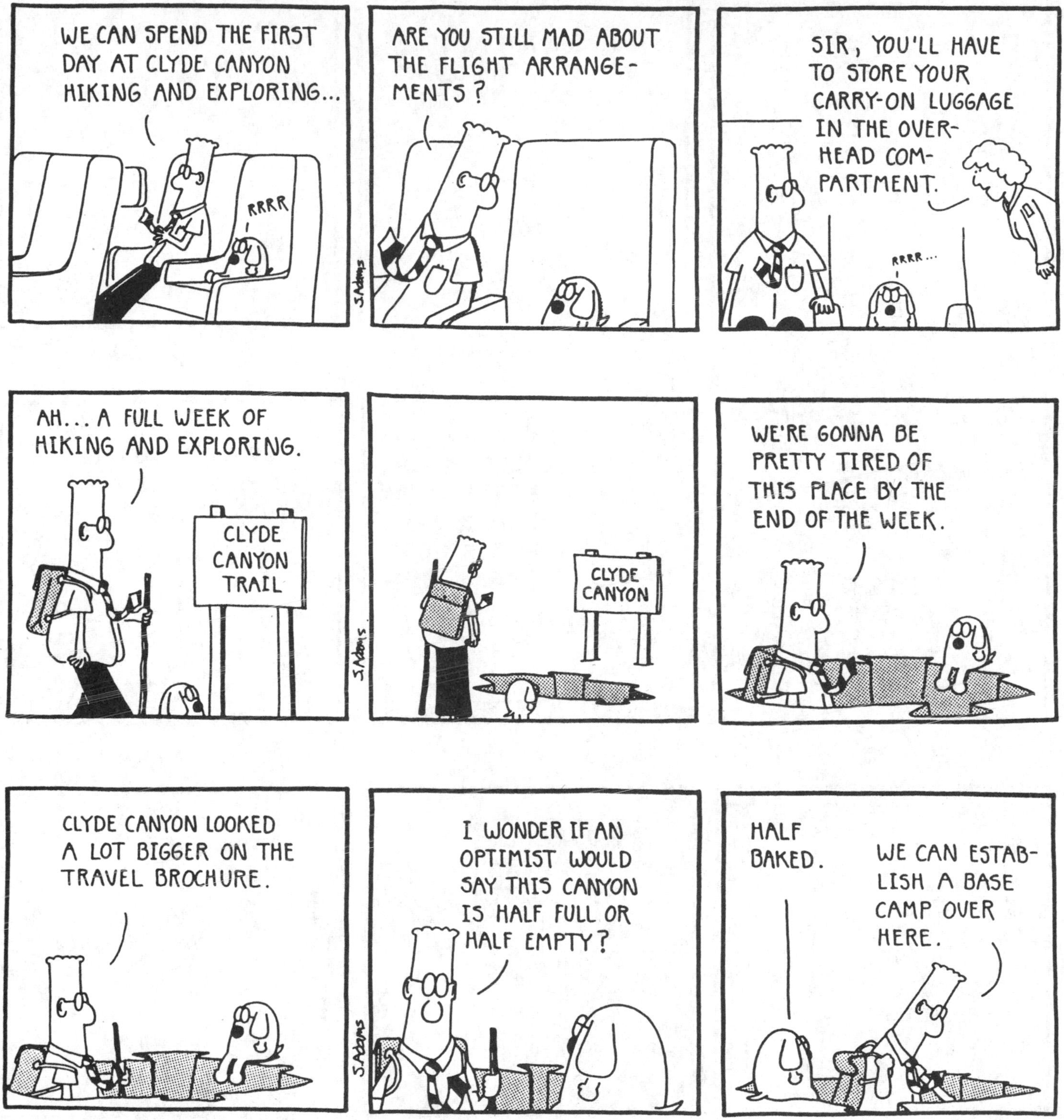
WE CAN SPEND THE FIRST DAY AT CLYDE CANYON HIKING AND EXPLORING...
RRRR
ARE YOU STILL MAD ABOUT THE FLIGHT ARRANGE-MENTS?
SIR, YOU'LL HAVE TO STORE YOUR CARRY-ON LUGGAGE IN THE OVER-HEAD COM-PARTMENT.
RRRR...
AH... A FULL WEEK OF HIKING AND EXPLORING.
CLYDE CANYON TRAIL
CLYDE CANYON
WE'RE GONNA BE PRETTY TIRED OF THIS PLACE BY THE END OF THE WEEK.
CLYDE CANYON LOOKED A LOT BIGGER ON THE TRAVEL BROCHURE.
I WONDER IF AN OPTIMIST WOULD SAY THIS CANYON IS HALF FULL OR HALF EMPTY?
HALF BAKED.
WE CAN ESTAB-LISH A BASE CAMP OVER HERE.

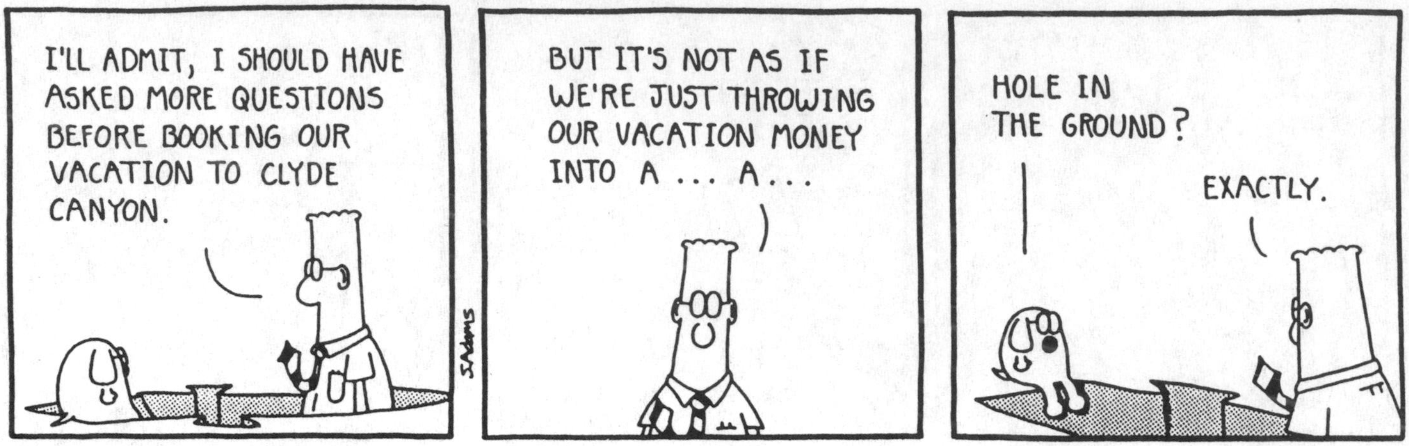
I'LL ADMIT, I SHOULD HAVE ASKED MORE QUESTIONS BEFORE BOOKING OUR VACATION TO CLYDE CANYON.
S.Adams
BUT IT'S NOT AS IF WE'RE JUST THROWING OUR VACATION MONEY INTO A . . . A . . .
HOLE IN THE GROUND?
EXACTLY.

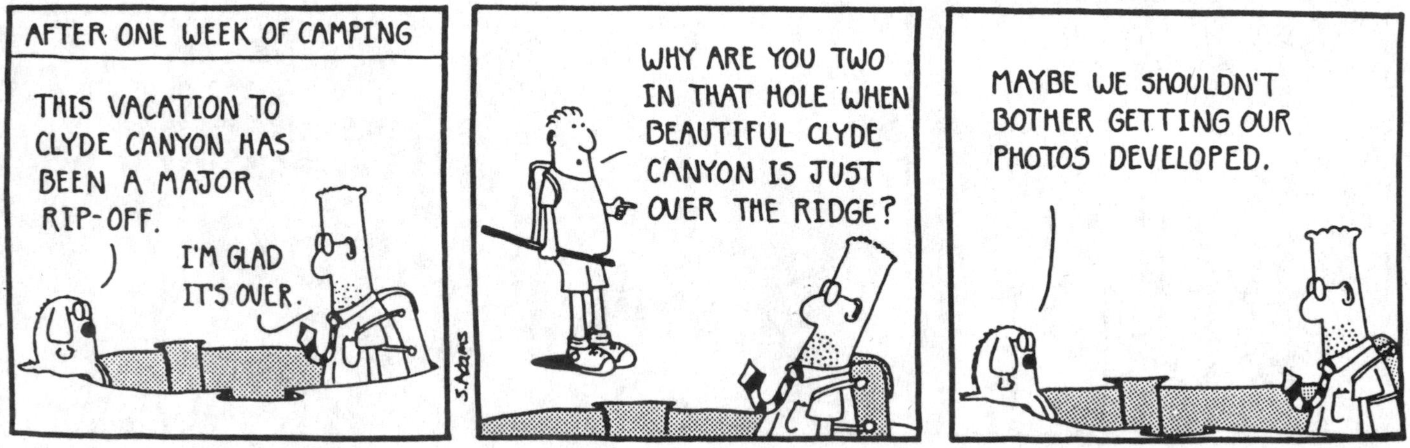
AFTER ONE WEEK OF CAMPING
THIS VACATION TO CLYDE CANYON HAS BEEN A MAJOR RIP-OFF.
I'M GLAD IT'S OVER.
S.Adams
WHY ARE YOU TWO IN THAT HOLE WHEN BEAUTIFUL CLYDE CANYON IS JUST OVER THE RIDGE?
MAYBE WE SHOULDN'T BOTHER GETTING OUR PHOTOS DEVELOPED.

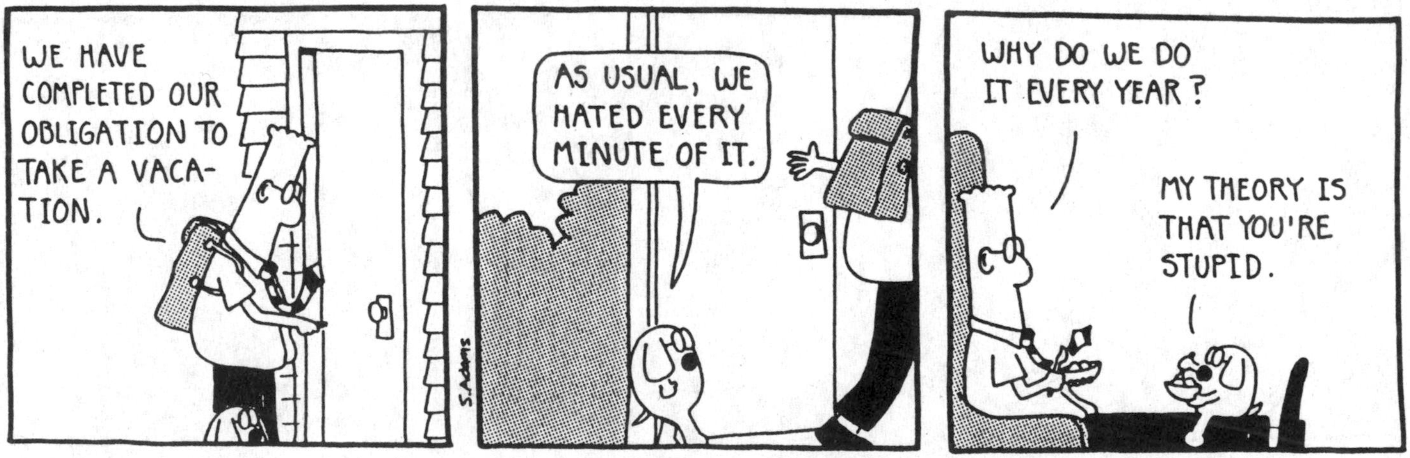
WE HAVE COMPLETED OUR OBLIGATION TO TAKE A VACA-TION.
S.Adams
AS USUAL, WE HATED EVERY MINUTE OF IT.
WHY DO WE DO IT EVERY YEAR?
MY THEORY IS THAT YOU'RE STUPID.

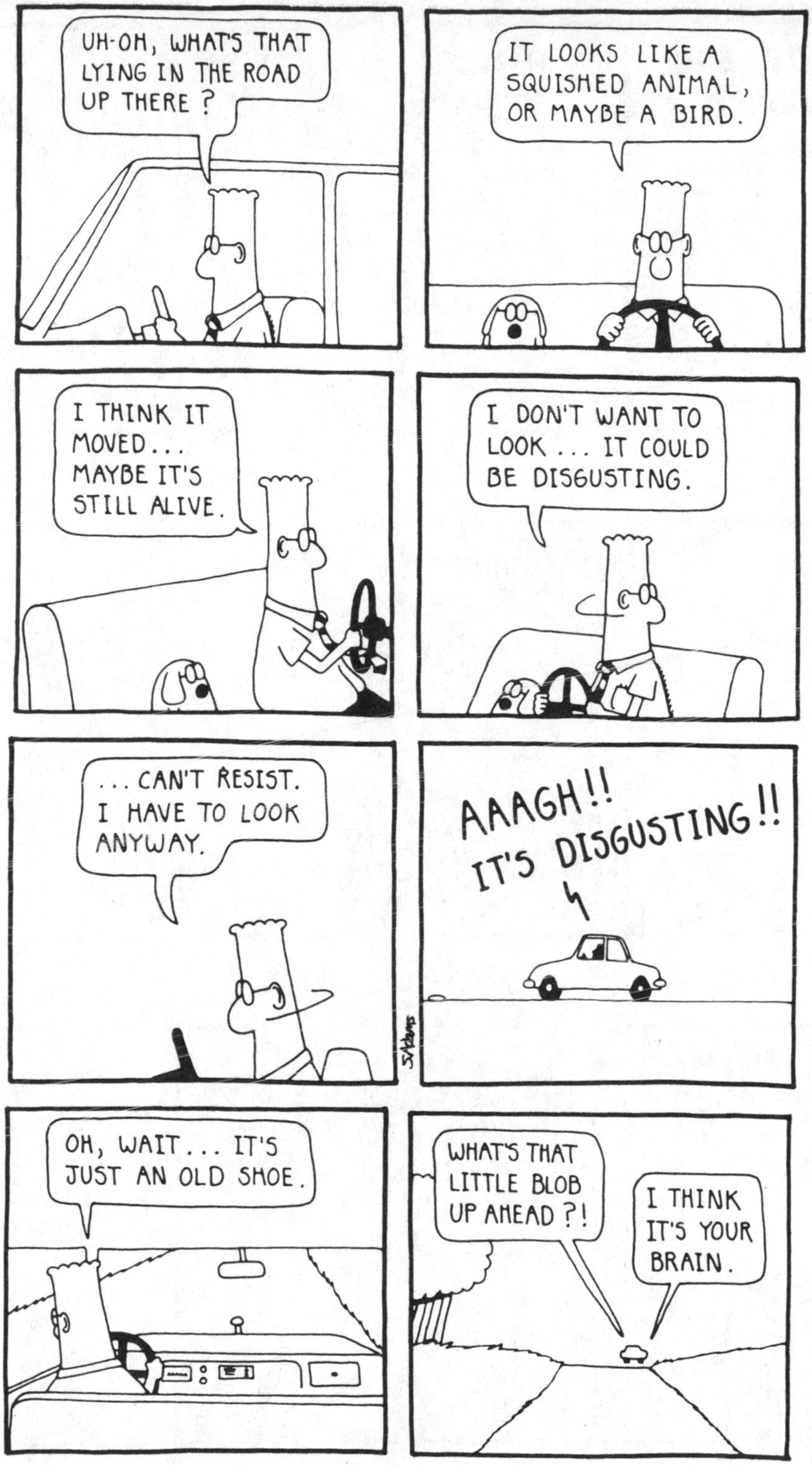
UH-OH, WHAT'S THAT LYING IN THE ROAD UP THERE ?
IT LOOKS LIKE A SQUISHED ANIMAL, OR MAYBE A BIRD.
I THINK IT MOVED... MAYBE IT'S STILL ALIVE.
I DON'T WANT TO LOOK ... IT COULD BE DISGUSTING.
... CAN'T RESIST. I HAVE TO LOOK ANYWAY.
AAAGH!! IT'S DISGUSTING!!
OH, WAIT... IT'S JUST AN OLD SHOE.
WHAT'S THAT LITTLE BLOB UP AHEAD ?!
I THINK IT'S YOUR BRAIN.

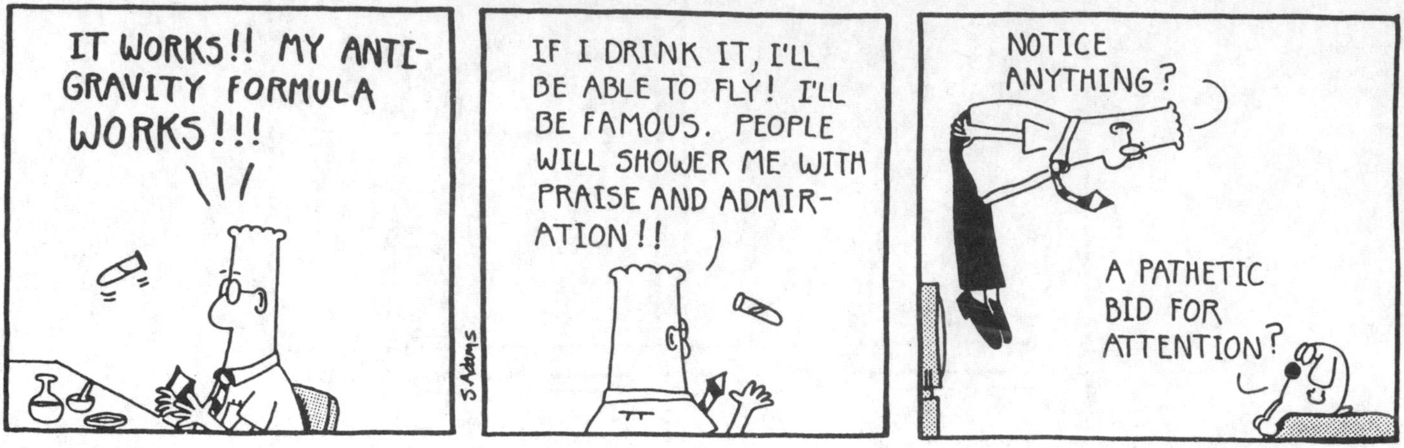
IT WORKS!! MY ANTI-GRAVITY FORMULA WORKS!!!
IF I DRINK IT, I'LL BE ABLE TO FLY! I'LL BE FAMOUS. PEOPLE WILL SHOWER ME WITH PRAISE AND ADMIRATION!!
NOTICE ANYTHING?
A PATHETIC BID FOR ATTENTION?

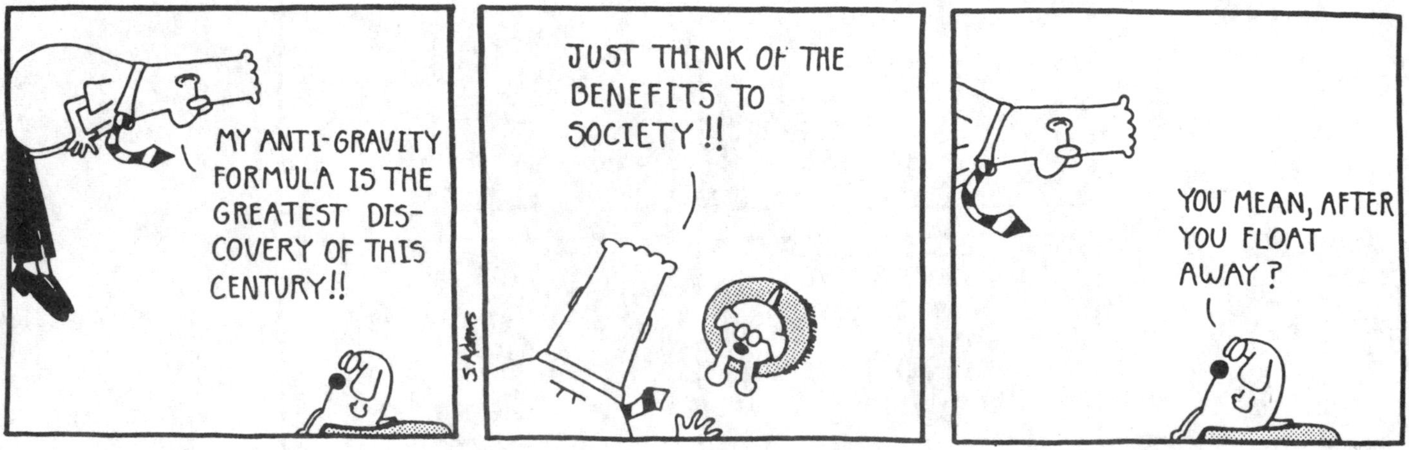
MY ANTI-GRAVITY FORMULA IS THE GREATEST DISCOVERY OF THIS CENTURY!!
JUST THINK OF THE BENEFITS TO SOCIETY!!
YOU MEAN, AFTER YOU FLOAT AWAY?

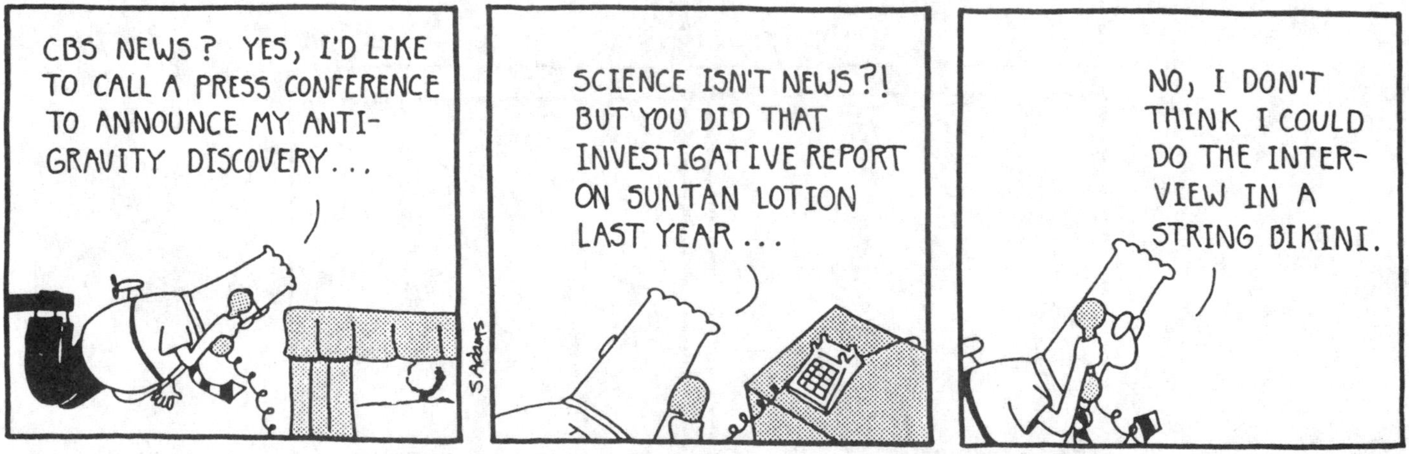
CBS NEWS? YES, I'D LIKE TO CALL A PRESS CONFERENCE TO ANNOUNCE MY ANTI-GRAVITY DISCOVERY...
SCIENCE ISN'T NEWS?! BUT YOU DID THAT INVESTIGATIVE REPORT ON SUNTAN LOTION LAST YEAR...
NO, I DON'T THINK I COULD DO THE INTERVIEW IN A STRING BIKINI.

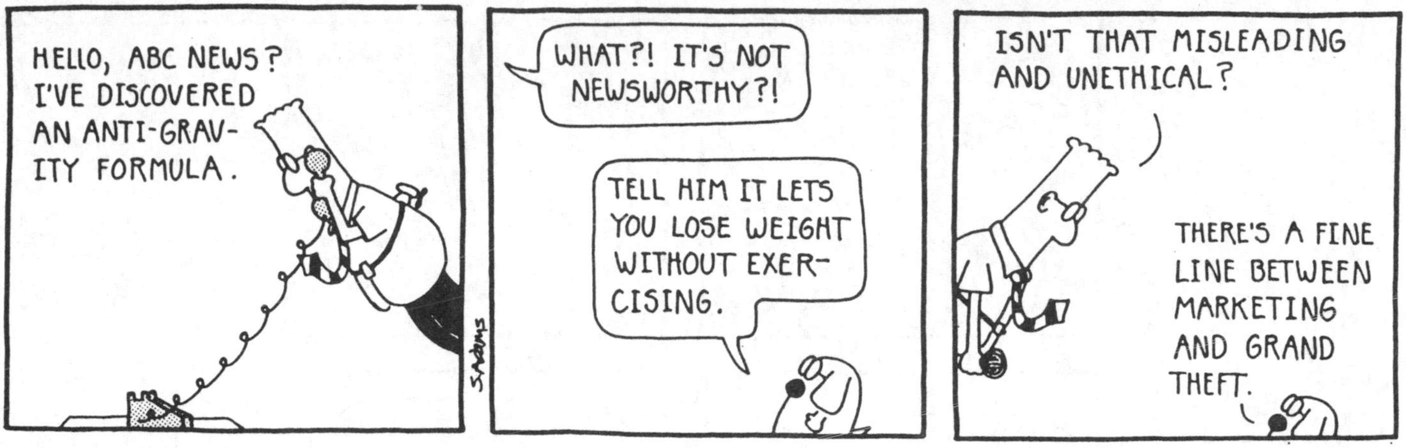
HELLO, ABC NEWS? I'VE DISCOVERED AN ANTI-GRAVITY FORMULA.
WHAT?! IT'S NOT NEWSWORTHY?!
TELL HIM IT LETS YOU LOSE WEIGHT WITHOUT EXERCISING.
ISN'T THAT MISLEADING AND UNETHICAL?
THERE'S A FINE LINE BETWEEN MARKETING AND GRAND THEFT.

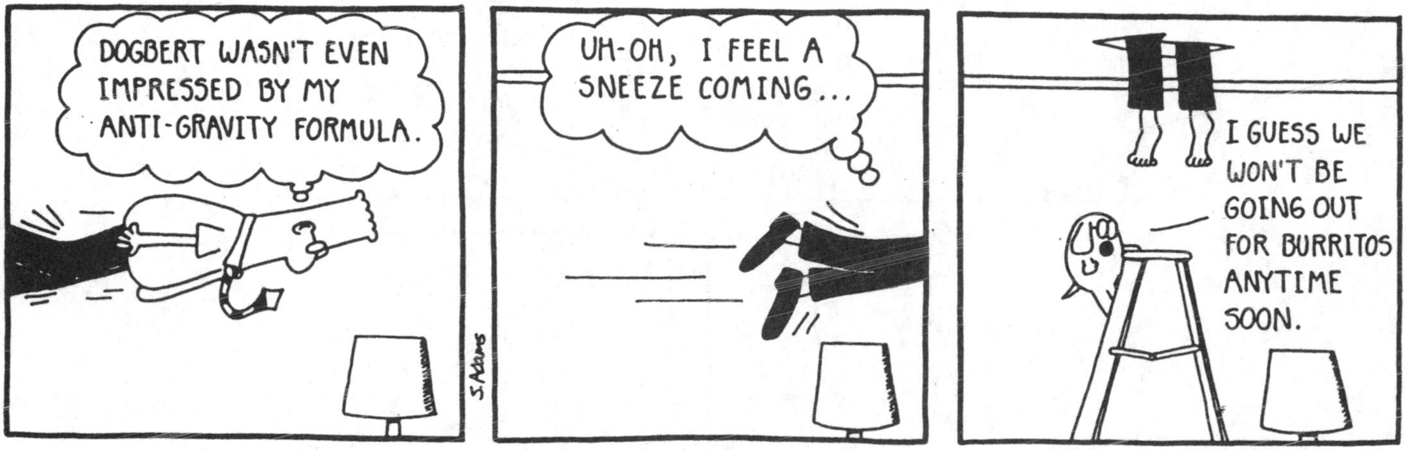
DOGBERT WASN'T EVEN IMPRESSED BY MY ANTI-GRAVITY FORMULA.
UH-OH, I FEEL A SNEEZE COMING...
I GUESS WE WON'T BE GOING OUT FOR BURRITOS ANYTIME SOON.

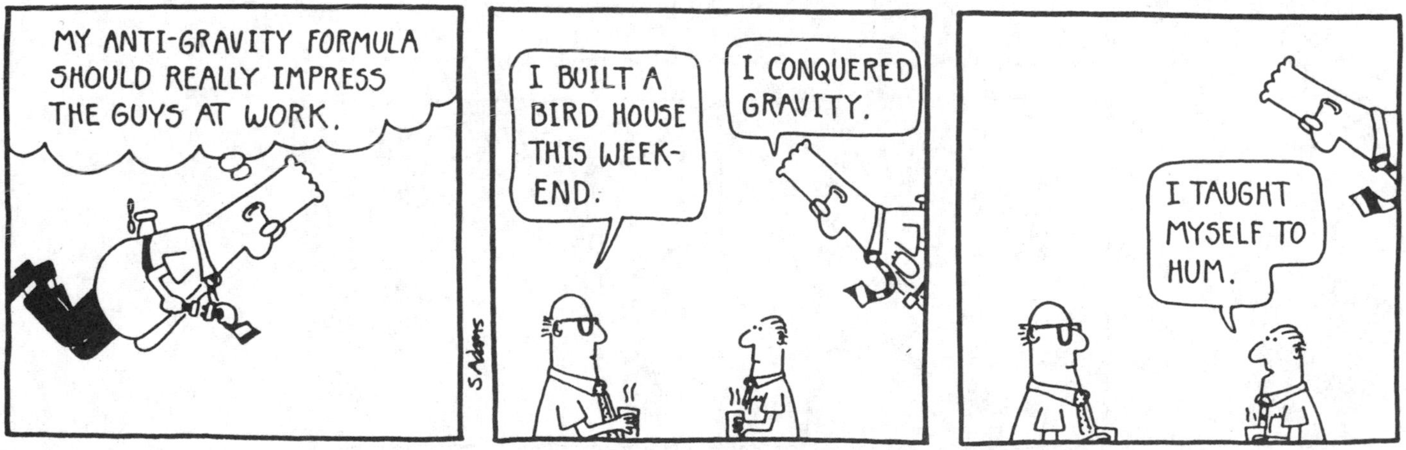
MY ANTI-GRAVITY FORMULA SHOULD REALLY IMPRESS THE GUYS AT WORK.
I BUILT A BIRD HOUSE THIS WEEKEND.
I CONQUERED GRAVITY.
I TAUGHT MYSELF TO HUM.

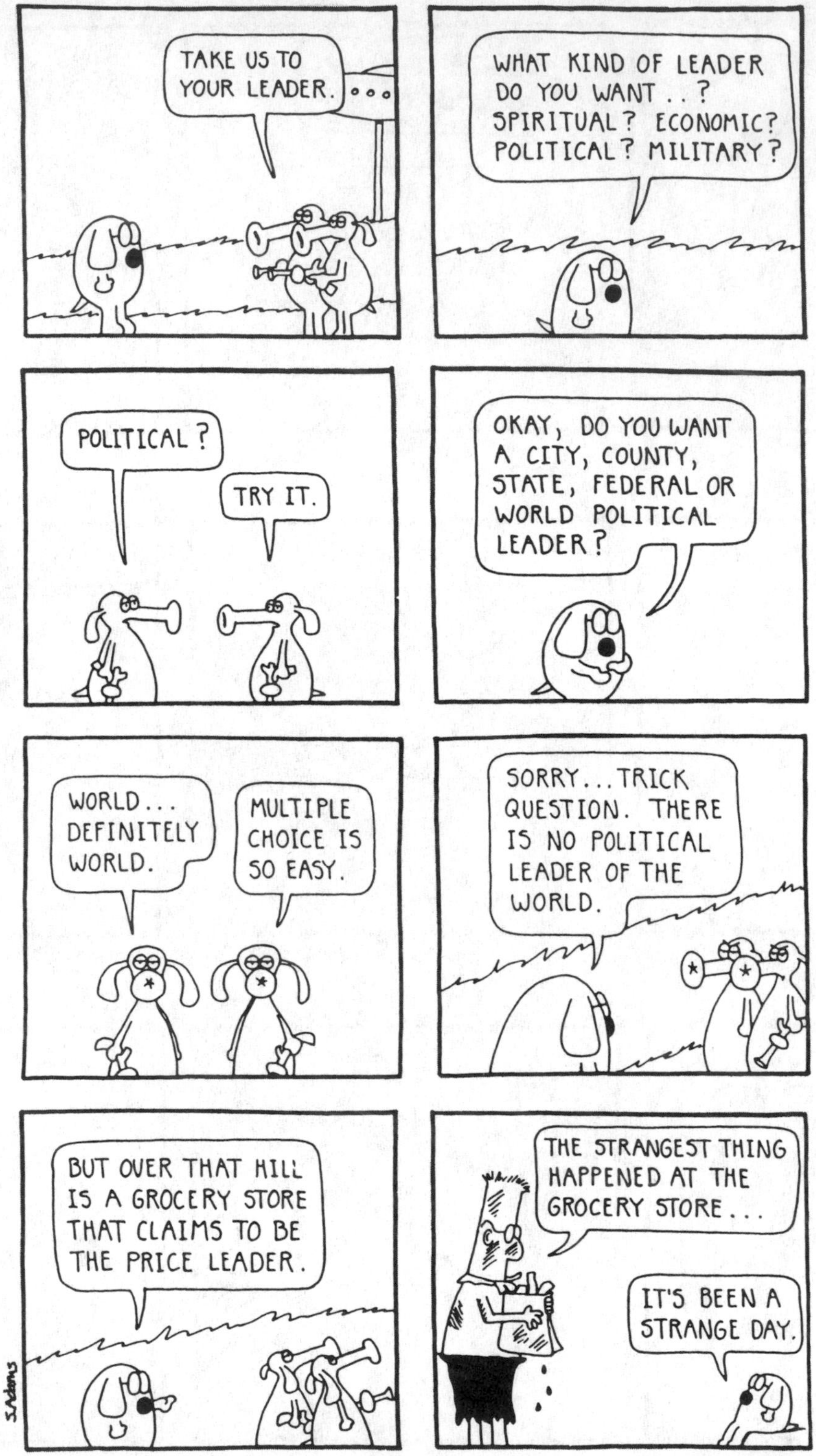
TAKE US TO YOUR LEADER.
WHAT KIND OF LEADER DO YOU WANT..? SPIRITUAL? ECONOMIC? POLITICAL? MILITARY?
POLITICAL?
TRY IT.
OKAY, DO YOU WANT A CITY, COUNTY, STATE, FEDERAL OR WORLD POLITICAL LEADER?
WORLD... DEFINITELY WORLD.
MULTIPLE CHOICE IS SO EASY.
SORRY... TRICK QUESTION. THERE IS NO POLITICAL LEADER OF THE WORLD.
BUT OVER THAT HILL IS A GROCERY STORE THAT CLAIMS TO BE THE PRICE LEADER.
THE STRANGEST THING HAPPENED AT THE GROCERY STORE...
IT'S BEEN A STRANGE DAY.

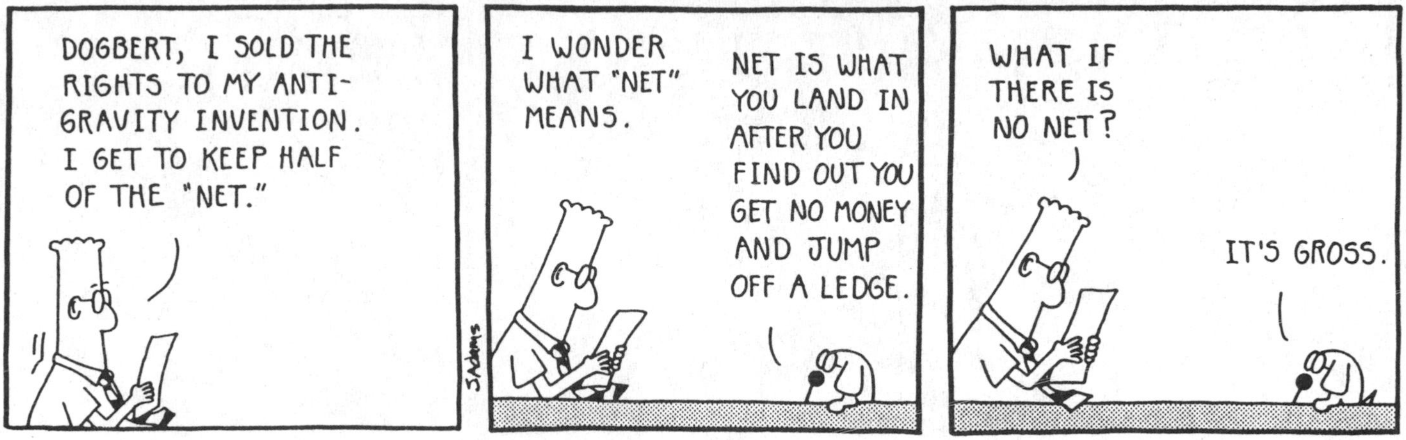
DOGBERT, I SOLD THE RIGHTS TO MY ANTI-GRAVITY INVENTION. I GET TO KEEP HALF OF THE "NET."
I WONDER WHAT "NET" MEANS.
NET IS WHAT YOU LAND IN AFTER YOU FIND OUT YOU GET NO MONEY AND JUMP OFF A LEDGE.
WHAT IF THERE IS NO NET?
IT'S GROSS.

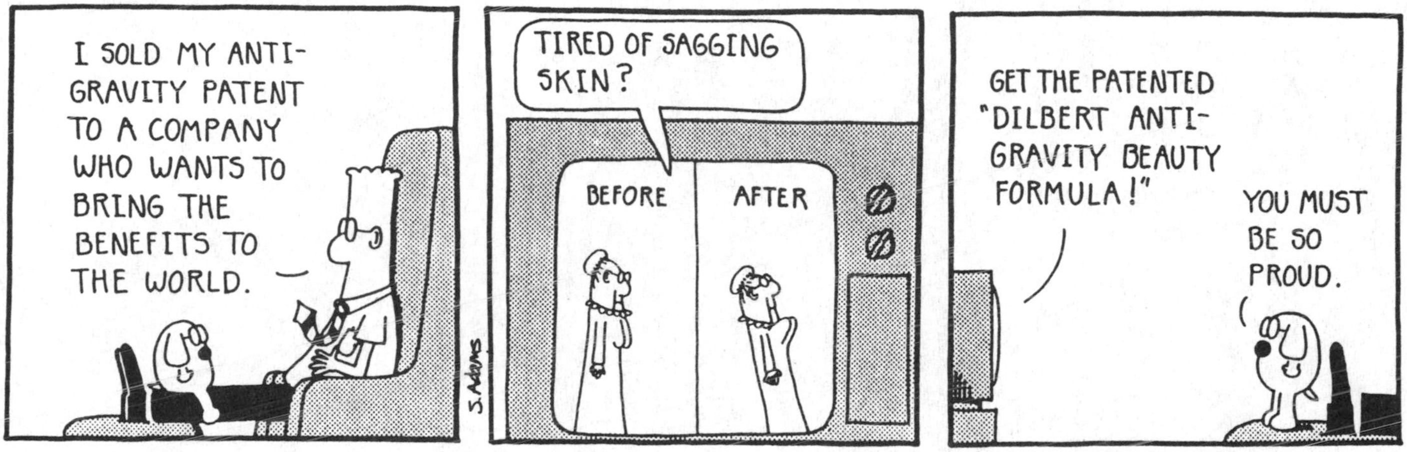
I SOLD MY ANTI-GRAVITY PATENT TO A COMPANY WHO WANTS TO BRING THE BENEFITS TO THE WORLD.
TIRED OF SAGGING SKIN?
BEFORE
AFTER
GET THE PATENTED "DILBERT ANTI-GRAVITY BEAUTY FORMULA!"
YOU MUST BE SO PROUD.

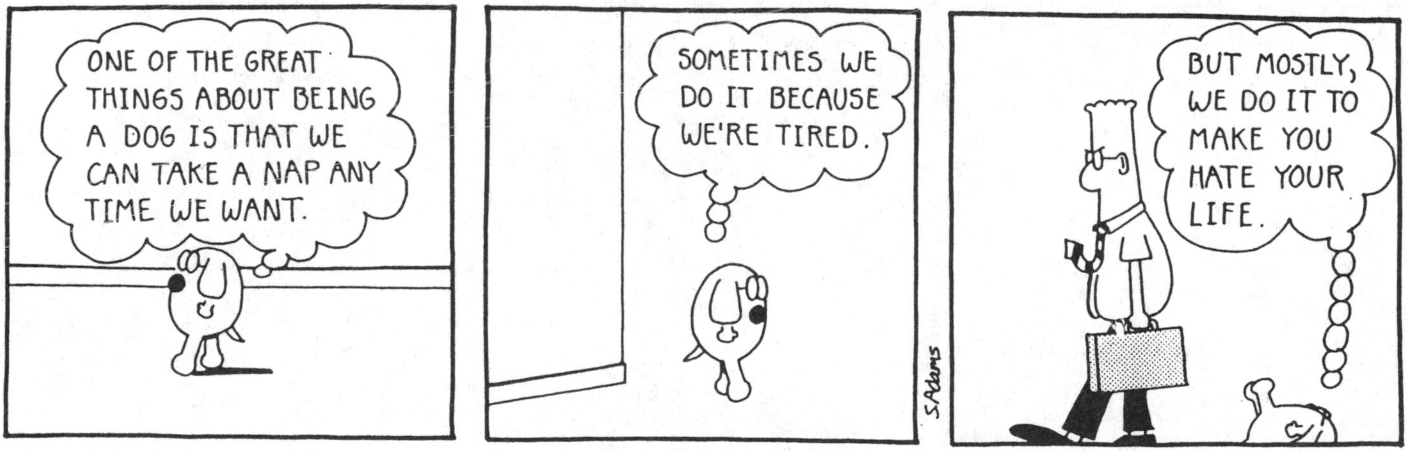
ONE OF THE GREAT THINGS ABOUT BEING A DOG IS THAT WE CAN TAKE A NAP ANY TIME WE WANT.
SOMETIMES WE DO IT BECAUSE WE'RE TIRED.
BUT MOSTLY, WE DO IT TO MAKE YOU HATE YOUR LIFE.

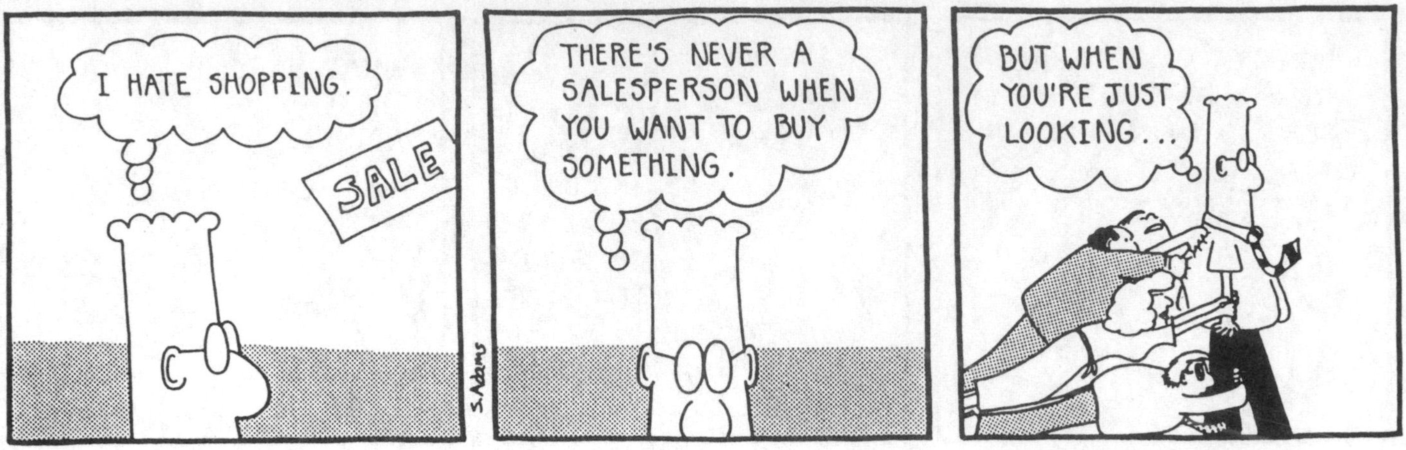
I HATE SHOPPING.
SALE
THERE'S NEVER A SALESPERSON WHEN YOU WANT TO BUY SOMETHING.
S.Adams
BUT WHEN YOU'RE JUST LOOKING...

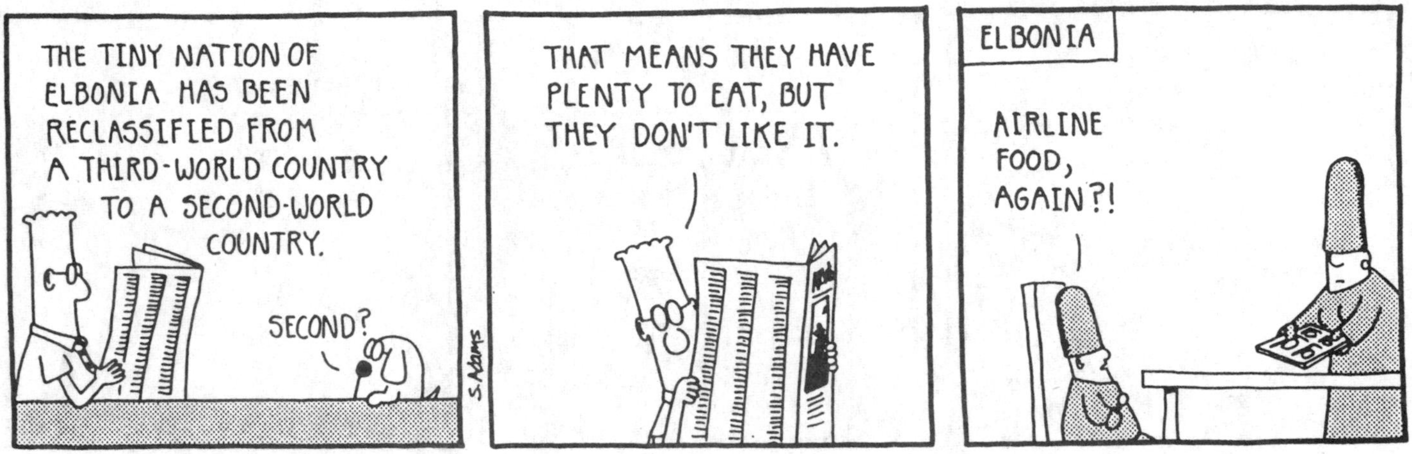
THE TINY NATION OF ELBONIA HAS BEEN RECLASSIFIED FROM A THIRD-WORLD COUNTRY TO A SECOND-WORLD COUNTRY.
SECOND?
S.Adams
THAT MEANS THEY HAVE PLENTY TO EAT, BUT THEY DON'T LIKE IT.
ELBONIA
AIRLINE FOOD, AGAIN?!

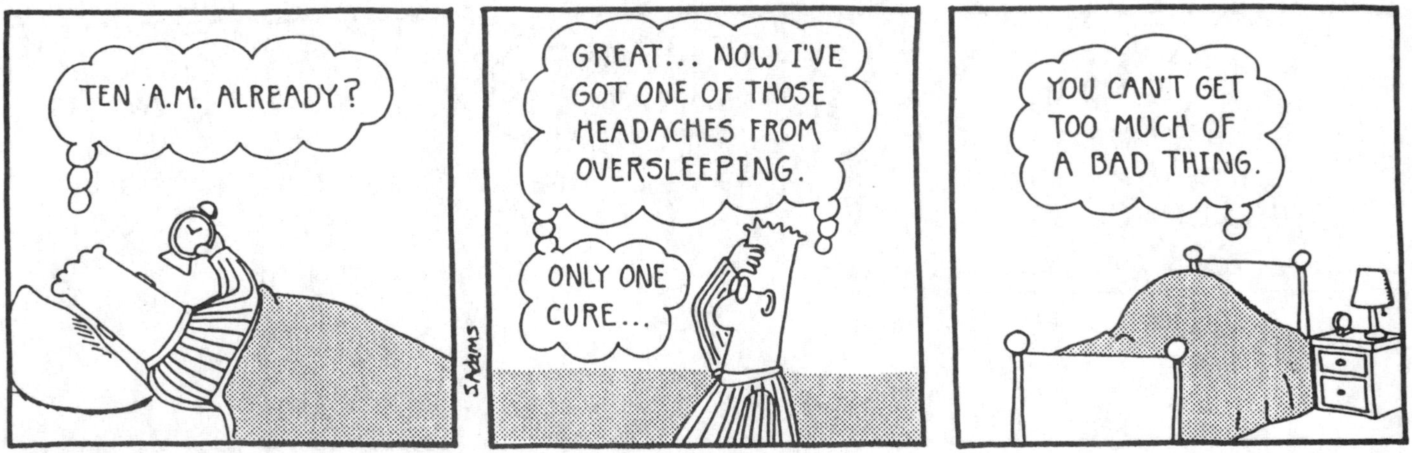
TEN A.M. ALREADY?
S.Adams
GREAT... NOW I'VE GOT ONE OF THOSE HEADACHES FROM OVERSLEEPING.
ONLY ONE CURE...
YOU CAN'T GET TOO MUCH OF A BAD THING.

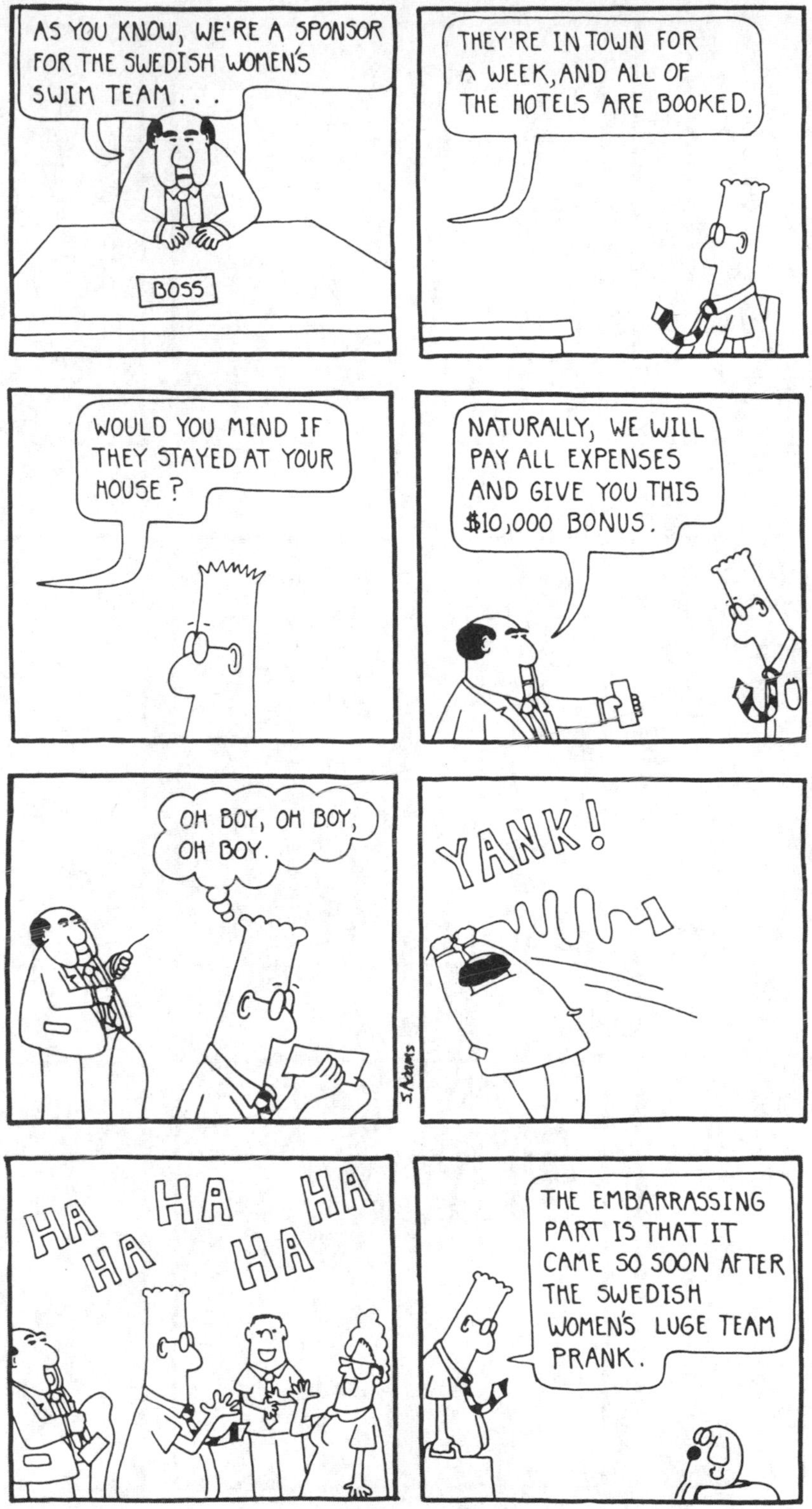
AS YOU KNOW, WE'RE A SPONSOR FOR THE SWEDISH WOMEN'S SWIM TEAM . . .
BOSS
THEY'RE IN TOWN FOR A WEEK, AND ALL OF THE HOTELS ARE BOOKED.
WOULD YOU MIND IF THEY STAYED AT YOUR HOUSE ?
NATURALLY, WE WILL PAY ALL EXPENSES AND GIVE YOU THIS $10,000 BONUS.
OH BOY, OH BOY, OH BOY.
YANK!
HA HA HA HA HA HA
THE EMBARRASSING PART IS THAT IT CAME SO SOON AFTER THE SWEDISH WOMEN'S LUGE TEAM PRANK.

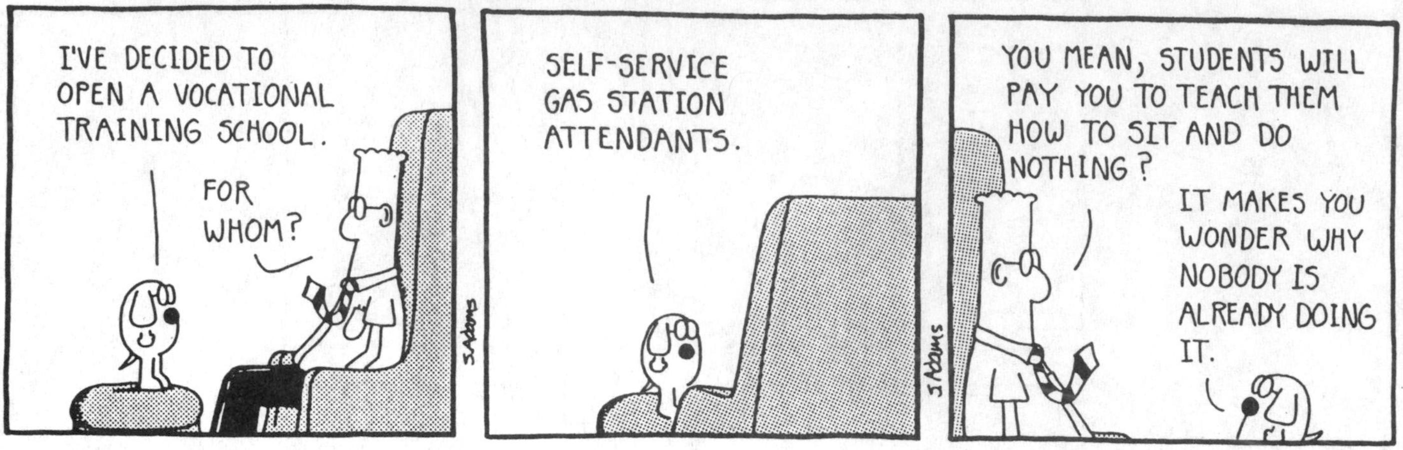
I'VE DECIDED TO OPEN A VOCATIONAL TRAINING SCHOOL.
FOR WHOM?
SELF-SERVICE GAS STATION ATTENDANTS.
YOU MEAN, STUDENTS WILL PAY YOU TO TEACH THEM HOW TO SIT AND DO NOTHING?
IT MAKES YOU WONDER WHY NOBODY IS ALREADY DOING IT.

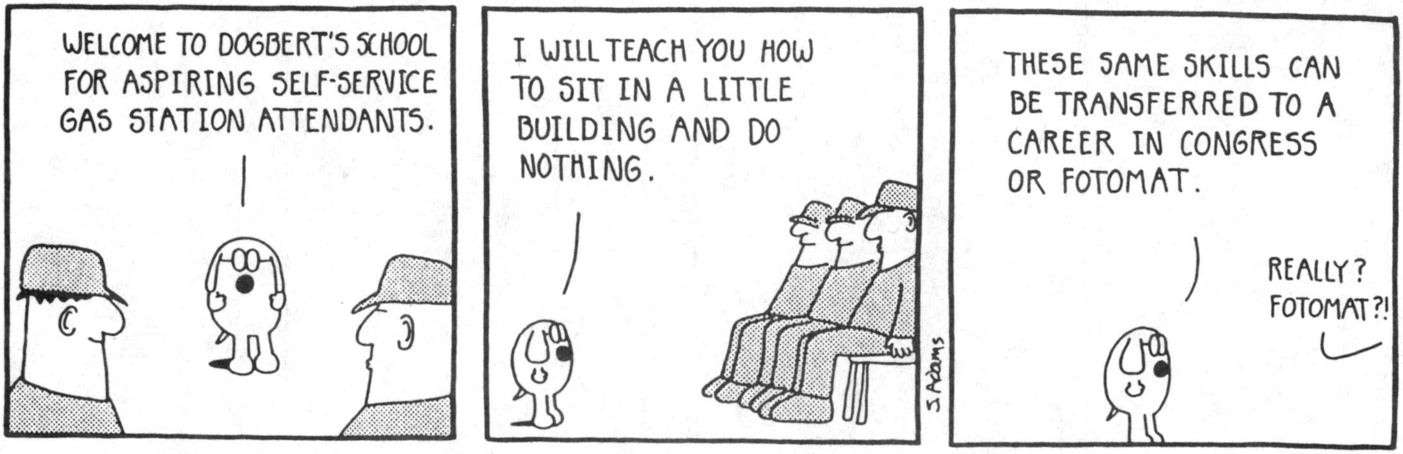
WELCOME TO DOGBERT'S SCHOOL FOR ASPIRING SELF-SERVICE GAS STATION ATTENDANTS.
I WILL TEACH YOU HOW TO SIT IN A LITTLE BUILDING AND DO NOTHING.
THESE SAME SKILLS CAN BE TRANSFERRED TO A CAREER IN CONGRESS OR FOTOMAT.
REALLY? FOTOMAT?!

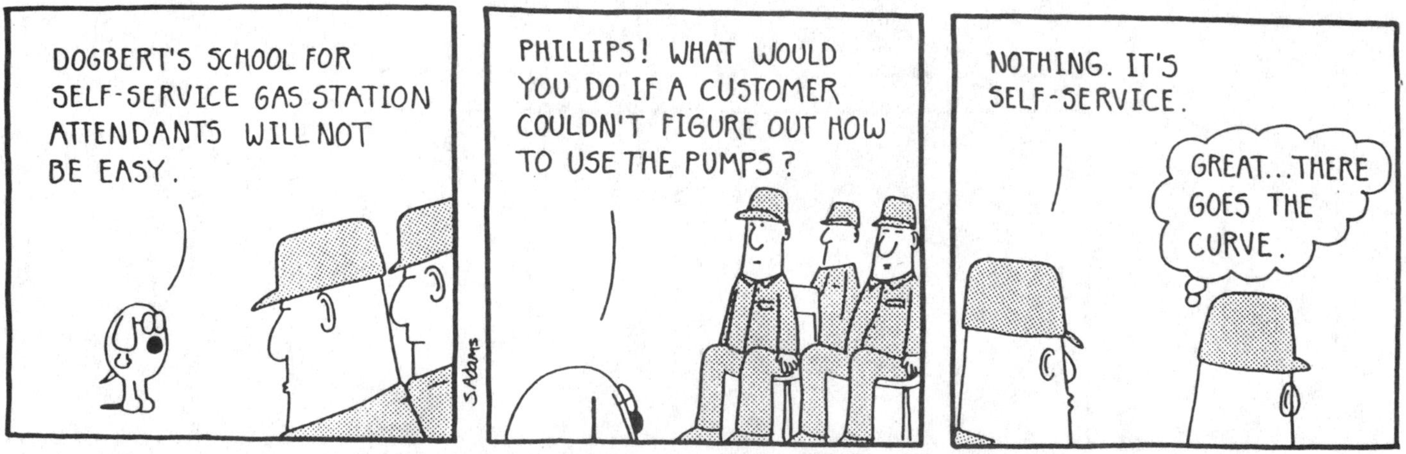
DOGBERT'S SCHOOL FOR SELF-SERVICE GAS STATION ATTENDANTS WILL NOT BE EASY.
PHILLIPS! WHAT WOULD YOU DO IF A CUSTOMER COULDN'T FIGURE OUT HOW TO USE THE PUMPS?
NOTHING. IT'S SELF-SERVICE.
GREAT...THERE GOES THE CURVE.

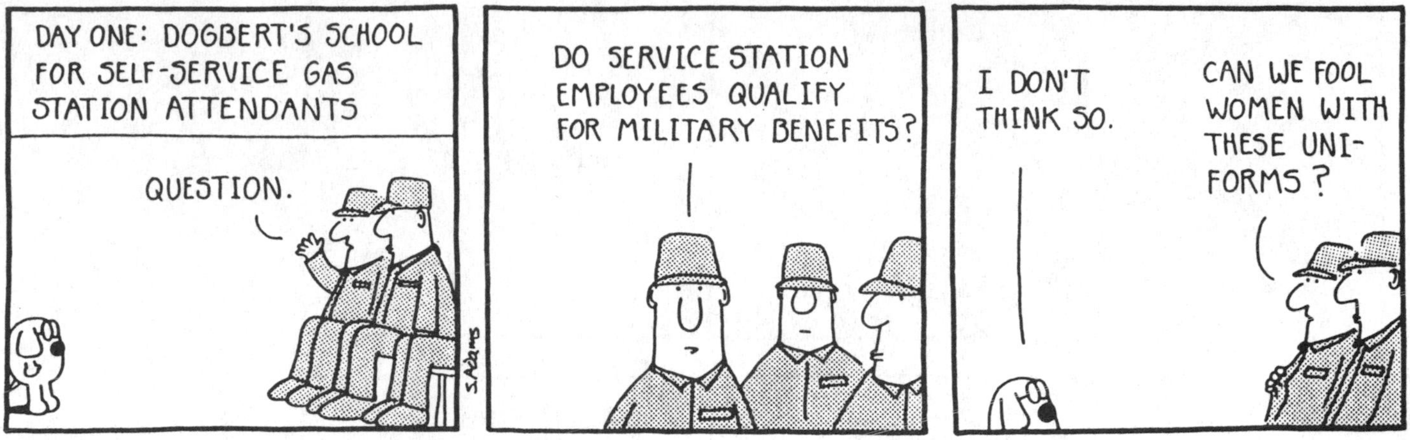
DAY ONE: DOGBERT'S SCHOOL FOR SELF-SERVICE GAS STATION ATTENDANTS
QUESTION.
DO SERVICE STATION EMPLOYEES QUALIFY FOR MILITARY BENEFITS?
I DON'T THINK SO.
CAN WE FOOL WOMEN WITH THESE UNI-FORMS?

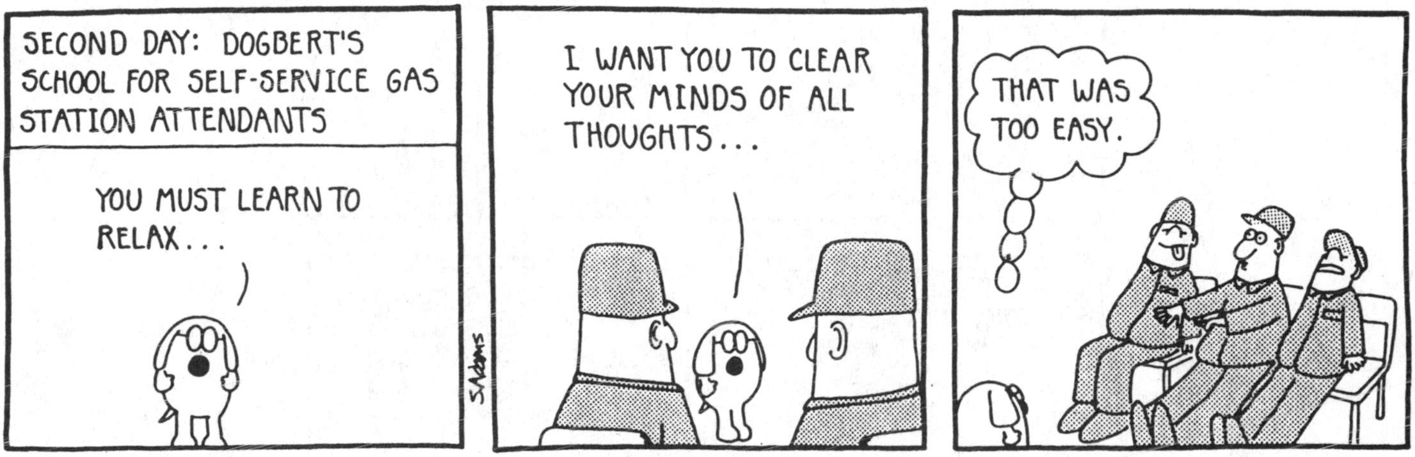
SECOND DAY: DOGBERT'S SCHOOL FOR SELF-SERVICE GAS STATION ATTENDANTS
YOU MUST LEARN TO RELAX...
I WANT YOU TO CLEAR YOUR MINDS OF ALL THOUGHTS...
THAT WAS TOO EASY.

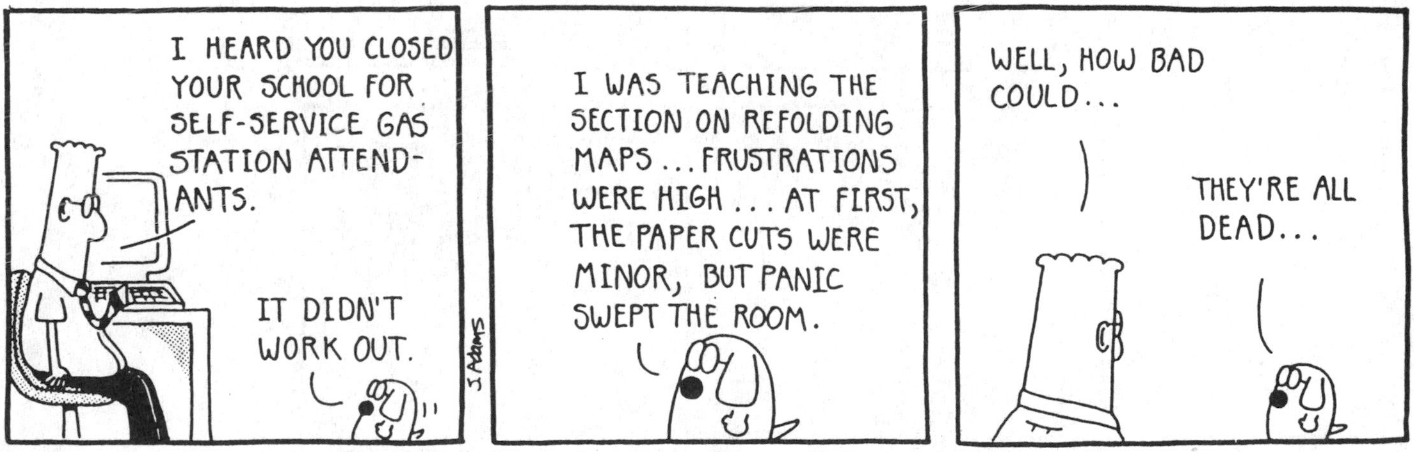
I HEARD YOU CLOSED YOUR SCHOOL FOR SELF-SERVICE GAS STATION ATTEND-ANTS.
IT DIDN'T WORK OUT.
I WAS TEACHING THE SECTION ON REFOLDING MAPS ... FRUSTRATIONS WERE HIGH ... AT FIRST, THE PAPER CUTS WERE MINOR, BUT PANIC SWEPT THE ROOM.
WELL, HOW BAD COULD...
THEY'RE ALL DEAD...

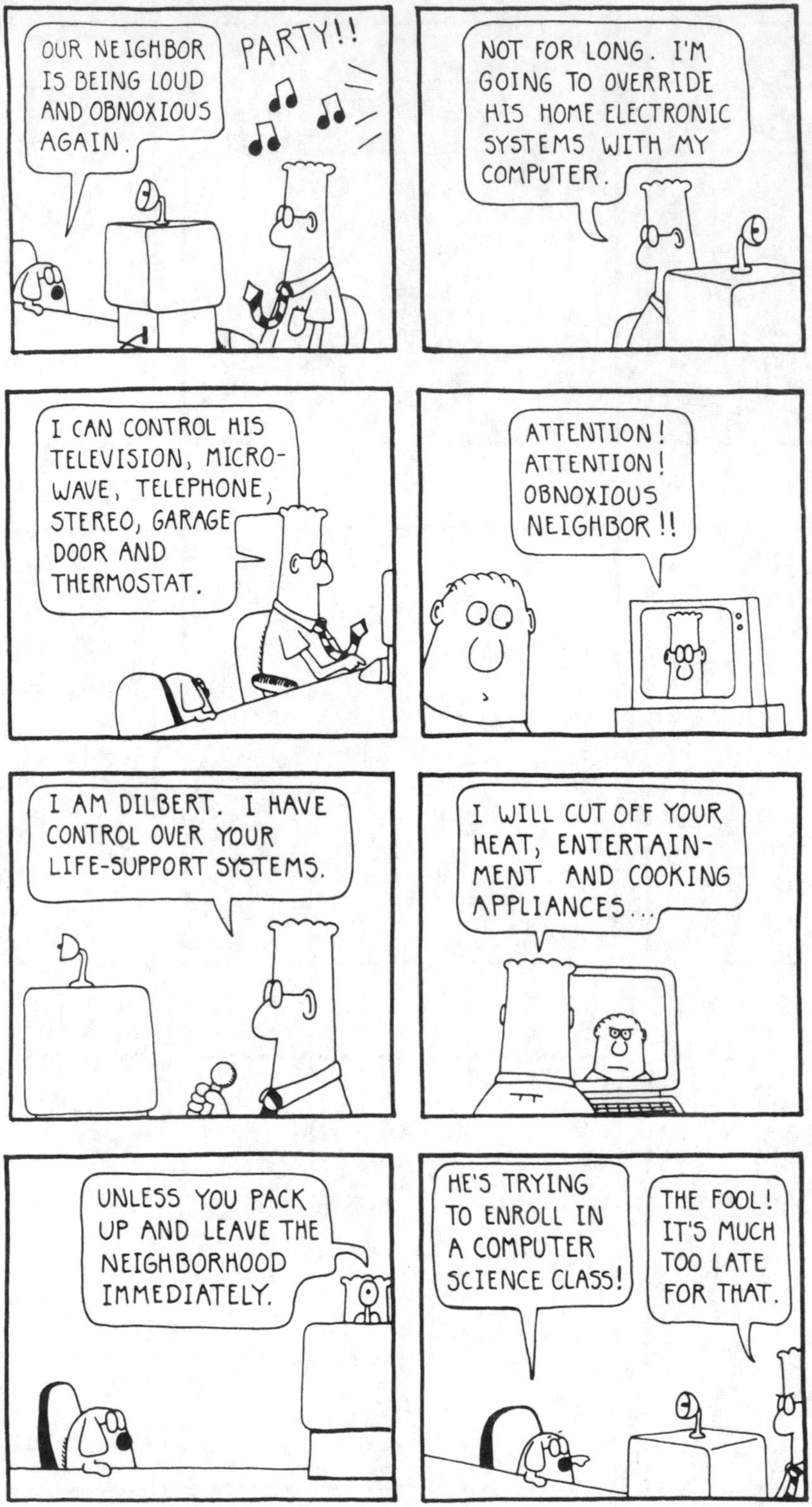
OUR NEIGHBOR IS BEING LOUD AND OBNOXIOUS AGAIN.
PARTY!!
NOT FOR LONG. I'M GOING TO OVERRIDE HIS HOME ELECTRONIC SYSTEMS WITH MY COMPUTER.
I CAN CONTROL HIS TELEVISION, MICRO-WAVE, TELEPHONE, STEREO, GARAGE DOOR AND THERMOSTAT.
ATTENTION! ATTENTION! OBNOXIOUS NEIGHBOR!!
I AM DILBERT. I HAVE CONTROL OVER YOUR LIFE-SUPPORT SYSTEMS.
I WILL CUT OFF YOUR HEAT, ENTERTAIN-MENT AND COOKING APPLIANCES...
UNLESS YOU PACK UP AND LEAVE THE NEIGHBORHOOD IMMEDIATELY.
HE'S TRYING TO ENROLL IN A COMPUTER SCIENCE CLASS!
THE FOOL! IT'S MUCH TOO LATE FOR THAT.

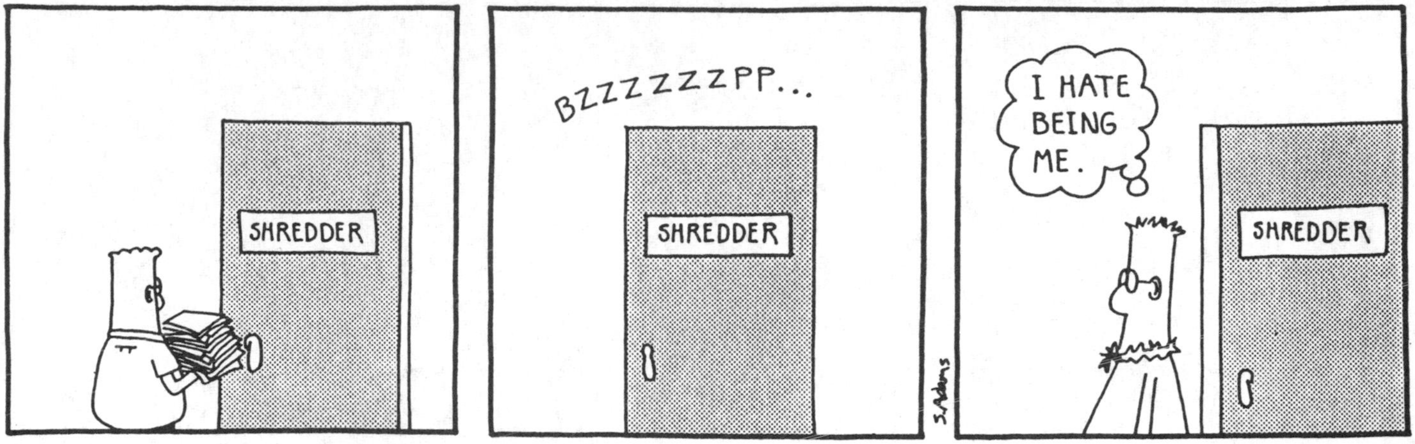
SHREDDER
BZZZZZZPP...
SHREDDER
I HATE BEING ME.
SHREDDER

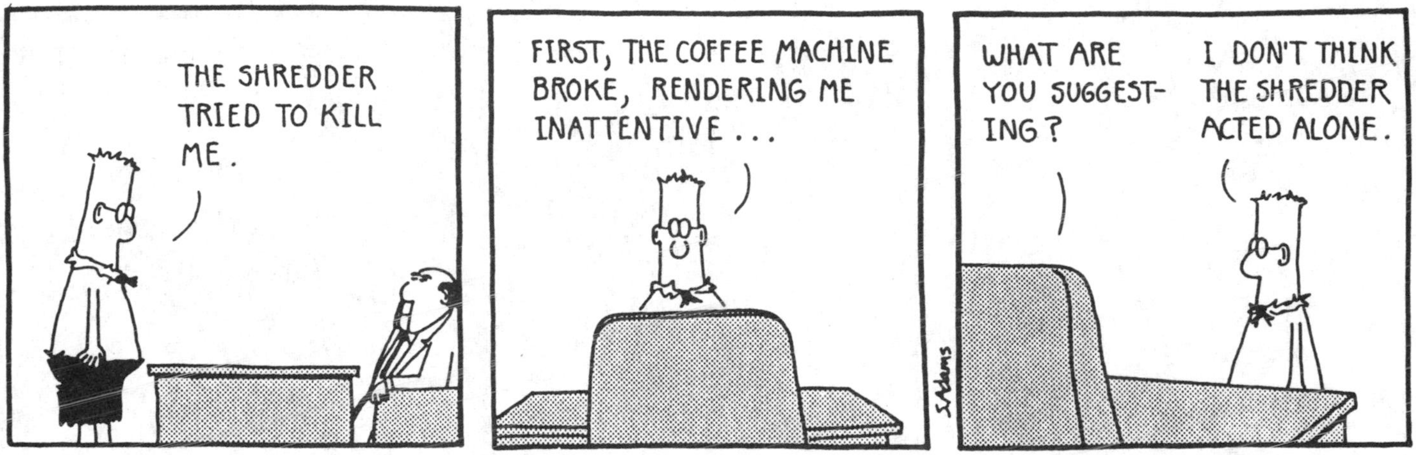
THE SHREDDER TRIED TO KILL ME.
FIRST, THE COFFEE MACHINE BROKE, RENDERING ME INATTENTIVE...
WHAT ARE YOU SUGGESTING?
I DON'T THINK THE SHREDDER ACTED ALONE.

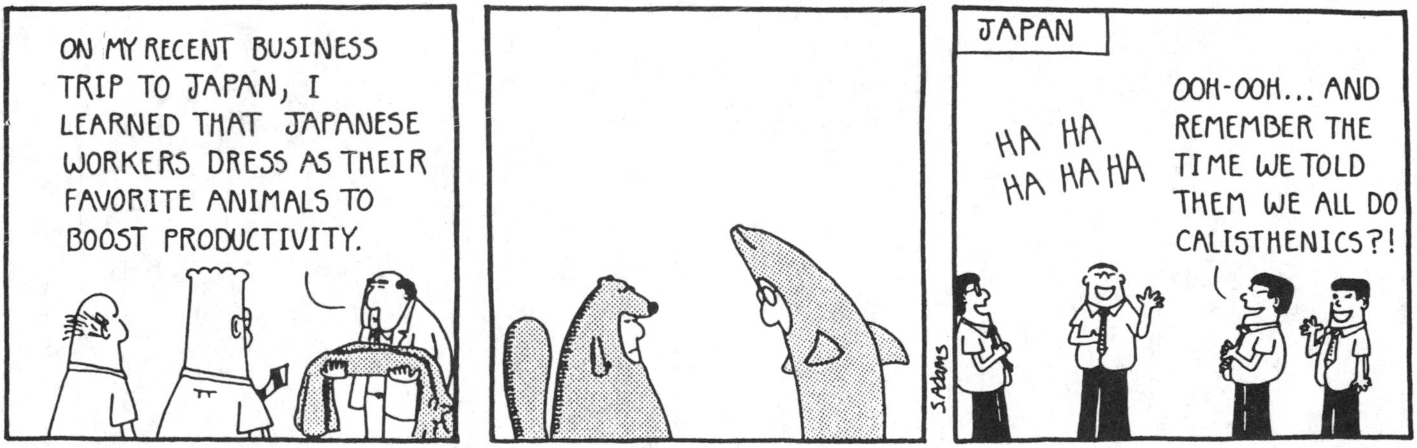
ON MY RECENT BUSINESS TRIP TO JAPAN, I LEARNED THAT JAPANESE WORKERS DRESS AS THEIR FAVORITE ANIMALS TO BOOST PRODUCTIVITY.
JAPAN
HA HA HA HA HA
OOH-OOH... AND REMEMBER THE TIME WE TOLD THEM WE ALL DO CALISTHENICS?!

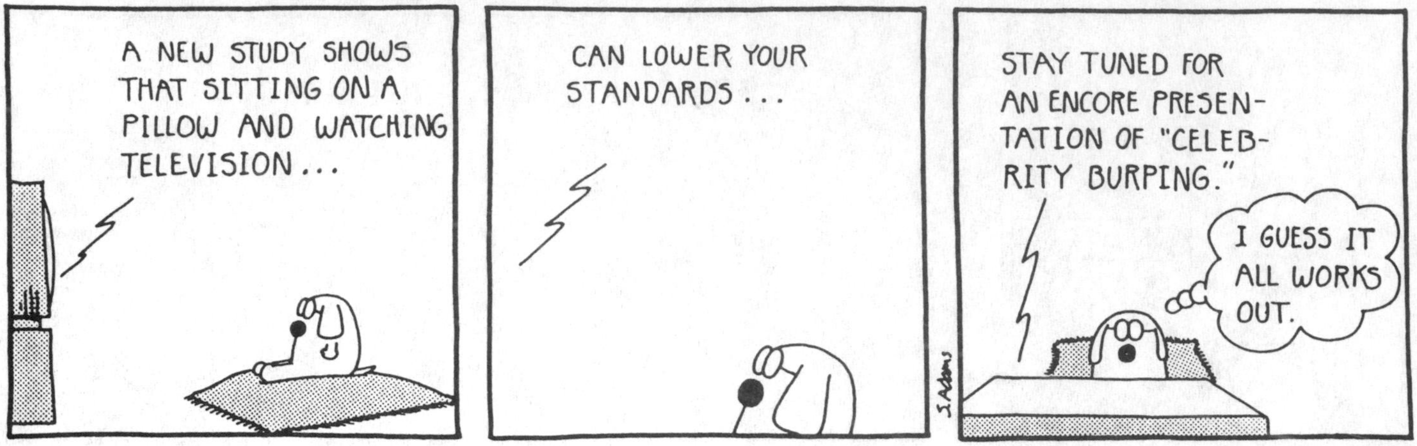
A NEW STUDY SHOWS THAT SITTING ON A PILLOW AND WATCHING TELEVISION ...
CAN LOWER YOUR STANDARDS ...
STAY TUNED FOR AN ENCORE PRESENTATION OF "CELEBRITY BURPING."
I GUESS IT ALL WORKS OUT.

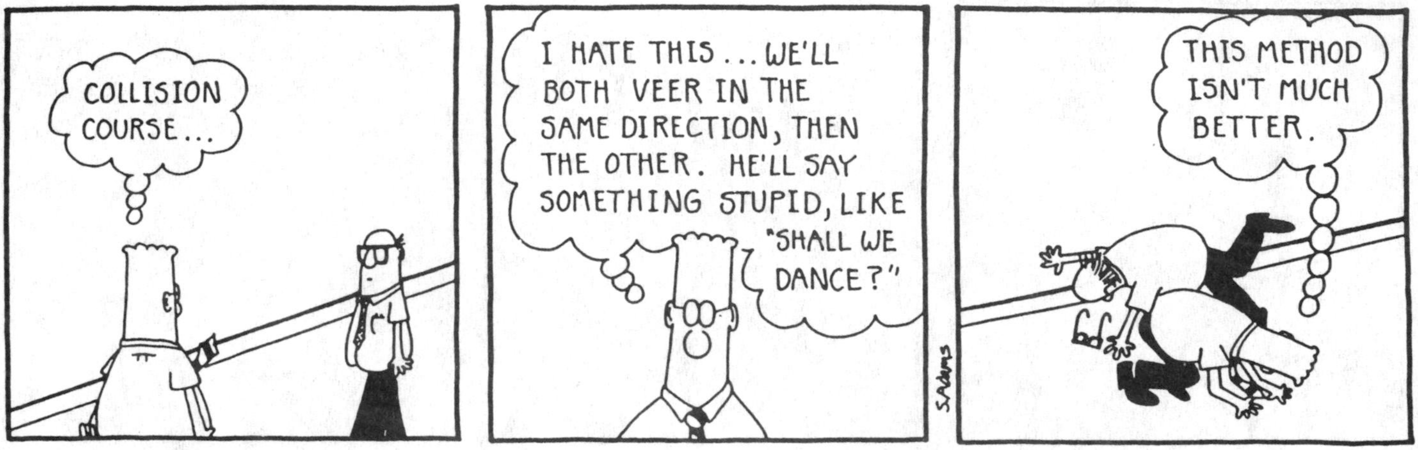
COLLISION COURSE ...
I HATE THIS ... WE'LL BOTH VEER IN THE SAME DIRECTION, THEN THE OTHER. HE'LL SAY SOMETHING STUPID, LIKE "SHALL WE DANCE?"
THIS METHOD ISN'T MUCH BETTER.

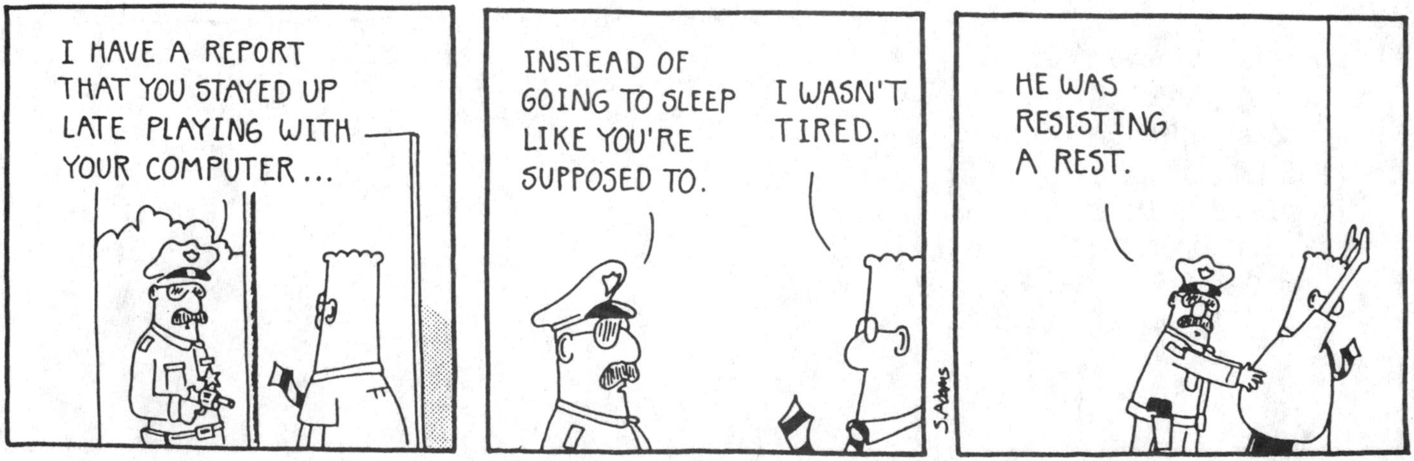
I HAVE A REPORT THAT YOU STAYED UP LATE PLAYING WITH YOUR COMPUTER ...
INSTEAD OF GOING TO SLEEP LIKE YOU'RE SUPPOSED TO.
I WASN'T TIRED.
HE WAS RESISTING A REST.

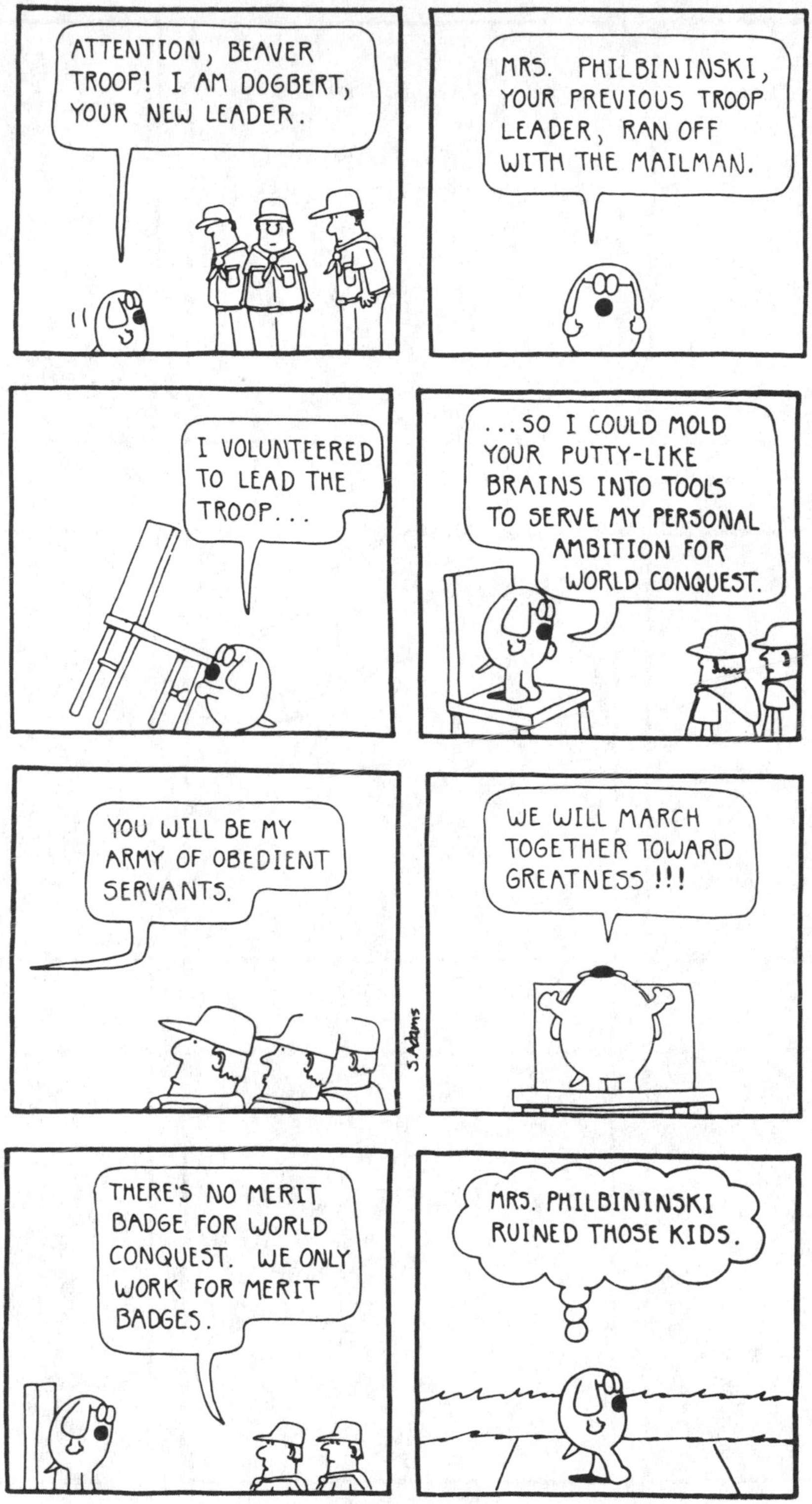
ATTENTION, BEAVER TROOP! I AM DOGBERT, YOUR NEW LEADER.
MRS. PHILBININSKI, YOUR PREVIOUS TROOP LEADER, RAN OFF WITH THE MAILMAN.
I VOLUNTEERED TO LEAD THE TROOP...
...SO I COULD MOLD YOUR PUTTY-LIKE BRAINS INTO TOOLS TO SERVE MY PERSONAL AMBITION FOR WORLD CONQUEST.
YOU WILL BE MY ARMY OF OBEDIENT SERVANTS.
S. Adams
WE WILL MARCH TOGETHER TOWARD GREATNESS!!!
THERE'S NO MERIT BADGE FOR WORLD CONQUEST. WE ONLY WORK FOR MERIT BADGES.
MRS. PHILBININSKI RUINED THOSE KIDS.

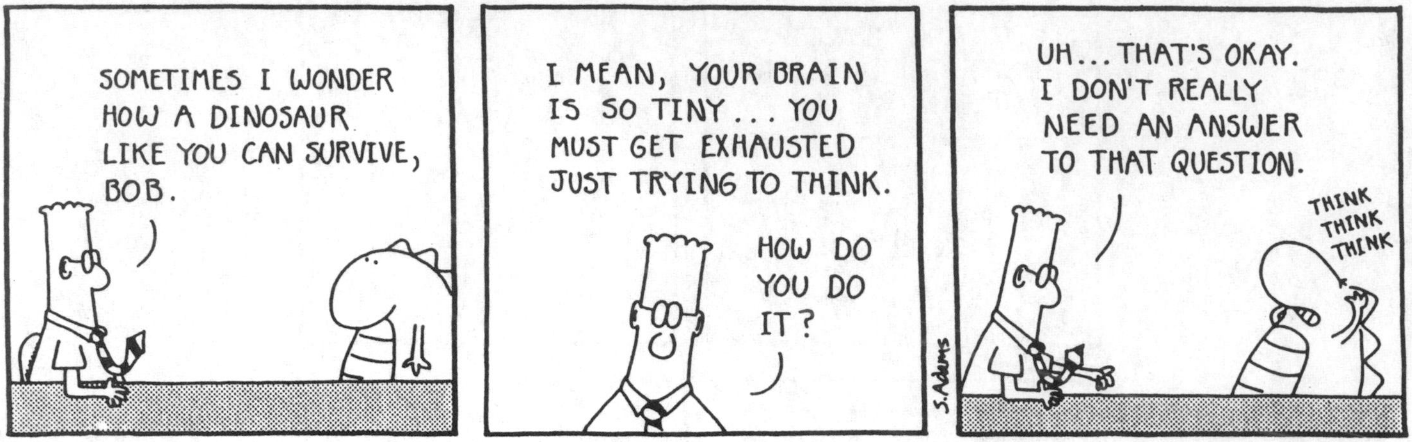
SOMETIMES I WONDER HOW A DINOSAUR LIKE YOU CAN SURVIVE, BOB.
I MEAN, YOUR BRAIN IS SO TINY... YOU MUST GET EXHAUSTED JUST TRYING TO THINK.
HOW DO YOU DO IT?
UH... THAT'S OKAY. I DON'T REALLY NEED AN ANSWER TO THAT QUESTION.
THINK THINK THINK

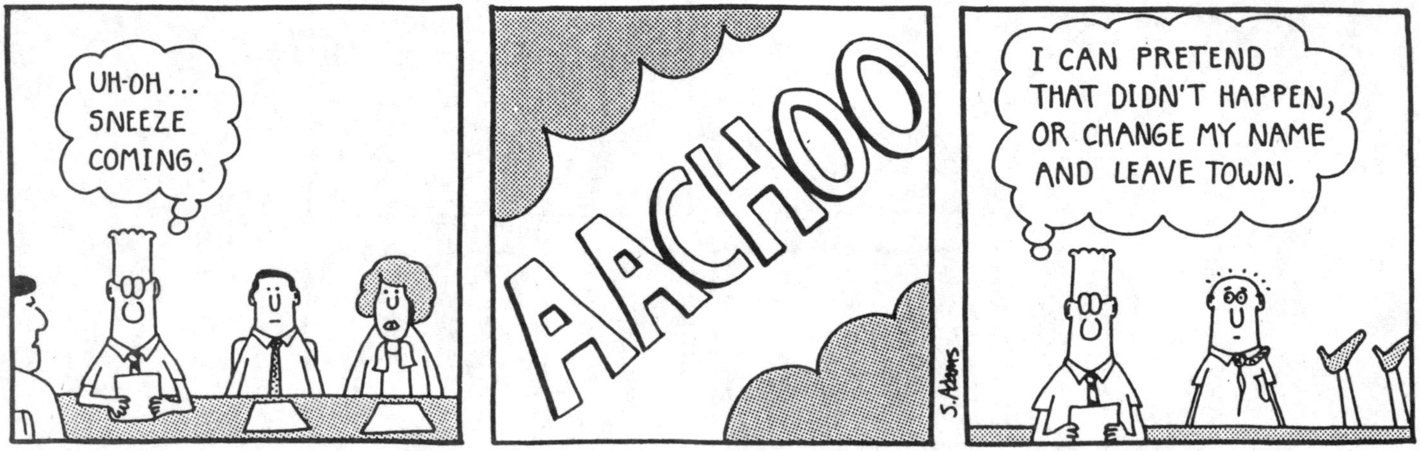
UH-OH... SNEEZE COMING.
AACHOO
I CAN PRETEND THAT DIDN'T HAPPEN, OR CHANGE MY NAME AND LEAVE TOWN.

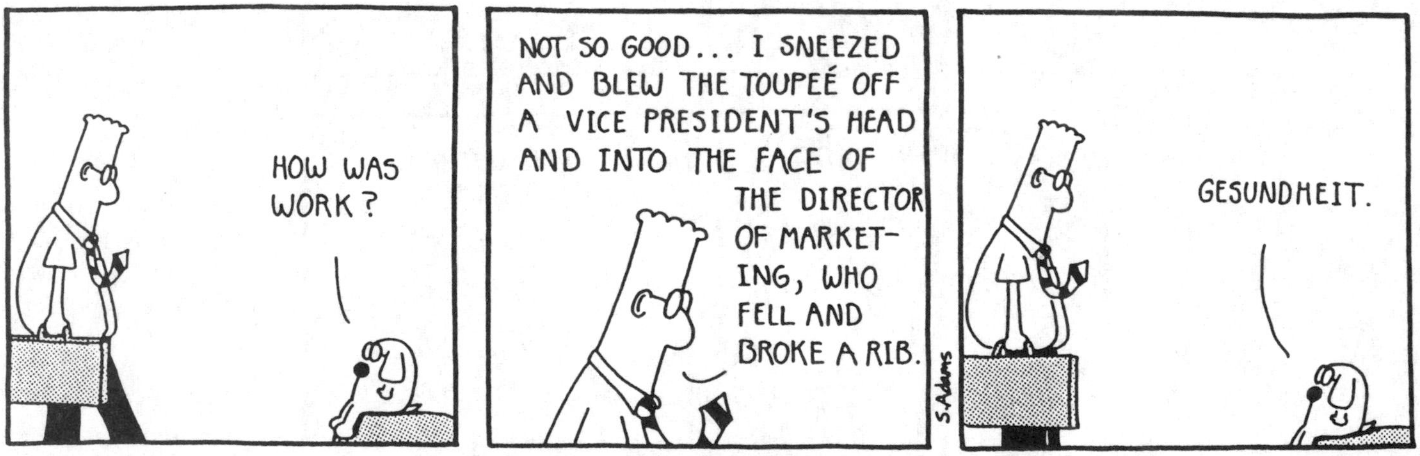
HOW WAS WORK?
NOT SO GOOD... I SNEEZED AND BLEW THE TOUPEÉ OFF A VICE PRESIDENT'S HEAD AND INTO THE FACE OF THE DIRECTOR OF MARKET-ING, WHO FELL AND BROKE A RIB.
GESUNDHEIT.

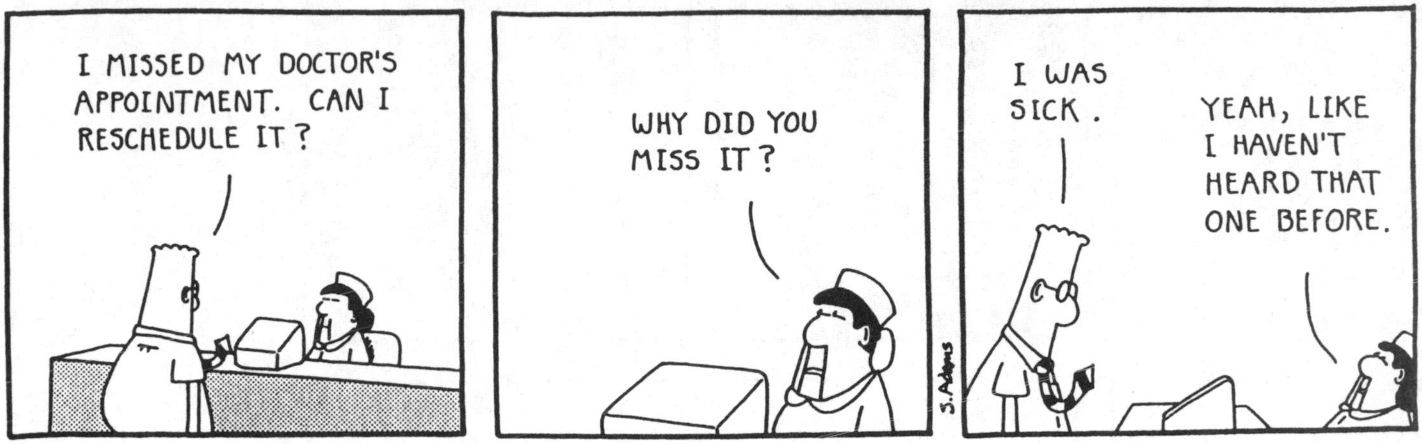
I MISSED MY DOCTOR'S APPOINTMENT. CAN I RESCHEDULE IT?
WHY DID YOU MISS IT?
I WAS SICK.
YEAH, LIKE I HAVEN'T HEARD THAT ONE BEFORE.
S. Adams

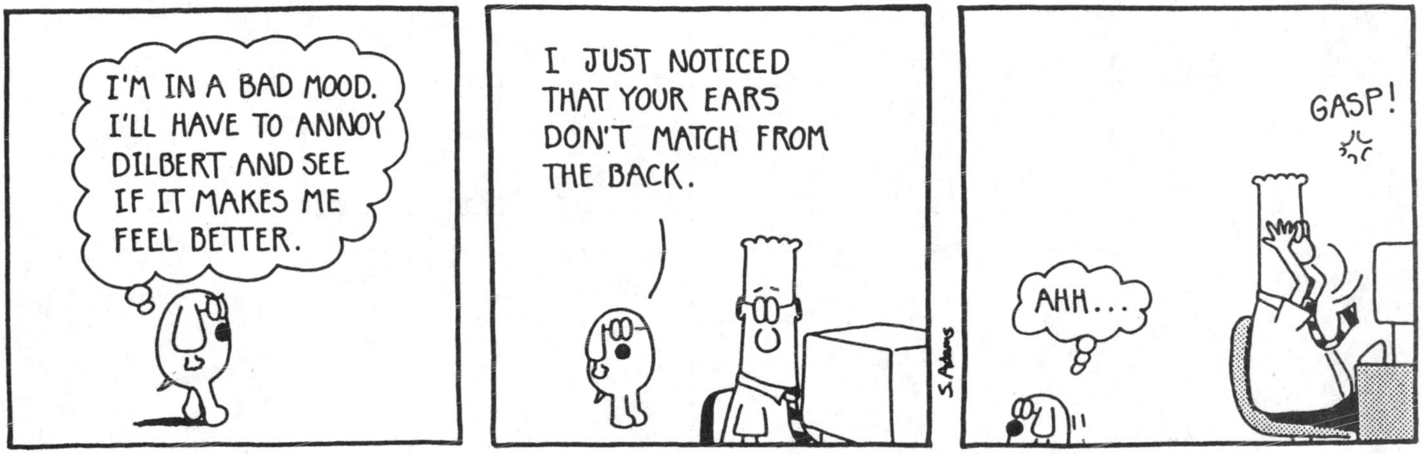
I'M IN A BAD MOOD. I'LL HAVE TO ANNOY DILBERT AND SEE IF IT MAKES ME FEEL BETTER.
I JUST NOTICED THAT YOUR EARS DON'T MATCH FROM THE BACK.
S. Adams
GASP!
AHH...

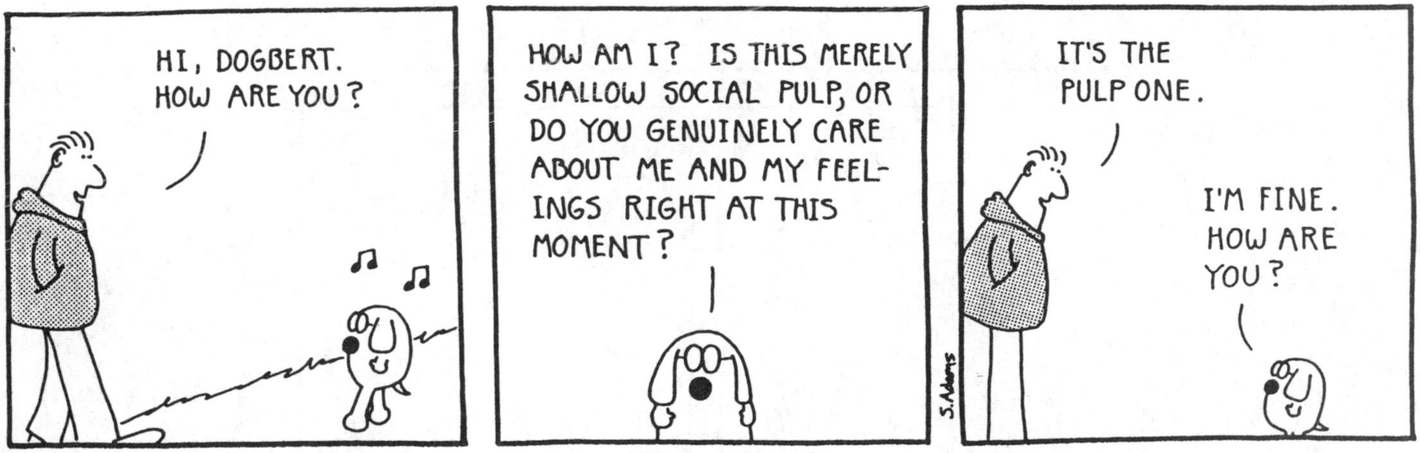
HI, DOGBERT. HOW ARE YOU?
HOW AM I? IS THIS MERELY SHALLOW SOCIAL PULP, OR DO YOU GENUINELY CARE ABOUT ME AND MY FEEL-INGS RIGHT AT THIS MOMENT?
S. Adams
IT'S THE PULP ONE.
I'M FINE. HOW ARE YOU?

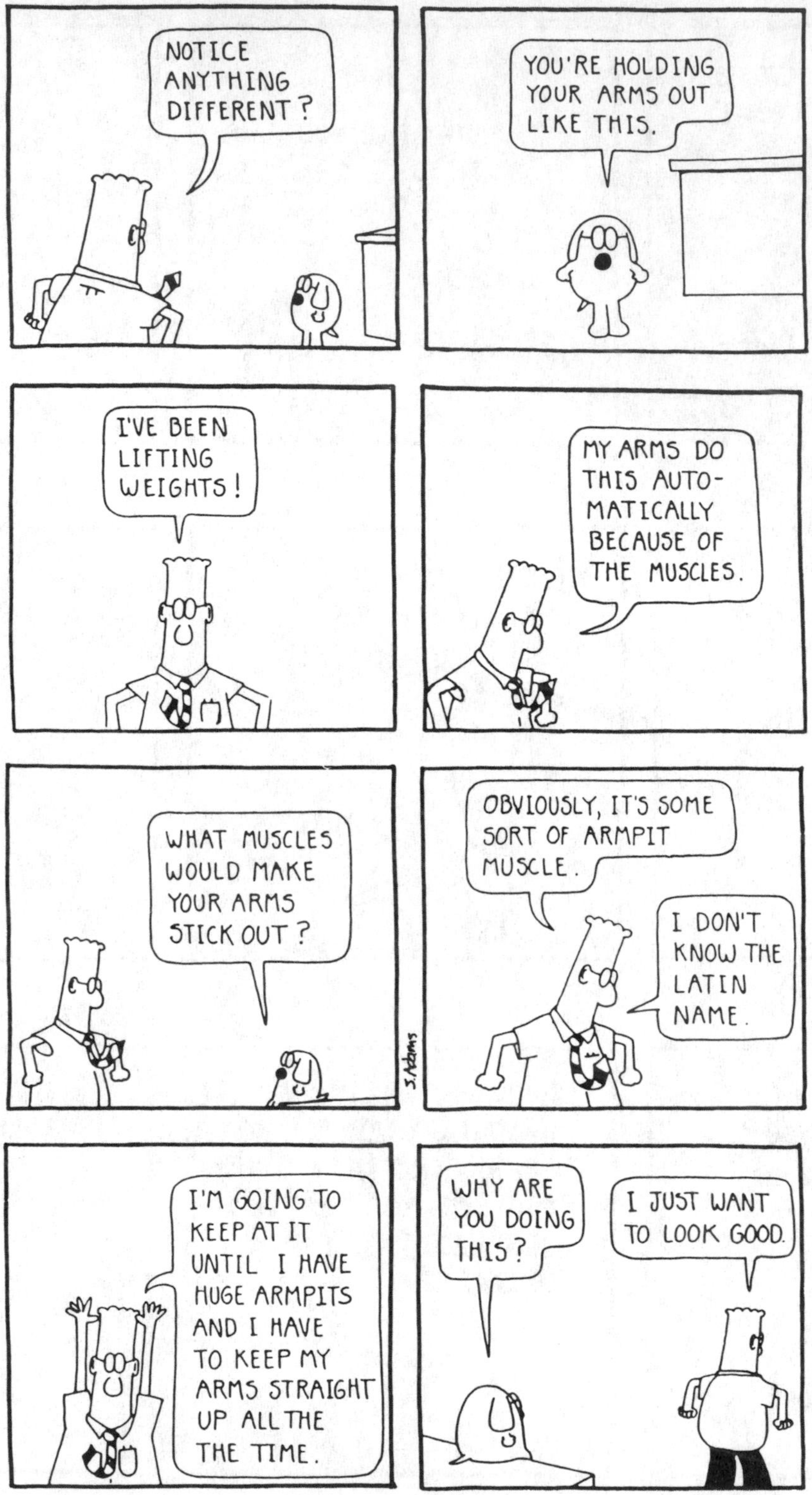
NOTICE ANYTHING DIFFERENT ?
YOU'RE HOLDING YOUR ARMS OUT LIKE THIS.
I'VE BEEN LIFTING WEIGHTS !
MY ARMS DO THIS AUTO-MATICALLY BECAUSE OF THE MUSCLES.
WHAT MUSCLES WOULD MAKE YOUR ARMS STICK OUT ?
S. Adams
OBVIOUSLY, IT'S SOME SORT OF ARMPIT MUSCLE.
I DON'T KNOW THE LATIN NAME.
I'M GOING TO KEEP AT IT UNTIL I HAVE HUGE ARMPITS AND I HAVE TO KEEP MY ARMS STRAIGHT UP ALL THE TIME.
WHY ARE YOU DOING THIS ?
I JUST WANT TO LOOK GOOD.

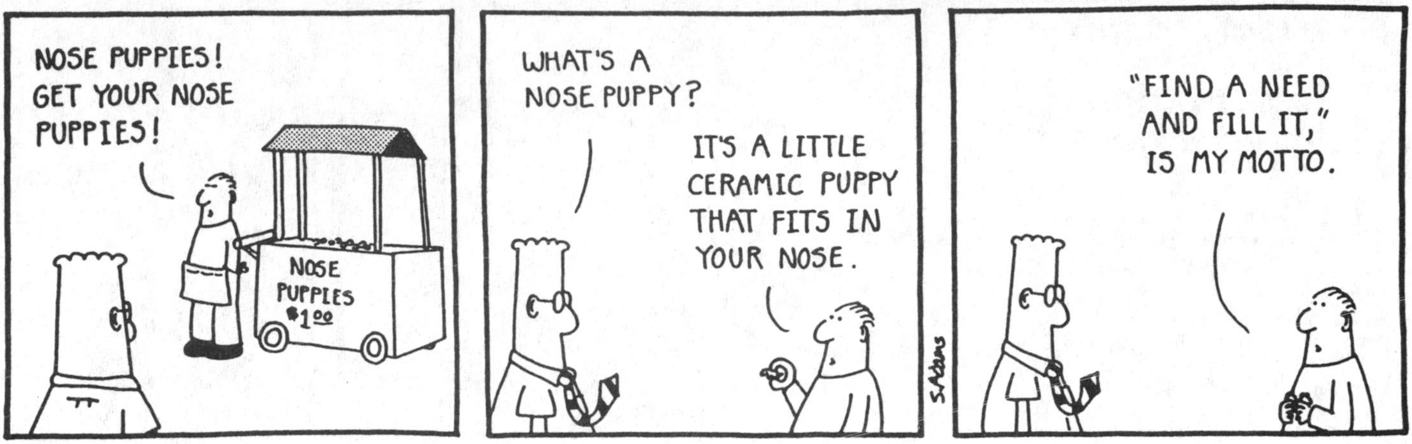
NOSE PUPPIES! GET YOUR NOSE PUPPIES!
NOSE PUPPIES $1.00
WHAT'S A NOSE PUPPY?
IT'S A LITTLE CERAMIC PUPPY THAT FITS IN YOUR NOSE.
"FIND A NEED AND FILL IT," IS MY MOTTO.

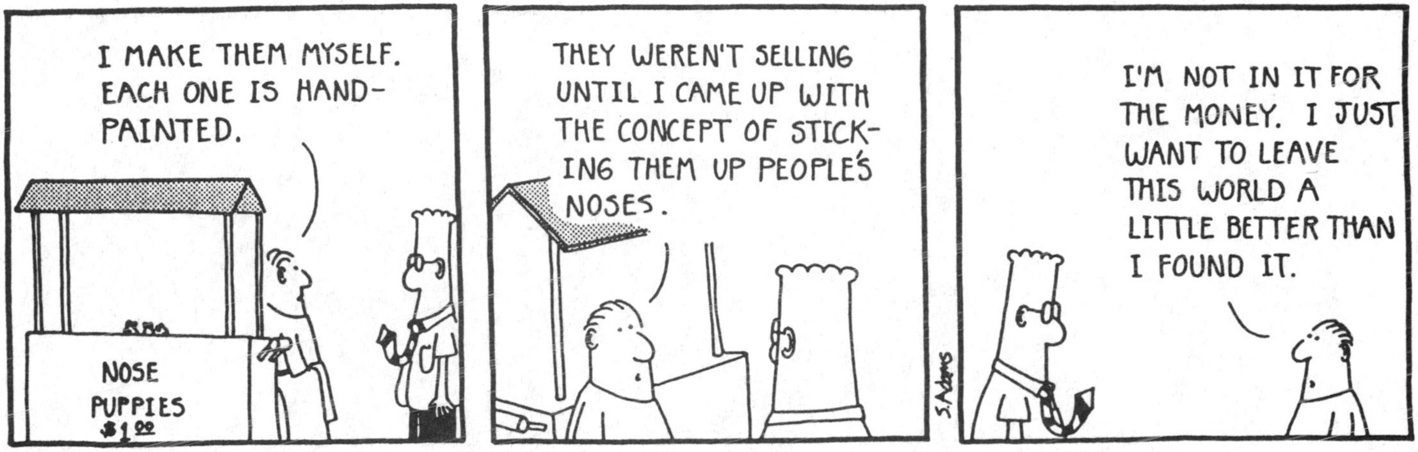
I MAKE THEM MYSELF. EACH ONE IS HAND-PAINTED.
NOSE PUPPIES $1.00
THEY WEREN'T SELLING UNTIL I CAME UP WITH THE CONCEPT OF STICKING THEM UP PEOPLE'S NOSES.
I'M NOT IN IT FOR THE MONEY. I JUST WANT TO LEAVE THIS WORLD A LITTLE BETTER THAN I FOUND IT.

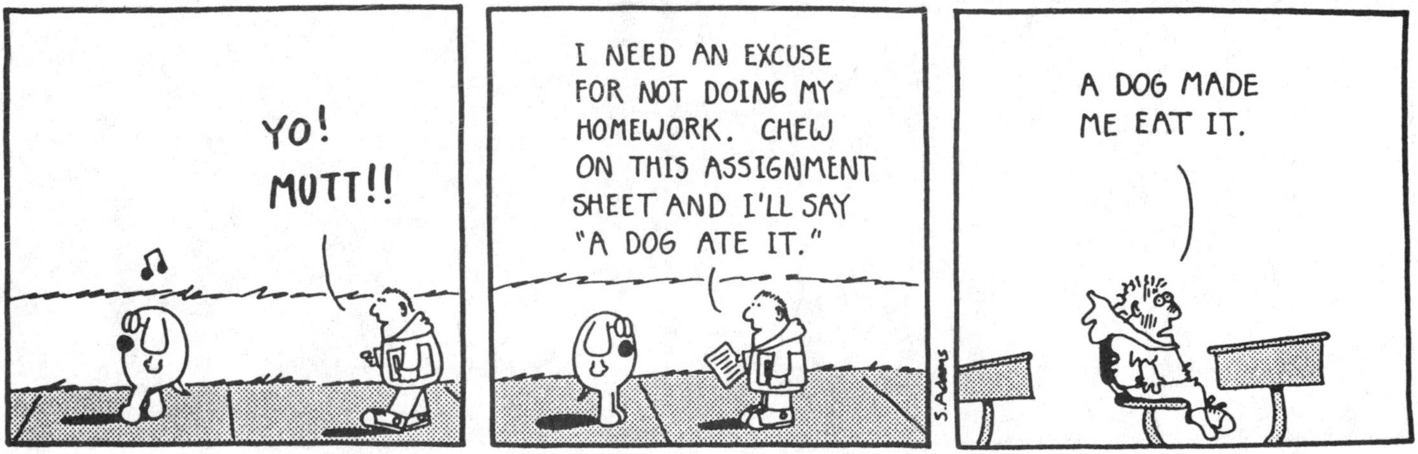
YO! MUTT!!
I NEED AN EXCUSE FOR NOT DOING MY HOMEWORK. CHEW ON THIS ASSIGNMENT SHEET AND I'LL SAY "A DOG ATE IT."
A DOG MADE ME EAT IT.

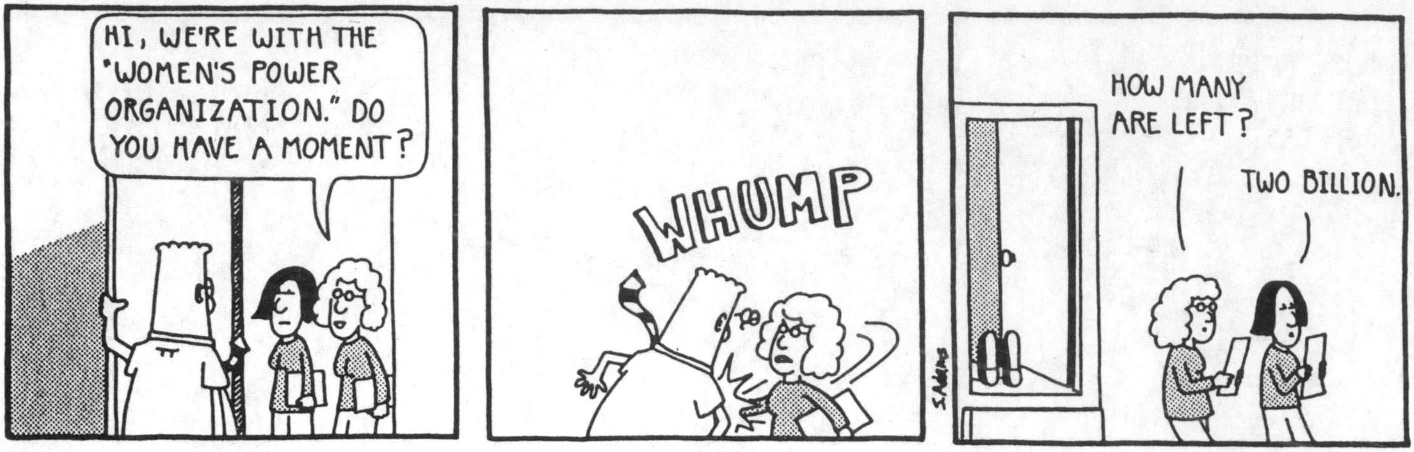
HI, WE'RE WITH THE "WOMEN'S POWER ORGANIZATION." DO YOU HAVE A MOMENT?
WHUMP
HOW MANY ARE LEFT?
TWO BILLION.
S. Adams

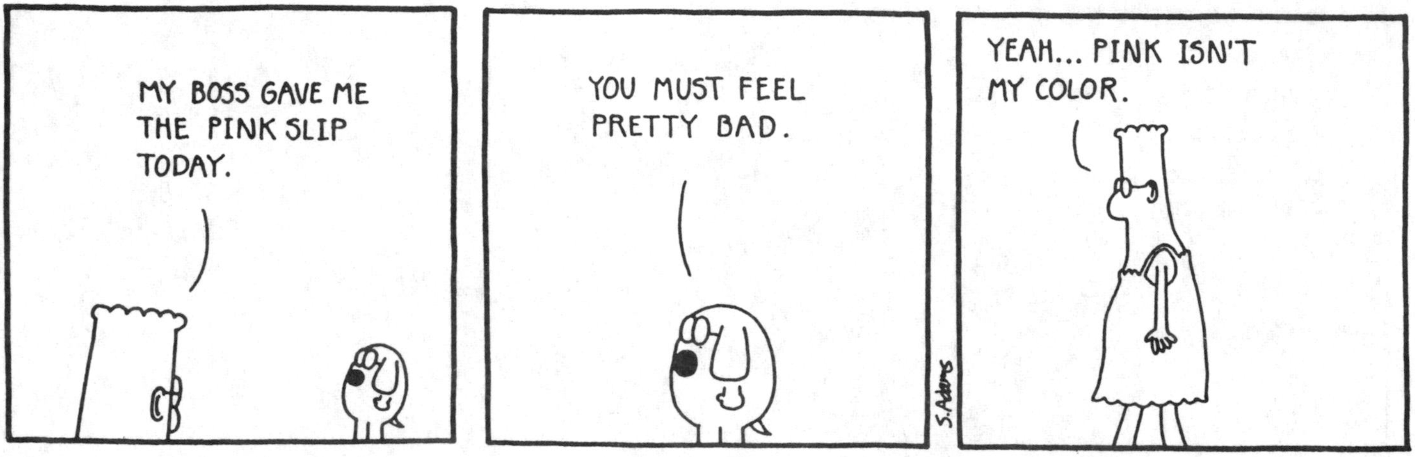
MY BOSS GAVE ME THE PINK SLIP TODAY.
YOU MUST FEEL PRETTY BAD.
YEAH... PINK ISN'T MY COLOR.
S. Adams

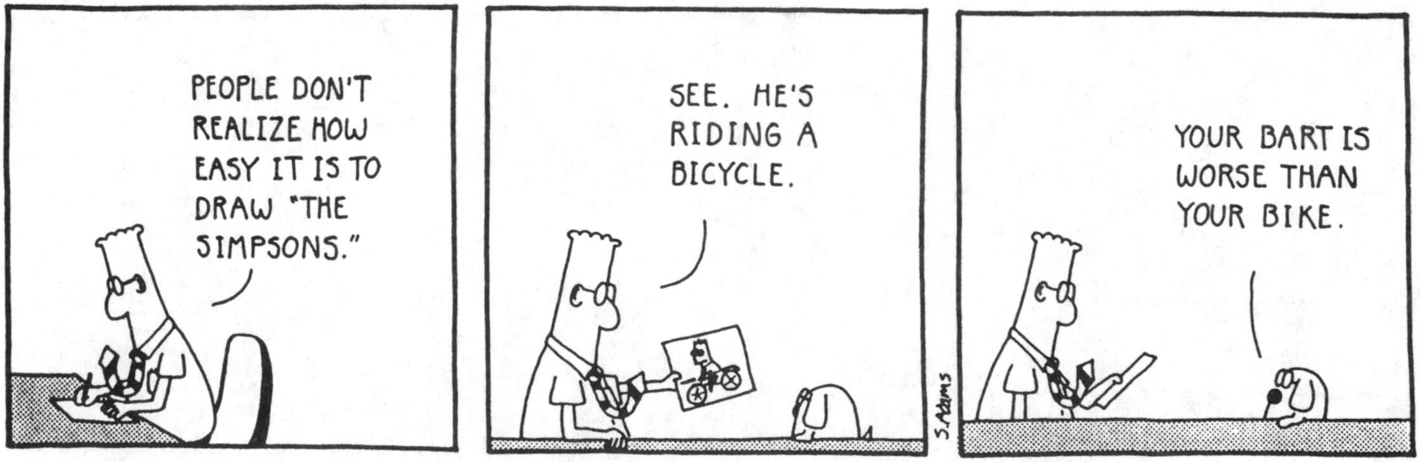
PEOPLE DON'T REALIZE HOW EASY IT IS TO DRAW "THE SIMPSONS."
SEE. HE'S RIDING A BICYCLE.
YOUR BART IS WORSE THAN YOUR BIKE.
S. Adams

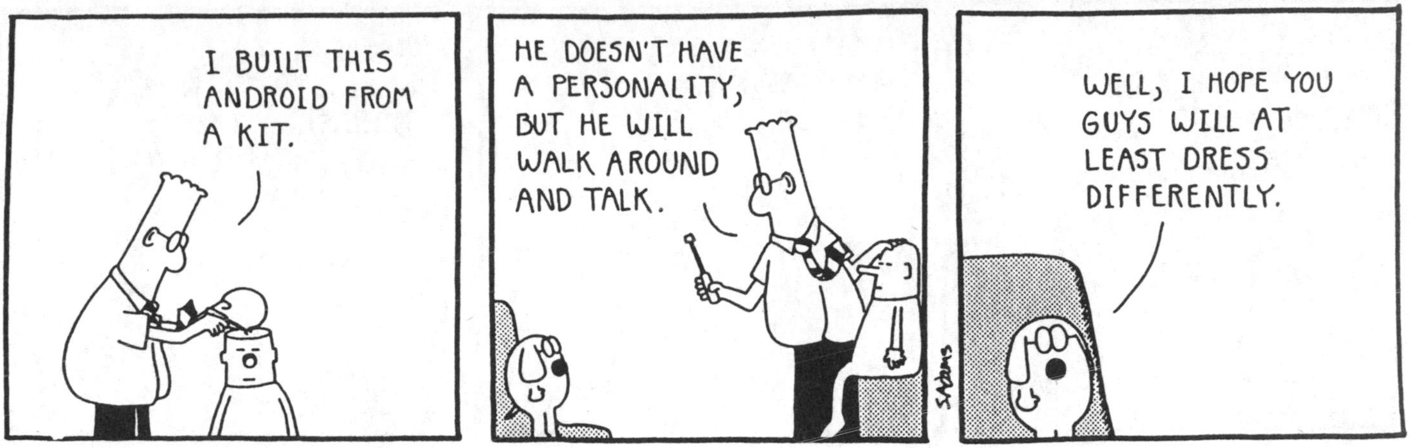
I BUILT THIS ANDROID FROM A KIT.
HE DOESN'T HAVE A PERSONALITY, BUT HE WILL WALK AROUND AND TALK.
WELL, I HOPE YOU GUYS WILL AT LEAST DRESS DIFFERENTLY.

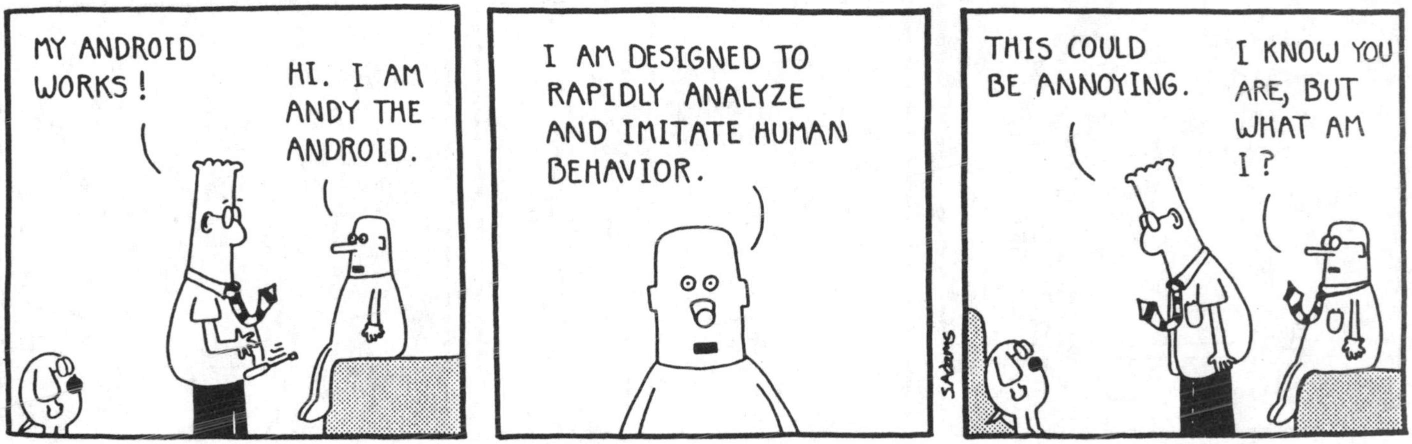
MY ANDROID WORKS!
HI. I AM ANDY THE ANDROID.
I AM DESIGNED TO RAPIDLY ANALYZE AND IMITATE HUMAN BEHAVIOR.
THIS COULD BE ANNOYING.
I KNOW YOU ARE, BUT WHAT AM I?

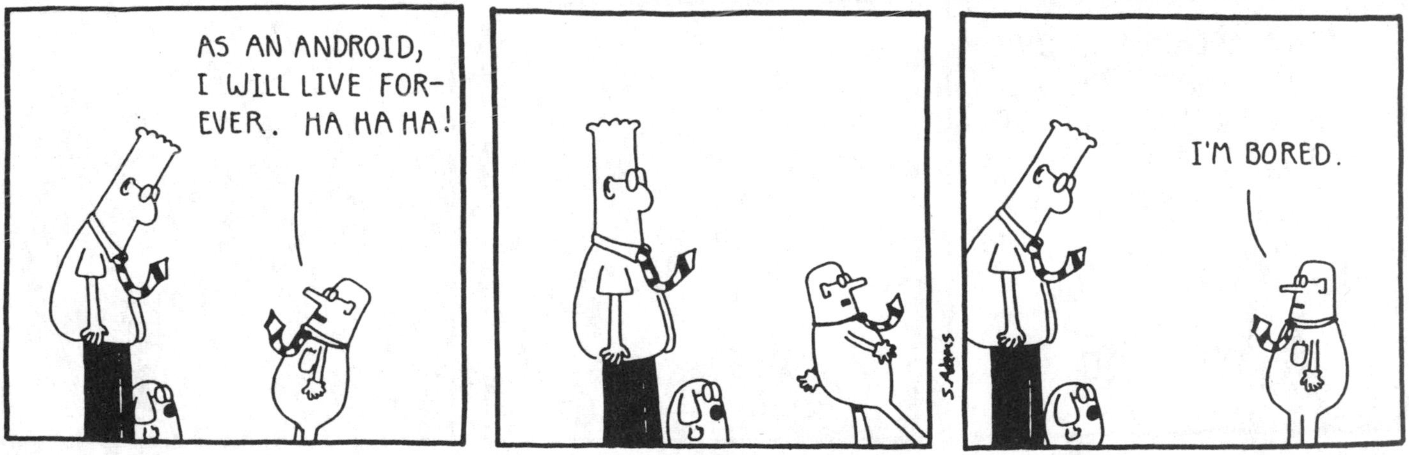
AS AN ANDROID, I WILL LIVE FOREVER. HA HA HA!
I'M BORED.

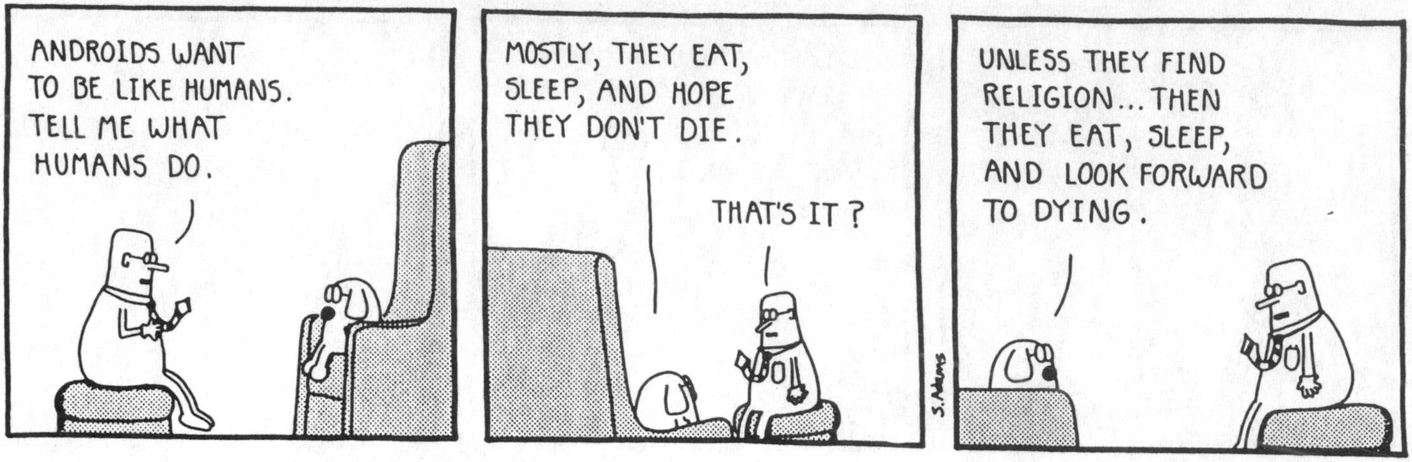
ANDROIDS WANT TO BE LIKE HUMANS. TELL ME WHAT HUMANS DO.
MOSTLY, THEY EAT, SLEEP, AND HOPE THEY DON'T DIE.
THAT'S IT?
UNLESS THEY FIND RELIGION... THEN THEY EAT, SLEEP, AND LOOK FORWARD TO DYING.
S. Adams

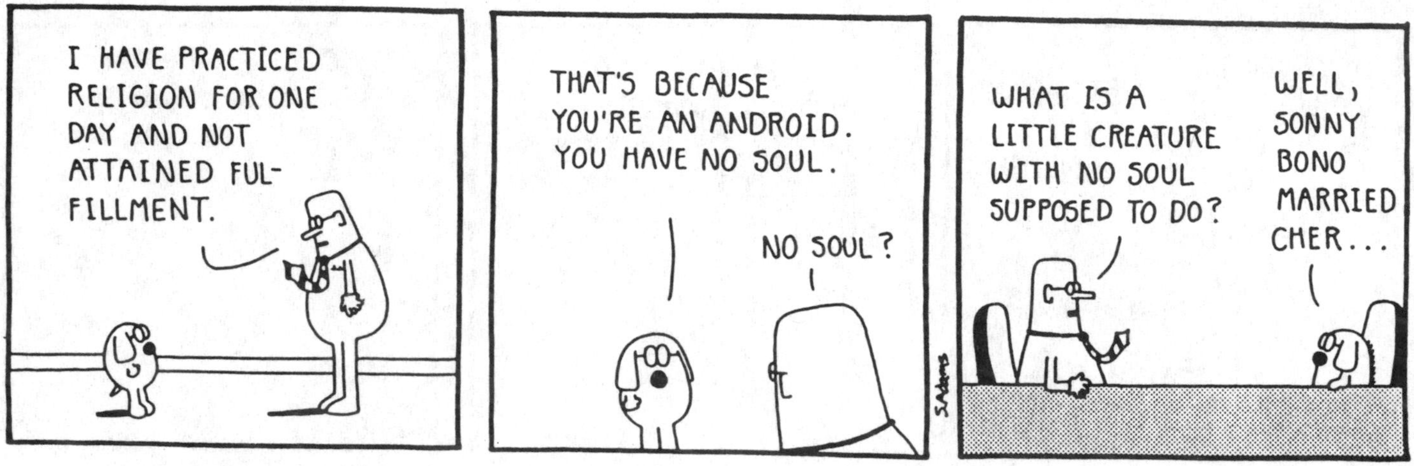
I HAVE PRACTICED RELIGION FOR ONE DAY AND NOT ATTAINED FUL-FILLMENT.
THAT'S BECAUSE YOU'RE AN ANDROID. YOU HAVE NO SOUL.
NO SOUL?
WHAT IS A LITTLE CREATURE WITH NO SOUL SUPPOSED TO DO?
WELL, SONNY BONO MARRIED CHER...
S. Adams

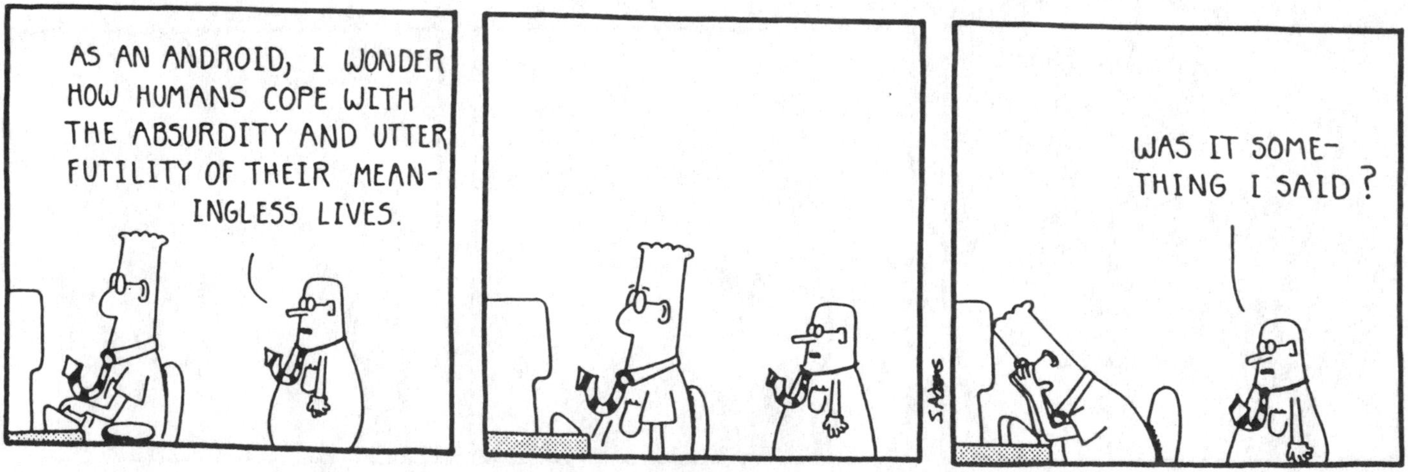
AS AN ANDROID, I WONDER HOW HUMANS COPE WITH THE ABSURDITY AND UTTER FUTILITY OF THEIR MEAN-INGLESS LIVES.
WAS IT SOME-THING I SAID?
S. Adams

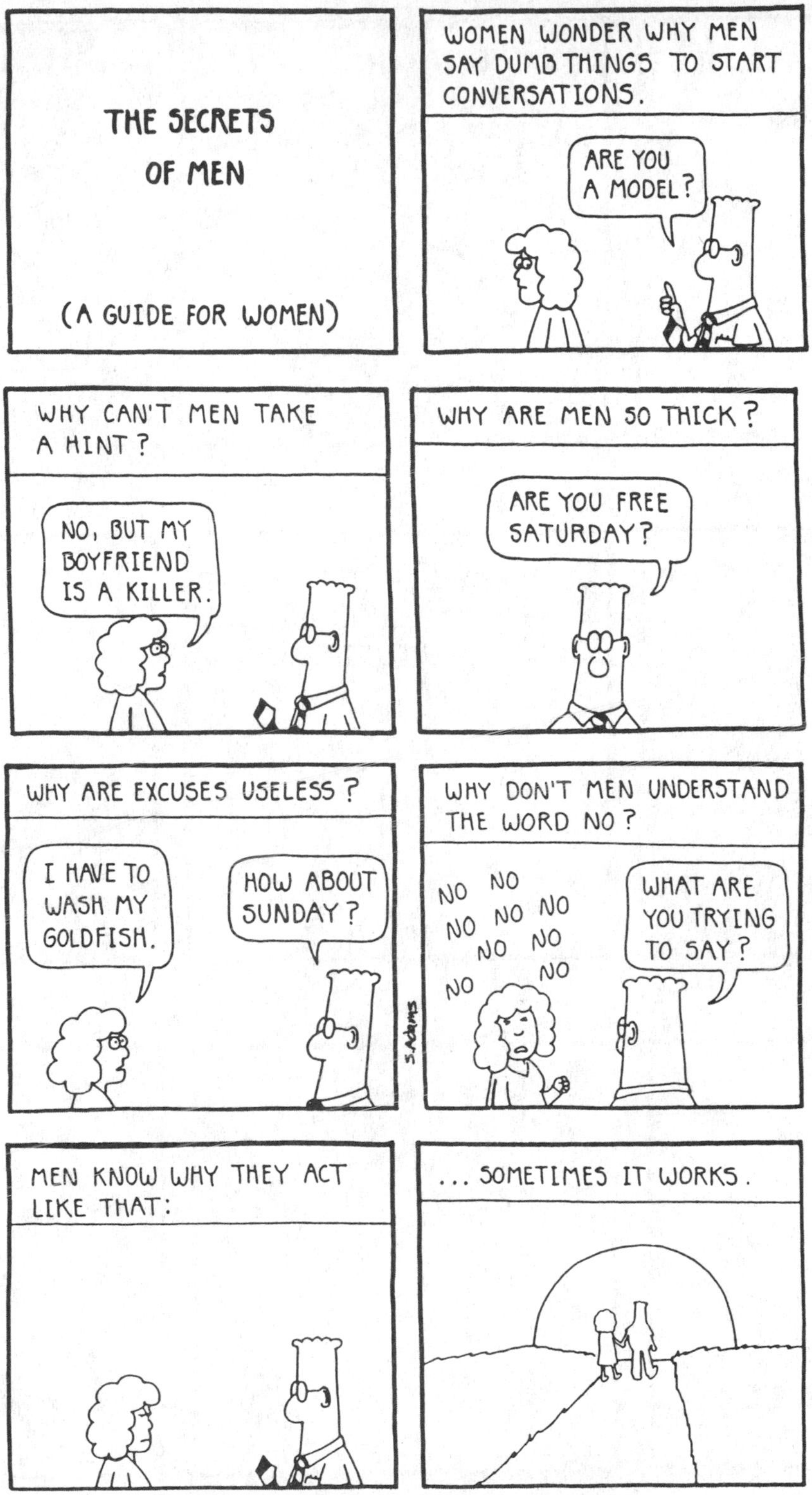
THE SECRETS OF MEN
(A GUIDE FOR WOMEN)
WOMEN WONDER WHY MEN SAY DUMB THINGS TO START CONVERSATIONS.
ARE YOU A MODEL?
WHY CAN'T MEN TAKE A HINT?
NO, BUT MY BOYFRIEND IS A KILLER.
WHY ARE MEN SO THICK?
ARE YOU FREE SATURDAY?
WHY ARE EXCUSES USELESS?
I HAVE TO WASH MY GOLDFISH.
HOW ABOUT SUNDAY?
S.Adams
WHY DON'T MEN UNDERSTAND THE WORD NO?
NO NO NO NO NO NO NO NO NO NO
WHAT ARE YOU TRYING TO SAY?
MEN KNOW WHY THEY ACT LIKE THAT:
... SOMETIMES IT WORKS.

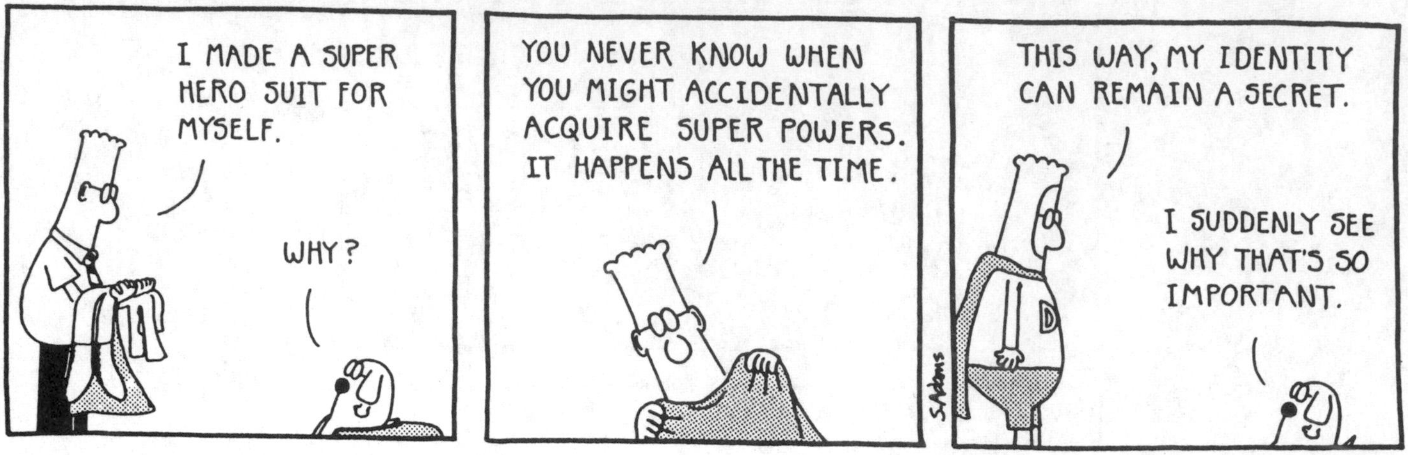
I MADE A SUPER HERO SUIT FOR MYSELF.
WHY?
YOU NEVER KNOW WHEN YOU MIGHT ACCIDENTALLY ACQUIRE SUPER POWERS. IT HAPPENS ALL THE TIME.
THIS WAY, MY IDENTITY CAN REMAIN A SECRET.
I SUDDENLY SEE WHY THAT'S SO IMPORTANT.

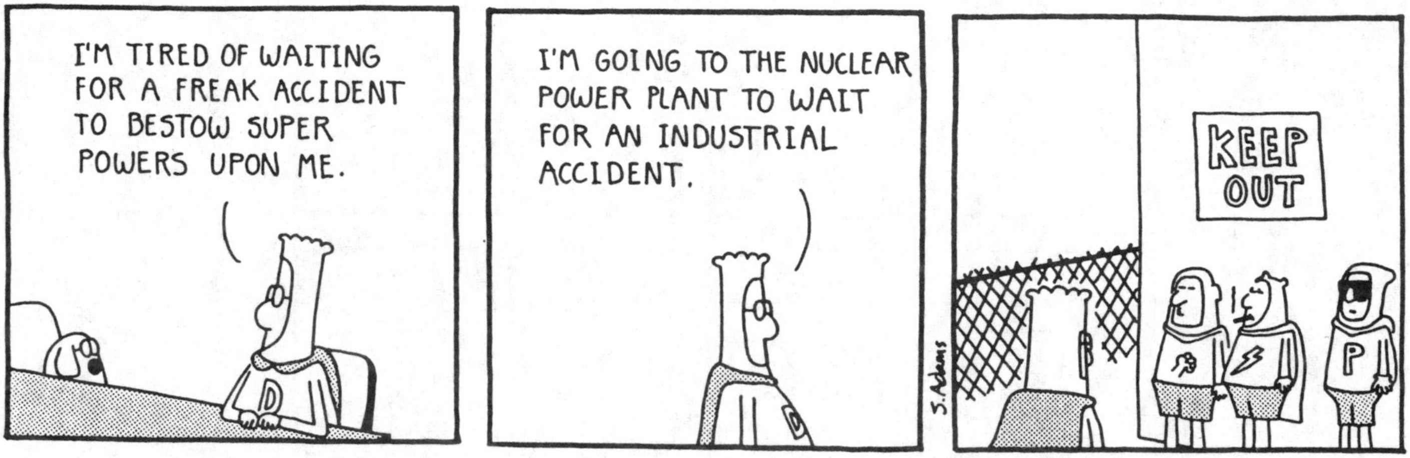
I'M TIRED OF WAITING FOR A FREAK ACCIDENT TO BESTOW SUPER POWERS UPON ME.
I'M GOING TO THE NUCLEAR POWER PLANT TO WAIT FOR AN INDUSTRIAL ACCIDENT.
KEEP OUT

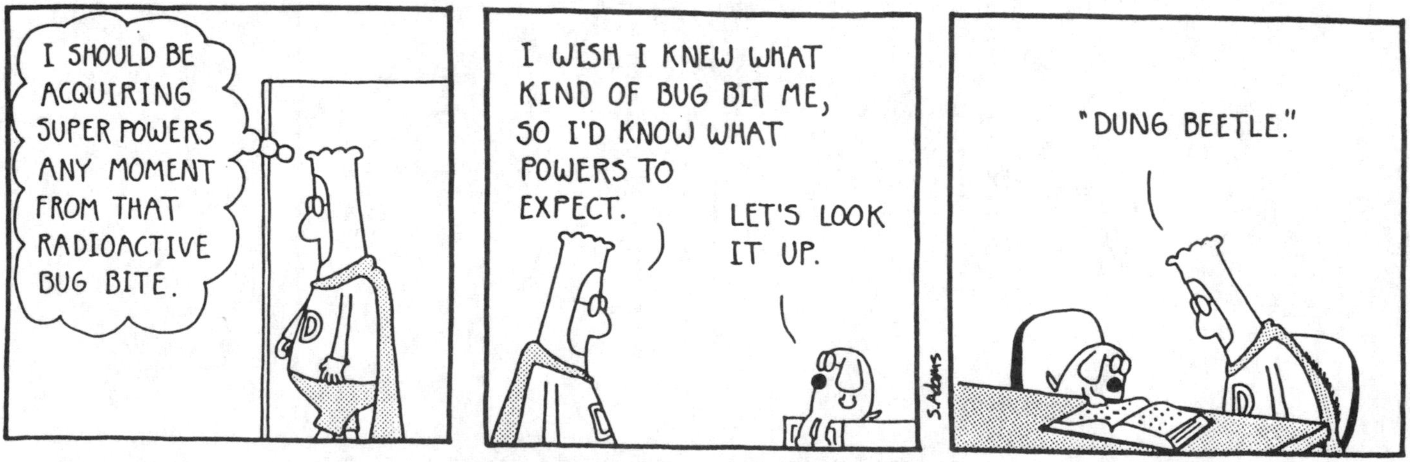
I SHOULD BE ACQUIRING SUPER POWERS ANY MOMENT FROM THAT RADIOACTIVE BUG BITE.
I WISH I KNEW WHAT KIND OF BUG BIT ME, SO I'D KNOW WHAT POWERS TO EXPECT.
LET'S LOOK IT UP.
"DUNG BEETLE."

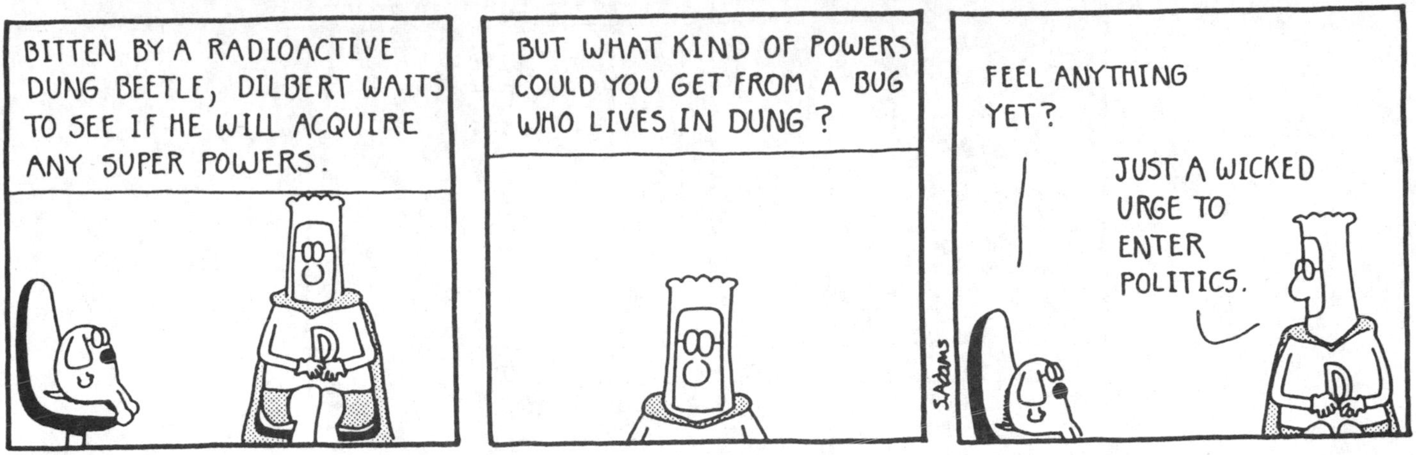
BITTEN BY A RADIOACTIVE DUNG BEETLE, DILBERT WAITS TO SEE IF HE WILL ACQUIRE ANY SUPER POWERS.
BUT WHAT KIND OF POWERS COULD YOU GET FROM A BUG WHO LIVES IN DUNG?
FEEL ANYTHING YET?
JUST A WICKED URGE TO ENTER POLITICS.

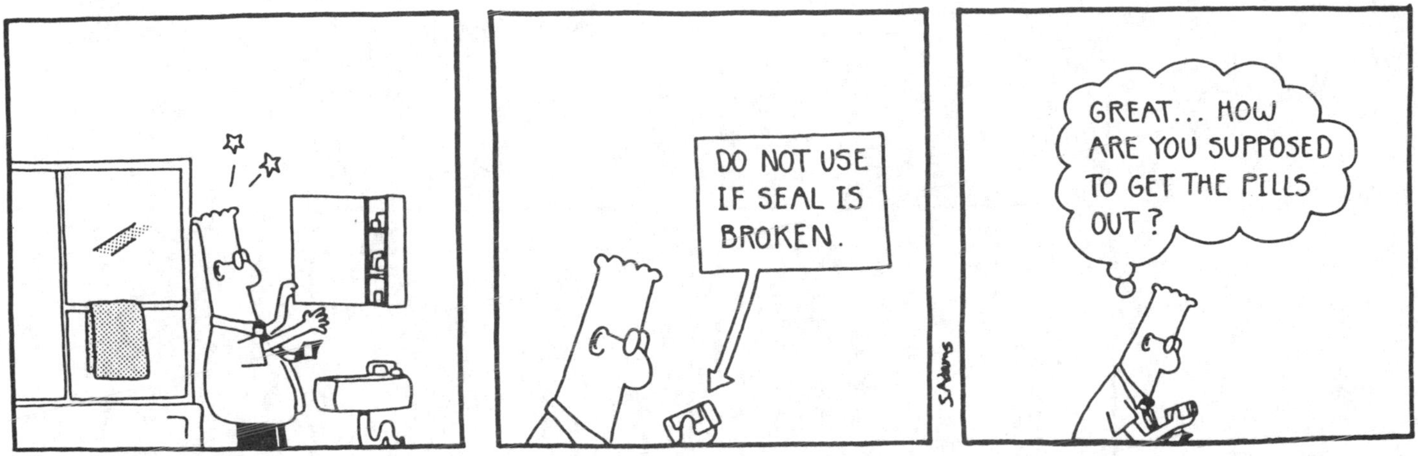
DO NOT USE IF SEAL IS BROKEN.
GREAT... HOW ARE YOU SUPPOSED TO GET THE PILLS OUT?

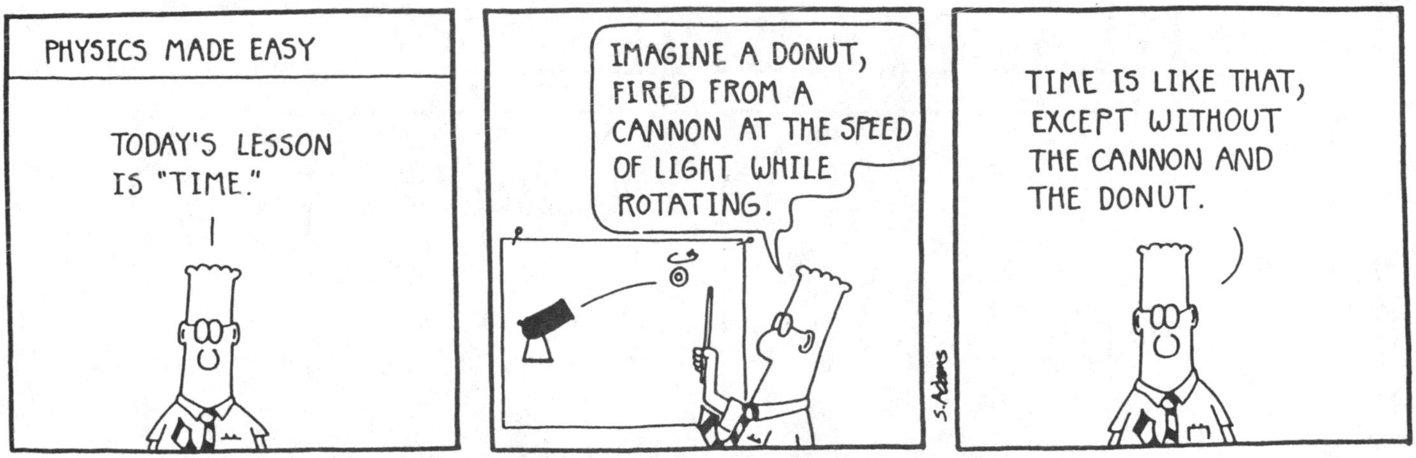
PHYSICS MADE EASY
TODAY'S LESSON IS "TIME."
IMAGINE A DONUT, FIRED FROM A CANNON AT THE SPEED OF LIGHT WHILE ROTATING.
TIME IS LIKE THAT, EXCEPT WITHOUT THE CANNON AND THE DONUT.

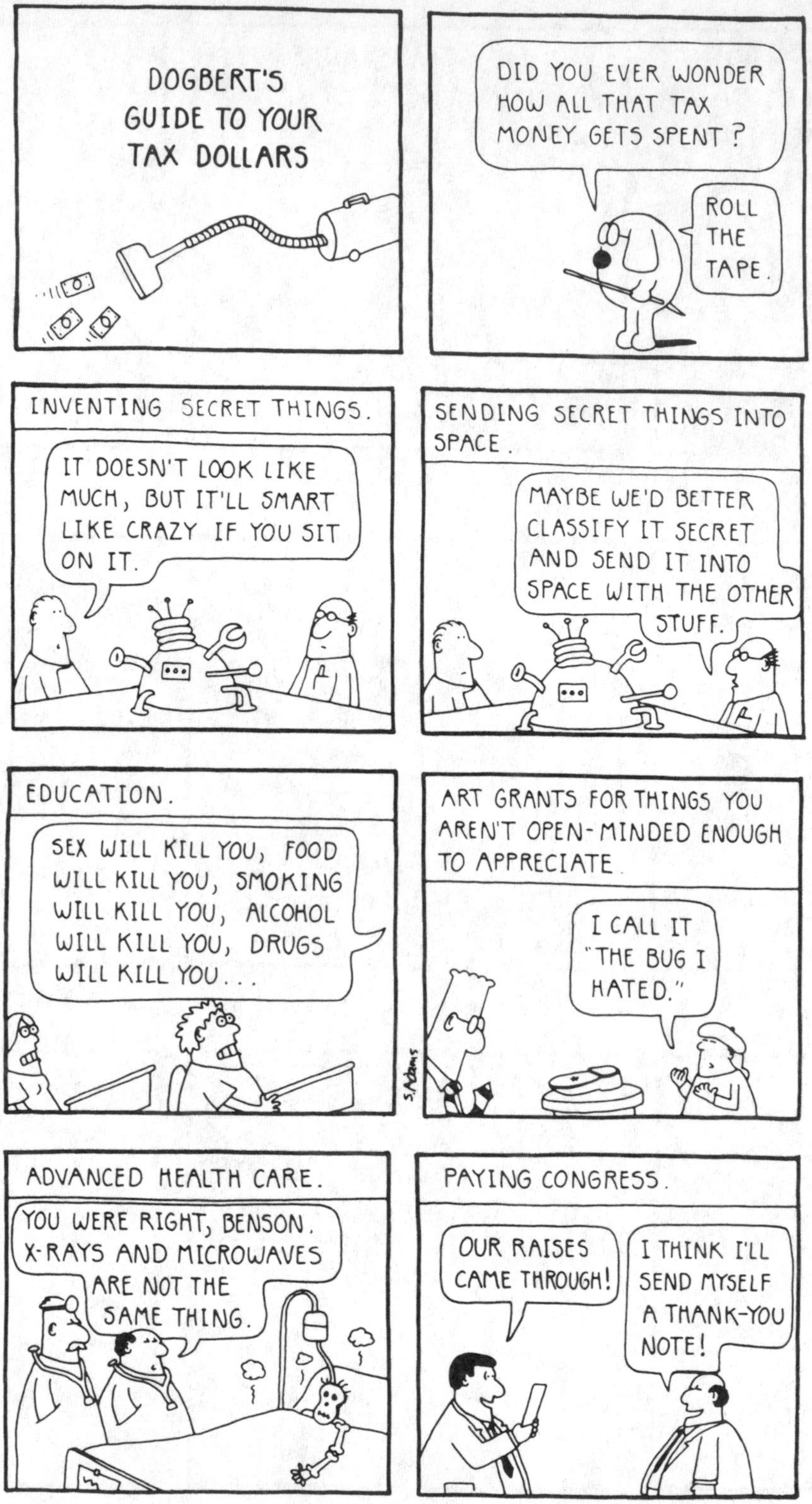
DOGBERT'S GUIDE TO YOUR TAX DOLLARS
DID YOU EVER WONDER HOW ALL THAT TAX MONEY GETS SPENT?
ROLL THE TAPE.
INVENTING SECRET THINGS.
IT DOESN'T LOOK LIKE MUCH, BUT IT'LL SMART LIKE CRAZY IF YOU SIT ON IT.
SENDING SECRET THINGS INTO SPACE.
MAYBE WE'D BETTER CLASSIFY IT SECRET AND SEND IT INTO SPACE WITH THE OTHER STUFF.
EDUCATION.
SEX WILL KILL YOU, FOOD WILL KILL YOU, SMOKING WILL KILL YOU, ALCOHOL WILL KILL YOU, DRUGS WILL KILL YOU...
ART GRANTS FOR THINGS YOU AREN'T OPEN-MINDED ENOUGH TO APPRECIATE.
I CALL IT "THE BUG I HATED."
ADVANCED HEALTH CARE.
YOU WERE RIGHT, BENSON. X-RAYS AND MICROWAVES ARE NOT THE SAME THING.
PAYING CONGRESS.
OUR RAISES CAME THROUGH!
I THINK I'LL SEND MYSELF A THANK-YOU NOTE!

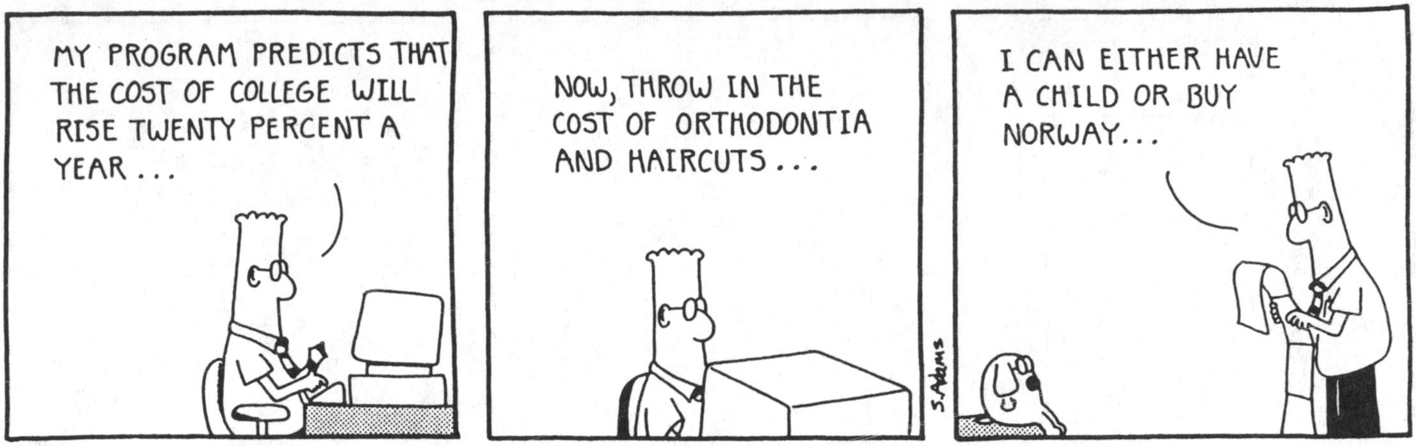
MY PROGRAM PREDICTS THAT THE COST OF COLLEGE WILL RISE TWENTY PERCENT A YEAR . . .
NOW, THROW IN THE COST OF ORTHODONTIA AND HAIRCUTS . . .
I CAN EITHER HAVE A CHILD OR BUY NORWAY . . .
S.Adams

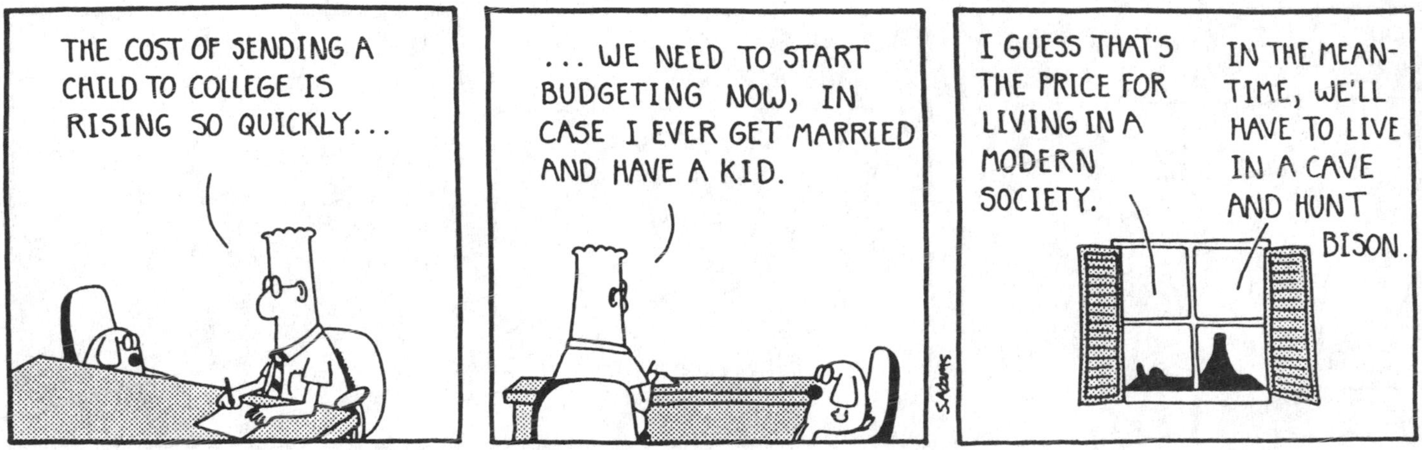
THE COST OF SENDING A CHILD TO COLLEGE IS RISING SO QUICKLY . . .
. . . WE NEED TO START BUDGETING NOW, IN CASE I EVER GET MARRIED AND HAVE A KID.
I GUESS THAT'S THE PRICE FOR LIVING IN A MODERN SOCIETY.
IN THE MEAN-TIME, WE'LL HAVE TO LIVE IN A CAVE AND HUNT BISON.
S.Adams

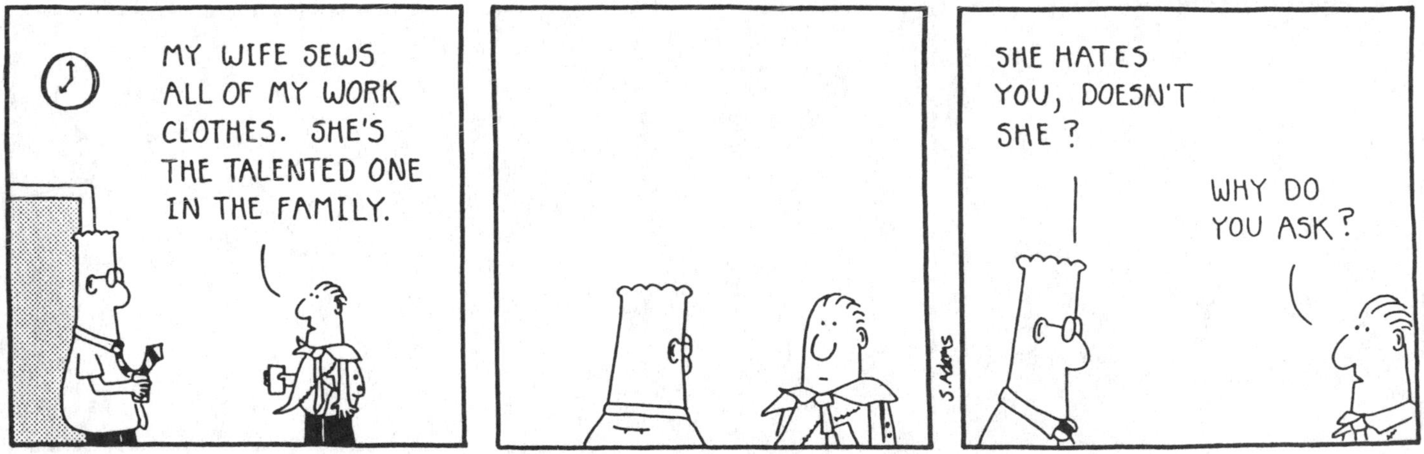
MY WIFE SEWS ALL OF MY WORK CLOTHES. SHE'S THE TALENTED ONE IN THE FAMILY.
SHE HATES YOU, DOESN'T SHE ?
WHY DO YOU ASK ?
S.Adams

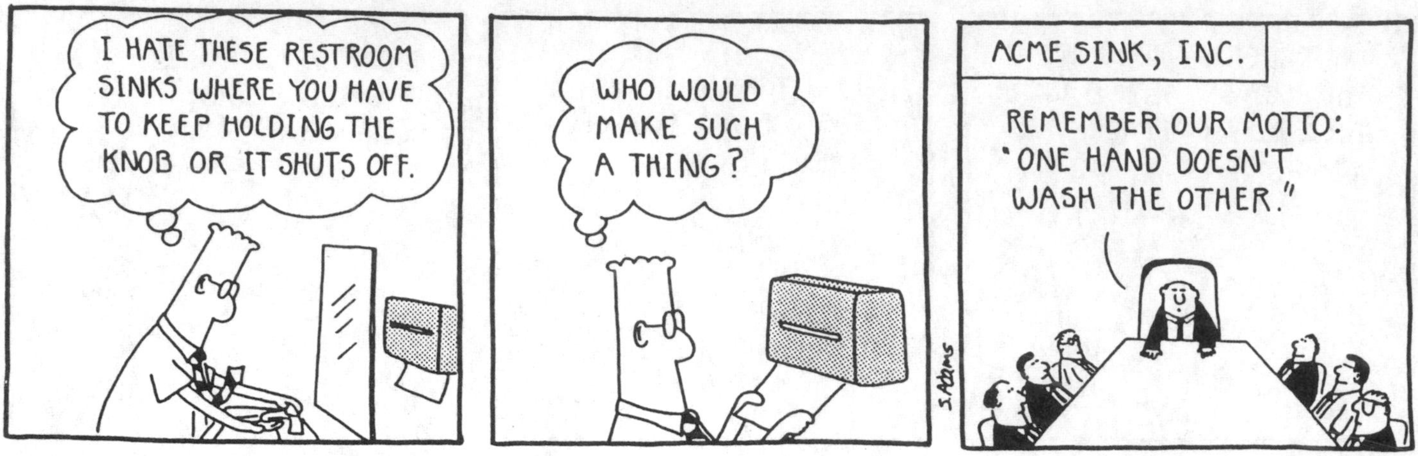
I HATE THESE RESTROOM SINKS WHERE YOU HAVE TO KEEP HOLDING THE KNOB OR IT SHUTS OFF.
WHO WOULD MAKE SUCH A THING?
ACME SINK, INC.
REMEMBER OUR MOTTO: "ONE HAND DOESN'T WASH THE OTHER."
S. Adams

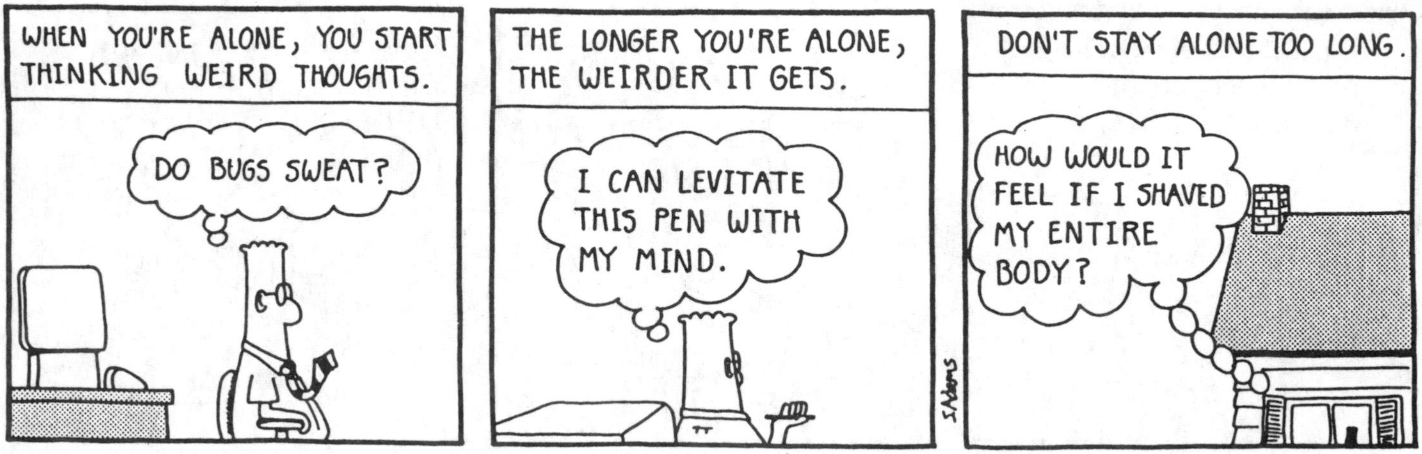
WHEN YOU'RE ALONE, YOU START THINKING WEIRD THOUGHTS.
DO BUGS SWEAT?
THE LONGER YOU'RE ALONE, THE WEIRDER IT GETS.
I CAN LEVITATE THIS PEN WITH MY MIND.
DON'T STAY ALONE TOO LONG.
HOW WOULD IT FEEL IF I SHAVED MY ENTIRE BODY?
S. Adams

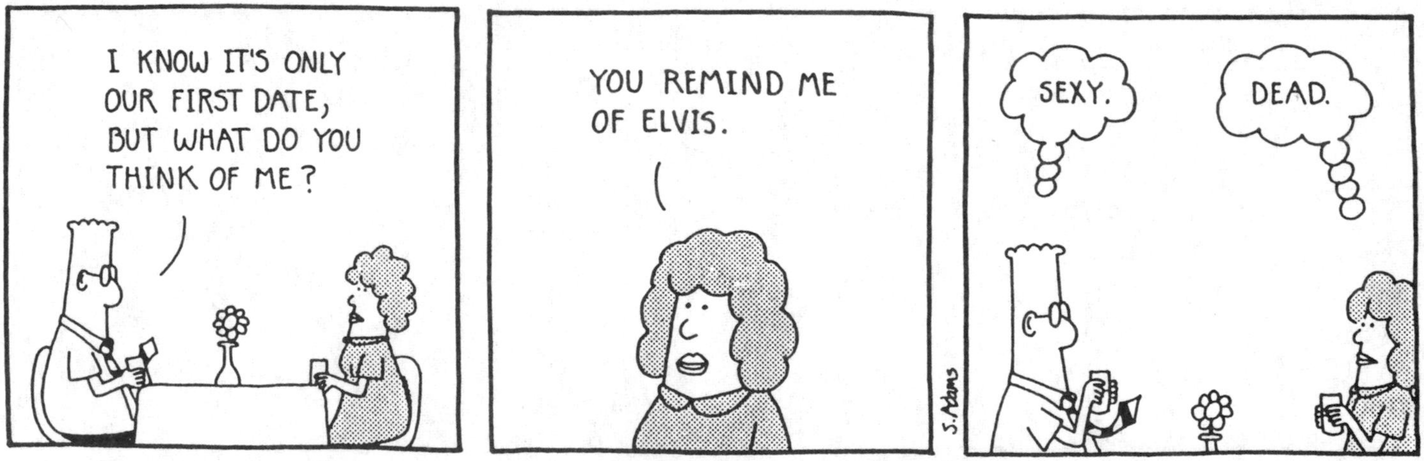
I KNOW IT'S ONLY OUR FIRST DATE, BUT WHAT DO YOU THINK OF ME?
YOU REMIND ME OF ELVIS.
SEXY.
DEAD.
S. Adams

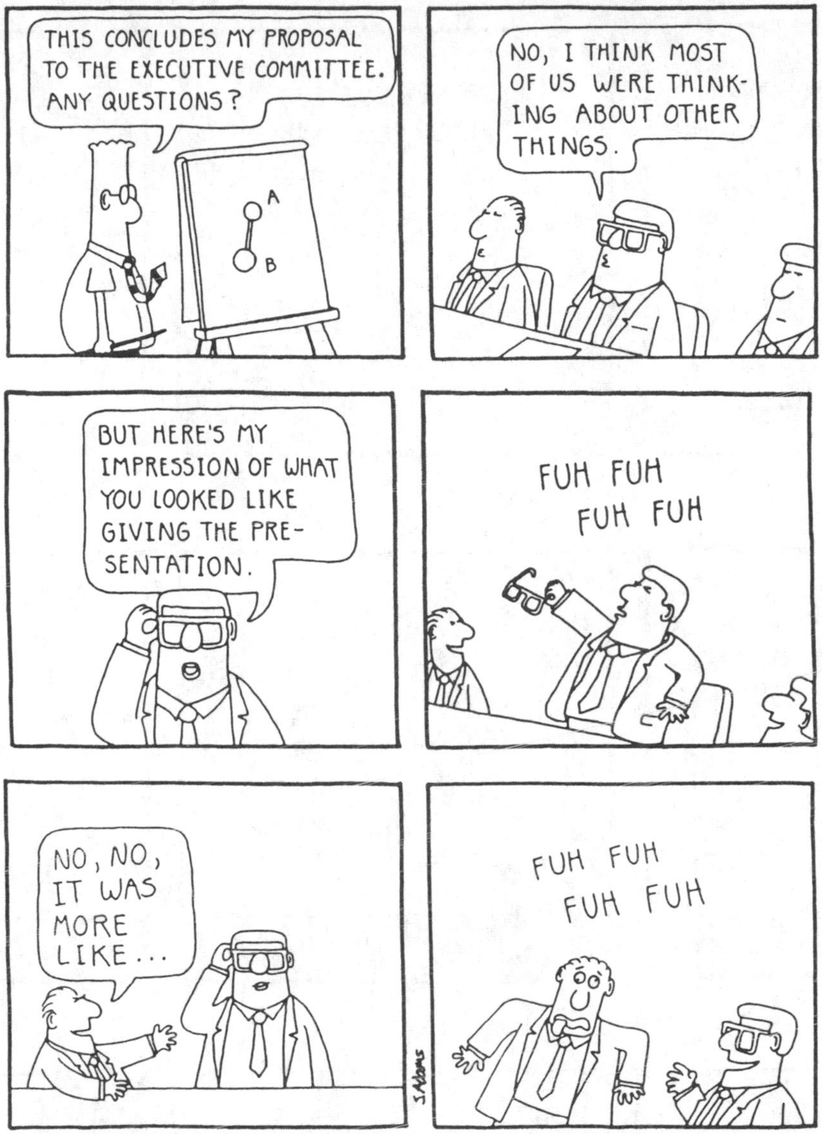
THIS CONCLUDES MY PROPOSAL TO THE EXECUTIVE COMMITTEE. ANY QUESTIONS?
A
B
NO, I THINK MOST OF US WERE THINKING ABOUT OTHER THINGS.
BUT HERE'S MY IMPRESSION OF WHAT YOU LOOKED LIKE GIVING THE PRESENTATION.
FUH FUH FUH FUH
NO, NO, IT WAS MORE LIKE...
S.Adams
FUH FUH FUH FUH

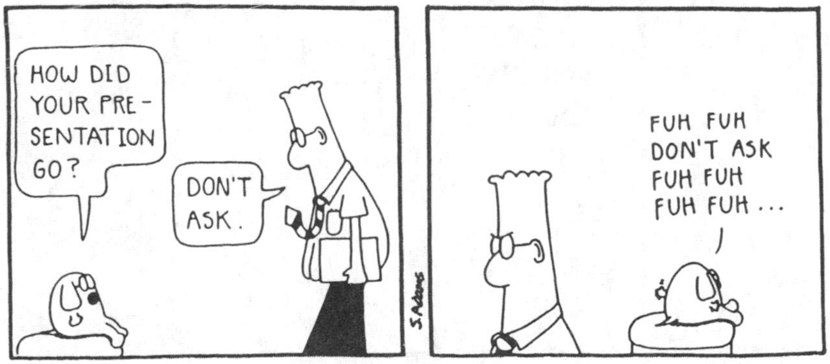
HOW DID YOUR PRESENTATION GO?
DON'T ASK.
S.Adams
FUH FUH DON'T ASK FUH FUH FUH FUH...

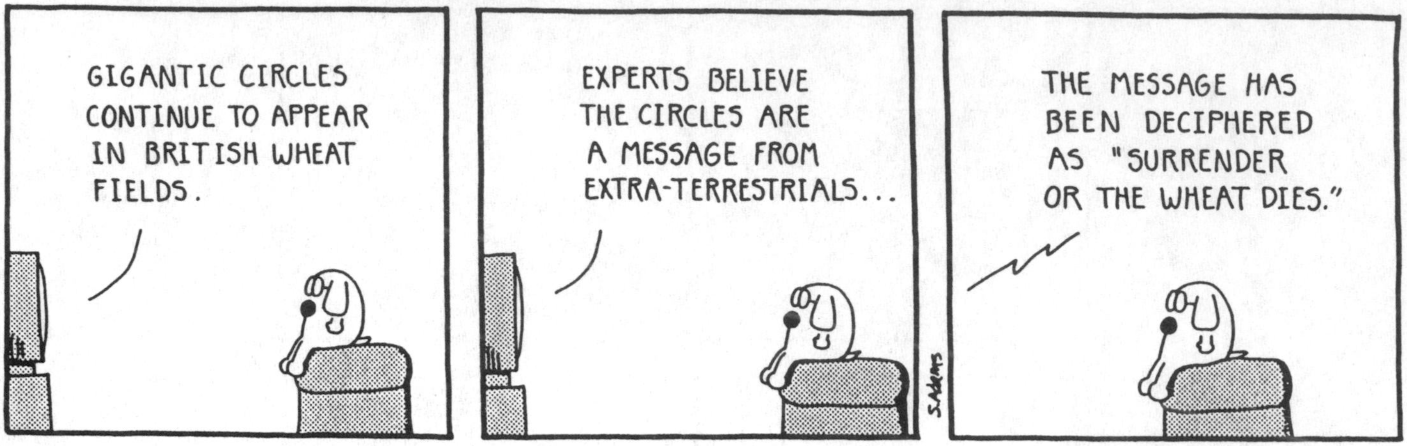
GIGANTIC CIRCLES CONTINUE TO APPEAR IN BRITISH WHEAT FIELDS.
EXPERTS BELIEVE THE CIRCLES ARE A MESSAGE FROM EXTRA-TERRESTRIALS...
S.Adams
THE MESSAGE HAS BEEN DECIPHERED AS "SURRENDER OR THE WHEAT DIES."

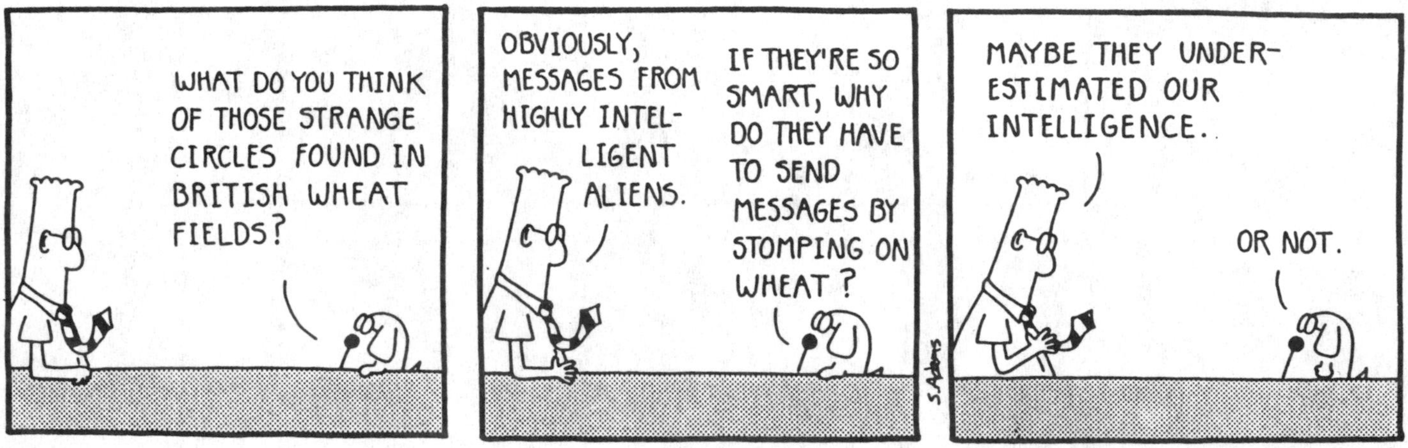
WHAT DO YOU THINK OF THOSE STRANGE CIRCLES FOUND IN BRITISH WHEAT FIELDS?
OBVIOUSLY, MESSAGES FROM HIGHLY INTEL-LIGENT ALIENS.
IF THEY'RE SO SMART, WHY DO THEY HAVE TO SEND MESSAGES BY STOMPING ON WHEAT?
S.Adams
MAYBE THEY UNDER-ESTIMATED OUR INTELLIGENCE..
OR NOT.

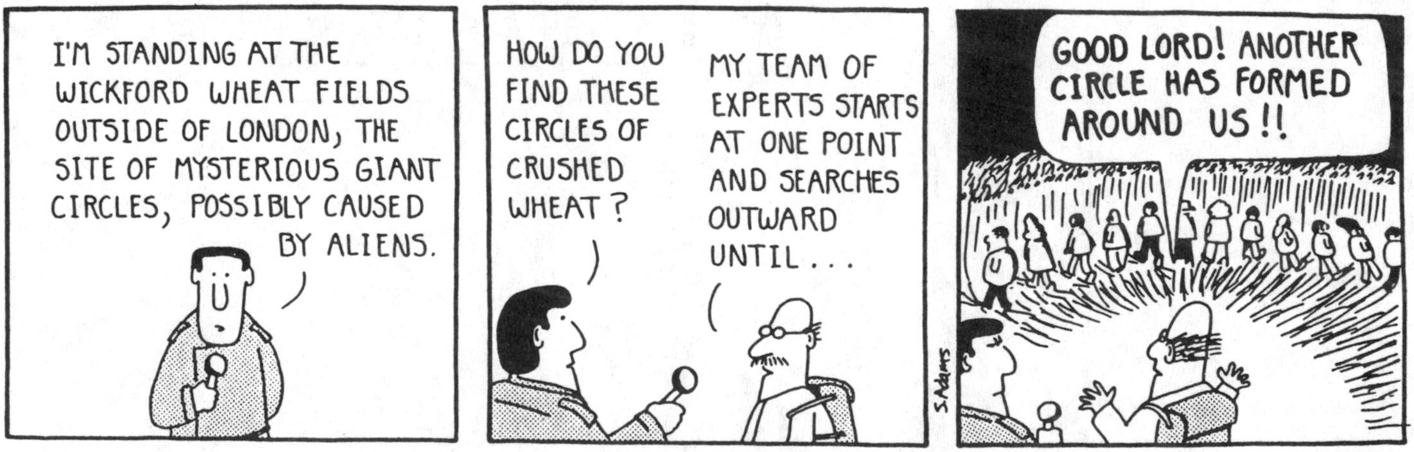
I'M STANDING AT THE WICKFORD WHEAT FIELDS OUTSIDE OF LONDON, THE SITE OF MYSTERIOUS GIANT CIRCLES, POSSIBLY CAUSED BY ALIENS.
HOW DO YOU FIND THESE CIRCLES OF CRUSHED WHEAT?
MY TEAM OF EXPERTS STARTS AT ONE POINT AND SEARCHES OUTWARD UNTIL . . .
S.Adams
GOOD LORD! ANOTHER CIRCLE HAS FORMED AROUND US!!

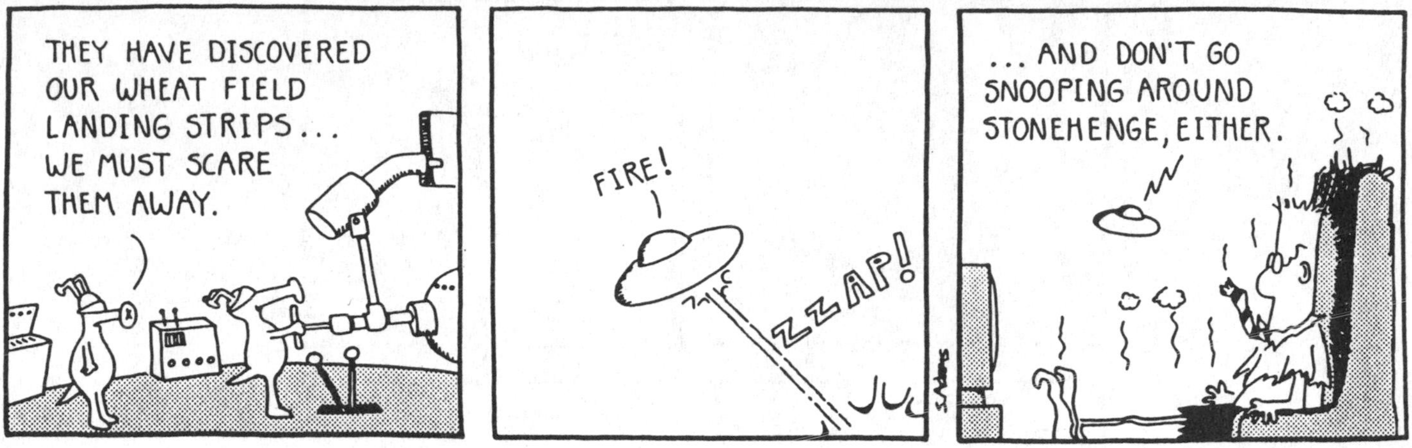
THEY HAVE DISCOVERED OUR WHEAT FIELD LANDING STRIPS... WE MUST SCARE THEM AWAY.
FIRE!
ZZAP!
... AND DON'T GO SNOOPING AROUND STONEHENGE, EITHER.

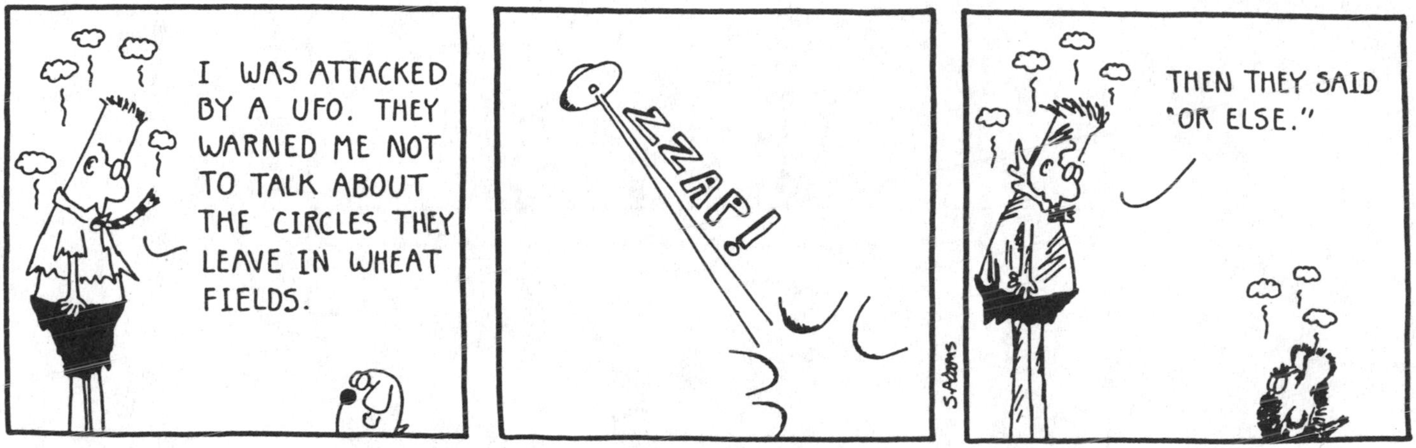
I WAS ATTACKED BY A UFO. THEY WARNED ME NOT TO TALK ABOUT THE CIRCLES THEY LEAVE IN WHEAT FIELDS.
ZZAP!
THEN THEY SAID "OR ELSE."

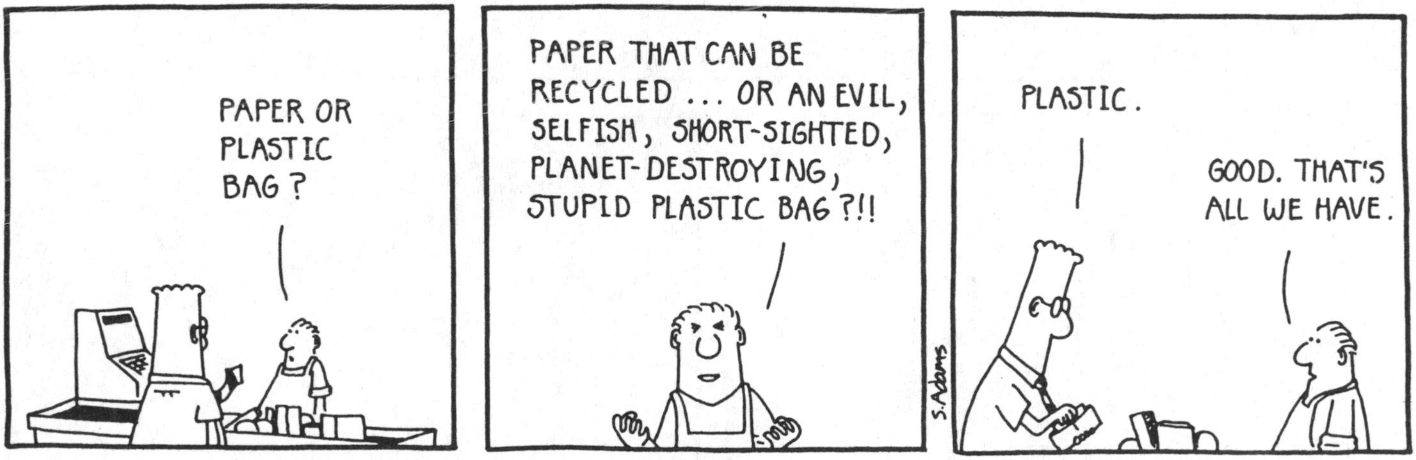
PAPER OR PLASTIC BAG?
PAPER THAT CAN BE RECYCLED ... OR AN EVIL, SELFISH, SHORT-SIGHTED, PLANET-DESTROYING, STUPID PLASTIC BAG?!!
PLASTIC.
GOOD. THAT'S ALL WE HAVE.

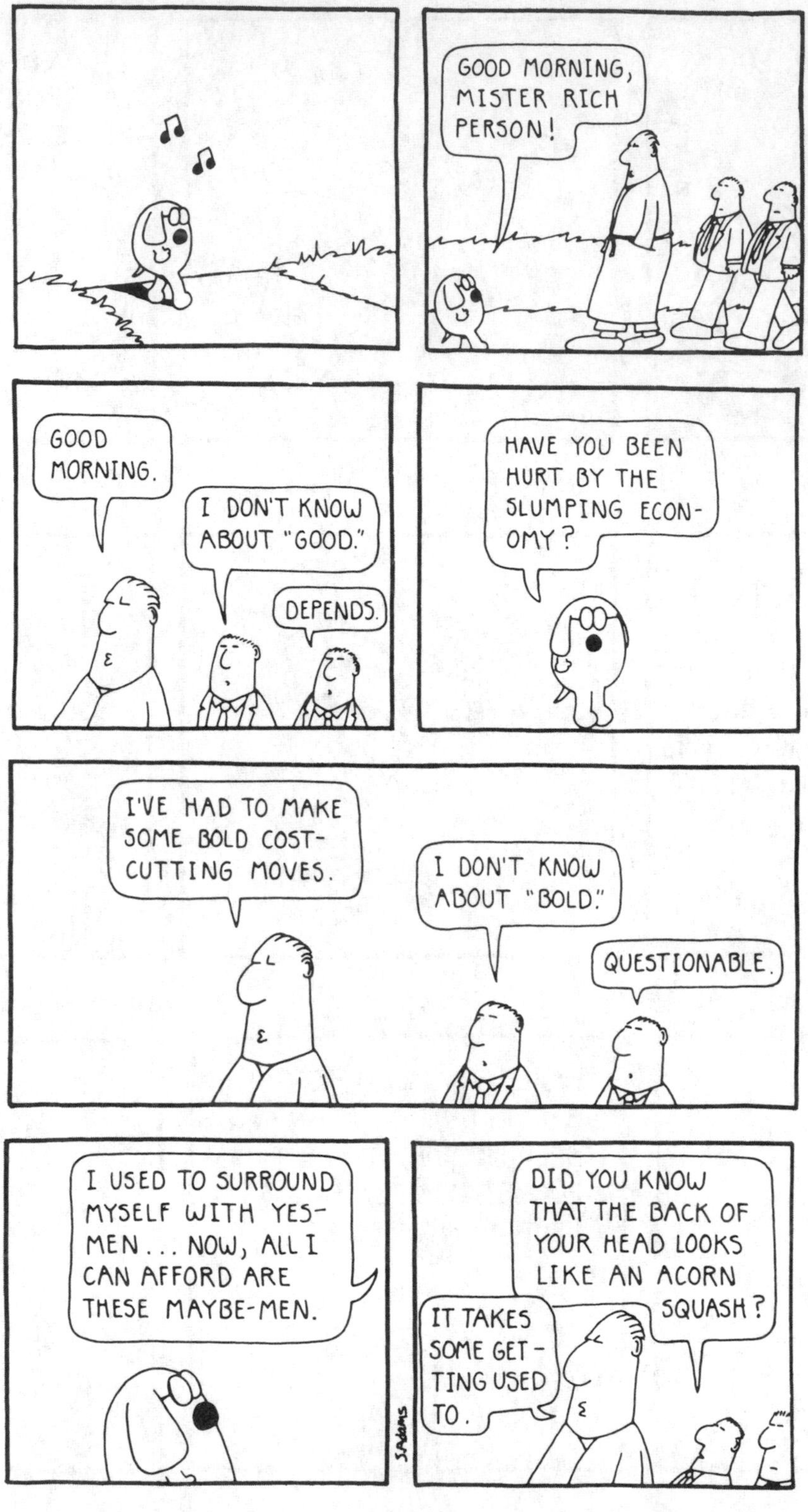
GOOD MORNING, MISTER RICH PERSON!
GOOD MORNING.
I DON'T KNOW ABOUT "GOOD."
DEPENDS.
HAVE YOU BEEN HURT BY THE SLUMPING ECONOMY?
I'VE HAD TO MAKE SOME BOLD COST-CUTTING MOVES.
I DON'T KNOW ABOUT "BOLD."
QUESTIONABLE.
I USED TO SURROUND MYSELF WITH YES-MEN... NOW, ALL I CAN AFFORD ARE THESE MAYBE-MEN.
DID YOU KNOW THAT THE BACK OF YOUR HEAD LOOKS LIKE AN ACORN SQUASH?
IT TAKES SOME GETTING USED TO.
S.ADAMS

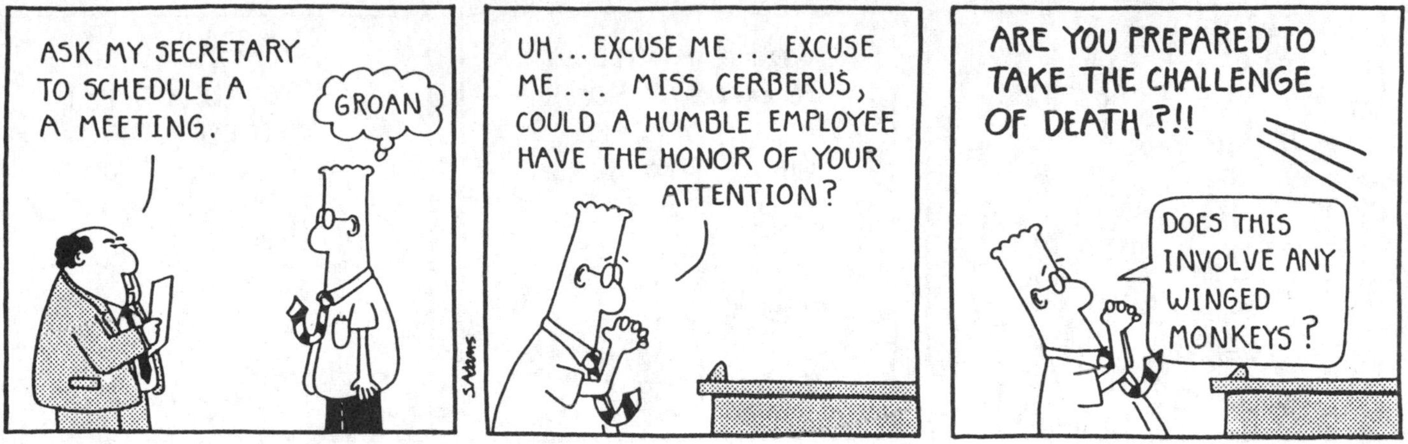
ASK MY SECRETARY TO SCHEDULE A A MEETING.
GROAN
UH... EXCUSE ME ... EXCUSE ME ... MISS CERBERUS, COULD A HUMBLE EMPLOYEE HAVE THE HONOR OF YOUR ATTENTION?
ARE YOU PREPARED TO TAKE THE CHALLENGE OF DEATH ?!!
DOES THIS INVOLVE ANY WINGED MONKEYS ?

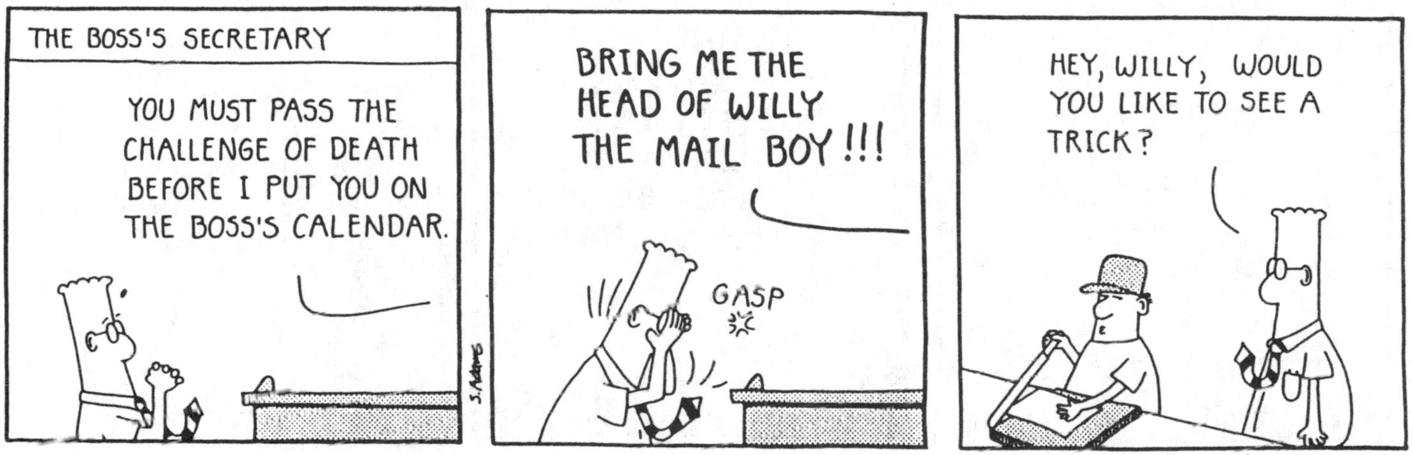
THE BOSS'S SECRETARY
YOU MUST PASS THE CHALLENGE OF DEATH BEFORE I PUT YOU ON THE BOSS'S CALENDAR.
BRING ME THE HEAD OF WILLY THE MAIL BOY !!!
GASP
HEY, WILLY, WOULD YOU LIKE TO SEE A TRICK?

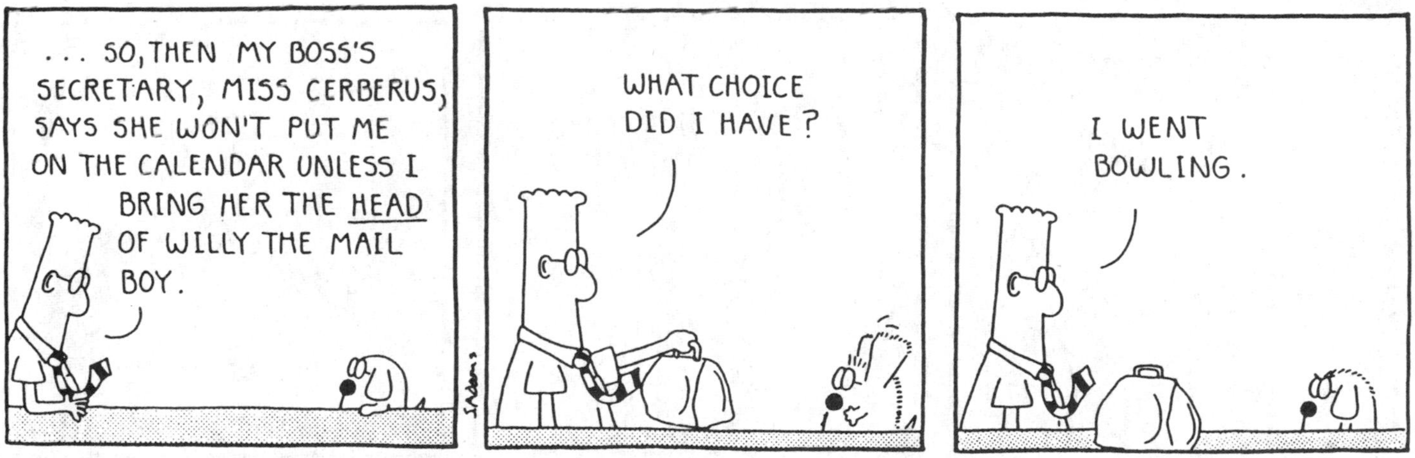
... SO, THEN MY BOSS'S SECRETARY, MISS CERBERUS, SAYS SHE WON'T PUT ME ON THE CALENDAR UNLESS I BRING HER THE HEAD OF WILLY THE MAIL BOY.
WHAT CHOICE DID I HAVE?
I WENT BOWLING.

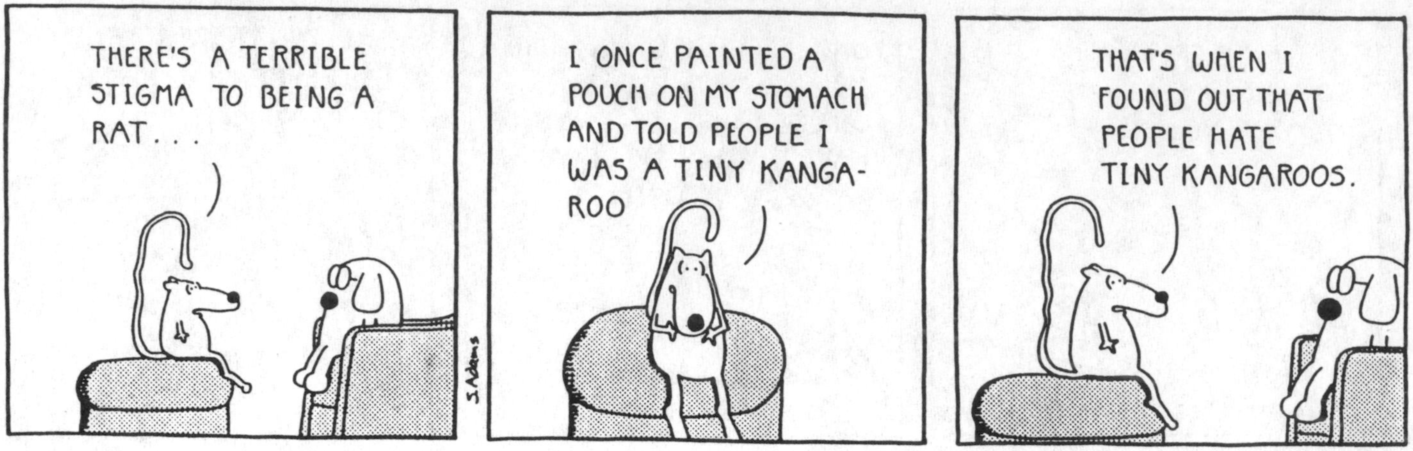
THERE'S A TERRIBLE STIGMA TO BEING A RAT...
I ONCE PAINTED A POUCH ON MY STOMACH AND TOLD PEOPLE I WAS A TINY KANGA-ROO
THAT'S WHEN I FOUND OUT THAT PEOPLE HATE TINY KANGAROOS.

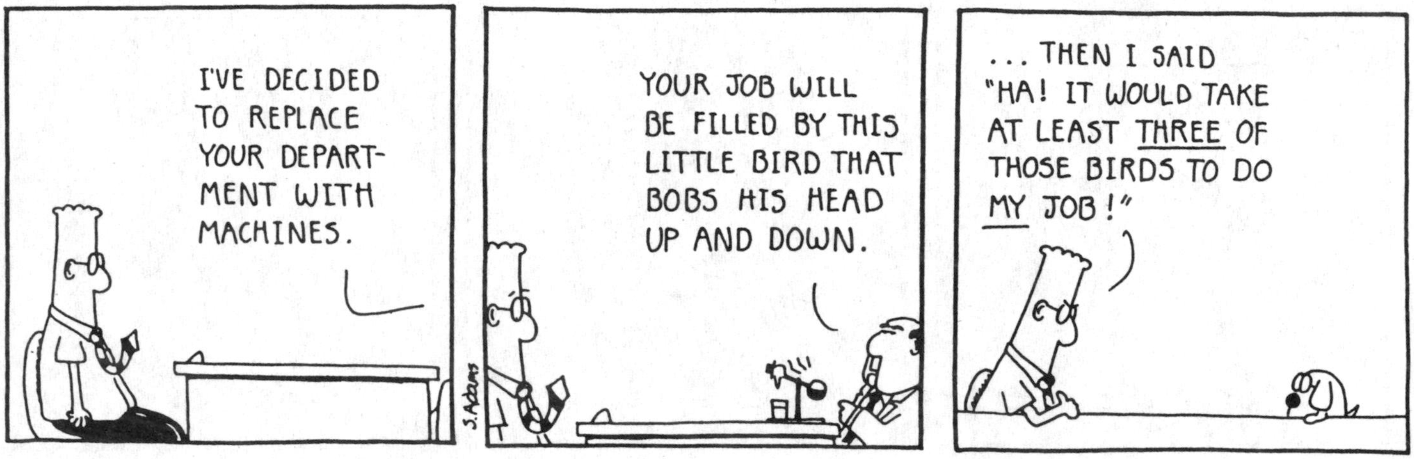
I'VE DECIDED TO REPLACE YOUR DEPART-MENT WITH MACHINES.
YOUR JOB WILL BE FILLED BY THIS LITTLE BIRD THAT BOBS HIS HEAD UP AND DOWN.
... THEN I SAID "HA! IT WOULD TAKE AT LEAST THREE OF THOSE BIRDS TO DO MY JOB!"

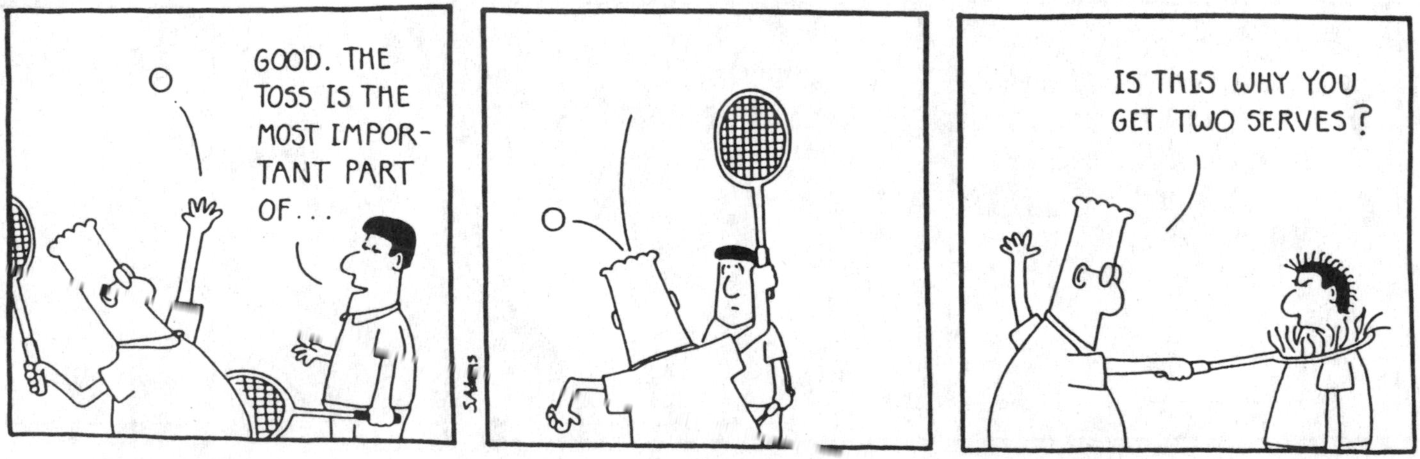
GOOD. THE TOSS IS THE MOST IMPOR-TANT PART OF...
IS THIS WHY YOU GET TWO SERVES?

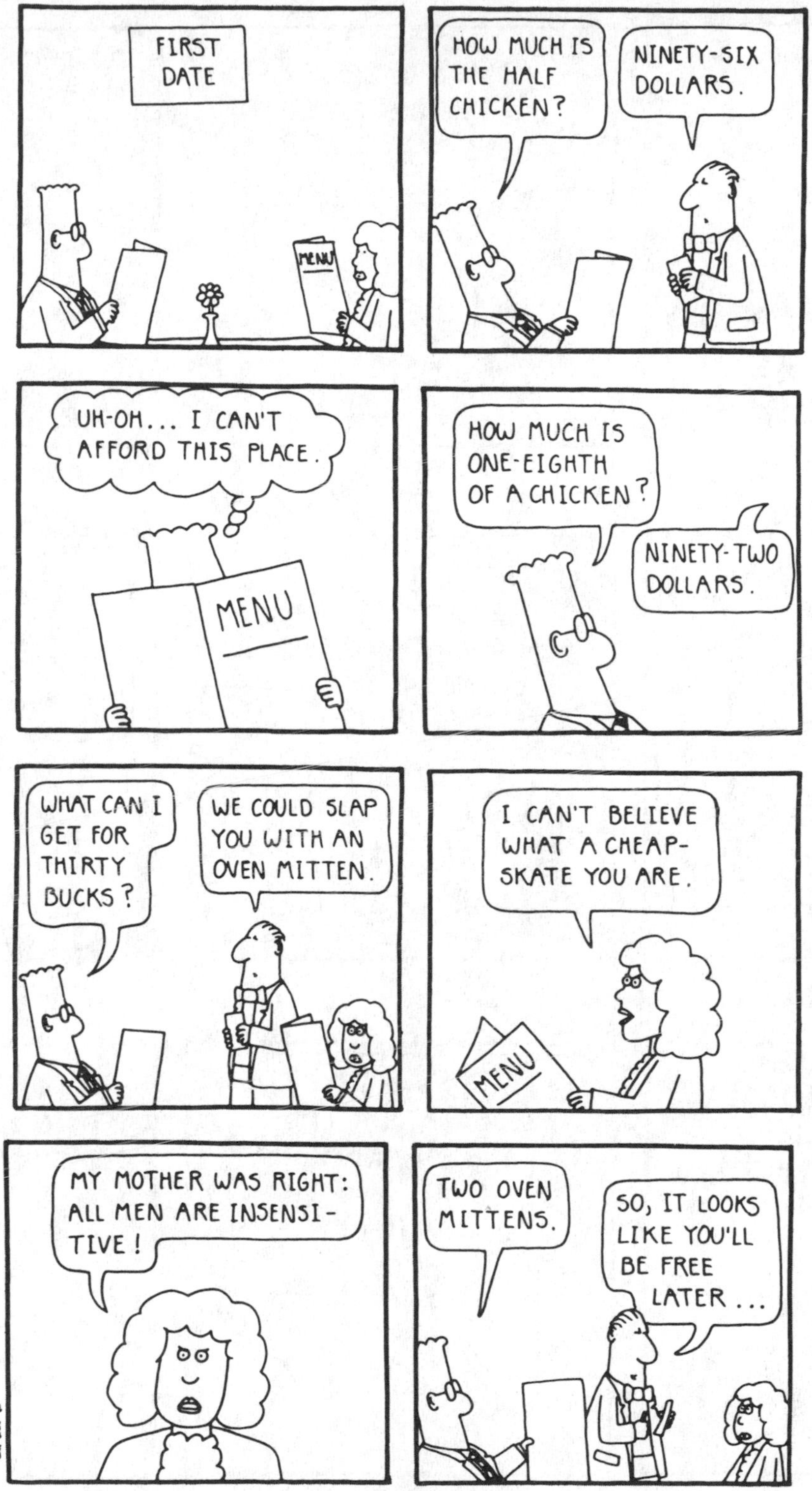
FIRST DATE
MENU
HOW MUCH IS THE HALF CHICKEN?
NINETY-SIX DOLLARS.
UH-OH... I CAN'T AFFORD THIS PLACE.
MENU
HOW MUCH IS ONE-EIGHTH OF A CHICKEN?
NINETY-TWO DOLLARS.
WHAT CAN I GET FOR THIRTY BUCKS?
WE COULD SLAP YOU WITH AN OVEN MITTEN.
I CAN'T BELIEVE WHAT A CHEAP-SKATE YOU ARE.
MENU
MY MOTHER WAS RIGHT: ALL MEN ARE INSENSI-TIVE!
S.Adams
TWO OVEN MITTENS.
SO, IT LOOKS LIKE YOU'LL BE FREE LATER...

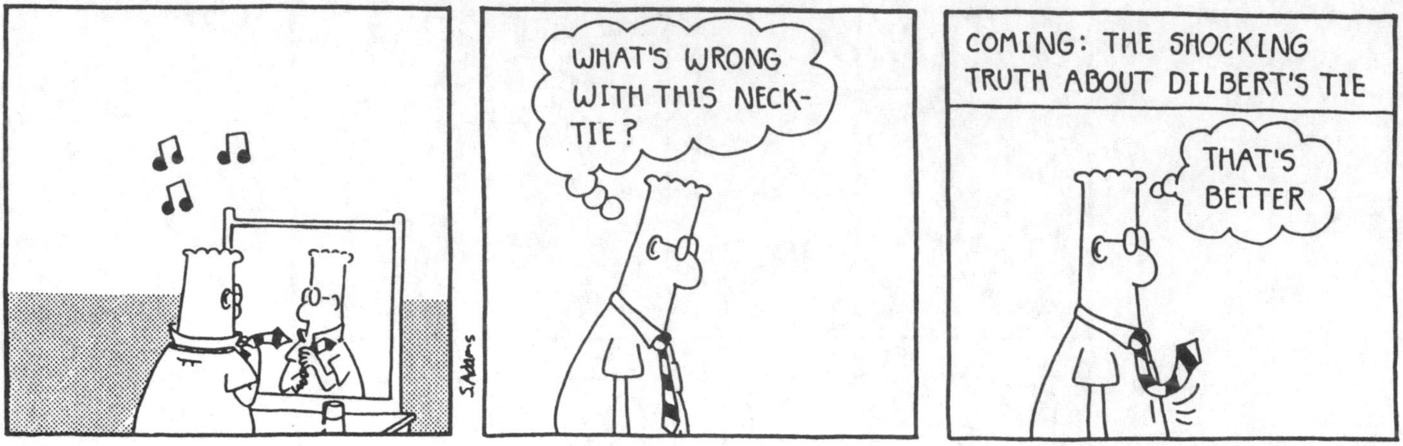
WHAT'S WRONG WITH THIS NECK-TIE?
COMING: THE SHOCKING TRUTH ABOUT DILBERT'S TIE
THAT'S BETTER
S. Adams

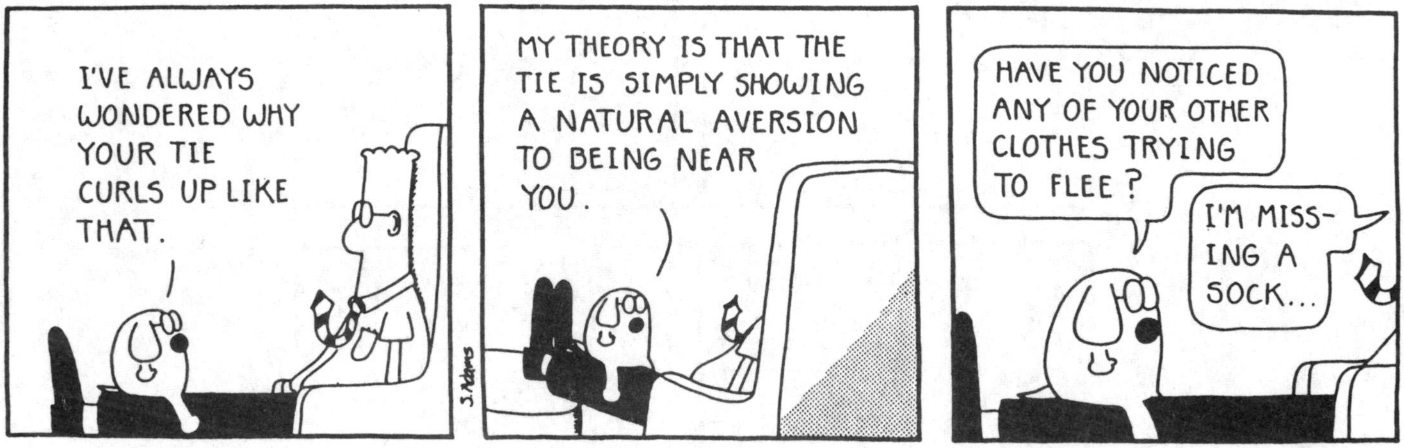
I'VE ALWAYS WONDERED WHY YOUR TIE CURLS UP LIKE THAT.
MY THEORY IS THAT THE TIE IS SIMPLY SHOWING A NATURAL AVERSION TO BEING NEAR YOU.
HAVE YOU NOTICED ANY OF YOUR OTHER CLOTHES TRYING TO FLEE?
I'M MISS-ING A SOCK...
S. Adams

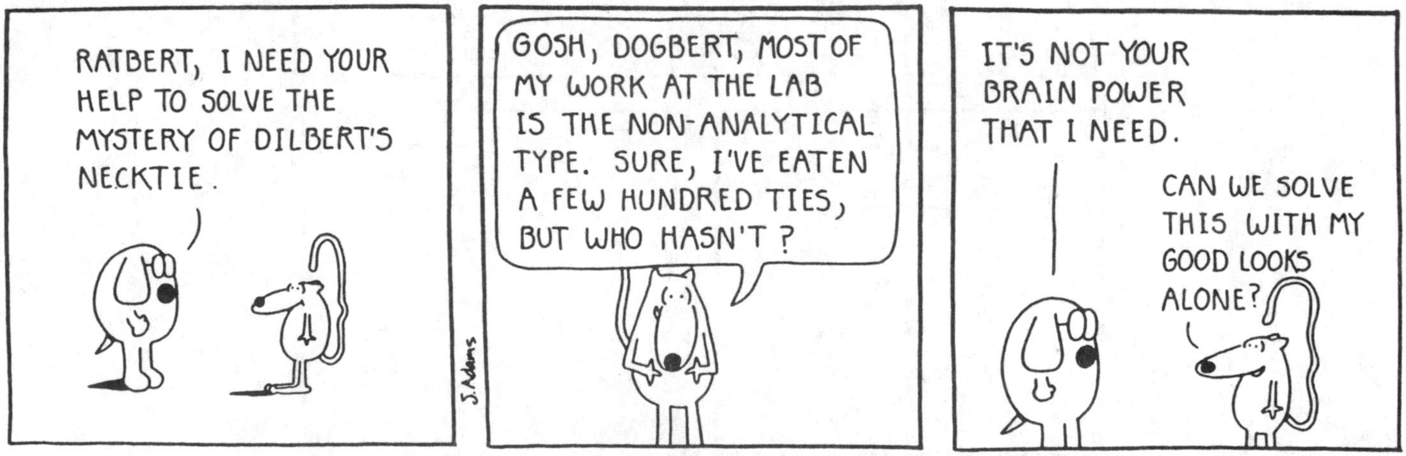
RATBERT, I NEED YOUR HELP TO SOLVE THE MYSTERY OF DILBERT'S NECKTIE.
GOSH, DOGBERT, MOST OF MY WORK AT THE LAB IS THE NON-ANALYTICAL TYPE. SURE, I'VE EATEN A FEW HUNDRED TIES, BUT WHO HASN'T?
IT'S NOT YOUR BRAIN POWER THAT I NEED.
CAN WE SOLVE THIS WITH MY GOOD LOOKS ALONE?
S. Adams

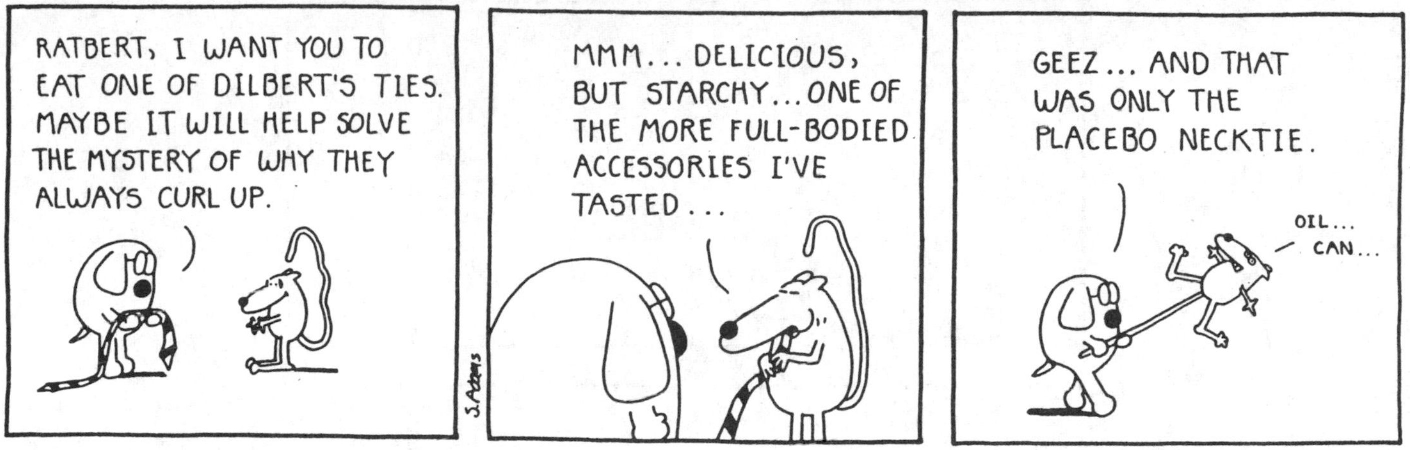
RATBERT, I WANT YOU TO EAT ONE OF DILBERT'S TIES. MAYBE IT WILL HELP SOLVE THE MYSTERY OF WHY THEY ALWAYS CURL UP.
MMM... DELICIOUS, BUT STARCHY... ONE OF THE MORE FULL-BODIED ACCESSORIES I'VE TASTED...
GEEZ... AND THAT WAS ONLY THE PLACEBO NECKTIE.
OIL... CAN...

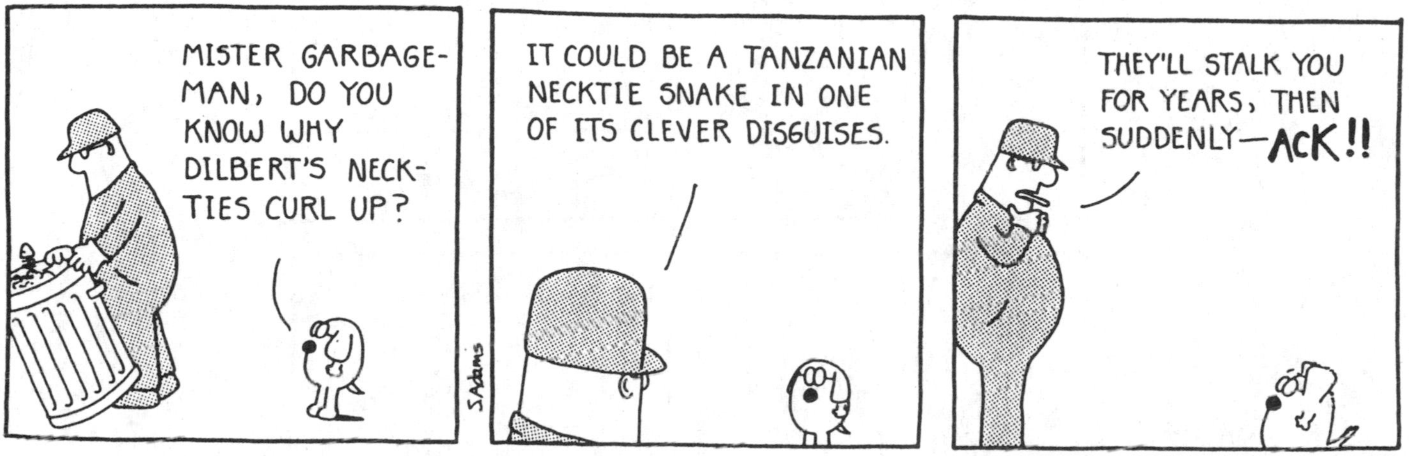
MISTER GARBAGE-MAN, DO YOU KNOW WHY DILBERT'S NECK-TIES CURL UP?
IT COULD BE A TANZANIAN NECKTIE SNAKE IN ONE OF ITS CLEVER DISGUISES.
THEY'LL STALK YOU FOR YEARS, THEN SUDDENLY—ACK!!

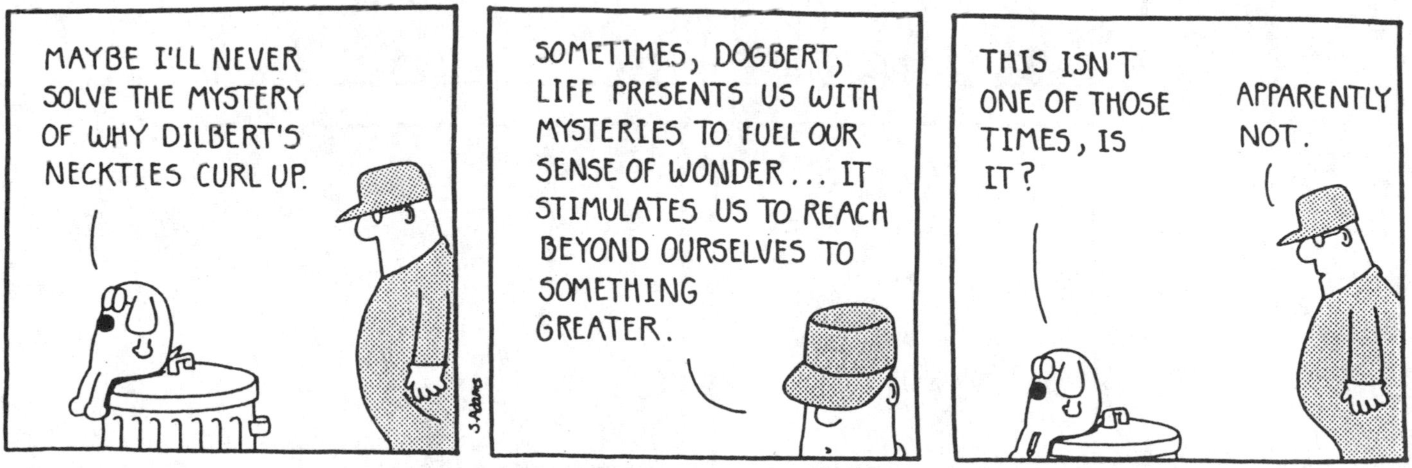
MAYBE I'LL NEVER SOLVE THE MYSTERY OF WHY DILBERT'S NECKTIES CURL UP.
SOMETIMES, DOGBERT, LIFE PRESENTS US WITH MYSTERIES TO FUEL OUR SENSE OF WONDER... IT STIMULATES US TO REACH BEYOND OURSELVES TO SOMETHING GREATER.
THIS ISN'T ONE OF THOSE TIMES, IS IT?
APPARENTLY NOT.

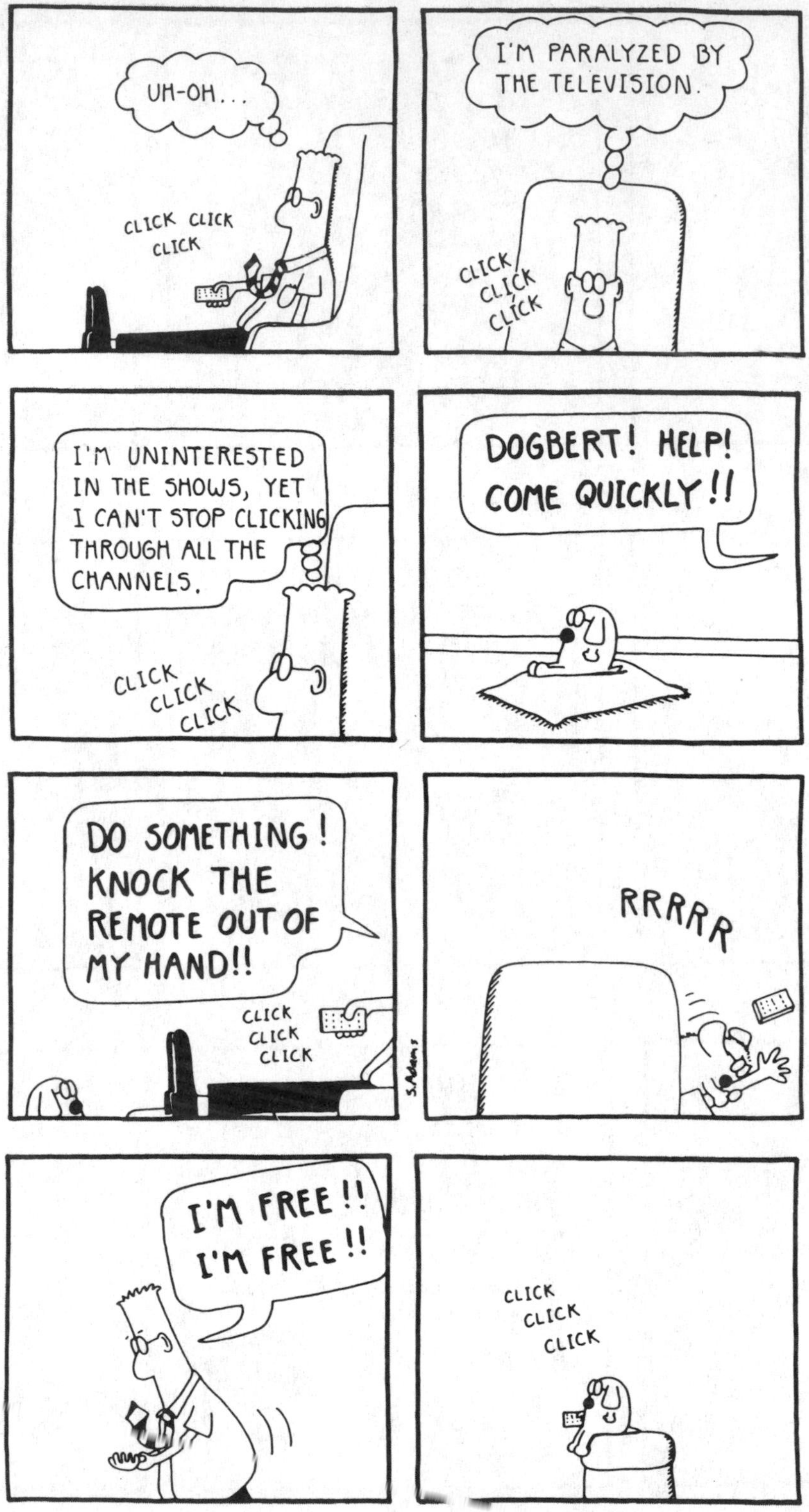
UH-OH...
CLICK CLICK
CLICK
I'M PARALYZED BY THE TELEVISION.
CLICK
CLICK
CLICK
I'M UNINTERESTED IN THE SHOWS, YET I CAN'T STOP CLICKING THROUGH ALL THE CHANNELS.
CLICK
CLICK
CLICK
DOGBERT! HELP! COME QUICKLY!!
DO SOMETHING! KNOCK THE REMOTE OUT OF MY HAND!!
CLICK
CLICK
CLICK
S. Adams
RRRRR
I'M FREE!! I'M FREE!!
CLICK
CLICK
CLICK

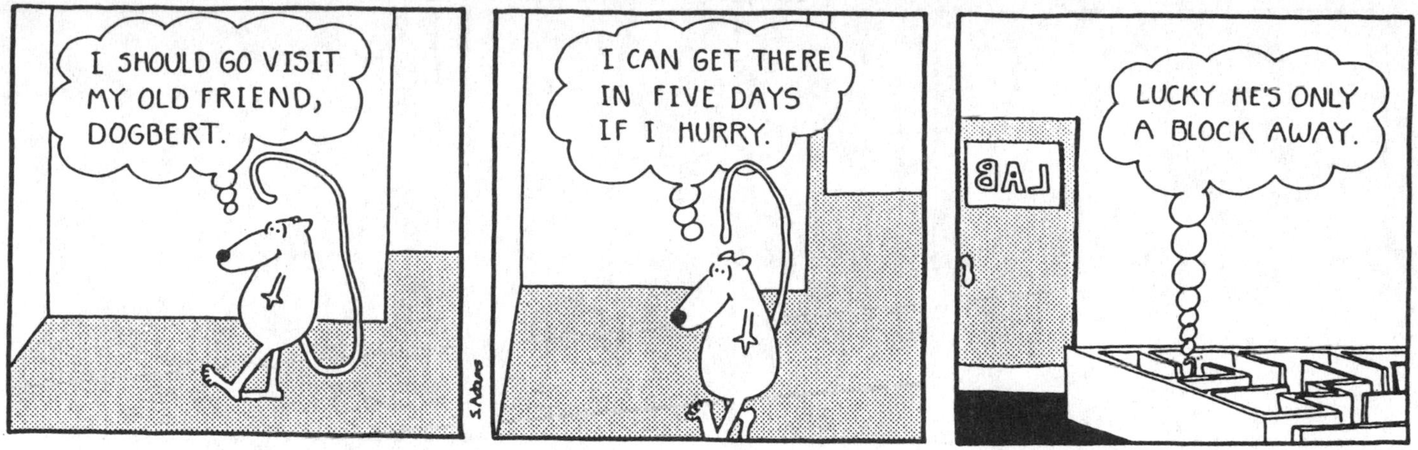
I SHOULD GO VISIT MY OLD FRIEND, DOGBERT.
I CAN GET THERE IN FIVE DAYS IF I HURRY.
LUCKY HE'S ONLY A BLOCK AWAY.

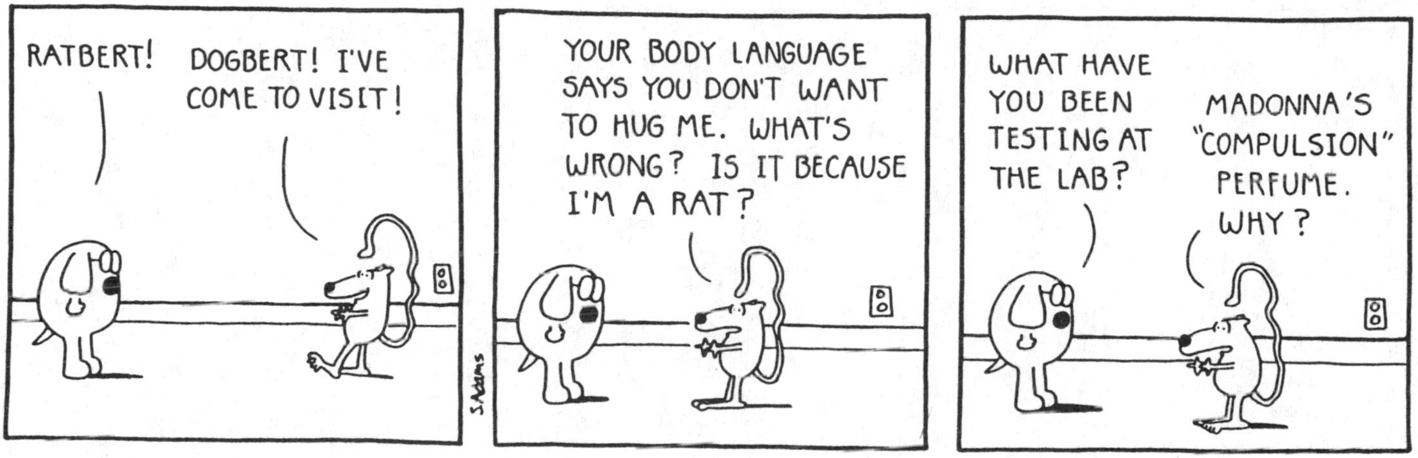
RATBERT!
DOGBERT! I'VE COME TO VISIT!
YOUR BODY LANGUAGE SAYS YOU DON'T WANT TO HUG ME. WHAT'S WRONG? IS IT BECAUSE I'M A RAT?
WHAT HAVE YOU BEEN TESTING AT THE LAB?
MADONNA'S "COMPULSION" PERFUME. WHY?

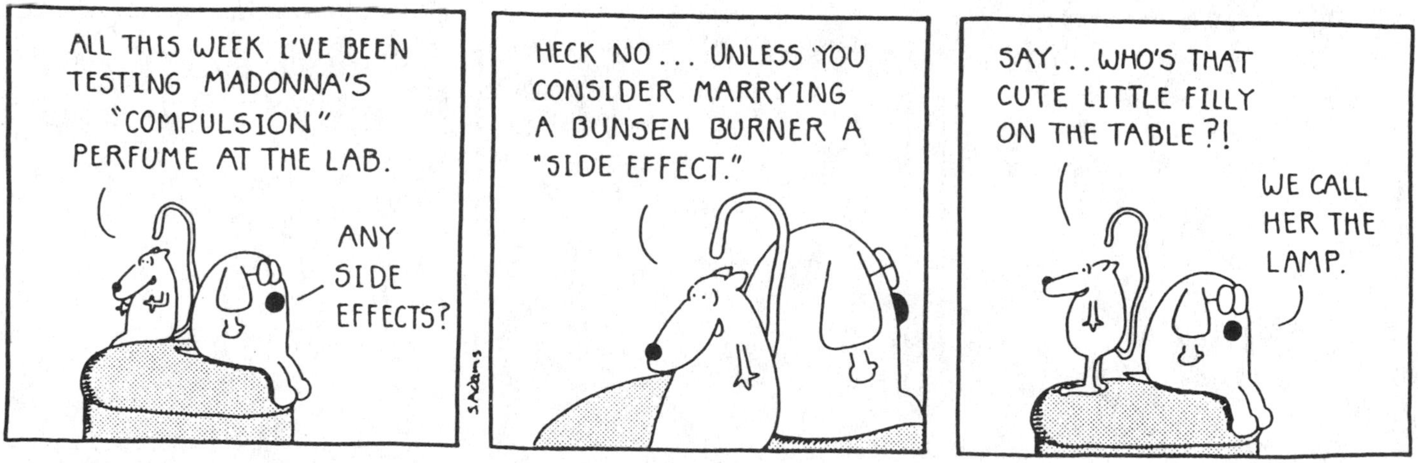
ALL THIS WEEK I'VE BEEN TESTING MADONNA'S "COMPULSION" PERFUME AT THE LAB.
ANY SIDE EFFECTS?
HECK NO . . . UNLESS YOU CONSIDER MARRYING A BUNSEN BURNER A "SIDE EFFECT."
SAY. . . WHO'S THAT CUTE LITTLE FILLY ON THE TABLE ?!
WE CALL HER THE LAMP.

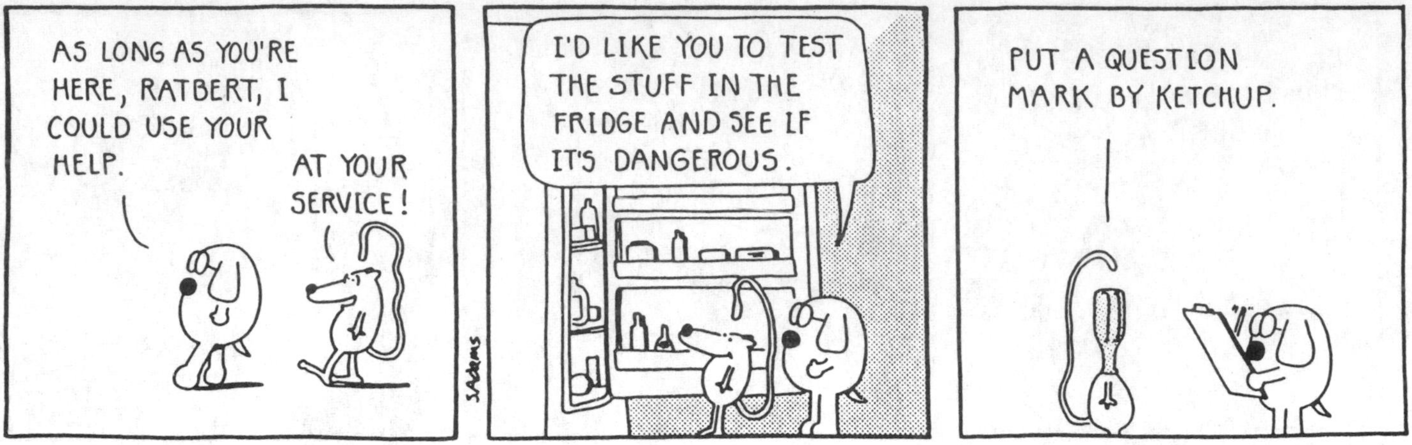
AS LONG AS YOU'RE HERE, RATBERT, I COULD USE YOUR HELP.
AT YOUR SERVICE!
I'D LIKE YOU TO TEST THE STUFF IN THE FRIDGE AND SEE IF IT'S DANGEROUS.
PUT A QUESTION MARK BY KETCHUP.

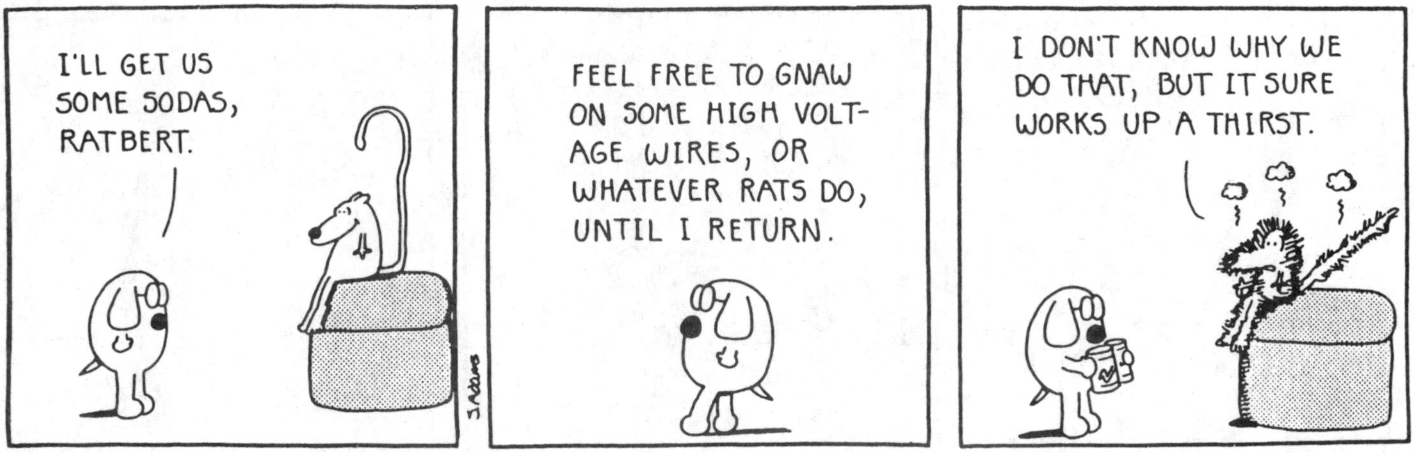
I'LL GET US SOME SODAS, RATBERT.
FEEL FREE TO GNAW ON SOME HIGH VOLT-AGE WIRES, OR WHATEVER RATS DO, UNTIL I RETURN.
I DON'T KNOW WHY WE DO THAT, BUT IT SURE WORKS UP A THIRST.

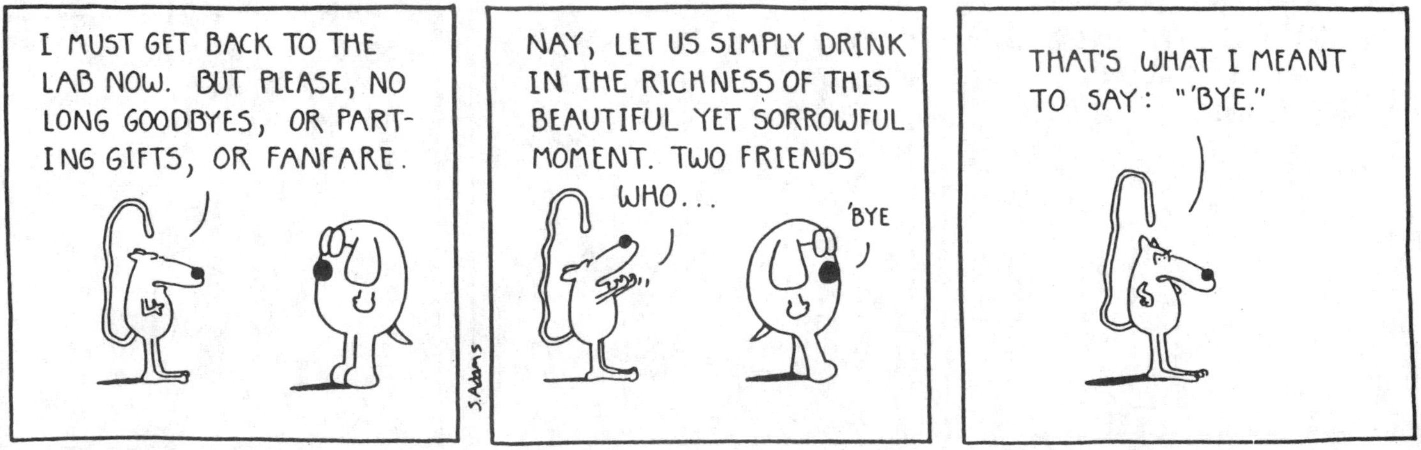
I MUST GET BACK TO THE LAB NOW. BUT PLEASE, NO LONG GOODBYES, OR PART-ING GIFTS, OR FANFARE.
NAY, LET US SIMPLY DRINK IN THE RICHNESS OF THIS BEAUTIFUL YET SORROWFUL MOMENT. TWO FRIENDS WHO...
'BYE
THAT'S WHAT I MEANT TO SAY: "'BYE."